THE TIME TUNNEL

A HISTORY of THE TELEVISION PROGRAM

MARTIN GRAMS JR.

Published in the USA by:
BearManor Media
PO Box 1129
Duncan, Oklahoma 73534-1129
www.bearmanormedia.com

ISBN 978-1-59393-286-2

Printed in the United States of America.
Book design by Brian Pearce | Red Jacket Press.

TABLE OF CONTENTS

"Two American scientists are lost in the swirling maze of past and future ages, during the first experiments on America's greatest and most secret project...the Time Tunnel. Tony Newman and Doug Phillips now tumble helplessly toward a new fantastic adventure, somewhere along the infinite corridors of time..."

"I know it sounds crazy, but you must believe me..."

Dr. Tony Newman in the episode...
...well, just pick an episode. *Any* episode.

INTRODUCTION

Mark Twain reportedly invented the time travel story. Years later H.G. Wells perfected it and revealed its paradoxes. Between them, they left little for latecomers to do. Many have tried, successfully, thanks to the diverse theories and hypotheses of the consequences of time travel. Through a variation on a theme, every science fiction writer has attempted to preach his own theories. However, regardless of how many novels, stories, comics, motion pictures and television programs have been created, as author Robert A. Heinlein once wrote, "they are still fun to write." Enter stage left…Irwin Allen who, through the love of science fiction, brought the concept of *The Time Tunnel* to life. Almost fifty years later, fans of the short-lived television program still discuss the show as if it was the greatest series ever created and telecast. They may be right.

In 1964, Irwin Allen created a 45-page synopsis of a program he titled "The Time Tunnel." Seeking a new series to add to his already successful lineup of television programs, which included *Voyage to the Bottom of the Sea* and *Lost In Space*, Allen called upon a talented list of writers, directors, technicians and actors to bring *The Time Tunnel* to life.

The Time Tunnel was by no means a superb product of Friday night entertainment. If the plot holes were not as large as the tunnel itself, viewers noticed the same props from Allen's other television programs popping up on the show. Fan boys to this day still debate whether the futuristic episodes involving space aliens were better than the historic adventures, but few would deny that Lee Meriwether made a lab coat look sexy. Meriwether herself recalled how the cast received letters from school teachers who used *The Time Tunnel* to stimulate interest in history in the classroom. So why did a show so successful last a mere 30 episodes? That is one of the questions this book hopes to answer.

This tome was written for the purpose of documenting the entire history of *The Time Tunnel*, with detail level so comprehensive as to be definitive. Dates of production, salary costs, production costs, differences between first and final draft of the scripts, memories from cast and crew, bloopers, behind-the-scenes trivia and much more: if it's about *The Time Tunnel*, it's here.

A growing challenge with writing books about television programs of the past is the lack of personnel who could answer questions and relate fond memories. Not a calendar year goes by that someone who was involved with the series passes away, and a bit of *Time Tunnel* history becomes part of, well, history. Some actors, justifiably, are asked to remember the details of a one or two day shoot that happened 40-plus years ago. By the time I was convinced to do this book, more than half of the cast and crew had passed on. The only possible solution to document memories and recollections were from prior published reference guides and magazines. So many, in fact, that I chose to reprint a great number of these interviews and commentaries within the pages of this book, and for those who gave me permission to reprint from their published works, including Mark Phillips and Tom Weaver, I would like to express my sincere appreciation.

Reprint quotes, however, became problematic for two reasons. One, to continue to cite each and every quote would cause the book to read like an encyclopedia, and a few proof readers told me it breaks up the prose. Second, I discovered, after reviewing a few books about *The Time Tunnel* written by other authors, proper citation was not being given, misleading the readers of those books into believing those authors were responsible for the interviews. The solution was to eliminate the repeated reference of quote origin from the text whenever it became too repetitive and instead, listed the interviews in the back of this book in the bibliography. It is my hope that these individuals will be acknowledged for their hard work of the past and my sincere way of thanking them personally for their contributions.

A number of interviews in this book are from exclusive discussions I had with the actors, writers, directors, and so on. Courtesy of the Internet, I was able to track down and exchange e-mails with more than two dozen individuals who were involved with *The Time Tunnel*, making my job a lot easier.

This might come as a shock to most reading this, but I never personally interviewed James Darren, Robert Colbert or Lee Meriwether for this book. I value the privacy of actors: considering the fact that they have consented to numerous interviews over the years, I cannot imagine what they could have added that hasn't already been said about *The Time Tunnel*. Instead, I decided to use quotes from previously published interviews. After all, many hard-working individuals went to a lot of trouble to set up their interviews and have them published. It is only deserving that they get their names in print once again. I know how much fun it is to hear from the celebrities themselves, and it is appreciated that the actors have taken time from their busy schedules to contribute.

Another factor in the making of this book is the array of sources. Almost half a dozen books have been written about *The Time Tunnel*, each varied in size and comprehensiveness. One book was promoted to have memories from cast members (including Robert Duvall), only to discover that the celebs merely commented that it had been so long ago that they could not remember anything. Disappointment continued when I discovered one book featuring reproductions of Time Tunnel blueprints were original art and not copies of Irwin Allen's originals. Behind-the-scenes trivia in some of those books were very scarce. It was for this reason that I merely skimmed through previously published books and did not scrutinize every printed word. Ninety-nine percent of the information contained within this book comes from my own original research and not from books already published on the subject. All of the previous books written about *The Time Tunnel* are each with merit and acknowledgement, and should not be discarded.

One also has to be careful not to rely on newspapers and magazines as the gospel. Even trade periodicals and their reporters made their share of errors. Such examples include columnist Bob Protzman in the January 29, 1980, issue of the *New York Daily News*, who reported that *The Time Tunnel* ran two seasons. The November 1973 issue of *Films and Filming* reported James Darren as the star of 39 episodes, instead of 30. And one such example ("King Tut") found within this book will verify that even press releases issued by the network, which formed the background for most newspaper blurbs, are to be taken with a large grain of salt.

This book could not have been done without the assistance and charity of a number of individuals: Lesley Aletter; Jo Bagwell; Joel Blumberg; Roy Bright; Chris Briskin; Kevin Burns; Bill Chemerka, founder of The Alamo Society and editor of *The Alamo Journal;* Linden Chiles; Mike Clark; Robert Colbert; Paul Comi; John Crawford; James Darren; Brent Davis; Kevin Flynn; James Forgetta; Brian Garson; Ron Hamill; Susan Hampshire; Gary Haynes; Walden Hughes; Lew Hunter; Jon Jashni; Vitina Marcus; Jim McMullan; Lee Meriwether; Jan Merlin; Robert Mintz; Lawrence Montaigne; Ben Ohmart; Nehemiah Persoff; Mark Phillips; Rhodes Reason; Jim Rosin; Bill Saito; Terry Salomonson; John Saxon; Ken Stockinger; Joe Tata; Dick Tufeld; the staff at UCLA Library; and Tom Weaver. I would like to acknowledge the unprecedented access to Irwin Allen's archives and papers, courtesy of Sheila Allen of Irwin Allen Productions and Synthesis Entertainment. Without them, this book would not be anywhere impressive as it is today. If I forgot anyone, please accept my sincere apologies.

By arrangement of the publisher, BearManor Media, author royalties will be donated to the St. Jude Children's Research Hospital. If you enjoy this book, please recommend it to your friends who might also purchase a copy and help support a good cause along the way. I had fun writing the book and I hope you have just as much fun reading it.

Martin Grams
March 2012

THE HISTORY
OF THE SERIES

IRWIN ALLEN

His name is synonymous with colossal calamity, awesome screen spectacle and larger-than-life action. Irwin Allen's creativity was expressed in fantasy and science fiction on both the small screen and large. Born in New York in 1916, Allen attended public schools and later Columbia University, where he majored in journalism and advertising. He went to Hollywood as an editor

Irwin Allen gives special guests a tour on the set of the Time Tunnel Complex.

of *Key* magazine. Less than a year after his arrival, he was invited by radio station KLAC to produce a one-hour show. He wrote, produced, directed and narrated a program that enjoyed 22 sponsors and ran continuously for eleven years. The success of his radio show prompted Atlas Feature Syndicate to offer him a Hollywood news column. Allen took on the role of pillarist: his "Hollywood-Merry-Go-Round" column was soon appearing daily in 73 newspapers around the world.

With the advent of television, Allen created the first celebrity panel show ever produced in the United States. Through the show's four-year history, more than 1,000 film stars and Hollywood celebrities made their television debut on his *Hollywood-Merry-Go-Round*, named after his newspaper column of the same name.

While juggling his radio show and newspaper column, Allen opened a literary agency representing writers and literary material for radio and motion picture industry. He obtained the film rights to Rex Beach's *The World in His Arms*, which he sold to Universal-International. He subsequently was granted the franchise to represent all the Rex Beach material. He also represented such important literary figures as Fanny Hurst, P.G. Wodehouse, Ben Hecht and Louis Joseph Vance as well as the Duell, Sloan and Pearce, Barcourt-Brace and Putnam publishing houses.

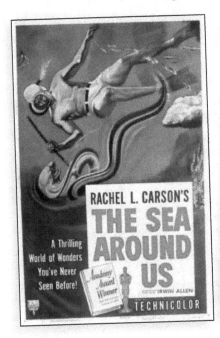 

Allen eventually became one of Hollywood's outstanding packagers of motion pictures. Inevitably he was drawn into production himself. His first production partnership was with RKO for the Groucho Marx-Jane Russell-Frank Sinatra starrer, *Double Dynamite* (1951). He followed with *Where Danger Lives* starring Robert Mitchum and Claude Rains and *A Girl in Every Port* starring Groucho Marx, William Bendix and Marie Wilson.

While still with RKO, Allen launched his production of Rachel Carson's *The Sea Around Us* (1953). Allen wrote the screenplay and produced the magnificently successful film for which he won an Academy Award. He then went to Warner Brothers to produce and direct *The Animal World* and *The Story of Mankind*. Then he co-wrote and produced the gigantic story of the big top, *The Big Circus*, with Victor Mature, Rhonda Fleming, Kathryn Grant, Peter Lorre, Red Buttons and David Nelson. It was one of the biggest money-makers of the year. The film was shot at MGM and released by Allied Artists.

In 1960, Allen moved to 20th Century-Fox Studios where his first film, *The Lost World*, with Michael Rennie, David Hedison and Jill St. John, was one of the studio's biggest box office hits of the year. In 1961, he co-wrote *Voyage to the Bottom of the Sea* as a motion picture, then produced and directed it with Walter Pidgeon, Joan Fontaine, Frankie Avalon, Peter Lorre, Robert Sterling and Barbara Eden in starring roles. This was the basis for his 1964 television series of the same name. Riding on the success of that television series, Allen brought *Lost In Space* to CBS, and began to conceive of a third network television program that would be just as rewarding. The result was *The Time Tunnel*.

IRWIN ALLEN'S CONCEPT

In 1964, Irwin Allen created a 45-page treatment consisting of five possible plot outlines for use as the pilot episode, establishing the characters and the format of the series. At the Institute for Advanced Research in the Theoretical Sciences, a sprawling, windowless complex of buildings on the outskirts of Silvermine, Connecticut, two brilliant young scientists are in the final stages of testing a gigantic device designed to carry man through the fourth dimension into a time warp that will deposit him in another time period. The two men, who have dubbed their long, chamber-like machine the "time tunnel," are Dr. Peter Phillips and Dr. Tony Newman. Phillips, thirty-two, a Rhodes Scholar, historian, mathematician and theoretical physicist

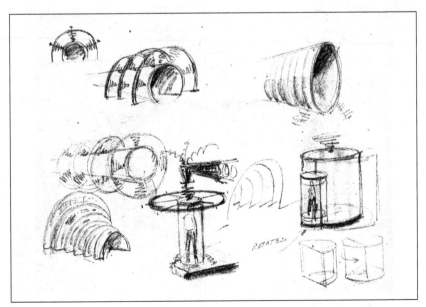

This page and following pages: Time Tunnel conception sketches.

is tall, athletic, a former All-American Quarterback. His partner, Tony Newman, is thin, wiry, with limitless nervous energy, a short temper and an endless appetite for coffee. A boy prodigy at the University of Chicago where he made astonishing contributions in the fields of physics and chemistry, Newman won his chair at the Institute at age twenty-one.

The "tunnel" is finally completed and Phillips and Newman run a first "live" test. A white mouse is placed in the convergence chamber at the end of the tunnel and Newman seats himself in the control cubicle deep inside the huge computer that is the "brain" of the device. With Phillips carefully monitoring his every move, Newman starts the massive power build-up. Finally, with billions of volts coursing through the circuits, Newman forces the three laser beams on the mouse in the convergence chamber. Moments later, he throws the master switch — and the tiny mouse is gone. For a moment neither man speaks. Then, with a grin, Newman turns to Phillips as he cuts the main switches and the screaming generators begin to unwind.

"There is now one more mouse in Hamlin for the Pied Piper to contend with," Newman remarks.

The next test, the final test, the conclusive test, must send a man into time. Phillips and Newman explain to the director of the Institute that only a man can travel into the millions of space-time continuums around us and return because only a man can carry with him and activate the tiny ion generator the "tunnel" requires in order to zero in on the time traveler and return him to the present. Since neither Phillips nor Newman has any idea what they

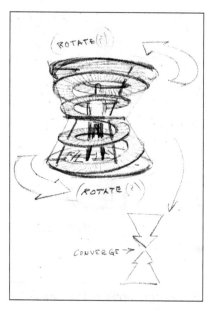

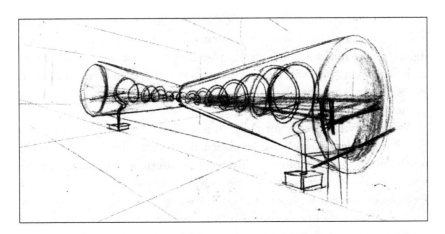

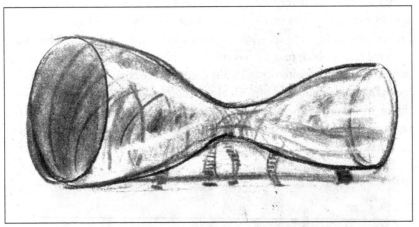

may encounter in other time periods, they have built the ion generator into a simple crest ring to be worn by the traveler. Like a photographer's strobe light, the miniaturized generator is depleted each time it completes a circuit with the "tunnel" and will require several days to build up again to its peak. When it is peaking, the filament concealed in the clear "stone" in the center of the ring will glow a soft orange.

With everything ready for the final test, Phillips picks up the ring and puts it on his left hand. Newman objects but Phillips finally wins out. He will be the one to step into the convergence platform and, hopefully, be the first man since the beginning of time to actually cross over through another time dimension to a separate moment in history.

Because of their uncertainty as to what stresses he might endure in the actual moment of divergence, Phillips and Newman decide that Phillips should wear a pressure suit not unlike that worn by present-day astronauts. He will also carry a small supply of auxiliary oxygen and a small but high-powered radio, which may or may not be usable. With all preparations finally made, Phillips steps into the grid-like convergence chamber. The chamber is locked and Newman seats himself at the console. Watching Phillips through the quartz crystal viewing shield, Newman starts the power build-up. The tapes on the computer whirl into action, setting the circuitry. The scream of

Conception sketch of the tunnel interior, ala *Cabinet of Dr. Caligari.*

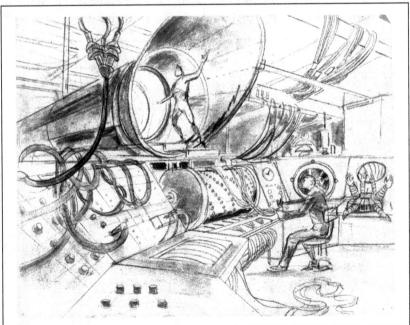

Conception sketches of control center and tunnel entrance.

power becomes almost unbearable as Phillips stands, feet firmly planted on the steel plates of the platform, and Newman double-checks all instruments. Finally, the needle-like laser beams are slowly brought into focus on the three critical points surrounding Phillips and then, in a blinding moment, Newman throws the switch. An instant later, the convergence chamber is empty!

After a moment of stunning silence, Newman immediately turns to the controls of the high velocity transceiver at his elbow. He throws several switches, carefully adjusts a series of wave bands and then picks up the microphone. Quickly he repeats Phillips' name over and over while continuing to keep the laser beam steady in the convergence chamber. Then, suddenly, there appears in the viewing reflector at the end of the tunnel the shadowy image of a human being. The image fades in and out and in and then there is a sudden burst of static on the transceiver, followed by Phillips' voice, garbled by static and hollowly distant.

"Newman —- can — you — hear — me?"

Instantly, Newman cuts in. "I hear you. Are you all right?"

"Feel nothing…Only sensation of falling…Nothing but the blackness all around…flashing lights…no horizon…like standing in space…no way to –"

The image in the viewing reflector is gone. Try as he will, Newman can get no further communication. Finally, after hours, he cuts the master switches. The screaming generators slow to a final sigh and are at last silent. Newman sits as one transfixed — staring into the tunnel as we dissolve to…

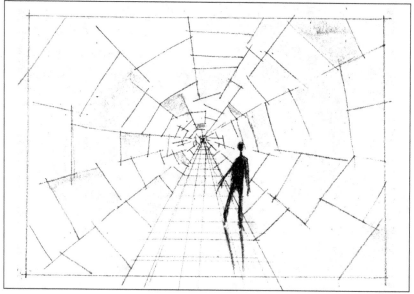

Conception sketch of the tunnel interior with mirrors.

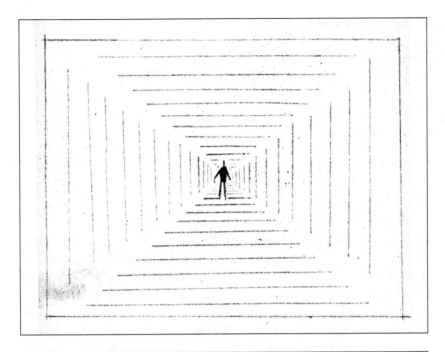

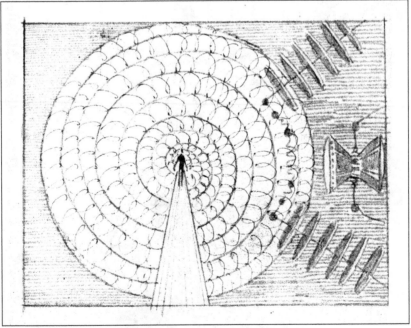

Conception sketches of the tunnel interior.

The remaining 40 pages of Irwin Allen's proposal consisted of five story ideas, designed to illustrate the handling of five basic story situations in the series.

a) The Immediate Past (1956)
b) The Recent Past (1927)
c) The Distant Past (1863)
d) The Ancient Past (200,000 B.C.)
e) The Future (2065)

The Immediate Past (1956)

Peter Phillips finds himself in Grand Central Station and after sneaking aboard a train bound for Connecticut, he turns to the empty seat beside him and idly picks up a folded newspaper left there. He opens it to the front page and is startled to find the headlines and the stories all about the Eisenhower-Stevenson presidential election coming up "next month." He quickly looks at the date on the paper — October 3, 1956. For a moment, he tries to believe he has stumbled onto an old paper, then he realizes that everything around him confirms that date. The newest cars on the road are vintage 1956. The

Conception sketch of the tunnel interior.

women's skirts are longer, there are no commercial jet planes, and John F. Kennedy is a U.S. Senator.

At Silvermine, he gets off the train and starts the long walk to the Institute. Once there he heads immediately for the main gate. But the policeman on duty will not admit him. He pleads to be identified by the director of the Institute. But when contacted at home, the director claims no knowledge of any Peter Phillips. When he sees Newman at the wheel of an older car, he throws himself at the auto as it passes and manages to bounce off unhurt. The "accident" causes Newman to stop. He gets out to see if the man is injured. Phillips shakes himself to clear his head, then smiles up to Newman.

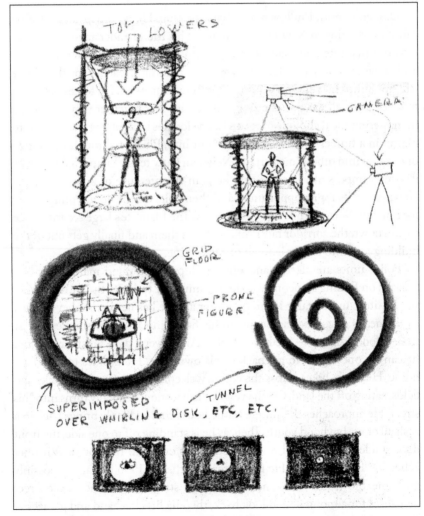

Conception sketches of the tunnel chamber.

"Thank God it's you, Tony," Phillips sighs. I'm finally home. But for a terrible moment Newman stares blankly back.

"Are you sure you're all right?" Newman asks concerned.

"Of course, I'm all right. I'm your partner, Pete Phillips. For God's sake say you know me." Newman is apologetic but carefully explains to Phillips that there is no Peter Phillips at the Institute and they have never met before. Newman starts to get into his car. Phillips tries to hold him back but Newman gets angry.

"Look mister, we've never met. If you're hurt, I'll be glad to get you to a doctor but I don't know you and you're not my partner." With that, Newman drives off.

Desperate now, Phillips remembers the ring. He is convinced that if he can show the ring to Newman, he can make his friend understand. He sneaks into the Institute and manages to get into Newman's lab. Newman enters and convinced now that he is up against a madman, reaches for the phone. Phillips jumps him and prevents him from making a call. He forces Newman to listen as he shows him the ring, telling him that together they succeeded in mastering the technique of relativistic velocities by applying laser beams to matter in a tunnel-like structure that sent him, Phillips, through the fourth dimension into other time periods. Newman flatly tells Phillips that the story is utterly impossible. Positive that he is in the presence of a raving lunatic, Newman waits for an opportunity and then bolts for the door. Phillips dives for him but Newman manages to get away. The Institute's large security force rushes down the corridor but Phillips eludes them and finally gets out of the building and into the little town of Silvermine.

Police units are alerted and now Phillips is a hunted man, his efforts focused on finding someone who knew him prior to 1956. But he didn't join the Institute until nearly 18 months later and he has neither money nor any other means of contacting people in his home in Ohio. The simple necessities — food, shelter — are beyond him. And several days must pass before he can try once again to get back to his own time. He decides to try to get home. He hitch-hikes across the country, sleeping in farmers' haystacks and fields, eating off the land. On the verge of exhaustion, he finally turns into "his" street. He approaches the simple frame house that suddenly brings back in a rush all of his boyhood youth. Then, as he is standing off to one side, the front door suddenly opens and his mother comes out onto the porch. With her is her son Peter Phillips. He finally realizes that in 1956 he cannot possibly go home. Slowly, he turns and starts up the street. At the end of the street he pauses for a moment and look back, then he lifts his hand and glances at the ring. It glows a soft orange. With a slight smile he reaches over and gives

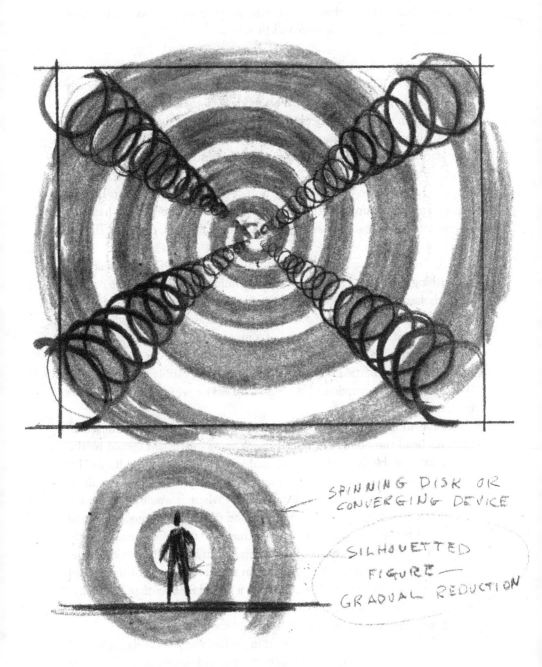

SPINNING DISK OR
CONVERGING DEVICE

SILHOUETTED
FIGURE
GRADUAL REDUCTION

Conception sketches.

the case a half turn and then starts up the street, knowing that any moment his image will begin to shimmer and then vanish.

The Recent Past (1927)

Dr. Peter Phillips finds himself in New York City in May 1927. Shortly after a woman laughs at the sight of his modern clothes, he discovers another young woman trying to murder him. The strangely attractive girl at the wheel of a car attempts to run him over. In spite of his exhaustion, brought on by near starvation, he finds the strength to sprint westward, looking frantically for the mission where he expects to find a temporary refuge. But the young woman catches up to him and forces him at gunpoint into her car. The girl glances around, making sure they have not been observed, brings her handbag up and crashes it against his temple. He slumps forward, out cold. The car speeds away.

Back in the laboratory at the Institute, Dr. Anthony Newman makes an astonishing discovery. His frantic and continuing attempts to make contact with his associate, lost in time, seem suddenly on the verge of success. The impulses from the ring device worn by Phillips are registering clearly on the instruments. The ring is in need of a massive recharging. He also gets a second reading. To Tony's knowledge, Phillips had only one ring, not two. He begins some frantic calculations in search of a possible explanation for the apparent fragmentation of the signaling device which has become lost back somewhere in the past.

At mid-morning of a May day in 1927, Phillips slowly regains consciousness, his head throbbing. He finds himself in an apartment owned by the young woman. He is further astonished when she addresses him as "Dr. Phillips." Then she explains. She had intended to kill him, planning to drive him into the country and dispose of the body where it would not be easily found. But before actually shooting him, she rifled his pockets, hoping to confirm what she was already certain was true. And that was when she made the exciting and astonishing discovery of his identity. He is the world famous Dr. Phillips…the same brilliant pioneer in the development of time travel. She, herself, is a time traveler, but one from a period far later than his own. It is a period when his invention has been developed and perfected to a degree where travel in time is possible for vast numbers of people.

She explains that she is a fugitive from justice. She was falsely accused of a crime she did not commit and was convicted and sentenced to die. Since her brother is a highly placed official in the International Time Travel Bureau and he risked everything to arrange her flight back in time, she needs to avoid anyone from another time period who might be on the lookout for her. Meanwhile, her brother is working on clearing her and has promised to find her here with new supplies for a new time destination.

Phillips' problem is a much different one and one that the girl is quick to understand. With the added knowledge that has come with the years, she is able to tell him a way to draw off the necessary electro-magnetic power that will recharge his ring in time for the next try at getting back to his own time period. Together, they are able to tap the sources of power and recharge the ring. Now all he can do for himself is wait until Tony makes the attempt in the lab.

After walking into a trap, the two flee in a desperate chase around the city…a chase that ends at last in the woman's tiny apartment. Cornered, they must wait until the agents close in for certain capture. Her brother arrives in the nick of time and thanks Phillips for what he has done and then both the girl and her brother disappear as the agents break into the apartment to find only Phillips.

Back in Silvermine, Tony at last decides to risk another attempt to get Phillips back in spite of the existence of the baffling, contradictory signals. He activates the instruments and waits…to discover he has failed once more.

The Distant Past (1863)

Peter Phillips now finds himself along the rich farm countryside with green rolling fields under a hot morning sun. It doesn't take long for Phillips to discover where he is: July 2, 1863. The place is a sleepy Pennsylvania town called Gettysburg. A place where 150,000 men, some in blue uniforms, others in butternut brown, have met in the bewildering confusion of a three-day battle that will change the course of history. Jed Fowler, a Confederate deserter, surrenders himself to Phillips, hoping to reach the Union lines. Because the boy is frightened, Phillips is sorry for him and agrees to help him escape if he can. But their position is difficult. They are between the lines and the pickets on either side will more than likely shoot before challenging in the heat of the long, drawn-out battle.

As the story of Jed Fowler unfolds, Phillips discovers the southern boy has seen too much disease and death over two long, discouraging years; he is weary of war and all it means. The young farm girl they encounter detests war and killing, yet her passionate love of the land makes her willing to lay down her life to defend it. And Phillips finds himself in the midst of this personal conflict, knowing too well how the larger conflict around them will end.

Back in the present time, the director of the Institute, the only individual besides Newman who is aware of the terrible plight of Phillips, tells Newman that they can no longer postpone reporting the failure of the experiment and the loss of their friend. But the release of such information to the world entails great and unknown risks. For this reason, the director is forced to agree to maintain their secret for at least a little while longer.

And a hundred years ago, Phillips risks entering the Union lines to search for a medical officer who could help tend wounded soldiers at the farm house owned by the young girl. While Phillips is gone, a looter shows up and attempts to assault the girl. Jed rescues her and kills the looter. The experience has a strange effect on the young Confederate officer. Much as he loathes killing, he has now come to understand that there are certain values even more important. Ashamed of his desertion, he resolves to return to his post. Phillips returns from his mission with a medical officer and some Union soldiers who manage to evacuate the wounded. Now that he knows no more fighting will take place in this sector, Phillips looks down at his glowing ring and slowly turns it to the activating position.

In his laboratory, Newman receives the long-awaited signal and prepares for one more attempt to move his colleague forward to his own place in time.

The Ancient Past (200,000 B.C.)

As Peter Phillips slowly looks around, he knows that he is not lucky enough to be back in the 20th Century. There is a wild, uncivilized "something" in the air that signals him to be wary and alert. Awe and wonder at the realization that he is now alive in the Old Stone Age, the Paleolithic Period, of some 200,000 years ago. And fear at the sight of the animal—alive—that established the time period: a mighty Mammoth. After witnessing men half-covered in animal pelts attempting to battle the large creature, Phillips is forced to blend in with the scenery and don the skins of a dead hunter. He starts a small fire by rubbing two sticks together. Using a flaming torch, Phillips impresses the hunters, who profusely thank their rescuer and take him to their village.

The chief of the village formally presents him with a young and comely maiden as his wife. A shouted challenge comes from a young, stalwart warrior who evidently thinks he has a prior claim to the lady in question. As is customary, a challenge must be settled by a fight that leaves only one man left alive. The brute strength of the challenger is no match for the karate-trained Phillips, who easily vanquishes his opponent. Instead of killing the Neanderthal, Phillips helps the befuddled young man to his feet, brushes him off and, with a smile, hands back his girlfriend. Later, both of them become good loyal friends to the time traveler. Phillips also leaves a contribution — the Neanderthal is introduced to the art of cooking when Phillips puts meat on the fire.

As the days pass, Phillips becomes a member in good standing. They have occasional brushes with a neighboring antagonistic tribe, but nothing serious. During a tribal meeting, Phillips tells the men that if they join forces with neighboring tribes, he will show them how to capture hundreds of mustangs roaming the countryside…and keep them alive as a plentiful source of food throughout the seasons. The tribe is rocked back on their heels by this radical suggestion to join forces with their enemy for the common good. The plan works perfectly and the tribes throw a raging orgy to celebrate its success…and most important, pledge, by their gods, to continue their mutual cooperation.

When Tony's instruments flash to indicate a location contact, the scientist waits until Phillips twists his ring in answer to the signal. Phillips tells his good friends (the boy and the girl) that the time has come for him to journey onward and asks for their help in making an escape. During the past weeks, his advice has become so valuable that he has been closely guarded by the men of the tribe. Thanks to the boy and girl, Phillips leaps on the back of a young pony — "breaks" it after a few moments of furious bucking — then gallops away. The guards, alerted, drop their spears and flee in terror. Up to this time, man had never ridden a horse. Phillips waves good-bye and gallops off to his rendezvous with the time tunnel, twisting the ring that will permit his transfer to another time and place.

The Future (2065)

Peter Phillips, dressed in the rough buckskins of the early American frontiersman, wearing hand-sewn moccasins and carrying a muzzle-loading long-rifle over his shoulder, trudges along as the cold light of dawn faintly illuminates the endless desert. He is badly in need of a shave. A rugged-looking all-purpose vehicle pulls up to Phillips and asks if he wants a lift. Gratefully, Phillips climbs in and the vehicle starts off with, to Phillips' slight surprise, no apparent effort from the driver. The man does not appear to shift, or clutch and there is no engine sound.

During conversation, Phillips discovers that what he has taken to be the Southwestern part of the United States in a time period near his own, is actually the barren surface of another planet — Mars. He further recognizes that the silent running car is probably a development of the future, powered by a tiny reactor, and the man's all-black clothes are designed to help gather the meager heat offered by a distant sun. Anyone not clean-shaven and wearing nothing but black is subject to discipline from the Keeper of Alpha. On the way, the driver explains that he is one of many members of an underground organization trying to overthrow the self-styled ruler of the American colony on Mars.

"We were sent up here by a free democracy," the driver explains, "and first thing you know this dirty little Sergeant in the Space Corps sets himself as 'Keeper of the Peace,' 'Keeper of Public Morals,' 'Keeper of Public Funds' and — well, you know the story as well as I do." Phillips plays along as if

he knows what the driver is talking about. At the first stop, Phillips shaves
and changes his clothes to fit in with the futuristic society. A group of secret
rebels explains that they are trying to get word back to the proper authorities
on Earth about what has happened on Mars. But the Keeper controls every
means of communication and the elected officials are virtually prisoners.

"And he's got a gang of cut-throat thugs he calls his special corps who

**beyond the known...
into the future!**

**beyond history...
into the past!**

THE TIME TUNNEL takes a young
physicist of the 20th Century through the
black emptiness of the fourth dimension
to the first landing on the moon; back to the
crossing of the Delaware with the first
Continental Army; then on to the Battle of
Midway; back to the French Revolution;
down to the center of the Earth; to a
thousand present lands; to countless fabled
yesterdays; to untold mysterious tomorrows.

boldly imaginative!

vividly prophetic!

the fantastic future!

the incredible past!

The spine-tingling reality
of Man coursing through
the complex of the most ingenious
time-warp ever conceived,
beyond the mist of all
known spacial relationships
into the deep mysteries of: *The TIME TUNNEL*

'eliminate' anybody who speaks up," a young girl explains.

"It's like a page out of history 150 years back," another man adds.

"Perhaps we can take another leaf out of the history books and do something," Phillips muses.

From then on, each time the mail truck makes a run from Alpha to
Beta, it stops on the way at the line shack where a piece of the vehicle is
removed and replaced with an exact duplicate, hand-made, of heavy armor
plate. Under Phillips' guidance, the truck is converted into an impregnable
tank. Like modern Trojans, Phillips, the girl and the other two men arm
themselves and climb into the back of the truck. Finally, the vehicle reaches
a large, heavily patrolled compound. Once inside, they enter the building and
make their way to the block of cells where the elected officials of the colony
are held. Taking the guards completely by surprise they free the officials and
race back to the armored vehicle. As they speed out the gateway the alarm is
sounded. Traveling at top speed the vehicle heads for the Communications
Center. At the entrance to this building they are met by a barricade of guards
who confidently open fire as the truck approaches. But the bullets ricochet

harmlessly off and the mail truck roars through the barricade and crashes into the communication building.

One of the men immediately leaps to a huge radio console and starts tapping a message to Earth while the others hold off the rampaging special corps. With the vital message received, the party piles back into the armored truck and crashes their way back to the open road. They head for the desert-like outlands, abandon the vehicle and walk off into the sandy emptiness. Now, they must survive through the inhumanly cold Martian nights until help comes.

Several days later, huddled around a tiny fire in the desert, the group suddenly looks skyward. A ship from Earth arrives and the International Police Unit comes out. Phillips looks at his ring, notices the glow, turns to the others, and remarks, "Yes, I guess our job is done." With that, he gives the crown of the ring a half turn, knowing that momentarily he will shimmer and vanish into the time warp that he hopes will return him to his own time.

BIOGRAPHIES

The following are biographical material composed for the two lead characters. These were created along with Irwin Allen's initial concept.

Dr. Anthony Newman

Tony Newman is the perfect complement to his working partner, Pete Phillips, in almost every way. Thin, wiry, with dark hair and darting eyes, Newman consumes coffee by the gallon through each working day. He is a tireless, totally dedicated researcher who has neither time nor patience for the disinterested or the imperfect. He is a raging terror when at the console of the gigantic device he and Phillips have created but in rare moments of relaxation his quick smile and love of fine music, post-impressionist art and gourmet cooking make him suddenly and wonderfully human. He is Phillips' junior by several years and his respect and admiration for his partner and best friend are boundless.

Newman was born in the typical big-city middle class environment of Chicago. From the moment he could read, his consuming interest was only the sciences. He was a boy prodigy throughout grammar and high school, winning science awards by the hatful. His single-mindedness ruled out his participation in any extra-curricular activity that wasn't science oriented. In his fourteenth year he built a model ram-jet engine that produced more thrust-per-cubic-inch than any yet designed. This won him a scholarship to the University of Chicago where he took his degree in physics and chemistry and to the Institute he has also served the National Aeronautics and Space Agency as a consultant on solid and liquid propellants.

Dr. Peter Phillips

Pete Phillips is the kind of soft-spoken, good looking young man who might well be called typically American. Tall, rugged, he looks every bit the All-American quarterback he was in college. Phillips, born in a small town in Ohio, distinguished himself scholastically and in athletics through both high school and college. Upon graduation from a large mid-western university, he won a Rhodes Scholarship to Oxford. For three years he studied in England with numerous holiday trips to the continent. His interests, then as now, ran to history, mathematics and theoretical physics. His contributions to the latter eventually won for him a top post at the Institute for Advanced Research in the Theoretical Sciences at Silvermine, Connecticut, where he met and teamed with Tony Newman to work on the theoretical possibility of producing a controlled time-warp. At thirty-two, Phillips is the Institute's four-wall handball and boxing champion. Like Newman — he is a bachelor. In general, he tends to be a remarkably well-rounded citizen for one so intellectually gifted. He still finds time to make weekly appearances at the local Boys Club, plays a devastating game of bridge, once gave a year of his life to help elect a governor he felt was genuinely needed to make his state's government honest and effective. He is, in other words, a man who cares.

ENTER SHIMON WINCELBERG

The date was July 22, 1960. George Pal, the same man responsible for destroying the Earth in *When Worlds Collide* (1951) and bringing Martians to life in *War of the Worlds* (1953), revealed what would become his latest box office success, *The Time Machine*, unaware that he was about to imprint a milestone of cinematic history. There was saturation booking on opening night in Chicago. The lines to buy tickets in New York extended a city block. And Americans were transported into another world as Rod Taylor sat in his time machine, traveled far into the future, discovered the horrors of mankind and saved the life of a beautiful woman at the risk of his own life, combating a race of flesh-eating Morlocks. MGM made of ton of money and television producers, Irwin Allen among them, wondered if the same kind of formula would work on a weekly basis.

Also pre-dating *The Time Tunnel* is *The Time Travelers* (1964), written and

directed by Ib Melchior, and distributed by American International Pictures. When scientists at the campus of USC begin testing their time viewing device, drawing enormous amounts of power, they observe a window 107 years into the future. They discover the window also serves as a portal to the future and they set out to explore a future yet unexplored. They soon learn that after a nuclear holocaust, the world is in tatters and human survivors must constantly defend themselves against mutated beasts. The surviving humans have built a defense against the mutants and are completing a starship that will (hopefully) take them to a planet orbiting a distant star. Upon seeing the future of the earth, the men would like to return to their own time and attempt to reproduce the same time travel technique they established back in 1964. Regardless of what science-fiction fans theorize, the movie bears no similarity to Irwin Allen's *Time Tunnel* series.

In 1964, Shimon Wincelberg, a script writer for numerous television programs including *Have Gun — Will Travel, Route 66, Johnny Staccato,*

Rawhide and the pilot episode of *Lost In Space,* was hired by Irwin Allen to create a pilot script for the proposed time travel series, based on Allen's 45-page conception, summarized into a five-page proposal (reprinted in Appendix B). Wincelberg threw away most of Allen's concepts and added a few scientists for weekly supporting roles, and chose a more appropriate incident in world history for man's maiden launch through time: the sinking of the Titanic on its maiden voyage. The title was "The Man Who Killed Time" and the script was dated October 26, 1964. As proposed, the year is 1967 and Dr. Peter Phillips of the Institute for Advanced Research and Theoretical Sciences at the University of Silvermine, Connecticut, decides to become the first human guinea pig to travel through time, thanks to the unperfected Convergence Chamber. Phillips soon finds himself in 1912, floating in the icy, Atlantic waters, and manages to be rescued by the crew of a passing luxury liner. There, he meets his grandmother, Althea Phillips, a passenger on the Titanic. Althea is struggling with Uncle Brian, an uncaring individual, who feels her young son, Walker, should have a proper upbringing in England — not the United States. Phillips, meanwhile, makes a number of efforts to get word out about the up-coming disaster, all of which makes him suspect in the eyes of the passengers and crew, with the belief that the Americans are attempting to thwart the British to beat a record for the fastest transatlantic crossing.

Back at the Time Tunnel, Tony Newman, described as the senior partner and ten years older than Peter, is furious. Washington bureaucrats have already been breathing down his neck, believing that funding has been wasted on a pile of electronic computers. Phillips' disappearance may even look like murder in the eyes of a few. The project will no doubt be shut down. Dr. Loman Kirk, administrative head of the Institute, introduces Tony to Blanche Putnam, an inspector from Washington, who wants to do just what Tony fears. The doctors quickly convince her that the Time Tunnel is a success, even while flawed in its earliest stages, and retrieving Phillips has now become their top priority.

Back on the Titanic, the iceberg incident has created panic and Phillips orders Althea to go to the lifeboats. He'll find Walker and bring her to him. Amidst all the chaos, Phillips succeeds, moments before the Time Tunnel personnel attempt to retrieve him. He doesn't return home, however, but instead lands in the prehistoric era. Phillips is forced to fight off a Tyrannosaurus Rex by starting a fire in the mouth of a cave and hiding inside. In desperation, the Time Tunnel personnel randomly places him into another time — which is about all they can do for him until they figure out why they are unable to bring him back.

On the viewing screen, they discover Phillips is now outside the Silvermine Installation. Kirk, Blanche and Tony, along with security, rush out to meet Pete, only to discover he is still out of time. Phillips is in 1956, a month before he began work at the Institute. Jiggs, head of security, doesn't recognize Dr. Phillips, nor does Tony. Phillips becomes furious and runs away, once again with the same luminescent glow that appears moments before

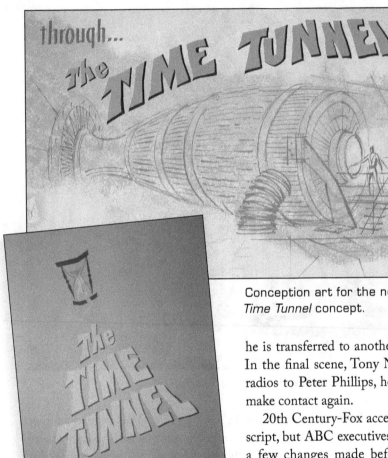

Conception art for the new *Time Tunnel* concept.

he is transferred to another time... In the final scene, Tony Newman radios to Peter Phillips, hoping to make contact again.

20th Century-Fox accepted the script, but ABC executives wanted a few changes made before they would proceed with a purchase. "We had a great deal of excitement about putting the series on the schedule," recalled Thomas W. Moore, Vice President of ABC. The network was placed third in competition and wanted 1966 to be the year of color, insisting existing programs shot in black and white now had to be filmed in color. A five-second bumper before each program bragging that the series was "In Color" became the season necessity. "TV Westerns were dying and science fiction was the perfect genre with which to attract viewers," recalled Moore. "Irwin Allen was a brilliant, take-charge producer and he hired the best people to work for him. He loved special effects and those costs were *Time Tunnel*'s biggest detriment. It's remarkable what he accomplished with limited technology and modest budgets." Even with the network's interest, and budgetary concerns, the concept contained within the initial script was the selling point.

Susan Hampshire on the deck of the Titanic.

As Wincelberg told Mike Clark in *Starlog* #159, "ABC wanted another script. I said I would do it, but Fox said, 'No, your name is already associated with the first script,' and even though everyone at Fox liked my script, they felt, for tactical reasons, there should be another writer's name on [the new one]. I was pretty annoyed at the studio's lack of loyalty after they had been so high on my script. There was still a lot of stuff left in the final script, mostly involving the establishing of the tunnel and some *Titanic* material."

Irwin Allen chose to hire Harold Jack Bloom, whose credits included *The Man From U.N.C.L.E.*, *Have Gun-Will Travel* and *12 O'Clock High*. Bloom co-wrote motion pictures as varied as the MGM Western *The Naked Spur* (1953) to Howard Hawks' ambitious *Last of the Pharaohs* (1955). After reviewing Wincelberg's premise, Bloom made a number of major revisions to please ABC executives, finishing a rough draft of the shooting script sometime around Christmas of 1965. The most notable difference was Bloom's insistence of two time travelers instead of one.

While Allen and his crew produced the pilot, constructing the sets and working out the technical details such as costumes, props and sets, Bloom

Irwin Allen directing a scene for the pilot episode of *The Time Tunnel.*

revised various pages throughout the month of January to accommodate the necessary production changes. Bloom was paid $10,000 for producing the first and final draft of the teleplay, and probably would have stayed on either as a script writer or as a story consultant had it not been for Harry Saltzman and Albert Broccoli's invitation to script the next James Bond film, *You Only Live Twice*, beginning in February after Irwin Allen admitted the final draft and all the revised pages were sufficient.*

* Wincelberg received screen credit for creating the first draft of the pilot, and received a payment for every episode that was produced; Bloom received $500. Kent Productions received $1,000, a total of $1,900 per episode. Ironically, Bloom suffered a similar fate when he went to England to script the James Bond film — Bloom would eventually be retired from the 007 project in favor of Roald Dahl, even though Dahl's screenplay contained most of Bloom's invention.

Bloom's script, when compared to Wincelberg's, included the removal of Peter Phillip's family from the *Titanic* and substituted hot-blooded Tony Newman as the scientist who hurls himself into the tunnel when a U.S. Senator playing devil's advocate wants to know if all the funding was worth a fool's dream. "I was a fair-haired boy of Mr. Allen's at that time," recalled Bloom to author Mark Phillips in the September 1991 issue of *Starlog*. "I

Irwin Allen directs Susan Hampshire for the pilot episode of *The Time Tunnel*.

had my interminable meetings with him, then he told me to start on page one of the script and I did. I thought the pilot was satisfactory."

Another major revision of Bloom's was to incorporate two time travelers, not one, to the series. Wincelberg's premise was based on Irwin Allen's, that of a solo time traveler on the move. According to an early press book following the completion of Wincelberg's treatment: "*The Time Tunnel* takes a young physicist of the 20th Century through the black emptiness of the fourth dimension to the first landing on the moon; back to the crossing of the Delaware with the first Continental Army; then on to the Battle of Midway; back to the French Revolution; down to the center of the Earth; to a thousand present lands; to countless labeled yesterdays; to untold mysterious tomorrows."

Before leaving for England to script the latest Bond adventure, Bloom gave Allen some advice. "I warned him that projecting our characters into the future wouldn't have the same impact as playing in the past because the latter gave the audience a sense of superiority, which had entertainment value," the writer recalled. "The best affirmation of that is the *Back to the Future* theatrical series."

Irwin Allen directs Dennis Hopper in a scene for the pilot episode of *The Time Tunnel,* which would ultimately end up on the cutting room floor.

Other changes (courtesy of Bloom) included the location of the Time Tunnel, Kirk became a General instead of a doctor, the name and sex of the Washington dignitary was changed, as well as the character of Pete Phillips (now changed to Doug Phillips). It would be Tony, not Pete/Doug, who went into the Time Tunnel (sans Convergence Chamber), and the radio which Tony communicated with Pete was substituted for the visual screen now evident on the telecasts.

The plot was finally resolved to fit within the constraints of both budget and weekly production. When the Time Tunnel project faces scrapping, Dr. Tony Newman volunteers to be an experimental subject. Before anyone can stop him, he sets the controls and is sent off through time. Tumbling onto the deck of the ocean liner, he finds a life preserver labeled "Titanic."

Astounded, he rushes off to find Captain Smith and warn him of the impending disaster. Meanwhile, at the Time Tunnel Complex, Dr. Doug Phillips, Dr. Ann MacGregor and Dr. Swain work to locate Tony, finally discovering him on the liner by following the sound of the ship's bells. Aboard the ship, Tony is having great difficulty persuading the Captain to change his course; Smith at first thinks he's mad, then, becoming convinced

Irwin Allen with James Darren and Robert Colbert on the set of *The Time Tunnel.*

he's a spy from an enemy steamship line, has him imprisoned. With Tony located, Doug goes through the Time Tunnel to his rescue and after freeing him, the two attempt to use the wireless to summon help. Captain Smith still remains unconvinced, until the ship hits the iceberg late that night. Asking the men how they knew this would happen, they only tell the extremity of his position, then plunge into rescue operation. Doug

Irwin Allen joins in the fun with James Darren on the set of *The Time Tunnel.*

and Tony are extracted just as the ship goes down, and are then separately hurled forward into time.

When the idea of the Time Tunnel was finalized, including storyboards and blueprints, Allen surrounded himself with the best in Hollywood to pull off the biggest disappearing trick on national television: the construction of the Tunnel itself and the Time Tunnel Complex, so viewers would seriously believe a man can vanish to and from the tunnel. "The time tunnel prop was fantastic," recalled actor Patrick Culliton, who stood in for brief roles in many of the episodes, including the role of a Time Tunnel technician. "I've walked onto a lot of sets, but you don't see something like that every day."

"For the pilot, they had two back-to-back stages and we used both of them for the Tunnel," recalled Robert Colbert. "The Tunnel went from one stage right on through to the other, another 40, 50 feet. After that, they just used the half of it [used one stage]. At the back of the Tunnel they put a scrim that showed sort of an infinity type of twirl, and away they went on one stage."

ABC insisted the television series be filmed in color, in an attempt to compete against the rival networks. NBC provided the catalyst for rapid color expansion by announcing that its prime-time schedule for fall of 1965 would be almost entirely in color. ABC and CBS quickly joined the bandwagon and over half of their combined prime-time programming was also in color that season. Irwin Allen by this time had switched both *Voyage to the Bottom of the Sea* and *Lost In Space* from black and white to color. Ironically, ABC, which had delayed its first color series until 1962, now found itself competing with rival networks by adding "In Color" bumpers at the beginning of all their prime-time programs, and by 1966, insisted every program was to be shot in color. For *The Time Tunnel*, the use of stock footage from older movies was handicapped because black and white movies could not have been used.

Cinematographer Winton Hoch, with three Oscars (*Joan of Arc, She Wore a Yellow Ribbon* and *The Quiet Man*) and an Emmy (*Voyage to the Bottom of the Sea*) under his belt, was taken off *Voyage to the Bottom of the Sea* and permanently assigned to *The Time Tunnel*. Educated at the California Institute of Technology, Hoch became a color specialist for the Technicolor corporation, working to develop their three color system. Allen needed the best man available to ensure *The Time Tunnel* productions matched the stock footage as closely as possible, so Hoch was shifted to the new science fiction series,

This page, facing page: the two stages at Fox where the Time Tunnel control center and the tunnel itself would be constructed. Photos taken by Irwin Allen personally on the day he inspected the stages to envision the construction.

where he set to work making it appear *The Time Tunnel's* budget was larger than it really was.

At the 19th Annual Awards Presentation of the National Academy of Television Arts and Sciences, held on June 4, 1967, L.B. Abbott, A.S.C., for the third consecutive year, received the Emmy statuette in the Photographic Special Effects category — this time for his work on *The Time Tunnel*.

Abbott was the head of the 20th Century-Fox Photographic Special Effects Department and competed against himself because he was also nominated for *Voyage to the Bottom of the Sea*. At the 14th Annual Golden Reel Awards, a banquet of Motion Picture Sound Editors, Irwin Allen's *Time Tunnel* series won the television award for best series. The crew responsible for the editing, who were acknowledged during the ceremony, was comprised of Don Hall, Jr., Robert Cornett and Mike Colgan.

With *The Time Tunnel* magnificently photographed by Winton Hoch, A.S.C., the series was bound to receive acknowledgement beyond critic reviews in trade columns. Abbott earned his reputation for wizardry by being able to conjure spectacular and seemingly complex effects with a minimum of time, equipment and budget. All of which were enormously important items in television production.

For example, it was necessary to create a unique illusion that could symbolize the actual repeated journeys of the time travelers through a vortex to the past or the future. To this end, a drum 9 feet in diameter with a band 5 feet wide was covered with scraps of colored cellophane, Christmas wrappings

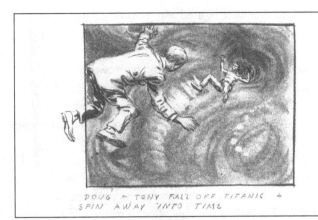

DOUG + TONY FALL OFF TITANIC +
SPIN AWAY INTO TIME

DOUG + TONY TUMBLE INTO
LIMBO

TONY + DOUG ARE SEPERATED
DOUG MOVES OUT OF FRAME
TONY RECEDES TO FAR BG

and other tinted items that were lighted with colored gelatins over the lamps. A camera with a Kinoptic 9.8mm ultra wide-angle lens was set up very close to the surface of the drum and framed so that the image photographed would fill exactly one-half of the frame as the drum revolved toward it.

Subsequently, the scene was flipped over to fill the blank half of the frame and the two complimentary images were printed through a "ripple" glass to form the master background scene. The result was a stunning, jewel-like kaleidoscopic effect of colorful "time fragments" flying by.

To play against this background, scenes were shot of Colbert and Darren suspended by wires in front of a blue screen in such a way that they could be revolved about an axis. The camera, mounted on a crane, was equipped with an image inverter prism before the lens which created the illusion of the actors revolving in the opposite direction. Filmed at 64 frames per second, the players seemed to float gracefully end over end. When these scenes were optically matted against the above described background scene, the characters did, indeed, appear to be soaring through a glamorously colorful Time Tunnel.

"We were each rigged up with a harness, and we were hangin' in front of a huge blue scrim," recalled Robert Colbert. "They had big Ritters [wind machines] on us as we hung suspended against this blue backdrop. And later, of course, they superimposed those kaleidoscopic images [over the blue]. So, yeah, that was us up there, twisting and turning!"

Both Abbott and Hoch were involved with all 30 productions. Bob Kinoshita, who worked on *Lost In Space* as the art director for the first two seasons, was asked to help out on *The Time Tunnel* with some designs for (according to Kinoshita) "some labs and stuff."

JAMES DARREN

Receiving top billing was James Darren, playing the role of Tony Newman, the hot-headed scientist who often acted on impulse and emotion. Darren came in on the wave of latter-day James Deans, all of whom seemed to shoot up with a minimum of acting experience. Back in 1954, at the age of 17, Darren used his savings from an apprentice job at his uncle's jewelry store, plus a loan from his father, to finance a fruitless trip to Hollywood with the sole aim of being "discovered." He hung around Schwab's drugstore for six months and finally left town, tail between legs. Later, he was riding an elevator in mid-Manhattan one day when he was spotted by a talent executive from Columbia Pictures. In a matter of days, Darren was in Hollywood. In a matter of weeks he was on a soundstage in his first starring picture, *Rumble on the Docks*. Said Joyce Selznick, his discoverer, "He was not one of those

James Darren publicity photo.

untouchable stars. He got right down there with the fans. And he was so beautiful."

Before his stint as a time traveler, Darren was already an accomplished actor and singer, a teen-age idol and co-star of three beach-party flicks: *Gidget* (1959), *Gidget Goes Hawaiian* (1961) and *Gidget Goes to Rome* (1963). While Sandra Dee managed to be an appealing little hard-head as she became smit-

ten with James Darren, it was the title song for the first *Gidget* that resulted in his recording contract and a whole separate career in the music biz. But with success comes the ultimate price: fandom. "At times it was Chinese torture," Darren recalled. "In San Francisco a crowd of girls age 13 to 16 tore down the TV studio doors, pulled me out and pinned me to the ground, tearing my jacket, ripping my clothes off and pulling souvenir hairs from my head." In a New England town, the police chief saved him from rapacious fans by pushing him into a waiting squad car in the manner of The Beatles. Once in Hollywood he found his car fenders, doors and trunk painted with the names and phone numbers of four girl fans. Another time a fan inked her phone number on the bottom of his new trench coat. "It's a nice thing to look back on," said Darren, "but it wasn't much fun at the time."

With Darren's popularity cinched among teenage girls, adding sex appeal to the television series was as easy as signing the singer up for a contract to star in a weekly television program. *The Hollywood Reporter*, reviewing the series in September 1966, once commented, "It is a little more difficult to believe the young, handsome Darren as an electronics genius with a doctor's degree and years of experiences on the *Tunnel* project, than it is to believe in the tunnel itself. But Darren should draw the femmes."

"Irwin called my agent [at William Morris] about my doing the role of Tony Newman, and my agent told me what it was, a science fiction series

called *The Time Tunnel*," recalled Darren. "I had not read the script or any-thing, but I told him I wasn't interested in doing television and not interested in doing a science fiction TV series. My head really wasn't there about doing science fiction. I might have looked at *Voyage* or looked at *Lost In Space* and figured I didn't want to deal with monsters and things like that. It was some-thing that just didn't really appeal to me at the time. And as far as doing a TV

series, at that point in my career I didn't really want to do a series, I wanted to continue doing films. Well, they called repeatedly, and finally my agent told me that Irwin wanted to talk to me. I called his office and he set up a meeting. I went into the meeting, and by the time I left, he had talked me into doing *The Time Tunnel*. He said, 'This is something you have to do. I know you don't want to do this, but I think you're perfect for this role and I want you to do it,' and he convinced me. Irwin was one of the great salespersons of our time. I accepted the role because of my meeting with him."

"What made it interesting was that we got to travel to so many time peri-ods in the show," Darren continued. "*The Time Machine* had been done a few years before as a film, which I thought was wonderful. To utilize that premise on a weekly basis was great. When Irwin told me about the initial episode, about the sinking of the *Titanic*, and all the other areas the show would get into, like the assassination of Abraham Lincoln, I was interested. I thought the public would be interested as well, since time-traveling is something most people have probably thought about at some point in their lives. I can't speak for other people, but I know if I could travel through time, it would be a kick in the pants; it would be great."

During filming of *The Time Tunnel*, Darren locked himself up in his trailer dressing-room every day right through the lunch break. "I'd rather think," he told a columnist for *TV Guide*. "I hate the commissary. It's worse than a Hollywood party, everybody staring at you, saying 'Hiya, baby,' 'Hiya, Sweetheart'." Darren was also recording a new album for Warner Brothers at the time he was filming *The Time Tunnel*.

"I always thought the world and all of Jimmy — he's a talented guy," Colbert said. "And he looks today pretty much like he did when we did the show, he looks like it's still '66 and he just stepped off the set. The portrait in the attic must be ripped and rancid and smelly by now [laughs], because he looks great. Back when we did the show, I think Jimmy was prematurely gray, and he dyed his hair. Now he has a little bit of gray that he lets come through. But it's just so funny, he's one of those guys that never ages, he's just the same size, the same look exactly as he did 40 years ago. Jimmy's a terrific guy, everybody likes him, he's got a lot of buds, and they all usually are from the crowd in Philly [South Philadelphia] — he's a real home boy. We didn't hang together, but — friends? I think he hung the moon, I just love the guy, he's a wonderful dude to me, I think the world of him. He came over the house a few months ago and we had a great time."

"That reminds me that Irwin and I had little disagreements because my sideburns would be a little long," recalled James Darren. "He'd say, 'No, no, no, no, no. Scientists don't have long sideburns, they have short sideburns.' I said, 'Really? Gee, I guess I don't know many scientists…' [Laughs] So I had to keep my sideburns short. But what I would do is grow them longer and then have the makeup department put a white line on the bottom part of each sideburn, to make it look as though they had been cut. It was just an illusion. A person's skin is usually a little tanned, so when you cut your sideburns, the skin that was under the hair is usually lighter. We would play those little tricks on Irwin. But he was hard to get things over on; you didn't fool Irwin too many times."

Reportedly, Irwin Allen, always the perfectionist, was upset with the actors during filming of "Rendezvous With Yesterday" because they were not following direction. Out of anger, he announced in a booming voice that he was going to create a series that would have no actors whatsoever.

"Irwin also felt scientists should not laugh. They were to be taken seriously," Darren added. "One day he discovered what we were doing with my sideburns and threatened to come down. He didn't threaten, he really did come down. Makeup quickly deceived him by putting white there to hide the sideburns and they fooled him. But that was Irwin. He wasn't a fan with actors and once told me that if he could direct robots, he would. Actors had their own way of playing a role and Irwin had his way."

ROBERT COLBERT

Colbert made his first screen test when he was five years old. "It was for MGM," he recalled. "The studio was having some sort of a contest to find new child stars. I don't remember too much about it except that I had long curly hair, sang a couple of songs and told a sad story. I hated it. At best, it's still in MGM's vaults somewhere. I guess I wasn't cut out to be a male Shirley Temple."

Colbert's next brush with fame came several years later. "I was to be a child prodigy on the violin. The only hitch was that I had no talent for music." He did perform a violin solo at the 1939 New York World's Fair in San Francisco. "I studied violin for seven years," he continued, "although my heart was never in it. I think I got started because of a neighbor — a 5-year-old across the fence from our house. He played violin beautifully, and I guess I was jealous."

During a stint in the Army, Colbert took a disc jockey job at radio station KSBK in Shuri, Japan. One day he received a call from Jerrietta Hayes, a civilian employee in charge of entertainment for Air Force Special Services, who was mounting a production of *The Caine Mutiny Court Martial*. She liked Colbert's deep, rich radio voice and was convinced he could be an actor. "I told her I had no interest in doing that, because the eight dollars a night was very important to me. I did not have time to perform my duties as a clerk-typist and run the radio station at night, and do anything else. To do her play would mean I'd give up my radio job, and, boy, that job was awfully important to somebody making 33 bucks a month. She said, 'Oh, come down and just try out for it. Read the part, see what you think. You might be interested and have some fun.' So I did, I went and I read for the part of Greenwald, the Jewish attorney. Those were, to this day, the greatest lyrics [lines of dialogue] I ever had — his soliloquy about how his grandmother was melted down into a bar of soap in Germany, and everything else. It was just an amazing experience. So I opted to give up my job at the station and go down and do this play, and we performed it in various places, including the Ryukyuan Islands."

"One little adventure took us to an island where we performed *The Caine Mutiny* in front of a small American contingent, and a huge Ryukyuan contingent," Colbert remembers. "Well, except for about four [Ryukyuan] corporals and a pfc, they couldn't understand a damn word we were sayin'!

And then I fell through the stage at one point, it was so rickety! It was the funniest experience in my life, it was a hoot and a holler, and I'll never forget it as long as I live."

After that, he was bitten by the acting bug. After he was discharged, Colbert, then living in Oregon, started doing a little theater with the Oumansky theater group. "We did theater in the round, a lot of little plays here and there, and I did some Shakespeare at the Portland Civic Theater. While I was doing *The Little Hut* in a theater in the round at a place called Amatos Supper Club in Portland, Mickey Shaughnessy saw the performance. He was a nightclub performer, and he also was in movies like *Don't Go Near the Water* (1957) with Glenn Ford and *Designing Woman* (1957) with Gregory Peck. He was pretty hot at the time. He saw *The Little Hut* and he came up to me afterwards and introduced himself and he said, 'Listen, if you ever wanna come down to L.A., I have an agent in Beverly Hills. I'd like him to meet you and see if they'd be interested in handling you. I think you got a career in films and various stages of the theater.' I said, 'Well... when's the next plane?' [Laughs]"

Robert Colbert as Brent Maverick

Colbert continued to explore stage work and small bit roles in movies such as *Under Fire* (1957) and *Macabre* (1958), followed by a contract with Warner Brothers. Like Robert Conrad, Van Williams, Clint Walker, Jack Kelly and Connie Stevens, Colbert was one of the "kids from Warner's," appearing on weekly television programs. Colbert soon found himself helping rescue a television series that was in trouble due to a studio dispute with James Garner. "Lo and behold, because of my resemblance to Garner, they took me out of *Black Gold* and put me into *Maverick* as Brother Brent," Colbert continued. Colbert never liked the role because the series was already taking a hit from viewers, and he only played the lead for two episodes.

When Colbert played the role of Thomas J. Morely in Warner's *A Fever in the Blood*, the studio attempted to create publicity with a press release in

February of 1961, heralding Colbert's motion picture debut, in which he appeared alongside his Maverick "brother," Jack Kelly, and Carroll O'Connor, who would later make a guest appearance in the fifth episode of *The Time Tunnel*. Warners failed to mention that Colbert appeared in a total of six motion pictures prior to his Warner contract, including the Three Stooges epic, *Have Rocket — Will Travel* (1958), and *Fever* was not his motion picture debut.

James Darren and Robert Colbert prepare for their scene with Michael Rennie.

After his Warner contract ended, Colbert moved over to Universal for two years, then jumped to MGM where he was to star in an E. Jack Neuman-scripted television pilot, "The Mayor," for NBC, which failed to sell in 1965.

Irwin Allen strangely enough signed actor Robert Colbert as a lead without even the benefit of a screen test. Colbert only met his new boss when he went in for wardrobe fittings. There can be no doubt that Allen had seen enough of Colbert on television to know what he was getting for his money. His previous experience on television westerns, including *Maverick*, no doubt helped with the riding sequences when the character of Doug Phillips had to ride a horse or face off against notorious gunslingers. (For a scientist, he was pretty quick on the draw when he faced off against Billy the Kid.)

"My agent sent me out to 20th, to meet Irwin Allen. I went in, I met him and I sat there with him, and he was interviewing me. There was no mention about any screen test or anything, we were just talking and so forth," recalled Colbert to author Tom Weaver. "Then he took me into a room where he had his storyboards — black-and-white drawings, 11x14s, maybe a little bigger, all around the walls of this room, depicting practically every scene in

this upcoming *Time Tunnel* pilot, which was set on the Titanic. There were renderings of costumes, all kinds of stuff. I thought, 'This is really incredible. Such great detail.' I didn't know Irwin from a rock. I didn't know what his past was, I didn't know at the time how many other shows he had going. But he was telling me about how this pilot was going to be the most expensive pilot ever filmed. It was like a half a million bucks, and that was a lot of money in '66. When I saw the storyboards and all this other stuff, and he was telling' me how much money they were gonna spend on it, and that Michael Rennie would be in it…it was quite impressive. And it was like he was tryin' to sell me on the idea of goin' to work for him."

"I don't know where he knew me from, but apparently when I came in, I was the one he wanted, 'cause that was that, I had the job," continued Colbert. "And I wanted that job, once I saw Irwin's dog and pony show there. I saw the storyboards, and found out that it was gonna be the most expensive pilot ever

filmed, and that Michael Rennie was going to be in it — I loved Michael from *The Day the Earth Stood Still* (1951). There was nothing about it that made you not want to do it! I didn't know Jimmy Darren or Lee Meriwether, but I wanted the part and he said, 'Well, you got it'...Michael Rennie was just the best, and we ended up spending a lot of time together. We were just buddies, chasin' chicks and drinkin' Margaritas and havin' a good time. I had a good relationship with Michael, we had fun. We didn't play golf or anything, we just were drinkin' buddies at a club that's no longer there."

To help convince Colbert to take the role, Irwin's office had a number of charcoal drawings and storyboards for the pilot episode, on display. The drawings depicted the camera angles, the sets, the costumes the cast would wear, which Paul Zastupnevich designed, and as Colbert once described, he could almost see the entire story in black and white. "That was when I knew this was going to be something special."

"Bob was great. From Day One, we hit it off. We just were friends, there was no competition," recalled James Darren. "Well, he got upset because he didn't have as many lines as me sometimes [laughs], but I would tell him, 'Do you really care?' He'd say, 'Well, look at all this stuff you have to say.' I'd say, 'I tell ya what: I don't even want to learn it. You say it. You say it, and I'll say this. Take this part of my dialogue.' And it was all done without any kind of animosity. We had a good time on the set, and I loved working with him. And I loved working with Lee as well. Even though we didn't have many scenes together, we were on the same lot, we'd get to see Lee and Whit Bissell and John Zaremba and all those people quite a bit."

"Incidentally [laughs], talking about Bob and me...we were two of a kind in many ways," Darren continued. "He would say, for instance, 'Y'know, I think we should get phones in our dressing rooms,' and I'd say, 'Yeah, we should.' But they wouldn't do it. Finally Bob and I said, 'Look, we need phones in our dressing room.' It didn't entail anything — they put a phone line to your trailer. It became just a matter of principle. So we finally, after about maybe, Christ, the 18th or 20th episode, we finally got our phones. Now today, we would not have to argue for that, because we have cell phones."

Observant fans of *The Time Tunnel* will notice how Doug and Tony's clothes would get dirty during a brawl with a combatant, but miraculously get clean again for the next scene. Because there was more than one sweater, the same dirt stains reappear on the same areas of the sweater in multiple episodes.

LEE MERIWETHER

Presumably it is the dream of many an American girl to be chosen Miss America. In 1955, a beautiful and talented woman named Lee Meriwether of San Francisco, California, was chosen Miss America with much fanfare at Atlantic City, New Jersey. It was the first Miss American Pageant to be televised and she was delighted because the money she received would

help her realize her lifelong ambition of becoming an actress. She applied her $5,000 pageant scholarship to studying acting in classes taught by Lee Strasberg and Curt Conway. Prior, she studied radio, television, theater arts and English for a year at City College of San Francisco, where a fraternity entered her into the Miss San Francisco pageant. She won the title, then the Miss California and Miss American crowns.

In 1955, Meriwether established herself as a major television personality during a 14-month assignment as fashion/women's editor on Dave Garroway's *Today* show. During her residence on *Today*, Meriwether met Marlene Olsen, the 1957 March of Dimes poster girl, famous French chefs, celebrated authors and even worked alongside the irrepressible J. Fred Muggs, a chimpanzee mascot for the NBC television program. During this same period, Meriwether made her television acting debut on *The Philco-Goodyear Television Playhouse* in two plays written especially for her. Attempting to avoid cheesecake photos and establish herself as an actress with dramatic talent, she asked Jack Webb for a chance to play a small part in a *Dragnet* television episode. Later, he confessed that he suffered misgivings about her

ability when he saw her name on the casting board because he identified her as a bathing beauty queen. But he went ahead and was delighted with her performance. It was Webb who phoned other Hollywood producers, with the result that she was cast on a number of television programs, including *The Millionaire* and *Omnibus*.

Meriwether continued to accept guest spots on numerous television programs, including brief recurring roles on *My Three Sons* as Phyllis Allen and *12 O'Clock High* as Captain Phyllis Vincent. The April 30, 1966, issue of *TV Guide* was among the earliest to break the news: "Lee Meriwether has landed a continuing role in *The Time Tunnel*, the forthcoming ABC series starring Robert Colbert and James Darren." The former Miss America and television host of the *Today* show was now signed to play the role of Dr. Ann MacGregor, an electronuclear biochemist, whose sole job was to look up historical facts in numerous encyclopedias, consult computer printouts and adjust controls to get a "fix" on Doug and Tony. While *The Time Tunnel*

was being produced and broadcast, Meriwether was married to actor Frank Aletter, who played the role of Capt. Glenn McDivitt ("Mac") in *It's About Time*. Together, they constituted the only husband-wife acting duo of the 1966-67 television season to star concurrently in different prime-time series (both, very incidentally, having the word "Time" in their titles).

"I really don't know how I was cast for the part," recalled Lee Meriwether.

"I don't remember doing any reading for the part. There was no screen test. I was around the 20th Century-Fox lot at the time for *12 O'Clock High* and the *Batman* movie so maybe that was how they came across me. I never met Irwin Allen until I was on the set."

The studio issued a number of press releases to help publicize the series. *The Reading Eagle* (Pennsylvania) quoted Meriwether as saying, "It has a good concept and it's an exciting series to work on for someone who was never meant to be in the acting business, as well as for someone who considers themselves as primarily a parent."

One press release quoted Meriwether's "ambition" to take a peek at the past.

Lee Meriwether is responsible for transporting stars James Darren and Robert Colbert through time while she attempts to return them to their own era. Busy pushing buttons, she has little opportunities to trip through time herself. But if given the opportunity to enter The Time Tunnel, she has several ideas of where she would like to be "time locked" too. "Of course I would want a guarantee that I can come back," she says cautiously. "And I would not want to go alone. I would like to have my husband, Frank Aletter, with me. I would love to go back to the Elizabethian age and see Shakespeare plays with their original casts. It might be nice to get some

acting pointers from "Willy" himself too. And it would be interesting to see London as it was then. In fact, I have never seen London in person, ever. Anyway, using The Time Tunnel would be one way for me to get to Europe. Then I would like to go back to just before the birth of Christ and then live from that point on to see if everything happened the way that it is written in The Bible. I would then find out what kind of reporters the Apostles really were. Going back through history before cameras were invented would be wonderful. When you see actual photographs of the past, your imagination of those times can take off from there. But when you only see paintings, you want to find out how accurate they are." Would Lee, who was Miss America in 1955, like to go back to the first Miss America contest, wearing her 1955 bathing suit, which she wore when she won her title? "NO!" she says emphatically. "I would lose hands down. The swimsuits and granny caps they wore back then were pretty daring by their standards. I don't think they were at all ready for one-piece bathing suits with ruffles!"

Victor Jory as Captain Beal.

Colbert and Darren's scenes were usually shot in five days, followed by a one day film shoot on Stage 18, housing the Time Tunnel Complex.

"Jimmy and I would work usually in the field," recalled Robert Colbert. "Most of it was shot on the back lot at 20th or, if we had to go to location, out at the 20th Ranch, Malibu Canyon and various places. So we would do five days in the field, Jimmy and myself having whatever adventure the episode was about. Then after we'd done our five-day shoot, the *Tunnel* people [actors Lee Meriwether, Whit Bissell, John Zaremba, etc.] would come in on the sixth day and they would work on the Tunnel set, doing various scenes that were interspersed throughout the script. Outside of the pilot, Jimmy and I never, except on rare occasions, worked with them. We hardly ever crossed paths or even saw each other."

"We were really looking at little round dots placed on sticks in the tunnel," Meriwether recalled. "Since Robert and Jimmy's scenes were filmed before we shot ours, the director could tell us how close the pirate's knife was to Robert's throat or how close Jimmy was to stepping on a land mine. It wasn't the easiest acting job!"

Del Monroe and Lee Meriwether in "The Kidnappers."

In the episode "Pirates of Deadman's Island," Victor Jory played the role of Captain Beal, who found himself accidentally misplaced in the Time Tunnel Complex. Meriwether recalled how Jory overplayed his part in using Ann MacGregor as human shield. "I still carry a small scar on my right thumb from Victor Jory's pirate knife. I got a scraped knee on that show, too." In other interviews, Meriwether revealed she discovered a number of bruises on her arms and legs a few days after the shoot. One stunt that would have been much safer was traveling through the vortex. Because Ann was kidnapped by space aliens in "The Kidnappers," and never traveled through the tunnel itself, she never had the opportunity to travel through the vortex. "I longed to do the time tunnel tumble," she commented. "That would have been fun. It would also have been interesting to play one of Ann's ancestors, perhaps an evil one. Robert Colbert and I also thought that Doug and Ann should have had a romance, but it never came to be."

"She's a princess. She's more beautiful now than she was then — she's a stunning-looking woman today," remarked Robert Colbert. "You talk about a high-class, top-flight human being, why, she's it. She gets an 11 in every aspect of her life. She loves the theater, she works all the time, she's married to a wonderful guy, Marshall Borden, and she's got Kyle and Lesley, her kids, and her little granddaughter Ryan. Lee Meriwether is one of the most beautiful, one of the finest, classiest women I've ever met in my life."

Because the Time Tunnel Complex scenes were usually shot within one day, the supporting cast was paid on a per-day basis. According to the salary contracts, had *The Time Tunnel* continued beyond the first season, their scenes would have been extended and perhaps more involved such as the episode, "The Kidnappers," in which Dr. Ann MacGregor's role goes beyond the Complex.

JOHN ZAREMBA

Before becoming an actor, John Zaremba was a successful reporter and journalist for newspapers such as *The Grand Rapids Press* and *The Chicago Tribune*, which makes it difficult to comprehend how a man of such literary accomplishments could happily utter such lines as "Check all channels, from 100 through to infinity" on *The Time Tunnel*.... but he did.

Having made the move to Hollywood in 1949 or 1950, he bounced from studio to studio, accepting any job that opened, from Columbia cliffhanger serials to low-budget westerns. After appearing on such television series as *Waterfront* and *Dragnet*, Zaremba got a big break courtesy of Frederick W. Ziv, producer of *I Led Three Lives*.

Next to *The Time Tunnel*, fans of classic television recognize John Zaremba for playing the recurring role of Special Agent Jerry Dressler of the F.B.I., on the popular *I Led Three Lives* program. Actor Richard Carlson played the role of Herbert A. Philbrick, a counterspy who each week secretly met an agent employed by the U.S. Government to provide information that would help fight against Communist infiltration in suburban America. There was more than one agent on the program, on a rotating basis, but the producer recognized the chemistry between Zaremba and Carlson, and made sure Special Agent Jerry Dessler showed up on the program more often than any other character, appearing in more than half of the episodes of the series.

After *The Time Tunnel*, Zaremba went on to guest spots on numerous television programs, usually typecast playing the role of a judge or a doctor. He was a series regular only once after *The Time Tunnel*, that of Dr. Harlen Danvers for 13 episodes of *Dallas*. During the 1970s, Zaremba supplemented his acting income with commercials, and was known to millions as the Hills Brothers Coffee spokesman.

"John was a very good actor, with a gentle, easygoing nature," recalled Meriwether. "I'll always remember his warm, easy smile and witty personality."

WHIT BISSELL

When a movie buff hears the name Whit Bissell, science fiction classics often come to mind. Bissell played the mad scientist in *I Was a Teenage Werewolf* (1957) and *I Was a Teenage Frankenstein* (1957), and secured screen immortality in the latter film for uttering the line, "Answer me! I know you have a civil tongue in your mouth! I sewed it there myself!" On *The Time Tunnel*, Bissell might have expected a weekly television gig would be a chance to bust his acting chops (such as playing two different roles in the episode "Reign of Terror"), but instead, in the episode "The Kidnappers," he was forced to deliver what might possibly have been the dumbest line in the series: "You know, he looked like he might be a time traveler!"

Whit Bissell made his share of high profile mainstream movies, not least of which are *Hud* (1963) and *Seven Days in May* (1964). But it is among the science fiction movies that his face is most recognizable. From *The Lost Continent* (1948) to *Creature from the Black Lagoon* (1954), *Invasion of the Body Snatchers* (1956), *The Time Machine* (1960), and *Soylent Green* (1973), Whit Bissell found immortality through the genre of science fiction and then secured it with *The Time Tunnel*, playing the role of Lt. General Heywood Kirk, known as "Woody" to his closest friends at the Complex. (Zaremba retained discipline throughout by simply referring to him as "General"). In

September 1994, Bissell's screen career was immortalized at the Los Angeles-based Academy of Science Fiction/Fantasy/Horror when they honored the actor with a special Career Achievement Award.

The September 1990 issue of *Filmfax* featured an interview with Whit Bissell, courtesy of Pat Jankiewicz, and the actor recalled that *The Time Tunnel* "was a fine program. The only trouble is that the scripts weren't very good

because we didn't have enough good writers. We had great special effects but we would have lasted a whole lot longer if we had better writers. The story always comes first."

THE PILOT

With the final draft of the script written by Harold Jack Bloom, Allen and his crew began preparations to film the pilot. On Wednesday, Thursday and Friday, November 10, 11 and 12, 1965, Irwin Allen and his crew conducted three separate meetings regarding the formation of the series, script revisions, production details and other pertinent details that needed to be ironed out before a budget could be created. Irwin Allen hoped to keep the cost under half a million dollars, and the preliminary designs and shooting schedule would help determine the estimated costs.

During the meeting of November 10, William J. Creber was assigned the task of designing the "Time Tunnel" insignia. Technical effects such as the images projected on the Time Tunnel screen (initially cube in shape) were

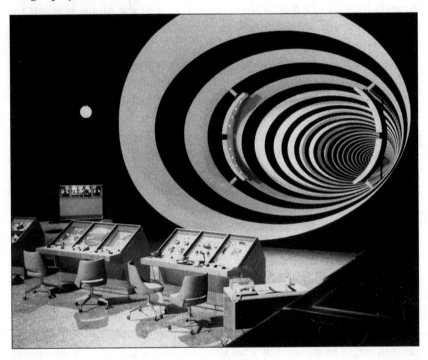

discussed. Burn ins or a projection system? Which was more effective? The cost factor was also taken into consideration. It was initially decided that all of the film seen on the cube should be tinted the same. This would excuse the use of black and white footage from *The Titanic* on the screen. Bill Abbott, at a Special Photo Effects meeting, agreed to start experimenting with tint treatments on the Titanic footage.

"At first we tried a kaleidoscopic effect, lights flashing and whirling," Irwin Allen explained for the June 10, 1966, issue of *TV Guide*. "Then we tried using old newsreel shots, blurring them to give the impression of time telescoping, but it looked like dirty soap. We finally went for an op art and came up with this tunnel, built at a cost of $84,000, out of Styrofoam, sheets of aluminum, and mostly paint for *trompe l'oeil* effect. It rests on an enormous concrete base. The consoles and ancillary equipment cost $45,000 and we used war-surplus material. The thing really works. Wheels turn and lights blink. The power towers are made of iron works put together piece by piece like Tinker Toys. They stand 45 feet tall."

"The set fills a complete soundstage at 20th Century-Fox," Allen continued. "The infinity segment of the tunnel at the rear goes back an additional 26 feet into another stage, and is built on wheels so that it can be moved into position to join the body of the tunnel or moved back to increase the tunnel's illusion of infinity. The front segment of the tunnel is wired for both lighting and special effects, and can shoot lagged streaks of colored lights and smoke."

Bill Welch and Irwin Allen agreed to re-write the beginning of the script right away in order to bring about a visual concept. William J. Creber's sketches, continuity drawings and plans were sufficient. Pete's costume was put into question, and Paul Zastupnevich was requested to design an appropriate wardrobe. It was also decided that Pete would never change clothes. Tony and Pete could change into clothes and costumes of the times, to blend in, but would always revert back to their original clothing at the end of each adventure, to ensure continuity with the beginning of the next adventure.

"Few people realize the number of costumes needed for a show like ours," Paul once pointed out for the Marion, Indiana, *Chronicle*. "If a costume is soiled, and a re-take is necessary, a clean duplicate set of apparel must be immediately available. With the lead players, we keep as many as four different copies of each costume on hand. Dressing the extras is a major headache. They keep changing shape. Many times we have fitted clothes to people for a crowd scene, and at the next day's shooting different extras report in. A short, fat man might be replaced by a tall thin one, which means quick alterations. We had a problem in the very first episode deciding what Darren and Colbert would wear to go back to the Titanic. Their outfits had to be generic as they never return to the Time Tunnel headquarters."

Paul decided to dress Darren in a turtle-necked sweater, which he believed was universally worn in recent eras. Colbert's suit was chosen because the Norfolk jacket had repeated itself as a perennial masculine favorite. In this way, they would rarely seem completely out of place.

"In a story about Devil's Island we had quite a close call," Zastupnevich recalled. "Prisoners in that penal colony historically wore suits of red and white stripes. Half an hour before the costumed actor was to go before the cameras, the producer felt sure it would draw laughs. I whipped the outfit off the actor, rushed off to tint it charcoal gray, hand-dried it with hot irons — and got the actor on the set within two minutes to spare. In one [episode] about 16th century pirates, a young actor plays a boy of royal blood. Nothing could be found ready-made to fit that role and a triple set of everything was required. A tailor ran up some velvet breeches, and a brocade vest was made. However, shirts and shoes found in a woman's apparel shop were used with only slight changes needed. Then, in a story about the Trojan War, we needed gowns for Helen of Troy. The fashion model playing the role had a contemporary gown which, again, with a few minor changes, fitted the era perfectly."

Dee Hartford as Helen of Troy.

Al Gelman of the legal department began looking into whether or not the names of characters on The Titanic, such as the ship's captain, would need prior approvals.

Initial concepts in the first draft of the pilot script that were written out of the second draft of the script, due to technical and cost factors, included an electronic security lock mechanism with a visitor count indicator. Allen

Irwin Allen directs Michael Rennie for the pilot episode.

originally intended for the design of tubular apparatus to come down from the ceiling to bathe each person, one-by-one, with a hand imprint "podium" to come up from the floor to meet the hand print. Fifty people in the control area. (Fewer actors were hired for that task, since clever camera shots could give the illusion of 50.) The Time Tunnel door was intended to be solid sound with a crystal type cube in the center. The Time Tunnel personnel (and the television viewers) could look through and see a semi-distorted view.

During the November 10 and 11 meetings, it was decided to change the Recreation Hall to a canteen, eliminate the country club atmosphere, and eliminate the cards, chess and billiards. Ultimately, the canteen was written out because of the expense involved. On The Titanic, the interior of the Ballroom was changed to the "Main Salon." The dancing, band and buffet was replaced with 25 people and a pianist. The characters of two Corbeau daughters were removed from the entire story.

The most notable difference between the first draft and the final draft was the selection of Time Tunnel personnel. Pete was originally sent back in time, not Tony. When the problem and a possible solution presented itself, it was Tony who chose to dress for the time period and go into the tunnel to fetch his friend.

In the filmed pilot, Marcel distracted a guard by pulling the hose off the

The evacuation of the Titanic as seen through a camera lens.

reel and running off with it. The original script called for a fire alarm, which Marcel would quickly pull and run. This prop was replaced with the second draft of the script.

During the sinking process, Pete and Tony ran onto the bridge. To eliminate the need for constructing a bridge set, their location on the boat was revised to areas that were already used prior in the pilot, such as the upper deck.

Since the innovation of the motion picture — and carried over later into the television medium — film-makers steadfastly relied on technical advisors to authenticate their film fare. In war films, they used professional soldiers, sailors and marines (among others). In medical films they consulted doctors, nurses and interns. In religious pictures they used priests, ministers or rabbis. And in love stories they drew upon their own backgrounds.

One of the best-informed "technical advisors" in the annals of the breed was used at 20th Century-Fox Television Studios during the filming of the

Dr. Doug Phillips (Robert Colbert) finds himself on board the Titanic.

pilot episode of *The Time Tunnel*. Irwin Allen spent considerable money to consult historians who looked over the script and provided a list of essentials. During each script revision, facts were corrected and revised as research went into verifying the exact terminology. The radio room thus became the Marconi room. Althea's London address had to become a slum area, but not one that truly exists in case someone presently resided at the address given. The exact number of people aboard the Titanic and how many survived were verified in advance. The time of the sinking was also verified, to ensure no errors (daylight vs. nighttime) was featured. One scene features Doug Phillips glancing at a sign posted on the wall: "H.M.S. Titanic, Constructed by Harland & Wolff, Ltd., Shipbuilders and Engineers, Belfast, England. Launched May 31, 1911." This sign was accurate, revealing Allen's attention to detail and intent of ensuring as much historical accuracy as possible for his pilot film. (Allen also consulted set drawings from the 1953 Fox film *Titanic*.)

During the November 12 meeting, it was agreed that Dave Constable would do all the burn-in and process drawings. William J. Creber, by this time, had created three small signs for the Time Tunnel Complex fence: "U.S. Government," "Danger, High Voltage" and the Time Tunnel logo. Since a fence was not created for the pilot, the signs were never used for the reasons they were created.

Dr. Tony Newman finds himself restrained outside the Time Tunnel Complex.

A change in the opening of the complex layout was approved. The beginning of the pilot should grab the television audience's attention within the first couple minutes. It was found necessary to eliminate the car elevator, and instead have the car drive down into a tunnel (Century City) where they would drive underground into the Security Area, cross a bridge, into an elevator and be lowered down to the Control center, as seen in the filmed pilot. Location shots were scouted on November 9, and it was quickly decided that using the Standard Oil garage elevator to lower the car into Century City would be unacceptable. Instead, the Century City drive-in tunnel would be filmed on location at the LAX passenger tunnel, with filming on location approved by the airport in advance.

More revisions to the script included the final moments on board the Titanic. Pete and Tony run to the upper deck. Pete is thrown due to an explosion. He falls through a broken chain and as he falls, grabs the deck lip or gutter and then falls toward the water, disintegrating before he can make a splash.

For the desert scenes, a 1956 military caterpillar half-track desert vehicle would be needed, along with four extras for military detail. Two special 1956 license plates were needed: 1 U.S. Government and the other from Arizona.

Filming on location for the desert sequence.

These would be used for the scene that ultimately became the five-minute sequence with Tony arriving near the entrance of the Time Tunnel Complex, ten years before he began working for them, and Sergeant Jiggs questioning his story. The initial draft called for Jiggs and his men working on the desert opening, hence the Time Tunnel Complex had not yet been built.

According to the "Schedule of Operations," drawn up on November 22, 1965, the Time Tunnel pilot, (prod. #6034) titled "Rendezvous With Yesterday," budget meeting commenced on the afternoon of Monday, November 15, 1965. Based on the written teleplay, an outline had now been drawn up listing the costumes, props, effects and cast needed to pull off a re-creation of the sinking of The Titanic. The crew went to the task of verifying price quotes for the materials needed to construct the sets and costumes.

Bill Abbott had scheduled a photo effects meeting with Irwin Allen and his cameramen on Tuesday, but the meeting was postponed until Wednesday.

There, it was decided to cut a number of scenes and props including the physical fence, wall and drive in hole on the desert location. No matte shot and no outside guards. A security guard system in the mountains would be established. This idea, however, was discarded for the more dramatic opening we see today: the creation of the disappearing ramp in the ground. The car disappeared into a hole that suddenly opened and closed again

Conception sketches of the generators used to power the Time Tunnel.

(entirely a foreground miniature on a table used on location with actual physical backgrounds).

At the same meeting, it was decided to eliminate the use of the "Titanic" miniature in a water tank.

For the interior of the Time Tunnel Complex, two complex bridge shots had to be accomplished. The first bridge shot was a miniature composite with the tunnel complex. The second was a composite of the bridge and power control, shot on location. Stacey, William J. Creber and Lydecker checked out possible power plants (Long Beach, El Segundo, Burbank and San Fernando) for use with the second bridge matte composite. Two weeks production time would be needed for the bridge mattes once the photo effects team received the completed film. (The futuristic hallways in the Time Tunnel Complex can be seen in the *Voyage to the Bottom of the Sea* episode, "Time Lock.")

The design for the huge subterranean city seems to have been inspired by the futuristic sub-level colony featured in the 1956 MGM film *Forbidden Planet*. In addition to the glowing, burping, flashing mechanisms on a gigantic scale needed to operate the Tunnel's mysterious mechanism, there was a need to create the illusion of an 800-story, ultra-modern living quarters for the staff. These were connected by ramps and causeways which the inhabitants

A comparison snapshot of the generators from the pilot episode.

could scurry across and where security guards would make their presence known in times of emergency.

In order to create this colossal illusion on a television budget, a large miniature 30 feet high and 10 feet across at the top was constructed, which presents the view one might see when looking down between buildings from 800 stories up. Glowing elevators are seen plummeting through translucent tubes on the outer surfaces of the buildings. At various levels (presumably every 100 stories) people could be seen crossing the connecting ramps on foot or in vehicles.

Again the 9.8mm ultra wide Kinoptic lens was brought into play to exaggerate the perspective of the miniature, making it seem to plunge for miles. After the miniature had been photographed with elevators dropping at full tilt, there remained the problem of putting in the multiple ramps with the live action.

Conception sketch of the tunnel and a comparison snapshot from the pilot episode.

An area of floor limited by railings was photographed on the sound stage with people moving and driving across it. Several takes were made with different action patterns. Then these scenes were matted off and reduced down in diminishing perspective so that seven ramps of decreasing size (each with its own moving figures) could be seen extending the full length of the towers. In order to assemble the total effect from its various bits and pieces, 15 separate

This page, facing page: The cameramen film this scene so matted effects would create the illusion of Century City passageways.

runs of film through the camera were necessary.

The Time Tunnel itself was pictured in the pilot as being housed in a cavernous hall crammed with impressive electronic gadgetry. In reality, only the bare shell of the tunnel was built on the stage along with railings enclosing a ramp and working area. The remainder of the intricate set was a skillfully executed painting which gave the scene tremendous scope and perspective when matted in with the live action portion.

One of the most striking effects — that in which the surrealistic patterns flash up as the elevator with Doug and the Senator drops 800 stories in "free fall" (original intention was to have the car drop below ground, not the actors) — was created simply by poking the camera lens through the cardboard tube of a toy kaleidoscope to film the ever-changing design.

On Thursday, November 11, at 9 a.m. in Room #9 at 20th Century-Fox, *The Titanic* (1953) was screened for everyone on Irwin Allen's crew. Footage of the sinking of the ship and the initial striking of the iceberg was examined, along with a study of how the director re-created the atmosphere within a self-contained movie studio. According to an inter-office memo, a number of other

> During the early development of the pilot script, the opening featured a car chase with a helicopter (supposedly owned and operated by the enemy) shooting at the car, and the helicopter ultimately exploded. The car then approached the trench in the ground, the ramp door opened and the car drove in, moments before the ramp door closed. Two helicopters would have been needed: one with a camera to film the action and the other for the shot. The helicopter would, during a thrilling, opening action sequence, explode. According to an inter-office memo, Irwin Allen was looking at *From Russia With Love* (1963) for possible stock footage to use for the helicopter explosion scene. (Inter office memos proposed using that same stock footage for *Dr. No* (1962), but they were mistaken about which James Bond movie the footage originated from.) It remains possible that Irwin Allen wanted to reuse some of the chase footage featured in the opening scene of "Eleven Days to Zero," the pilot episode of *Voyage to the Bottom of the Sea*.

movies were examined for possible stock footage including *The Unsinkable Molly Brown* (1964), *Forbidden Planet* (1956), and "No Time Like The Past," an episode of television's *The Twilight Zone. Kwaidan* (1964), a Japanese film, was also consulted for special title treatment. (There is a general myth circulating that claims Irwin Allen pulled stock footage from films solely in the 20th Century-Fox film library. This is not so. Allen had a binder at least three inches

thick listing production companies and the movies that were available at Allen's request. Each movie was featured with a list breaking down all of the footage available, the action on the scene and the length of time the footage ran. Films from MGM, Columbia and Republic were listed in the binder. One episode of *Voyage to the Bottom of the Sea* featured stock footage from Columbia Pictures' 1955 classic, *It Came from Beneath the Sea*.)

On November 18, additional script changes were made. The spread eagle method which allowed a man to travel through time in the Time Tunnel was discarded for a radiation bath (blue mist) and a run through the tunnel itself. On Friday, November 19, the financial estimates were ready. By this time, the blueprints of the Titanic were completed.

On Monday, November 22, the art department consulted the cameramen regarding the Time Tunnel sets. On Tuesday, the budget was approved and construction began on the Titanic sets. It was also decided to eliminate the regular type of elevator in the complex and instead create a futuristic pressure shaft. The original concept was to have the passengers strapped into "gravity drop" chairs and, while in the express shaft, explanatory dialogue would be exchanged for the benefit of the television audience. Later it was changed to have the actors standing instead. The Captain's Cabin was eliminated and now Tony would encounter Captain Smith on the deck where he arrived when he landed on the Titanic.

On Wednesday, the photographic effects department tested the "burn in" material, and a survey for the "Steam Plant" for the second bridge matte was conducted. On that same day, a major script revision was made. Tony would be the first time traveler. Pete, Ann and the technicians are relaxing with a

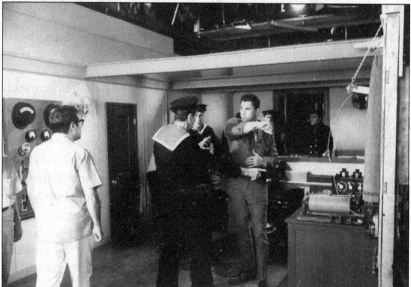

Robert Colbert receives instructions on how to swing a mean punch.

cup of coffee in the canteen when, through the window, they witness Tony adjusting the controls for his departure

By this time, the property department created preliminary set dressing with Norman Rockett: four 12-foot copper coils mounted in glass insulators, wired for power arcing. These were mounted on low platforms with wheels for stage area fill-ins and cutting pieces. Coil sets were to create visual excitement and the illusion of power. The preliminary property budget justification list had been revised to save money from the initial proposal, to read as follows:

Additional Electronic Equipment.. *$1,500 (cut $1,000)*
2 Plexiglass Paneled Synchronized computers*..................... *$3,000 (cut $3,000)*
was 4 units
1 Biological Table .... *$1,000 (cut $1,000)*
was 2 units
1 Control Panel Unit with Electograph unit .... *$1,000 (cut $2,000)*
(using components from Lost In Space *and* Voyage to the Bottom of the Sea*)*
4 Copper Coil Units *$1,500*

All Time Tunnel Complex components were required to be the same height except for the Master Control panel, which was agreed to be desk height in order to see over the top into the Time Tunnel itself. The computers, control panels and other equipment for the Time Tunnel Complex was created by Mars Aviation in San Francisco, California.

The Art Department began work on a recent script change: painting a large, luminous clock pattern in the center of the Time Tunnel Complex floor. Technicians' uniforms had to be dyed with luminous colors for use under "black light" in order to create a fluorescent effect with the clock. Paul Zastupnevich worked the costume colors out with William J. Creber.

On Friday, November 26, the Time Tunnel blueprints were ready. James Darren and Robert Colbert began what would ultimately become a two-week process of wardrobe fitting, tailoring of suits and costumes, wig and mask measurements. The latter of which would be used for photo and stunt doubles.

"I really hated the green turtleneck," recalled James Darren. "It was made of the cheapest wool. It was very, very scratchy. What I had to do was line

---

* Many of the computers on *Voyage to the Bottom of the Sea* and *The Time Tunnel* were supplied by the U.S. Air Force's IBM and Air Division. The same computers also appear in episodes of *Batman* as part of Bruce Wayne's bat cave. On *Land of the Giants*, the same computers can be seen in the episodes "Brainwash," "Target: Earth," "Deadly Pawn," "The Clones" and never more obvious than "A Place Called Earth." The same computers can be seen in episodes of *Lost In Space* including "Two Weeks in Space," "Space Creature," "Kidnapped in Space" and "The Flaming Planet."

the neck portion with silk so I was comfortable with it." But having only one thing to wear in each episode was a lot cheaper than a new suit for every episode. "I loved that, because I hate wardrobe fittings, I really do. They're just the biggest drag. I still have my green sweater — there were many, but there's only one left. Once when I was at [an autograph show], there was a Japanese man who he offered me $5,000 for the sweater. I told him that I

had the sweater, and he said, 'Would you sell it?' I said, 'Well, what do you mean? How much?' And he said, 'I don't know. What do you think it's worth?' I said, 'Well, it's worth a lot to me, because I don't anticipate selling it.' He said, 'Would you sell it for $5,000?' I said, 'Would you pay $5,000?' He said, 'Yeah.' I said I wouldn't sell it. I mean, I don't need $5,000 — what am I gonna do with it? I'd wind up spending it on something that means nothing compared to the sweater. Today, $5,000, you can go to a good movie and have a great meal [laughs] — that's about it!"

Beginning Monday, November 29, the majority of the blueprints were completed for most of the sets. Matte shots and bridge miniatures began and would be completed in about a week. Most importantly, construction on the tunnel began.

On December 22, Dennis Hopper began a wardrobe test for the role of Tabor, a role that would ultimately end up on the cutting room floor, even though his role was substantial through the pilot film. Had the pilot not sold, Hopper's scenes would probably have made it to the finished film as the entire feature would have been released theatrically. Susan Hampshire did a wardrobe test on the morning of January 3, 1966. On that same afternoon,

Dennis Hopper in the role of Tabor. Photo taken on December 22, 1965, during the wardrobe test.

According to a memo casting meeting, dated November 30, 1965, Robert Colbert's character named Pete was changed to Doug. As for the description of Doug: "Try for an older look, grey in temples, moustache…"

PRE-PRODUCTION SCHEDULE
(Dated November 22, 1965)

DECEMBER 1: *Photo effects department tested backgrounds including "Falling Thru Time."*

DECEMBER 3: *Blueprints of two bridge mattes were completed (miniatures). Construction of the Titanic sets were completed.*

DECEMBER 6: *The crew began dressing and rigging the Titanic sets. The special effects crew began construction of the miniature for the bridges.*

DECEMBER 7: *Allen selected the material for "process" and "burn-in" plates from* Titanic *and* The Lost World. *Began wardrobe designs.*

DECEMBER 8: *Construction Department to Barstow: began construction (would take 4 days).*

DECEMBER 10: *Final script ready. Titanic sets ready.*

DECEMBER 12: *Stacey to Barstow — arranged housing, etc. for second unit.*

DECEMBER 13: *Second unit to Barstow (Pre-Production) began, lasted two days. Shot the desert ramp (matte) and helicopter for the car chase plates.*

DECEMBER 14: *Second unit to return to the studio.*

DECEMBER 15: *Second unit to shoot two bridge shots (matte) and power plant (matte).*

DECEMBER 16: *Second unit Century City ramp — blue backing #1 (Tony thru space).*

DECEMBER 17: *Second unit blue backing #2 (Tony and Pete thru space). Second unit finished pre-production.*

DECEMBER 20: *Photo effects department now supplied with film for the matte shots and blue screens. Wardrobe approvals.*

DECEMBER 21: *Second casting began.*

DECEMBER 24: *The Time Tunnel sets constructed.*

DECEMBER 27: *Start photography (14 days and one travel day). Began "dressing" and rigging "tunnel" set.*

DECEMBER 31: *Tunnel set ready.*

The schedule on the previous page was outlined a month in advance, and the exact dates of production were more than 30 days. December 22, 23 and 28, 1965, and January 3 to 7, 10 to 14, 17 to 21 and 24 to 26, 1966. The first three days consisted of blue backing, wire flying, second unit special photographic effects and matte shots on Stage 14 and 18. Chuck Couch was the stunt double for Robert Colbert and Frank Graham was the stunt double for James Darren. On December 23, stunt man Chuck Couch had to run over to another set for a *Lost In Space* episode, as a result of an emergency on the set, so the crew lost 90 minutes of shooting time for *The Time Tunnel*.

Don Knight, Dennis Hopper, Michael Rennie and James Darren were filmed for the scene on the exterior Promenade deck and exterior deck and ladder to bridge scenes. These were the scenes in which Newman recently arrived and alerted the Captain of the Titanic about the impending disaster. This was the first day of principal photography.

JANUARY 4: *Interior Crew Cabin and Exterior Promenade Deck. Filmed on Stage 15. Darren, Hopper, Hampshire, John Winston and Frank Graham*

JANUARY 5: *Dennis Hopper did not show up at the set. He was scheduled off, but due to a clerical error, he was needed for a scene. This was also Robert Colbert's first day of filming. Interior crew cabin and passageway. Filmed on Stage 15. Gerald Michenaud, John Winston, Rennie, Hampshire and Darren.*

JANUARY 6: *George Pelling, Stage 15*

JANUARY 7: *Promenade Deck, Stoker Room, Stage 19. Dinny Powell, George Pelling, Gerard Michenaud and supporting cast.*

JANUARY 10: *Interior Maintenance Room and Interior Marconi room. Filmed on Stage 15. Paul Stader, Ann Dore, George Carter, Pat O'Hara, George Pelling. Dennis Hopper, Knight, Rennie, Darren and Colbert, Michenaud, Hampshire.*

JANUARY 11: *Interior Main Salon. Filmed on Stage 15. Don Lawton, Paul Stader, Ann Dore and Gerard Michenaud*

JANUARY 12: *Barstow Location, Exterior Southwestern Desert, Exterior Desert Tunnel Entrance, process plates. Gil Perkins was stunt driver.*

JANUARY 12: *Exterior Promenade — Boat Decks and panic scene. Filmed on Stage 15. Darren, Colbert, Hopper, other regulars, John Neris, Nadine Arlyn, William Beckley, Eric Michelwood, Paul Stader, Marilyn Moe, Frank Graham. George Robotham, Sol Gorss, Roy Sickner, Ann Dore, Norman Bishop*

JANUARY 13: *Exterior Boat Deck–third class passageway. Filmed on Stage 15. Colbert, Darren, Hampshire, Eric Michelwood, Marian Simmons, Paul Stader, Roy Sickner, George Robotham, Frank Graham, Don Knight.*

JANUARY 14: *Interior Tunnel Control area, Observation Loft. Filmed on Stage 18. Merrill, Darren, Colbert, Bissell, Meriwether, Zaremba, Mariam Schiller and Bret Parker.*

JANUARY 17: *same as above.*

JANUARY 18: *same as above.*

JANUARY 19: *same as above, with Wesley Lau in the cast, not Mariam Schiller.*

JANUARY 20: *same as above.*

JANUARY 21: *Exterior Security Lock Shaft — Bridges Process. Filmed on Stage 18. Darren, Colbert, Merrill, Bissell, Zaremba, Meriwether, and Lau.*

JANUARY 24: *Interior William Lear Jet–Military Sedan Process, Interior Tropical Underbrush. Filmed on Stage 18 and Stage B. Darren, Colbert, Lau and Merrill.*

JANUARY 25: *Coyote Dry Lake Barstow, Exterior Barren Desert near Tunnel Entrance. Darren, Colbert, Merrill, Lau, Michael Haynes.*

JANUARY 26: *same as above.*

ORIGINAL CONSTRUCTION SCHEDULE

MONDAY, DECEMBER 13, 1965, *Art Director and Construction Foreman to Barstow. Stake out Tunnel ramp and HQ Desert Inn*

DECEMBER 14 AND 15, *dig tunnel ramp*

DECEMBER 16, *Construction Crew to Barstow (3 carpenters, 4 laborers and 1 painter)*

DECEMBER 17, *Construction Crew return to studio.*

DECEMBER 21, *Photo effects unit to Barstow, shoot matte shot and process plates.*

DECEMBER 22, *Photo effects unit returns to the studio.*

JANUARY 11, 1966, *Shoot the Century City Tunnel at LAX Airport Tunnel at night.*

JANUARY 12, *First unit travel to Barstow location.*

JANUARY 14, *Return from Barstow location.*

To have the entire cast synchronized in action, leaning toward one direction when the boat rocked, Irwin Allen used the bucket and spoon system that worked when filming *Voyage* and *Space*. "Irwin Allen was a witty man whose bark was worse than his bite," recalled Lee Meriwether. "When he directed the pilot, he climbed a tall ladder and sat there banging a pail with a hammer. It made a horrendous noise, but that was his way of generating energy for everyone on the set. It worked! There was a method to his particular madness."

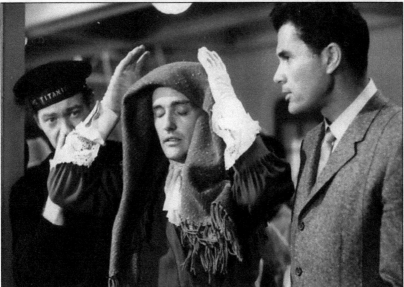

Tabor (Dennis Hopper) attempts to sneak on board the lifeboat
dressed as a woman. This scene never made it to the final cut of the
pilot film.

"As a director, he was very low-key. Competent. Great authority. There was a lotta respect for him among the crew and the cast," recalled Robert Colbert. "When he was around, we all deferred to Mr. Allen as the leader of the pack, and everybody was very pleasant to him, and vice versa, he was always nice to us. But, as I say, he was a very low-key director, he would go about his business, he didn't raise his voice. He'd get a little frantic once in

This page, facing page: Irwin Allen directing the pilot episode of *The Time Tunnel*.

a while, if he got in a bind, and it just became kinda comical. Incidentally, he had a comb-over that was one of the best I've ever seen. But one time he walked in front of a Ritter, which is like a big fan — it's a huge, three, four-blade airplane propeller inside a cage, and when they fire that thing up, it would be a huge wind machine. Well, when Irwin walked in front of it, you couldn't see the Ritter for the hair that flew up off the back of his head, straight up in the air! So he had to be very cautious about his hair [laughs]."

"He knew exactly what he was doing and exactly what he wanted," James Darren recalled. "You weren't looking at somebody who was saying, 'Gee, should I do this or should I do that? Let me see how it looks this way...' Because Irwin storyboarded everything. He knew every single shot he was doing and how he wanted it to end up and whatever. (I learned a few things from him which I later applied to my directing.) He was extremely well-prepared, he was very easy to get along with, and he did an excellent job. Think about the technical components he had to work with at that time; he did a damn good job of making everything look pretty decent. If he were living today, and had all the technical advantages that they have today in filmmaking, *The Time Tunnel* could look absolutely brilliant. For back then, I thought he did an outstanding job."

Susan Hampshire as Althea Hall.

Susan Hampshire, who flew in from England to play the role of Althea, recalled: "I was thrilled to be working in Hollywood. I remember my makeup was very thick, as was the style in those days, and it was very hot." Contrary to what has been printed in numerous books and web-sites, *The Time Tunnel* was not Susan Hampshire's first Hollywood appearance. In 1962, she had flown to the States for a guest spot on an episode of *Adventures in Paradise*, making her American television debut, before returning to her home in England. The actress returned a few years later for a guest spot on *Coronet Blue* (1967), her third and final appearance for a U.S. television production. When asked years later about her experiences in Hollywood, she remarked: "All the men have crocodile wives and ulcers and gold-and-diamond rings they twist around their hairy fingers. The big shots also had arms they kept putting around me that managed to be long enough to reach my left breast. I told them, 'I don't have to do that. I can act.'"

After principal photography was completed in late January, the photo effects department completed the matte and trick shots. Two editors took five days for post-production (phase one) and ten additional days for post-production (phase two). On February 10, 1966, Johnny Williams began composing the music, followed by the arrangement, conducting and recording of the theme song and music cues for the pilot film. Meanwhile, the sound effects were recorded and optical work was edited into the film. Re-recording of audio was then edited into the finished film and an answer print was delivered and completed by mid-February.

Cover of sheet music for *The Time Tunnel.*

According to an inter-office memo dated December 6, 1966, two versions of the lead-ins were created, one long and one short. These were the lines delivered by Dick Tufeld that opened each episode. The unused shorter version is reprinted below:

> *"Lost in a swirling maze of past and future, time travelers Tony Newman and Doug Phillips tumble helplessly toward a new, fantastic adventure somewhere along the infinite corridors of time."*

THE NETWORK

After viewing the pilot, ABC agreed to broadcast the series and *TV Guide* broke the news of *The Time Tunnel* in their February 12 issue, announcing what obviously originated from an ABC-TV press release: "James Darren and Robert Colbert star in a pilot, *The Time Tunnel*, which 20th Century-Fox is making for ABC. It is being produced by Irwin Allen."

According to the March 5, 1966, issue of *TV Guide*, the ABC network initially planned to have *The Time Tunnel* and *The Invaders*, two new shows in pre-production, telecast back-to-back on Wednesday evening. Nobody could be absolutely sure so far from September, and *The Time Tunnel* ultimately aired on Friday evenings. *The Invaders* did not premiere until January 1967, as a Tuesday night feature.

THE STORY LINES

Daily Variety reviewed the opening '66 episode of *Lost In Space* this way: "Second season preem of *Lost In Space* is simply a 1966 model of cliffhanger format that worked so well a generation ago. It's pure escapism and the situations and much of the dialogue are absurd." The younger audience, however, found the closing few minutes of each episode of *The Time Tunnel* one of the most addictive features of the series questioning, "Where will the boys land next?" The formula worked well with *Lost In Space* and Irwin

INITIAL CASTING PROPOSALS

GENERAL KIRK: *Whit Bissell, David Brian, Staats Cotsworth, Michael Fox, Bert Freed, Larry Gates, Lloyd Gough, Douglas Henderson, Tom Brown Henry, John Hoyt, Paul Lambert, Frank Marth, Frank Maxwell, Byron Morrow, Roy Roberts and Herbert Rudley.*

MASTER SGT. JIGGS: *Martin Brooks, John Doucette, Gene Evans and Charles Tannan.*

ALTHEA HALL: *Anna Maria Alberghetti, Elizabeth Ashley, Diane Baker, Senta Berger, Daniella Bianchi, Joan Collins, Susan Hampshire, Shirley Knight, Jocelyn Lane, Juliet Mills, Yvette Mimieux, Joanna Pettet, and Suzanne Pleshette.*

SENATOR CLARK: *Ed Begley, Thomas Gomez, Dean Jagger, Henry Jones, John McIntire, Carroll O'Connor, Ford Rainey, Mark Richman and Fritz Weaver.*

DR. SWAIN: *Barry Atwater and John Zaremba.*

CAPTAIN SMITH: *Brian Aherne and Alexander Scourby.*

DR. ANN MACGREGOR: *Barbara Bain, Lou Bryne, Shelby Grant, Nancy Kovak, Shary Marshall, Jane Massey, Diane McBain, Marian Moses, Pamela Searle, Joyce Taylor and Grace Lee Whitney.*

TABOR: *John Barrymore Jr., Linden Chiles and Dennis Hopper.*

Original photo used for a special feature in an issue of *TV Guide*.
© *1966, Gene Trindl.*

Allen and the writers believed it would work even better with the *The Time Tunnel* premise.

The tremendous library of stock film neatly catalogued from all the 20th Century-Fox movie epics provided inspiration for Irwin Allen and his writers, who reviewed films and worked out *The Time Tunnel* storylines based on what was available in the film library. Story and plot proposals often featured notes of what footage from specific movies could be inserted in various scenes that would normally cost a big scale arm and a leg to reproduce for the small screen.

"From a practical standpoint, it was a brilliant idea," recalled writer Ellis St. Joseph. "The studio backlot had everything from ancient Babylon to the Hawaiian islands. The centuries were built next to each other. Allen knew more about producing a series under budget than anyone else in Hollywood. He was extremely severe in his budget restrictions, but if you knew what he wanted, he was fine. If he didn't respect your talent, he could be arrogant and contemptuous."

"We did take advantage of a lot of the film Fox had in their library, Irwin used a lot of that old footage," James Darren commented. "He was brilliant in that sense too. Irwin was such a control freak — and I say that kindly — that he demanded as close as he could get to perfection, he demanded that whatever he visualized in his head be put onto that screen. And he did want to know everything that was going on — and you really

OUT-OF-THIS-WORLD PUBLICITY

A press release sent to *Hollywood Reporter* in December 1965 remarked: "Series, created by Allen and pilot scripted by Harold Jack Bloom, based on scientific fact data, is futuristic high-adventure serial concerning time travel from top-secret experimental stations throughout the world. Space experts from several countries will act as series consultants."

didn't do anything without Irwin knowing it, believe me. Because it just didn't fly. Everybody behind the scenes, maybe because of their respect for Irwin, did an outstanding job. I have to say that Irwin held that ship together, that's for sure."

After a plot proposal was accepted and commissioned, the script writers would write the plot around the desirable footage which turned out to be

a small percent of the hour drama, when you look back at the scheme of things. One exception was "One Way to the Moon," in which footage from *Destination Moon* was used for two key scenes. Allen had to rent the same costumes used in the movie and create a whole new set of the interior of the space ship, to ensure the new film would blend unobserving with the old.

Many times the Technicolor footage was more grainy than the newly filmed footage, or the color was faded, and the television viewers were not easily fooled. Viewers could easily differentiate between original footage in "Night of the Long Knives" and stock footage from *King of the Khyber Rifles* (1953) featured in that episode. For some episodes like "One Way to the Moon" and "The Walls of Jericho," the editing of movie footage was smooth enough that it could pass flawlessly to the casual viewer.

Arthur Weiss was the story editor who gave the final approval for stories used on *The Time Tunnel*, and commissioned the script writers to draft the first and final scripts, with revised pages to suit production needs. Weiss often consulted Irwin Allen for his opinion, and Jerry Briskin and Frank

La Tourette would review the first draft of each script with an eye toward the cost of production, costumes, sets, and so on to make suggestions for the final draft. "We worked well together," recalled Leonard Stadd. "With Arthur, rewrites were kept to a minimum." Pages revised for the final draft were of a different color other than white (usually yellow, green, pink and light blue), and dated in the corner of the pages, to verify they were revised

pages. This was a standard in television production and one of many ways a collector of television scripts can tell the difference between the first draft and the final draft of a teleplay.

"We held Arthur in great esteem," recalled Bob Duncan to author Mark Phillips. "He was a former Harvard lawyer-turned-writer and a soft-spoken, truly gentle man in the finest sense of the word. We immediately became good friends. More than once, Wanda and I wrote an ending showing Tony and Doug being killed. This startled Arthur, who was always relieved to find the real ending under the spurious page. Arthur was uneasy about this kind of joke for fear the wrong page would find its way to Irwin's desk."

The Duncans wrote a total of nine episodes for *The Time Tunnel*, almost a third of the scripts.* The Duncans began writing scripts for *Tunnel* after joining up with story editor Anthony Wilson for *Lost In Space*. "We worked with Tony when we first arrived in Hollywood," Duncan recalled to author Mark Phillips, "and we kept up with him when he came to the Irwin Allen stables. There was an unwritten rule that writers were hired according to a rating list

put out by the networks and studios. Writers were classified from A to D, A being the best, D being the dregs. We saw the lists once and there were only two writers in the A category, Howard Rodman and Shimon Wincelberg, both extraordinary talents. Wanda and I were B+ on one list and B on another, so Tony never had any difficulty clearing assignments for us. He told us that Irwin wasn't looking for geniuses; he was looking for hacks. By that, he meant writers who could deliver a script on time and on budget."

"While these shows were on the air, everybody considered them to be like Kleenex — to be used and then discarded," script writer Bob Duncan recalled. "We did *Time Tunnel* for the money, and from what we could see, so did the actors. It was definitely a money show in many respects, despite the many fine actors and technicians who worked on it. For one thing, it was strictly an action show without any great delineation of character. Irwin Allen had a strong dislike for what I call 'relationship scenes.' Sometimes you could write a scene with emotional content for the guest stars, but never for the regulars…We didn't enjoy writing for the two leads. They weren't really actors. They could have been replaced by any two other young men and no one would have known the difference. We approached one of the leads with the idea of providing him with more substantial material, only to have him ask us to keep his speeches short. He wanted simple action lines, like 'Let's go!' or 'We have to get out of here!' so we did so."

*Al Gail, Irwin Allen's cousin, was also his right arm and often credited as an Associate Producer.

James Darren later recalled, "The only thing that Bob and I got a little tired of was that line, 'Where are we?'"

"I was used to New York, where actors learned their lines," recalled Stadd. "In Hollywood, the idea of a speech is one line. Irwin was always worried about losing his actors if you didn't give them a good script, but the two guys on *The Time Tunnel* were easy going, nice people. I think they were well cast. However, *The Time Tunnel* was shot in five days and Irwin loved it when it was shot in three, and most Hollywood actors don't spend time learning their lines. When I did a *Honey West*, [the producers] flipped out; 'My God, this script doesn't need any rewrites!' Then, they said, 'Just one thing: Can you cut out the long speeches?' I said, 'You mean these three little lines?' 'Yeah, make them shorter. The actors can't learn them.' I said, 'Then, get yourself some other actors!' Eventually, that *Honey West* script ended up with a million rainbow pages because of that. It was a shame."

Leonard Stadd, who would go on to script numerous television programs including *The Man From U.N.C.L.E.* and *Room 222*, contributed three scripts for *The Time Tunnel*: an assassination attempt on Abraham Lincoln in Baltimore, a chance meeting with Robin Hood and the ghost of Nero. The latter of which produced a spooky, supernatural element to the series as Doug and Tony encounter a real ghost from the past — something scientists would normally dismiss with rational scientific reasoning. Stadd also proposed a story set aboard the "Marie Celeste," a sailing ship found adrift off the Atlantic Coast in 1872. The ship was intact, but her crew and passengers were missing, with no signs of a struggle or foul play. The sailors' fate remains a mystery to this day.

"I told Arthur Weiss that, as I saw it, a giant squid grabbed the ship and pulled the people overboard," recalled Stadd to author Mark Phillips. "Arthur said, 'Wait a minute,' and ran off to Irwin's office. He returned with, "OK, you've got the assignment.' My story had Tony and Doug landing on this ship and everybody's gone. They put two and two together and learn that everyone was killed by this squid. So, we had a production meeting and while the production people were explaining how they could make this giant octopus tentacle, I noticed Irwin getting more and more disturbed. Finally, he said, 'No, the octopus tentacle won't work.' A production guy said, 'Sure it will, Irwin. We'll use a big arm with a mechanical —' and Irwin said, 'No, the last time I used a giant tentacle, it cost me $30,000!' The production guys kept saying, 'It won't cost more than a few hundred dollars,' but they couldn't convince him. Irwin said, 'We had better put this one on hold,' and that was it. The episode wasn't filmed because it had once cost Irwin $30,000 to use an octopus tentacle on *Voyage!*"

A short time later, Christmas 1966, Leonard Stadd saw jars of octopus for sale. "I immediately thought of Irwin, so I bought a jar," Stadd recalled. "Then I remembered Irwin's threat with the club, so I bought a bullwhip. I sent them to Irwin with a note: 'From all the boys on the Marie Celeste.' That got Irwin really mad! Sheila Mathews [an actress], whom Irwin later married, told me Irwin loved the bullwhip but he was absolutely livid over the jar of octopus, claiming that my "Celeste" episode was his favorite script. He just couldn't afford that one lousy octopus arm."

"He was a megalomaniac with extremely high control needs," Bob Duncan recalled of his employer, Irwin Allen. "He made his fortune by developing concepts and sur- rounding himself with the finest talent in the business. I remember Irwin's shiny new Rolls Royce sit- ting out in front of this old office building on the Fox lot whenever he was in residence. The story editor was on the second floor, and this required writers to walk past Irwin's open door, with his desk facing out- ward. Over a period of years, we developed a feeling of dread that his

Jerry Briskin. *Photo courtesy of Chris Briskin.*

voice would ring out and call us in for one of his games. One day Wanda and I had come in early in the morning to work on a rewrite for a show destined to be shot the next day. We worked until 7:00 that night, and then started to leave.

"Irwin's voice rang out and he asked us into his office. Then, without saying another word, he stopped everybody who went past his door, called them into his office and asked them, 'Why are the Duncans leaving?' When they couldn't provide him with an answer, he had them sit down; then he called in the next person to walk by: 'Why are the Duncans leaving?' It was crazy. Most of these people had no idea who Wanda and I were, and we didn't know them. Finally, after a half-hour of this, Arthur Weiss passed by and Irwin called him in and asked, 'Why are the Duncans leaving?' Arthur, in his mild way, said, 'Because they've finished their script.' And Irwin released everyone to go home. We never saw Irwin as a genius of any sort, and we never consulted with him about a script. He would scribble comments for rewrites in the margins."

YESTERDAY, TODAY AND TOMORROW -- Turn the dials and set off a multi-billion-volt power charge. Set the switches for any century, any era, past or future. It's the thrill of a lifetime, heading your way via producer Irwin Allen's new 20th Century-Fox Television series "The Time Tunnel," debuting in color, Friday, Sept. 9 during ABC-TV's Advance Premiere Week. Actors James Darren (left) and Robert Colbert, stars of the series, are shown at the controls of the fantastic tunnel, which also produces a fascinating hour of television drama each week.

Those comments would often be handed over to Jerry Briskin and Arthur Weiss, who would address the issues in written form, typed in the form of either a letter or an actual list. Then the suggestions would be applied in revised pages. Carbon copies of the suggestions would be forwarded to everyone involved with story development, for backup and consultation in case an issue arose during production and filming.

An example of Jerry Briskin's input after reviewing a script was his inter-office memo dated June 10, 1966, after reading the first draft of "The Last Patrol."

> "I do not find this script to be too exciting. In fact, a great deal of it reads somewhat like a history lesson which I don't think is particularly entertaining," he wrote. "There is one section in the script in which approximately 20 pages go by and we never see Tony. It seems as though the fade outs are all the same — British soldiers or soldier either pulling the trigger to shoot our boys, or about to pull the trigger to shoot our boys, and in the last cut, our boys swerving out of the way of the bullets. I didn't think our men were supermen, just ordinary human beings. Jiggs is written into the script briefly and I suggest he be taken out as he doesn't really do anything. The sets are complicated, and unless we have Stage 6 or its equivalent, I don't know how we would do the wooded area, the bog, the British camp and the American camp. There is one shot that calls for General Southall to spin weightlessly in time and this would require Abbott to do a shot against blue and it would be much too costly. General Southall is sent out in time and lands exactly where he wanted to go. Again, is this going to make our viewers wonder why the Tunnel can't bring our boys back and yet can send people to exact locations?"

Another example can be found among the production notes from Jerry Briskin, for the episode "Massacre." "I suggest we reduce the Western Avenue page count by approximately 5 pages," Briskin wrote. "By making this change, we could then complete our work at Western Avenue in 2 days of shooting."

With a weekly television series taking an average of six days to produce an episode, scripts were often written steadfast. Leonard Stadd's first draft of "The Revenge of Robin Hood" was supposedly written in four days, after his plot proposal, "The Tyrant," was accepted by Arthur Weiss, the story editor. "Everything at Irwin's was done in a rush, and I wrote that script quickly," recalled Stadd. "I used to write the soap opera, *From These Roots*, without any help, and that was 261 scripts in one year, so I could write fast. Just after I got the assignment, Arthur called me and said, 'Irwin wants to see you,' and he tipped me off that Irwin wanted the script fast. I walked into Irwin's office and he asked me, 'When do I get your script?' 'Well, I just got the assignment. Today's Tuesday, you can have it by next Tuesday.' Irwin said, 'Wait, before you answer that,' and he reached into his desk drawer and pulled out this big club with a chain around it and spikes on the end. He held it in his hand and said, 'Okay, now tell me!' 'When do you want it, boss?' 'Get it to me by Friday and you've got yourself another assignment.' So I worked on it, and

Doug and Tony help assist with "The Revenge of Robin Hood."

on Friday, I went to his office and said, 'Here's the script, Irwin.' He barely looked up — 'Oh? That's nice.' he had forgotten his threat."

In 1957, when Irwin Allen produced and directed *The Story of Mankind*, he hewed to the line on such chronological technicalities as proper beards and bushes in scenery. For *The Time Tunnel*, Allen and his crew took a dramatic license with history, sometimes choosing production costs over historical accuracy. No one but history professors and the harshest movie critics took note of the historical blunders ranging from incorrect swords of the time period to uniforms that looked like they just came from a 20th century dry cleaner.

According to the July 17-24, 1966, issue of the Los Angeles *Herald-Examiner TV Weekly*, Irwin Allen described plot summaries that apparently never made it to fruition. During the Great Plague of Europe, 1800 people in the heat of London were unaccountably spared. It was proposed that Doug and Tony had a hand in this, creating penicillin. Another had the boys put down a mutiny aboard Columbus' flag-ship, thus enabling Chris to discover the New World.

"There is no limit, either in space or time, as to just how far we can go with *The Time Tunnel*," Allen was quoted in a press release. "We have a story concerning Halley's Comet and its plunge to Earth, as well as stories build around Dunkirk, the American Revolution, Columbus' discovery of America, the storming of Troy and the Babylonian revels." Apparently Babylon and Dunkirk were never featured dramatizations.

THE REVIEWS

"Prepare to enter a top-secret U.S. research project concealed beneath the Arizona desert, to plummet 800 floors and pass through the fourth dimension, to traverse the farthest reaches of time…"

ABC Television Network Press Release, dated August 31, 1966

When *The Time Tunnel* was selected for a preview showing at Tricon, the 24th World Science Fiction Convention in Cleveland, Ohio, it met with an adversary and guest speaker, Gene Roddenberry, who agreed to attend the event in the hopes that buzz would begin with his newly-produced *Star Trek* series. *Star Trek* was ultimately chosen as the "Best Science Fiction Telefilm Ever Screened for Conventioneers" and was predicted as the "best TV show of this coming season."

When the pilot was screened at Tricon days before its network debut, novelist Jerry Sohl recalled the reaction was mixed. "The fans there had very high standards for televised science fiction. When they saw thousands of soldiers running up and down the Time Tunnel corridors with sirens blaring, the fans hooted and booed. There was another scene where the desert literally rolls back and a car drives underneath it. Those scenes were over the top. Spectacle rather than true science fiction."

Andrew I. Porter, assistant editor of the magazine of *Fantasy & Science Fiction* (and later a Hugo winner for his semi-prozine Algol in 1974) was a 20-year-old Tricon attendee in 1966. "The one thing I remember from *The Time Tunnel* is that hilarious bit when they're trying to convince the Captain of the Titanic to turn around or slow down or something by holding up a copy of the newspaper that says, 'Titanic sinks.' Yeah, that oughta do it. *Star Trek* made a much bigger impression on fans than *The Time Tunnel* did."

The reaction from the hard core of the science fiction world: a citation for excellence in the presentation of "adult and true science fiction." Add to this the favorable reaction from such science fiction editors and writers as John

---

There was apparently no continuity drawn up for *The Time Tunnel* reflecting the rules writers were to abide by. In the pilot episode and "The Day The Sky Fell In," for example, Doug and Tony discover that no matter what they do, they cannot change the past. In "The Walls of Jericho," Tony and Doug were the two nameless spies described in passages of The Bible, and thus were principal participants already logged into history accounts. In "Billy the Kid," Doug and Tony, without commenting about their past adventures, fear they may have shot and killed William Bonney and thus changed the course of history — Doug is even relieved when he discovers Bonney alive and well. Other plot loopholes make the viewers question why Doug and Tony just don't sit back and watch history in the making, and wait for Tunnel personnel to pick them up again, when their involvement with the events is not always required.

W. Campbell, Frederick Pohl, Sara Moskowitz, Donald Wolheim, Robert Sheckley and Lester Del Rey. This gave reason for optimism on the part of the producer, who promoted the series with numerous press releases.

"One of the best jobs of adult and true science fiction programs I've ever seen. You've got a science fiction rather than a fantasy approach."

John W. Campbell, writer and editor of
Analog Science Fact and Science Fiction

"Nicely done; nice effects. I think this concept and series has fine possibilities."

Robert Sheckley, writer

"The most authentic appearing sets and background I have ever seen. Unlike so many, this is good science fiction done as it ought to be. I do not usually care for the science fiction productions on TV, but I was enthralled by this one. Should be a prize-winner."

Donald Wolheim, writer, anthologist, editor of *Ace Books*

"Science fiction in television has gone a long step forward with Time Tunnel. The production is superb, leaving out most of the clichés. The cast acts in parts instead of parodying them, and the story line is highly promising. Bearing in mind that this is adventure science fiction, not the cerebral kind, it is high quality."

Frederik Pohl, writer, anthologist, editor of *Galaxy* magazine

"Technical effects are highly effective. Acting, production, photography excellent."

Lester Del Rey, science fiction writer

The first two weeks of September were a busy time for promoting the series. Days before the series premiere, James Darren, Robert Colbert and Lee Meriwether were appearing in a 16-city tour to help promote the series. William Shatner, star of the *Star Trek* series, spent one week beginning September 5, making television appearances to promote his new series, with stops in Philadelphia, Hartford and New York City. MGM producer George Pal, meanwhile, made it public knowledge that science fiction on television was here to stay and began making preparations for an updated version of *Destination Moon* from his 1950 hit, which would be based on a new original story, "S.U.A.," to encompass the exploration of the moon's surface. (His proposal would not get off the launching pad, but he did manage to produce a brief pilot film for a proposed series based on *War of the Worlds*.) ABC-TV began promoting *The Time Tunnel* with print ads and radio spots,

and newspaper columnists across the country expressed their criticism after watching the premiere episode. (Some reviewers were treated to the unaired version and therefore made mention of the dinosaurs and not the rocket launch sequence that concluded the pilot.)

The September 14, 1966, issue of *Variety*

"ABC has given Time Tunnel *the onerous task of trying to bridge three proved rating busters on the other webs, and if the show is shot down by the tested competition it will not be for want of trying. If* Tunnel *were just a routine sci-fi meller, it might just as well have crept into its time device and projected itself into an easier slot. As it is, this elaborately wrought and well-scripted (albeit trickily) show should give a good account for itself."*

The September 12, 1966, issue of *Daily Variety*

"Intriguing plotting and advantageous time slotting appear immediately as solid plus factors for Irwin Allen's new sci-fi adventure series…Special effects on a big scale (at which 20th is becoming somewhat of an expert via other series and the Fantastic Voyage *feature) will, particularly on color sets, remain a continuing draw for viewers. The concept, probably and properly, will dominate the players, this placing a big load on scripting, direction and production. Prospects look good for at least one season, if the first half-hour is strong."* *

The September 12, 1966, issue of the *World Journal-Tribune*

"Two shows purporting to deal with Einstein's theory of time proved to be light years apart in taste and technique. The Time Tunnel *is a suspenseful adventure involving a time machine that plummets scientists into whatever year — past or present — they wish. Friday night's episode found James Darren aboard the Titanic on the night of revelry that preceded the iceberg collision. It sounds trite in capsule but fine acting and a highly professional production gave it all a gloss of wonder."*

The September 12, 1966, issue of *The Hollywood Reporter*

"Irwin Allen, creator and producer of Lost In Space *and* Voyage *to the* Bottom of the Sea *has successfully molded a new science fictioner for the tube in* The Time Tunnel. *It is a solid idea which appears to be getting the right treatment and which should pull the same audience as the other two shows… The special effects department contributed to the product's success."*

---

* Ironically, *Variety* reviewed the premiere episode of *Star Trek*, commenting, "…it could lure a small coterie of the smallfry, though not happily slotted in that direction. It's better suited to the Saturday morning kidvid bloc."

Marian Dern, columnist for *Cover Close Up*

"Time Tunnel *has some strong plus qualities: the concept is imaginative, with potential for great variety in storyline; the special effects, particularly in color, of the huge underground research lab — its tiers of platforms, its flashing lights and banks of computers, its vibrant electronic sounds, the mysterious tunnel itself — all live up to the wildest dreams of what a futuristic lab should look like; the cast is appealing, and competent.*"

Columnist Cleveland Amory in the October 29, 1966, issue of *TV Guide*

"*This show offered at least a new idea — that of taking us back, via the conquering of time, to the Good Old Days…All in all,* The Time Tunnel *is one of the most annoying shows we've seen. There is imagination and inventiveness in the photography and gimmickry, but the acting is stilted and unbelievable, the dialog is soap-opera-ish. And finally, it's preposterous to have bombs and things like that repeatedly coming up the tunnel. When Halley's Comet came up, Dr. Swain said quietly, 'I think the time has come to rethink this whole project.' We couldn't have agreed more.*"

The September 10, 1966, issue of the *Long Island Star-Journal*

"*…the sets are magnificent and the scientific gadgetry is amazing.*"

The September 9, 1966, issue of the *Niagara Falls Gazette*

"Time Tunnel, *a new adventure series with science fiction overtones, is so handsomely and expensively produced you wish it were better written. There seems an obvious effort to please younger viewers based on the first episode which too often employs childlike dialogue.*"

September 1966 UPI news brief by Rick du Brow

"The Time Tunnel *is an hour-long opus about a couple of young workers on a government research project who succeed in passing through the fourth dimension, opening them up to traveling into the past and future. The sets and special effects in this series are highly impressive and they must have cost a fortune! And though this show has obvious appeal for mostly children, the show is sometimes diverting in the realm of fantasy because it is played dead straight. In the opener, the two heroes wind up on the Titanic in mid-ocean before its disaster. They tried to warn everybody but I am sorry to reveal that the ship sank anyway.*"

Columnist Win Fanning in the September 13, 1966, issue of the *Pittsburg-Post Gazette*

"Time Tunnel, *whose debut James Darren, the show's co-star, and I, watched together on Channel 4, is presumably shooting a bit more widely than just for kids,* which its lead-in, The Green Hornet, *is aimed at. I mean,* Time Tunnel, *with what I have been told has the most expensive sets and is the most expensive pilot*

Doug and Tony are shocked when they meet Adolf Hitler in "The Kidnappers." Hitler was played by Bob May, the same actor who performed The Robot on *Lost In Space*.

film ever made in television history. I mean, would you believe one million dollars for the pilot alone, with half of that just for the series' sets, means that you've got to be aiming at somewhat above the teenage horizon in terms of viewers. If its production values alone, plus its quite acceptable acting can turn the trick, then Time Tunnel *may just make it with the science fiction group. But for those with a knowledge of the past, there may be serious questioning of the show's research. The tunnel moves people back and forth in time, keeping them in a sort of perpetual* Twilight Zone."

Columnist Percy Shain in the September 25, 1966, issue of *The Boston Globe*
   *"Looking over some of this season's shows...*The Time Tunnel *with Jimmy Darren and Robert Colbert is fascinating in concept, striking visually but absurdly written.* Star Trek, *starring William Shatner, is either clumsy or eerie, depending on your point of view.* Jericho, It's About Time, Tarzan *and* The Green Hornet *are all stinkeroos."*

The September 9, 1966, issue of the *St. Petersburg Times*
   "The Time Tunnel, *a new adventure series on ABC with science fiction overtones, is so handsomely and expensively produced that you wish it were better written. There seems to be an obvious attempt to please younger viewers based on its first episode which too often employs childlike dialogue. The Time Tunnel is a U.S. research project 800 floors below the American desert (and there are some breathtaking glimpses into this deep pit). What the machine can do is send a man backward or forward into time. In the first episode, Gary Merrill plays an itchy cost-conscious Senator who provokes regular James Darren, an eager-beaver scientist, into trying out the tunnel before it has been perfected. Amazingly, he lands on the Titanic on the eve of the ship's sinking in 1912. He is soon joined by another regular and scientist, Robert Colbert. There is some suspense as you wonder if the scientists can change history. The other regulars, all members of the American team, are Lee Meriwether, Whit Bissell and John Zaremba. They fret a lot."*

The September 10, 1966, issue of the *Christian Science Monitor*
   "The new TV season's score at the end of the first inning is three hits, five runs and six errors. The hits are all from ABC: The Monroes, Man Who Never Was *and* Hawk. *But there are two more possible runs with* Star Trek *and* The Time Tunnel. *Both deal with the breaking of the barriers of time and space...For the first episode it's a trip back to the Titanic, just before the fatal collision with the iceberg. But it is guest star Gary Merrill, as the investigative Senator, who steals the show. Both* Time Tunnel *and* Star Trek *have dizzyingly intricate machinery that contributes to their impact."*

The September 13, 1966, issue of the Utah *Desert News*

"Some of our televiewers are making comments on the new TV season. Says one viewer: 'The Time Tunnel *looks like a pretty good show!' However, from our reader mail, it seems no new TV series is yet emerging as a big favorite."*

The September 9, 1966, issue of the *Milwaukee Journal*

"This is a fine and suspenseful science fiction program, with a built-in dramatic attraction...This show, incidentally, has incredible sets...The show is occasionally unreal when the time travelers try to change the course of history but the photography and details are excellent...It's an outlandish premise but it is an all-around good show."

Columnist Clay Gowran in the September 10, 1966, issue of *The Chicago Tribune*

"Irwin Allen has something in this entry not only more spectacular than his other two television shows but with a better storyline, of traveling through time. A time tunnel lobs the characters, amid the best fireworks seen since the Fourth of July, from Pearl Harbor December 6, 1941, to landing on a doomed island called Krakatoa and through the storming of Troy...Filmed in color, The Time Tunnel *offers some of the finest trick photography ever brought to the home television screens and Darren and Colbert make an attractive team of video heroes. Lee Meriwether, Whit Bissell and John Zaremba play members of the scientific team, who made the time break-through possible. The continuing plot of* Time Tunnel *is that the malfunction prevents them from returning to 'now' so they will keep bouncing back and forth through the centuries, for as long as their ratings hold up."* *

The September 16, 1966, issue of *Time Magazine*

"The new shows this season are for 9 to 90...IQ, that is...Science fiction once again rears its preposterous head with The Time Tunnel, *providing a new dimension for last year's* Lost In Space *series. Project Tic-Toc headquarters is housed 800 floors below the Arizona desert and is developing the capability to thrust its explorers into any time period, past or present. The first human test pilot is propelled back five decades, finding himself in the Atlantic aboard the Titanic. The Captain naturally thinks his visitor is some kind of a nut and locks him up. Another lift from H.G. Wells'* Time Machine *gimmick..."*

---

*The review reached the desk of Irwin Allen, who wrote a personal letter to Gowran. "Your review of the *Time Tunnel* premiere episode just arrived and I want to warmly thank you for your kind words. Happily, critical response to *Time Tunnel* around the country has been delightful. To live up to this lavish praise, we have thrown away the budgets on the next half dozen episodes and are planning more exciting blockbusters for the future."

The August 21, 1966, issue of the New York *NEA Herald Tribune*

"It is a pleasure to report that the TV pilot crop for this season is better by far than anything seen in recent years. Not only are several pilots quite good but many are based on ideas that seem able to sustain a series. By far the best pilots are The Hero *and* The Man Who Never Was. *The Time Tunnel, with Robert Colbert and James Darren, is a fine science fiction series about two men who can be manipulated to any era but cannot be brought back to the present. Also,* Star Trek, *is a fine adult science fiction series which stars William Shatner."*

The September 12, 1966, issue of *The Toledo Blade*

"Variety in the settings will at least be provided in the weekly adventures of James Darren and Robert Colbert in the realm of past and future on Time Tunnel. *As a pair of scientists projected through the tunnel, first to the Titanic, where their warnings of disaster are, of course, ignored, they will then be ranging up and down the corridors of time. Next week, according to the show's teaser, the pair will be hurtled into a future flight as their colleagues back at mission control try to get them back to the present. This won't happen until the series is cancelled, I'm sure. Meanwhile, the series has a sort of* Fugitive *gimmick going for it and all the time in the world for its locations and stories."*

Columnist Hal Humphrey in the September 10, 1966, issue of *The Los Angeles Times*

"Science fiction impressio Irwin Allen has once again borrowed from Jules Verne for his latest venture, The Time Tunnel, *which debuted last Friday night on ABC. It's the tale of a highly classified research project and two young scientists (old scientists are passé these days) who end up ricocheting across time, from the prehistoric past to the future, unable to return to their own era because of a malfunction with their time machine. James Darren and Robert Colbert starred as the time travelers who are working on the project, 800 stories beneath the Arizona desert on an amazing time machine that propels men through the fourth dimension, forward or backwards in time. Into this labyrinth wanders a skeptical Senator (Gary Merrill) who wants to check on the government's seven million dollar investment. He's told that the tunnel still has flaws. And apparently, so does the project's security system because young Darren somehow sneaks past everybody in the control room in order to offer himself up as a guinea pig to the tunnel. As he enters, the huge cavern sputters, smokes, flashes lights and then produces an old film clip from 20th Century-Fox's movie,* Titanic, *which of course is where our young scientist lands, in 1912. Robert Colbert insists on going back to rescue Darren, over protests from his fellow scientists and even after an apology from the Senator who caused this crisis. 'Go ahead, sock me!' the Senator says disgustedly*

before young Colbert takes the plunge into the tunnel to help young Darren. The hour is clogged full of terms like 'polarization field' and 'radiation freeze,' which all of the scientists utter in solemn tones amidst acres of pulsating computers and electronic gadgets.

"Michael Rennie also guest starred as the Titanic's captain. Whit Bissell co-starred as the project's General and Lee Meriwether and John Zaremba were the

white-smocked project assistants at the tunnel who stood around holding clipboards and looking concerned.

"Well, anyway, we all know what happened to the Titanic but what happens to our young heroes, who, because of their flaw-bugged tunnel, were last seen facing a dinosaur? You'll have to tune in again to see the next thrilling episode. At the end of the show there was a trailer, giving viewers a sampling of what they'll witness in weeks to come, if viewers are still around."

Columnist Percy Shain in the September 11, 1966, issue of the *Boston Globe*
"ABC-TV's Shane *is miles ahead of the typical slam-bang TV Western and* The Time Tunnel, *starring James Darren as a time traveling scientist, shows promise but both shows still remain TV series of potential rather than actual realization. Time Tunnel's idea, in principle, of roaming through the corridors of time backward and forward, from the days of dinosaurs to heaven knows what in the future, is both intriguing and stimulating. The visual effects seen here are literally out of*

this world, with a fantastic array of consoles, corridors and eerie ellipses and flashing lights. They are all embedded deep beneath the Arizona desert in an 800 floor complex that ingeniously suggested, onscreen at least, that it is all done with mirrors. The series is, in fact, set in 1968. The concept, as I said, is great until they get down to the stories. The first yarn last Friday was titled 'Rendezvous With Yesterday' about the time transfer that lands our two heroes aboard the Titanic. Their frantic efforts to avert disaster is ludicrous and old-fashioned, the latter a fatal defect in a TV series geared to young viewers. Some of the storyline here is just plain humbug, particularly the part about the poor but pretty schoolteacher (Susan Hampshire) on board who is ready to die because she has a brain tumor. She is dissuaded from death when Jimmy Darren, who is certainly a young-looking scientist, tells her all about the wonders of neurosurgery ahead. Besides Darren, a formidable cast was lined up that included Robert Colbert as his co-scientist, Lee Meriwether as a pretty biologist who supplies up-to-the-date information, Gary Merrill as a surly Senator, Whit Bissell as a general and Michael Rennie as the captain of the Titanic."

THE RENEWAL

The series budget allotted $167,757 per episode. ABC, uncertain whether the series would be successful enough to warrant such a high price tag, contracted a partial season with the option to order additional episodes by a set date, should the network decide favorably. Contracts at the time usually granted a 17-episode deal, with an option for nine additional. *The Green Hornet* and *The Monroes* fell into this pattern. Both programs were given an extension of nine episodes, producing a total of 26 before they were cancelled. *The Rounders* (with Chill Wills) and *Hawk* (with Burt Reynolds) did not receive an extension and lasted only 17. When network executives decided to pull the plug, they found it more economical to have paid for only 17 or 26 episodes instead of 39. Nine weeks after the series premiere, right before Thanksgiving, the November 19, 1966, issue of *TV Guide* reported: "ABC has ordered nine more episodes of *The Time Tunnel*, ensuring the series a full season." Irwin Allen could not have been more thankful — but the ratings were a reflection of the network's attitude and only four more episodes would be ordered before Allen placed a new calendar on his desk for the New Year,

Via means of a gimmick ad in *TV Guide*, ABC-TV promoted *The Time Tunnel* in September 1966 with celebrity praise. "I find it a great escape mechanism," proclaimed Dr. Richard Kimble, the fictional man-on-the-run character from *The Fugitive*.

bringing the season to 30 episodes. One network executive, however, brought attention to brewing storm clouds when he was quoted as saying: "Trouble is, people don't look at television on Friday nights."

"The fact is, we never achieved any major ratings," Robert Colbert told author Kyle Counts. "We had a lot of competition — we were up against *The Man From U.N.C.L.E.* on NBC and *The Wild, Wild West* on CBS."

Fans, however, managed to visit the set just to get a peek at what was going on. "Carol Burnett came down one day when we were shooting — her daughter loved *The Time Tunnel*," James Darren recalled. "Jayne Mansfield came down, because she also loved the show, and Sugar Ray Robinson too." Tom Hanks, as a guest on Conan O'Brien's late-night show, once recalled how he was a fan of *The Time Tunnel* and would do a slow-motion tumbling on the sofa, imitating Darren and Colbert.* But the real stunts were performed by stuntmen who knew their craft, yet were still injured on occasion.

STUNT MEN

Doubling for the role of Doug Phillips in many of the episodes was Glen Colbert, brother of Robert Colbert. Glen was the same height and nine years younger than Robert. Paul Stader was the stunt coordinator on the show, and he originally assigned himself as Robert's stuntman. "At some point in the early stages of the show, I expressed a desire to have my brother be my stuntman," recalled Robert. "Well, Paul wanted the job of being my stunt-man so bad he could taste it — it meant a whole lot of extra money to him, because that was totally separate [from his stunt coordinator paychecks]. So when I said I wanted Glen, well, it wasn't the most popular thing I ever said in my life. I had to go through quite a bit in order to be able to get Glen the job, because doubling me meant a couple of hundred grand a year to Paul and it was nothing he wanted to lose. Paul was my same height and coloring and everything, he was a fine double for me, but not anywhere near as good as my brother; with my brother, you could hardly ever tell when he was working and when I was working. So I fought like hell and got Glen the job." For Stader, it was like somebody coming in and taking money right out of his pocket. "I hadn't realized the significance of it. These [stuntmen] didn't want my brother there at all, because they were all close to Paul who had hired them in the first place," Robert continued. "Anything Paul felt toward my brother had to trickle down from him to them in a heartbeat. Denver Mattson [another stuntman], all these top dudes didn't want anything to do with my brother. Well, they all ended up just respecting Glen completely, man. Before we finished the series, Glen was the most popular guy on the show in the stunt department. They thought he hung the moon, that he was the handiest, that he could kick anybody's ass. Glen was awesome: He could

---

*"You're talking with somebody who grew up with television," says actor Tom Hanks to columnist Jay Boyar of the *Orlando Sentinel* (July 23, 1998, issue). "I knew what time it was by what was playing on television. I never needed a clock. I was probably as affected by *Rat Patrol* and episodes of *Batman* and *The Time Tunnel* as I was by the theatrical films that were playing at the time, like the Elvis Presley movies every Saturday night."

do everything they could, and better, faster, more convincingly. My brother ran the gauntlet of everything they had to do and nobody could touch any of the stuff that he could handle, he was just terrific."

"After that first season ended, we thought we were gonna be coming back the next year, and during this hiatus Glen raced Triumphs," Robert concluded. "He got badly injured in a Triumph accident up in Idaho somewhere and he

Robert Colbert and Glen Colbert.

ended up in the hospital. One of his ribs had punctured his heart or lung, and he had broken an arm and stuff, but he was anxious to get back to L.A. So he got out of the hospital too soon, he jumped on a plane, and the pressurization wasn't just right and he formed blood clots. He then had to have a very serious operation where they had to tie off the veins to his legs, and he never recovered from that. He's still alive, but he's never had the use of his legs again...He's never been anything like he was. He was the most incredible physical specimen and stuntman and motorcycle rider and fighter — he could hit you, and before you landed on the ground he'd hit you eight more times [laughs]."

Another stuntman who made a splash was Charles Picerni. Having recently begun his career as a stuntman for television and motion pictures, Picerni was at 20th Century-Fox as a double for Cliff Robertson when the actor appeared on *Batman* in the character of Shame. He also performed a number of stunts for *The Green Hornet*. It was because of James Darren that Picerni got his job on *The Time Tunnel*.

"He was a friend, and his brother [actor] Paul Picerni was a friend of mine from almost my Day One in California, and is still a friend to this day," Darren explained. "Charlie and I, our looks are similar, and we're built

similarly. Being the star, quote-unquote, of a show, as I was on *The Time Tunnel*, you can pretty much dictate who you want to stand in for you and who you want to double you. I asked if Charlie could do it; and with Irwin, as I told you before, whatever I wanted, I would get. Within reason [laughs]! Charlie did double me and did a spectacular job, as usual. There was a guy named Paul Stader who was the stunt coordinator, and that's who Charlie and all the other stunt people had to work with. Now, Charlie wouldn't do the falling-and-rolling-into-the-frame, which was the first thing Tony and Doug [Robert Colbert] would do as each show was opening up, Charlie wouldn't do that stuff. Another stunt guy would do it from a ladder. It was really not a major stunt, so that wasn't something that Charlie did. He did the fights and the swordfights and things like that."

It was not uncommon for more than one stuntman to stand in for the characters of Doug and Tony on the same day. In "Attack of the Barbarians," for example, Paul Stader (filling in for Doug) and David Sharpe (Tony) did the pratfall from above in the scene where the time travelers arrive in Mongolia in 1287. Later that day, Glen Colbert and Charles Picerni were stuntmen for Doug and Tony. "The guy who did the falling-into-the-frame, that was all he did," recalled Darren. "But it was a pretty treacherous thing, because he was jumping from behind camera off a ladder sometimes. And, Jesus, Bob Colbert's brother Glen was doubling me one time, or doubling

Bob, either one, and, man, he landed right on his head — I thought he'd broken his neck. I didn't envy those guys!"

"Paul Stader and I were rolling down a big hill," recalled Charlie Picerni to Mark Phillips. "It was a very steep hill, two Mongolians rode up on horses trying to run us down with swords in their hand. As I turned, a stuntman named Gil Perkins pulled his horse up hard and the horse reared up. Gil fell backwards and caught his foot in the stirrup. The horse was galloping and kicking Gil at the same time, he broke his leg. As the horse was running up a hill, I ran and managed to cut him off and I grabbed the reins. I held him as he was rearing up and I managed to get Gil free with the help of the other wranglers."

This page, facing page: Rehearsal of the tent fight in "Attack of the Barbarians."

SCIENCE FICTION

As evident with the series' second episode, "One Way to the Moon," a turn of the dial at the hands of the modern scientists could not only push the two time travelers into the past, but forward in time. But space age drama was frowned upon, according to Charles Witbeck of the Columbus (Ohio) *Evening Dispatch*, "since Allen already has a corner on that market." The cost

This page, facing page: Outer space menace from "Visitors from Beyond the Stars."

of creating new props, costumes and rubber masks were essential for *Lost In Space* and *Voyage to the Bottom of the Sea*, with the weekly protagonists facing off against new other-worldly threats. The idea of reusing the same masks and props, even if painted a different color to avoid recognition from faithful television viewers, was also essential when the bottom line was scrutinized.

Future worlds, however, were a possibility from the start. After reading the first few scripts of the series, James Darren personally proposed a story to Irwin Allen. Doug and Tony would land in the future, on the planet Earth, following an atomic war. "They thought it was too depressing for viewers," said Darren. "I told them, why not make it another planet, then. That didn't go over, either."

The introduction of an outer space menace in "Visitors From Beyond The Stars" marked a new chapter in the *The Time Tunnel* saga, that of more frequent trips to the future and brushing encounters with extraterrestrials. The script writers were notified of the change and many of the writers expressed divided opinions.

Bob and Wanda Duncan wrote two episodes involving visitors from outer space. Had the series continued, Bob Duncan confirmed that more aliens were waiting in the wings. "The stories were definitely going to drift further

into that vein because we were running out of historical outtake footage," he recalled to author Mark Phillips. "Personally, I found many of *Time Tunnel*'s later episodes, including the ones we did, silly in the extreme. The series' basic premise had to be taken with more than a scientific grain of salt, but aliens from outer space were more than the show could handle. It was desperation, and it shifted away from *Time Tunnel*'s original and singularly better format."

Aliens abduct Adolf Hitler in "The Kidnappers."

"The aliens were a weakening of the series' format," recalled writer Ellis St. Joseph to author Mark Phillips. "They weren't necessary, but perhaps there was a vogue since other shows with aliens were successful."

Script writer Leonard Stadd theorized that the past may have had unlimited potential, but Irwin Allen and his staff wanted a fresher look. Research and historical accuracy were shelved for more action and excitement. "The conferences often lasted eight hours," Bob Duncan recalled for author Mark Phillips. "Wanda was especially good at basic story ideas and construction. Egos never worked into it. We had very few disagreements on scripts. We were also meticulous researchers at first. We had done a documentary film on the Alamo and had the rather small honor of being the first people permitted to bring a documentary film crew inside that Texas shrine."

Another early episode scripted by the Duncans was "Devil's Island." "We did considerable research for that story," Bob Duncan explained. "We wanted to ensure that the physical setting was as accurate as we could make it, right down to the leg irons. But there was absolutely no pressure on us to depict history accurately. Irwin's favorite saying was, 'Don't get logical with me.' Once we entered that combination of aliens from outer space woven into historical episodes, there was no need for accuracy."

To be fair, other television programs of the time were taking the same liberties. On *Daniel Boone*, starring Fess Parker, the frontiersman battled South American Incas. Asian tigers battled African lions while South American toucans flew overhead in *Daktari*.

The series was clearly aimed toward youngsters, not adults. "The early 1960s was a time to experiment, and we felt that next to sports, nothing worked better in the medium than science fiction," recalled Thomas Moore. "We believed the genre was of interest to teenagers and viewers in their twenties."

"When the show started becoming about people from other planets, it lost its substance," recalled Darren to author Kyle Counts. "It became too much like *Lost In Space*. To me, the most interesting thing about going forward in time is to see what the future will bring. To go there and meet a couple of guys with silver faces who speak mumbo-jumbo, doesn't mean anything. When *The Time Tunnel* started to lose its creative flair [in terms of the writing], I got concerned about the show's future."

Among the plot proposals never produced was a futuristic look at society dealing with the issue of overpopulation. "Around that time, there was a $10,000 award given to any writer who illustrated the population explosion properly," recalled Leonard Stadd. "So I thought, 'Here's an opportunity to show the result of this insane rush to have children, no matter what the cost.' I came up with a story set 5,000 years in the future, when the population is so great that the survivors are living in filtered, underground silos, each silo containing five million people. The manager of one city is overlooking the lives of 20 million people and when the computers explain that there isn't enough oxygen to keep everybody alive, he decides to let one silo perish, reasoning that it's better to let five million people perish

Planet Leader (Kevin Hagen) threatens Doug's life with a ray gun.

and thereby conserve the remaining oxygen for the 15 million others. He wasn't a bad guy, he was just under tremendous pressure to make a decision, and he was hoping that future generations would find new way of generating oxygen."

Tony and Doug, arriving on the scene, analyze the situation and from a fresh approach and concern for human life, propose a number of ideas to address the overpopulation problem. One proposal involved birth control to prevent children being born, thus less of a demand on the air supply.

Ultimately, Tony and Doug save the lives of the five million by turning the air valves on. "Arthur Weiss loved the script, he thought it was remarkable, but the next thing I knew Arthur was saying, 'Irwin wants a rewrite.' 'Has Irwin even read it?' I asked. 'No, but Jerry and Frank are unhappy with it.' Well, Jerry disliked every script, but Frank's reaction surprised me. He was one of my biggest fans, and I couldn't understand why he was equivocating

Robert Duvall, Vitina Marcus and Lew Gallo in "Chase Through Time."

on this. I went to Irwin, but I couldn't get him to read the script so I asked him, 'What's happening with Frank?' 'Talk to Frank. He'll tell you.' So I went to Frank and found him very vague. I said, 'Look, this is one of the few scripts that has some feel to it.' And he said, 'Well, maybe you should get rid of that overpopulation theme.' Finally, Irwin said, in front of witnesses, that he wanted me to write an entirely new script, without pay. 'You owe it to me,' he said. I refused. It was a matter of principle. I was being paid $3,000 per script, and I would be dead with the union. I said, 'Look, I'm capable of writing a lot, but this happens to be a very good script. You read it. Tell me exactly what you object to and why it won't fit into the series' concept.' Irwin finally said to me, 'Well, what do you think I should do?' and I said, 'Shoot it.'"

The script, naturally, was never filmed and Leonard Stadd never wrote another script for the series. "I resented the way Irwin operated by pitting one person against another. If Irwin liked a script, Al Gail always liked it. If there was a production chief who loved a script, Frank or Jerry wouldn't. Irwin would then get a consensus. However, most of the people there had reasonable opinions."

A year later, Stadd discovered what the real problem was with the futuristic script. One of the main ideas in the script dealt with the subject of birth control. Frank La Tourette found the theme objectionable. He had studied to be a Jesuit priest and the script shook him up badly, "and that got Irwin Allen upset, of course," recalled Stadd.

RATINGS

Promotional gimmicks, popularity polls and lavish productions never guarantee the renewal of a television program. The networks looked at the ratings reports, knowing full well the sponsors paid attention to the same. Low ratings meant a lack of sponsors. The September 20, 1966, issue of *The Boston Globe* reported the second week of the 1966-67 Nielsen ratings. Only five new shows broke into the Top Ten: *The Rat Patrol* was the leader, with *The Girl from U.N.C.L.E.*, *Pistols and Petticoats*, *Felony Squad* and *Occasional Wife*, which had a 22.6 rating, following. The rest of the new shows follow below with their high and low rating during their broadcast.

The Monroes: 13.2–15.4

Shane: 9.6–9.2

Hey Landlord: 15.3-10.0

Family Affair: 17.0–21.2

Jean Arthur Show: 14.4–14.3

The Road West: 15.6–10.7

The Iron Horse: 17.9–17.3

The Monkees: 11.3

Roger Miller Show: 13.7–12.2

The Rounders: 15.0–12.0

Mission: Impossible: 13.2–13.6

Run Buddy Run: 14.7

Love on a Rooftop: 17.9–18.4

ABC Stage '67: 16.6

It's About Time: 16.5–14.6

That Girl: 17.9–18.4

Hawk: 12.3–14.1

Star Trek ("Charlie X"): 16.5

Jericho: 14.4–14.1

The Hero: 9.0

The Green Hornet: 10.3–14.1

The Time Tunnel ("One Way to the Moon"): 13.4–17.2

The Milton Berle Show: 12.7–13.7

THE Cat: 11.7–12.1

Tarzan: 15.8–12.5

The Man Who Never Was: 15.4–16.1

The Garry Moore Show and *12 O'Clock High* both ranked near the very bottom out of the 91 shows in total. Moore ranked 89th, *12 O'Clock High* was 88th. It should be noted that a 16.0 rating was considered in 1966 to be a barely passing rating grade. Anything below that was deep trouble. A rating around 20.0 and higher was considered a genuine success. If you take a look at *The Time Tunnel*'s ratings, you'll see it built up from a terrible 13.4 to a fair 17.2, which was remarkable considering its *Green Hornet* lead-in was mired down in the 10-14 range. This may be partly why the ABC network considered *Time Tunnel* something of "an unsung hero" for building its rating as its hour progressed.

Looking over the first four weeks of the new television season, the Nielsen ratings for September 1966 to October 11, 1966, revealed the overall popularity of the programs. Out of 96 total programs, the following selected programs were placed in the following positions.

The Rat Patrol: 3

Bonanza: 4

Family Affair: 14

The Virginian: 15

Felony Squad: 16

The Man From U.N.C.L.E.: 17

Occasional Wife: 18

I, Spy: 19

The Girl From U.N.C.L.E.: 24

Pistols and Petticoats: 33

Batman: 34

Gunsmoke: 36

Star Trek: ("Where No Man has Gone Before"): 39

The Big Valley: 47

It's About Time: 49

THE Cat: 50

The Man Who Never Was: 51

Tarzan: 52

Road West: 54

Flipper: 54 (tied with *Road West*)

Run Buddy Run: 55

The Monroes: 56

The Rounders: 61

Jericho: 62

The Monkees: 66

The Time Tunnel ("End of the World") 67

Jean Arthur Show: 68

Mission: Impossible: 73

The Green Hornet: 78

The Roger Miller Show: 79

Hey, Landlord: 80

The Hero: 81

The Milton Berle Show: 82

The Tammy Grimes Show: 85

Hawk: 86

Shane: 87

12 O'Clock High; 88

ABC Stage '67: 89

The Garry Moore Show: 92

The October 11, 1966, issue of *The Boston Globe* did not hesitate to report the statistics for their readers. "*The Green Hornet* and *Time Tunnel* are the other novice ABC-TV entries this season which remain low in the rating standings, as are older fixtures such as *Combat!*, *Hollywood Palace* and *Voyage to the Bottom of the Sea*. A Florida newspaper, the *St. Petersburg Times*, held a popularity poll and reported the results in their November 13, 1966, issue. Eight hundred local TV viewers responded to the poll regarding the 1966-67 season's new shows (33 in total). In order of ranking best shows, according to the results, they are below, in order of favorites:

1. *Family Affair*
2. *The Monkees*
3. *The Time Tunnel*
4. *Star Trek*
5. *The Monroes*
6. *The Roger Miller Show*
7. *The Man Who Never Was*
8. *Mission: Impossible*
9. *Jericho*
10. *That Girl!*

The November 17, 1966, issue of the California *Press Courier* reported that according to TVQ, the major national rating service that measured people liking a TV program rather than just tuning in, the five best-liked new television shows this season were, in order: *Star Trek*, *The Time Tunnel*, *Family Affair*, *Mission: Impossible* and *Hawk*. The five least liked shows: *The Garry Moore Show*, *The Jean Arthur Show*, *The Tammy Grimes Show*, *The Milton Berle Show* and *The Roger Miller Show*.

"Although television has produced several duds this season, there are three new series that deserve a second season and they might not make it," reported Howard Pearson in the November 21, 1966, issue of *The Deseret News*. "They are *The Monroes*, *Family Affair* and *The Time Tunnel*. *Time Tunnel* presents history painlessly, with all of the suspense of a good mystery. The series has received many votes in a poll of teenage viewers but it has not been able to crack that magic circle in the general ratings, which is unfortunate. Its first

When *The Time Tunnel* aired on the West Coast, on the evening of January 27, 1967, the program was interrupted by an ABC News Bulletin regarding the death of three astronauts (Virgil "Gus" Grissom, Edward White, and Roger Chaffee) in a fire in the Apollo 1 command module, while preparing for launch of the first manned Apollo space mission, on the launch pad at the Kennedy Space Center.

episode, dealing with the Titanic, was a one-million dollar heart stopper, even if viewers did know what was going to happen. Although the production was uneven in the recent show about Krakatoa and its explosion, it was still a worthy production. The segment last week, about the French revolution, was a stirring hour and it had many moments which could have sent young viewers rushing to their history books!"

Doug and Tony find themselves on board a space ship in "One Way to the Moon."

Even though television critics were quick to point out in their reviews of the premiere episode that the ratings might dictate the success of *The Time Tunnel*, the series managed to limbo between favorable and unfavorable among the network. Only time would tell.

SCIENCE FICTION VS. SCIENCE FACT

Joan Crosby of the syndicated *TV Scout* column described the episode "One Way to the Moon" as "another wild adventure that will keep the kids in suspense." The reviewer for the TV Time Previews column in the Ohio *Youngstown Vindicator* referred to this broadcast as "a weird and complicated episode." The TV Previews reviewer for *The Milwaukee Journal* remarked: "It

198

LONG SHOT – DEPOT

(MINIATURE)

198 CONT. A

DEPOT ERUPTS IN GREAT FLAMING
EXPLOSION WHICH MAKES NO SOUND

Storyboard conception of the climatic explosion. In agreement with
Isaac Asimov, even the artist knew there was no sound on the moon.

is a suspenseful, exciting and convincing episode. The more this series stays in the future, and out of established history, the better it is." Not everyone shared Joan Crosby's opinion.

Isaac Asimov wrote about "One Way to the Moon" in his essay, *What Are a Few Galaxies Among Friends?* "In *Time Tunnel* every other character is a secret agent of That Other Nation, and there is a terrific fight between one of them and one of the heroes, both grunting and straining away under what was clearly Earth-gravity, when the Moon's gravity is only one-sixth Earth-normal. Furthermore, the secret enemy agent blows up some of the fuel stores on the Moon. There's a terrific noise although the Moon has no atmosphere to carry sound. The fuel dump goes blazing up in a gigantic bonfire, even though the Moon has no oxygen to support a fire."

Vera W. Heminger of Klamath Falls, Oregon, wasn't convinced, either. She wrote to *TV Guide* after viewing this episode, and her letter was accepted by the editor for amusement of the readers. "To quote the Encyclopedia Americana: 'Without air to transmit sound, the moon is a totally silent world…' In the episode called 'One Way to the Moon,' from the new series *Time Tunnel*, footsteps echoed, doors shut noisily, explosions were very loud and fires burned brightly — all on the moon. And those zippered spacesuits! Any high school student would know better, so why do producers of science fiction shows keep making the same glaring mistakes? Such inattention to scientific details in our space age detract from the value of a show. Please, producers of *Time Tunnel*, read an encyclopedia."

Her letter prompted a response from Andrew Porter, Assistant Editor of *Fantasy and Science Fiction Magazine*, in New York City. "The producer is interested in creating a series which will purely and simply sell him as a producer and sell the sponsor's product. *Time Tunnel* may eventually, heaven help us all, become as popular as *It's About Time* is. In summary, the producer of *Star Trek* is appealing to the intelligence of the viewer. He's using professional science fiction authors to write scripts. *Time Tunnel* is appealing to the audiences craving for monsters."

Star Trek was considered the only serious rival to compete against *The Time Tunnel*, even though neither program competed on the same evening or time slot. Still, science fiction fans across the globe couldn't help but compare the two — which could only hurt *The Time Tunnel* because *Star Trek* was being considered at the time a minor ground-breaker, offering a science fiction take on an adult Western. Ray Oviatti, a columnist for *The Toledo Blade*, wrote in his October 2, 1966, column: "The new *Time Tunnel* has the premise for wide-ranging adventures over the span of history and into the indefinite future. This series may develop into something a little bit special

Rehearsals during filming of "Rendezvous With Yesterday."

in the realm of science fiction. However, *Star Trek*, the other new venture in this realm, is right from the pulps."

Bob Shiels, columnist for *The Calgary Herald*, wrote in the April 5, 1967, Canadian paper, "I know I must be in the minority (perhaps of one) in this respect but if we have to have science fiction on television, I still prefer TV shows that go back in time rather than forward in time. Call it a whim if you will but to me a show that goes back in time at least has a thread and connection, however tenuous, to reality. This is the one and only reason why I have always had a soft spot for *The Time Tunnel* rather than for *Star Trek*. The two time travelers know what is going to happen, even though nobody else does and that adds up to drama that is built-in. It has to be a whim of mine because by all other criteria–acting, writing, you name it, *Star Trek* clobbers *The Time Tunnel* so badly that there is really no comparison. The only other explanation that occurs to me is that *Time Tunnel* may be so bad it's camp, like *Batman*."

Some viewers and critics believed the series was a deliberate rip-off of *The Time Machine* (both the novel and the movie). Any television series involving time travel would be compared to the H.G. Wells story and, sadly, the television program was looked down upon as a result. One television viewer of Mt. Washington, Pennsylvania, Charles Dugan, wrote to *The Pittsburg Press* and his letter was printed in the October 3, 1966, issue: "The perpetrators of *Time Tunnel* have dug their own way into a potential plagiarism suit. They have picked the brain of the late H.G. Wells, right down to the last bit of gray matter. They have snatched his brainchild, *The Time Machine*, like thieves in the night. Old H.G. must be spinning around in his coffin."

Barbara Gregan of Kansas expressed her opinion in a letter reprinted in the September 25, 1966 issue of *The Appleton Post-Crescent*: "*The Time Tunnel* should be recommended for people who cannot afford much excitement or who have a problem sleeping or need something to fill in between the commercials. The acting on this series bogged down while trying to convey a feeling of sincerity and realism. The dialog was far too simple for its wild background, which was probably the dream of an LSD user. The young man who went into the past to warn people of an impending disaster got just as far as all of the others have — nowhere. The 'tried and true' got tedious to watch. This program needs conflict and action, like the Time Tunnel blowing up and taking everybody with it!"

The harshest critic of all, however, was Carl Michael Galli. Author of The Eye Television column in *The Miami News*, he expressed his displeasure in the November 23, 1966, column. "This new TV season has seen a renaissance of science fiction and yet the failure of certain directors to produce something more than pabulum is noticeable. With the exception of NBC's *Star Trek* and a recent *Chrysler Theater* presentation, this year's crop has been mostly designed to appeal to those with a need for monsters and little time for thought. In this group we can lump *It's About Time* and the Irwin Allen shows. This includes *Lost In Space*, many episodes of *Voyage to the Bottom of the Sea* and *The Time Tunnel*. Good science fiction uses fact as a stepping

The cast rehearses a scene for "Rendezvous With Yesterday."

stone toward the fulfillment of its plot — it entertains, educates and even stimulates. Using this criteria for judgment, the new *Time Tunnel* program is all but wiped out.

"The original premise of the series concerns two Time Tunnel scientists, Tony Newman (James Darren) and Doug Phillips (Robert Colbert) who are hurled from one era to another because of technical difficulties with the six billion dollar tunnel. This can be accepted. What is hard to swallow is the show's unstated possibility that Tony and Doug may be imprisoned outside their present time, in the year 1968, for the rest of their lives. This is especially hard on us when we see the time tunnel scientists (played by Lee Meriwether, John Zaremba and Whit Bissell) bring back assorted Indians, Trojan soldiers and French political prisoners. But this is just one contradiction.

"There are also predictable plots, and a general lack of unconcern for viewer intelligence and the effect this series has on the stature of science fiction. *Time Tunnel* could be good but it is not. It is original and in view of this, it is a crime to have such potential go to waste. But perhaps there is one saving feature: *Time Tunnel* is often very funny. Just think what Channel 10 could do with its 6 to 7 p.m. time slot if it replaced *It's About Time* with *Time Tunnel*. Come to think of it, they had better leave *Time Tunnel* where it is, we couldn't stand anything worse."

REJECTED FIRST SEASON PROPOSALS

"I had hoped that after the first season, we would be able to mellow out and give our characters some depth. You bet your butt I thought it was a running and jumping show," Robert Colbert said for *Starlog* magazine. "It had the potential to be so much more. Little did I know that Irwin Allen was up in the office running the show with that mentality. We tried to make sense out of things in scripts that were absolutely ludicrous — some of them had holes you could drive a Mack truck through — but none of that filtered down to the set."

Among the plot proposals commissioned by Irwin Allen, a few were rejected during the first season, such as Charles Bennett's "Murder-Go-Round." (Story outline dated January 5, 1967.) Here, Tony and Doug joined up with the British Intelligence in London, during WWII, to thwart terrorist bombings by the Nazis. Jerry Briskin's commentary in a memo to Irwin Allen: "As this story outline now stands, I would have to recommend that we do not go any further. I believe the idea of a spy story with a WWII London buzz-boat background is an interesting thought but it is not worked out in the present outline. In fact, Tony and Doug are reduced to being bystanders in the action. It's possible this story could be altered, in that Tony and Doug are somehow accepted by the British and then assigned the task of trying to

Observant fans of *The Time Tunnel* will notice repetition in *Planet of the Apes* (1968), a 20th Century-Fox theatrical release. As Taylor's spaceship enters the planet's atmosphere, before crash-landing in a lake, the sound of the engines are replicated using the same sound effect used to power up the Time Tunnel.

locate the German spies in the city and notify the London authorities where and how the German spies plan to set their bombs. In addition to these story problems, this outline calls for magicians, trained dogs and music. I believe this would be very time-consuming and costly."

A 73-page script titled "Prehistoric Future" (drafted November 10, 1966), written by William Welch, was originally titled "The Time That Never Was."

Dr. Raymond Swain (John Zaremba) checks his calculations.

The story technically pre-dates the finale of *Planet of the Apes* (1968). In this script, Tony and Doug land in what appears to be the caveman era, and befriend a sensitive cave girl around a campfire. They are soon threatened and chased by fierce warriors. At one point, Tony and Doug find the apocalyptic ruins of New York City and realize this is not the past, but the far future. A memo from Arthur Weiss raved that, "This could be one of our best shows ever!" and that "there will be plenty of story material to use in this time zone…stock footage will also be used," says Weiss. Why this story was never produced during the first season remains unknown.

Also considered was Leonard Stadd's script (title and date unknown), the story of an over-populated future, after an atomic war, and Tony and Doug are arrested by security police chief Krim, but make their escape into a underground labyrinth. There, the travelers find a subterranean museum which houses parts of their old Time Tunnel. Filming this episode would have allowed a cost-effective measure for using the Time Tunnel Complex on Stage 18. Jerry Briskin's memo about this script to Irwin Allen criticized, "Is this museum underground or above ground? What kind of clothing do these people of the future wear? Don't any of these people have to be decontaminated? Police Chief Krim's search for Tony and Doug extends into the subterranean world, where the boys have taken refuge with a family. Why does this family go out on a limb to protect Tony and Doug and take this risk?"

In "The Savages," a plot outline by Robert Hamner, Tony and Doug materialize in a clearing near a farm and watch in horror as a band of savage war-painted Indians burn the farm buildings and kill a settler and his wife. Two Indian braves remain behind to loot the area and Tony and Doug barely manage to subdue them. They hear a sound in the wreckage and find two scared teens under the charred timbers, Tommy and his sister Angie. The travelers quickly take the

TV Week Magazine, October 1, 1966.

children into the safety of the nearby woods as the Indians return to look for their missing two braves. The Indians find their braves unconscious and pick up the trail of the time travelers. As the four reach a clearing, Tommy tells Doug and Tony that Geronimo is planning an uprising. Jerry Briskin proposed that "stock footage and plates will be made from the film, *River of No Return.*"

MID-SEASON

According to most popularity polls, *The Time Tunnel* was a favorite among teenagers who were not already hooked on the spy intrigues of David McCallum and Robert Vaughn. Tom Hoder, a 23 year-old teacher at Irwin Crown's Carpentersville high school in Illinois asked his teenage students (all 568 of them) for their reaction to the current new TV programs. They picked and praised ABC's *The Time Tunnel* as their overwhelming top favorite new show of the season out of over 30 new shows possible, with a rating of 3.56 out of 4.0. The four runner-ups were *That Girl*, *The Monkees*, *Star Trek* and

The Rat Patrol. The fact that *Time Tunnel* had two handsome young heroes, James Darren and Robert Colbert, plus a dramatic theme, helped *The Time Tunnel* with the school kids. The students also put Jean Arthur and Garry Moore, who had a 2.03 rating, as dead last.

Clay Gowran of *The Chicago Tribune* reported these facts in the October 2, 1966, issue, which prompted a letter from Max Slobodin, from Chicago.

Whit Bissell as Lt. General Heywood Kirk.

"Your recent article about the Carpentersville students in Irving Crown's high school and their choice of favorite TV show being *The Time Tunnel* was very interesting," Slobodin wrote. "You mentioned that *The Time Tunnel*'s young heroes, James Darren and Robert Colbert, helped the show out with those school kids. Well, you will be interested to know that I am 57 years old and I not only think *The Time Tunnel* is the finest science fiction series on television but it is the best of the new network shows this season."

In December 1966, Mrs. Jacqueline Sheppert, a teacher at San Gabriel High School in California, encouraged her class of 30 tenth-graders to write an essay about their favorite television programs. *The Time Tunnel* received the most votes. Mike Sollenberger, a student in the class, wrote a review that appeared in the Christmas issue of *The Daily Review*. "Original is the word that best describes *The Time Tunnel*. It is a refreshing break in the monotony of wild and woolly westerns, slinky spy plots and situation comedies that are anything but humorous. What better way is there to teach history than view it first hand on an exciting TV show? *Time Tunnel* has just enough surface know-how to satisfy the modern intellect but not so much that it leaves ordinary people lost in a maze of terms and gadgets, so that he knows where to pick up the loose ends. Each week the camera focuses on an interesting event in world history. This ranges from an invasion of ancient Troy to the modern day revolution in Hungary. *Time Tunnel* may not depict history exactly as it happened but it does stimulate interest in the past and it inspires research for one's own personal satisfaction. Learning history from books is usually dull. This certainly is not the case with *Time Tunnel*. The whole idea of men controlling time is very fascinating.

The Time Tunnel also keeps you in suspense. You know exactly what is going to happen yet in the back of your mind you have that great hope that history may be changed. The acting and plots on *Time Tunnel* are excellent. Few people would watch a show where they already know the ending unless it was exciting and interesting. It is regrettable that *Time Tunnel* must run with competition from two other fine TV shows but even though it is in its freshman season I am sure it will hold its own and come through with flying colors. With a little experience under its belt, it should enjoy a long and successful run."

George Woods, a columnist for *The New York Times*, felt differently in his December 11, 1966, column. "Thanks to *The Time Tunnel*, my younger boys have now become convinced that whenever a momentous event occurred in history, the Titanic disaster, Custer's last fling, the Trojan horse, there must have always been two young men present who, if history's participants had not been so obdurate, might have been able to stave the inevitable hand of the past."

"I am a high school student who was doing poorly in the subject of world history in school and then the TV show *Time Tunnel* came on and it changed my whole outlook on history," someone wrote to *The Chicago Tribune* (July 29, 1967, issue). "I would much rather learn the facts about true history by watching *Time Tunnel* rather than by watching *Hogan's Heroes* and learn false facts about prison camps."

Someone who preferred to remain anonymous, known simply as "A Country Girl," wrote to the Alabama *Times Daily*. "There is not a thing to look at that is not out-of-this-world," she wrote in the February 14, 1967, issue. "No wonder people are going crazy in this world and doing crazy things! We only get crazy things like *Voyage to the Bottom of the Sea*, *Batman* and *The Green Hornet*. And there is *Time Tunnel*, a show where all of these people have been dead for years. It's awful to see such messes on television. If you try to change the channel, you just get another mess."

The October 4, 1967, issue of *The Toledo Blade* reprinted a letter submitted to their TV Key Mail column: "I think *Time Tunnel* is a wonderful show.

Lee Meriwether and a V.I.P. on the Fox lot.

Why don't they take off *Rango* and Phyllis Diller instead? I don't like them at all. They act silly and crazy."

In January of 1967, Rick du Brow of the United Press International questioned whose minds the network was after. "Anyone measuring the worth of a television show should weigh its merits, if any, on the basis of the audience it is trying to reach. Therefore, it should either entertain, inform, stimulate or evoke a combination of all of those reactions. Clearly, most TV shows this season have failed on all counts. But again, just who are the people these shows are trying to reach? The question is not easily answered. *Captain Kangaroo* is perfect for his audience. *Batman* is fine for his. And presumably *Bonanza* has stolen into the maudlin hearts of viewers aged 16 to infinity.

"But what of a series such as *The Time Tunnel*, which airs every Friday evening? Who in the world is ABC-TV trying to reach with this nugget? What does producer Irwin Allen have in mind? The tots are in bed by that time. Teenagers are too hip to watch when they can go out on dates. And any adult who would watch it has got to be suspect. In the beginning *Time Tunnel* may have been based on a sound idea, perhaps the HG Wells novel, *The Time Machine*. The premise was to have two handsome young scientists flung back and forward through time from week to week and get involved in historic events which they have no control over. But the idea is too costly for execution for one thing. If you are going to put a couple of guys back into early Rome or into the War of the Roses, you had better have the money to make it look authentic. On this show it never does. The concept is handled clumsily, the acting is poor and the scripts unbelievably bad.

"But it cannot be written off so lightly. In reality, it is typical of TV executives who are determining what the public will be offered for viewing. But this isn't just to single out *The Time Tunnel*. It is no better nor much worse than the commercial TV fare American viewers have been slapped in the face with for too many years. The great misfortune is that good television, to say great television, is so rare that one is forced to leave the TV set off for most nights of the week. There are a lot of *Time Tunnels* of one kind or another on almost every hour of prime time. It is pitiful that a great and powerful medium, indeed America's mass medium, cannot or will not do better.""I noticed a letter to the editor of the CBC Times the other day and it suggested that *The Time Tunnel* is educational," Bob Shiels wrote in the November 5, 1966, issue of *The Calgary Herald*. "I guess there are several ways that you can look at *Time Tunnel*. You might call it educational or just escapist adventure. On the other hand, you might color it as funny. A case could be made that *Time Tunnel* contains more unconscious and unintentional humor than most of the so-called TV comedies that consciously try to make you laugh. This week our intrepid time travelers, played by James Darren and Robert Colbert, found themselves all mixed up in the siege of Troy. As usual they had a lot of trouble explaining to everyone where they came from. Ulysses, quite reasonably when you think about it, concluded that they must be Gods from Olympus. I started to wonder about the educational value of *Time Tunnel* at around the time those anxious knot of scientists at the other end of the tunnel got into the act and decided to send in reinforcements in the form of an older soldier named Sergeant Jiggs. Jiggs went back in time armed with a submachine gun and a bag of hand grenades. It is to wonder how Homer overlooked this rather startling development when he sat down to write *The Iliad*.

"One of *Time Tunnel*'s plus features is the very effective way in which the series works in old film footage into their stories. Back at Pearl Harbor a couple of weeks ago, the Japanese planes looked really menacing. This week had a most impressive Trojan horse clipped out of an old movie, which may

or may not have been directed by Cecil B. DeMille. The two stars of *Time Tunnel*, James Darren and Robert Colbert, are the weak link in the whole crazy chain. Neither of them is in any danger of winning an award for his acting ability."

R.E. Owen of Washington, D.C., wrote to Donald Kirkley of *The Baltimore Sun*. "I'm writing to you regarding your recent TV column and I am upset at you for suggesting that *Star Trek* in on the same level with *The Time Tunnel*. To state *Star Trek* and *Time Tunnel* are similar is to admit that you have only seen *Star Trek* superficially. Perhaps you have only seen a few curious characters, the few odd monsters and weird vehicles floating around in space without really seeing the show. You have apparently not attempted to appreciate the series and how it concerns human interests. Perhaps you, like the other critics, have been taken in by producer Irwin Allen's cheap special effects on *Time Tunnel*, while there a serious attempt to make *Star Trek* a very high quality show each week. Unlike *Time Tunnel* or *Lost In Space*, *Star Trek*'s producer, Gene Roddenberry, appreciates drama while it is Mr. Allen, the so-called king of science fiction, who is ruining the reputation of science fiction. *Star Trek* and *Time Tunnel* were both shown in Cleveland during the annual World of Science Fiction convention last year and *Star Trek* and its producer received applause while Allen's show received well deserved boos and hisses.

Over the years, both Darren and Colbert insisted they never clashed, but there appears to be evidence to the contrary during the early weeks of production. Whether the studio fed the story to tabloids for the purpose of picking up higher ratings or there was a real, though minor, difference of opinions, the actors today are good friends and continue to make appearances together at celebrity and autograph venues to meet and greet fans.

The news broke in the fall of 1966 when *The Hartford Courant* reported in their November 10 issue: "James Darren and Robert Colbert are co-stars of *Time Tunnel* but they rarely exchange dialog off-camera. The freeze between them is the result of clashing egos." Columnist Howard Pearson in the November 14 issue of the Utah *Deseret News* reported: "The grapevine had reported earlier that there was refrigeration between James Darren and Robert Colbert, the stars of *The Time Tunnel*. But that's been rectified. The freeze between them was reported to be due to clashing egos." Columnist Alex Freeman reported in the January 4, 1967, issue of *The Hartford Courant*, "James Darren and Robert Colbert, the co-stars of *The Time Tunnel*, started out as anything but pals. Both of them were seeking the star title on the show. But several months have changed things between them. The two boys are now closer together after realizing that this series won't make major stars out of anyone." (Salary contracts before the show went before the cameras dictated the star title, so this news brief appears to be a bit exaggerated.) Walter Winchell in his January 29, 1967, syndicated column reported: "The tantrumental scenes happening between takes of television's *Time Tunnel* series are often a lot more entertaining to watch."

"*Time Tunnel* was extremely over-praised by critics because they were suckered in by its special effects. But take a close look at the works of *Time Tunnel* and you'll see that the equipment used for the tunnel has been taken off the show *Voyage to the Bottom of the Sea*. They also use old footage from old Irwin Allen films to save costs. *Star Trek* is watched by enthusiasts and written by top writers in the field such as Harlan Ellison and Robert Bloch,

Robert Colbert on location for "Massacre."

the author of *Psycho*. I think you ought to be banned to the planet Vulcanis where Mr. Spock is from (Leonard Nimoy, one of the principal actors on the NBC series, has been spokesman for the National Space Club!)."

Donald Kirkley responded: "In terms of television science fiction, *The Twilight Zone* was superior to *Star Trek* because it relied on human problems and little scenery. And incidentally, science fiction writers worked on *Twilight Zone* too. If I ever equated *Star Trek* with *Time Tunnel* it is because both shows are time-wasters and have no relation to the important problems facing our society today. They are simply a part of the dream world of TV fiction and their audiences are made up of people who find an outlet for their fantasies by watching such shows."

"My love affair with *Star Trek* began after the fifth or sixth episode," recalled Leonard Nimoy for *The Bryan Times* (via UPI release). "I was always proud that

Star Trek dealt with worthwhile issues. We were ahead of our time in 1966. We were one of two new science fiction shows that debuted that season. The other was *The Time Tunnel*. The critic for *TV Guide* again picked *Time Tunnel* as the one with the most promise." Star Trek would ultimately last three seasons (one season more than the network was initially willing to give, as a result of a strong letter-writing campaign from viewers in late 1967 and early 1968).

FIRST SEASON REJECTIONS

A number of plot proposals never reached fruition for the first season. The most promising was "The Cro-magnons," a caveman story written by Rik Vollaerts, and "Hang, Witch, Hang" by Catherine Turney, in which Tony and Doug arrive to witness the Salem, Mass. witch trials.

Others, according to an inter-office memo from John D. Garr to Irwin Allen, dated July 12, 1966, can be found listed below.

Writer	Episode Title	Contract Date
Peter Packer	"Lunar Express"	May 13, 1966
Barney Slater	"The Human Monster"	April 11, 1966
Boris Sobelman	"Lions of the Coliseum"	April 11, 1966
Leonard Stadd	"The Marie Celeste Mystery"	April 11, 1966
Sheldon Stark	"Ashes of Fire"	April 11, 1966
Robert Tallman	"Cagliostro"	April 11, 1966
Robert Tallman	"Exploding City"	April 11, 1966
Catherine Turney	"Hurricane of Easter Island"	April 27, 1966

THE SECOND SEASON

Columnist Win Fanning was among the earliest news columnists to report that a *Time Tunnel* renewal was "doubtful, but not yet axed." In the January 23, 1967, issue of the *Pittsburgh Gazette*, Fanning reported ABC's Friday night line-up was "still very confusing." A month later, columnist Bob Hull reported that low ratings plagued the Friday night adventure show. The series, according to Hull in his February 26, 1967, issue of *The Los Angeles Herald Examiner*, "probably will not return to the screen next season." He cited a number of reasons for the dark outlook. "Adults just don't understand the wildly improbable premise of *Time Tunnel*. Children believe the stories about a pair of young scientists who invent and use a time travel machine which catapults them into the thick of historical events. The shows are 'unsuitable' to the unbending, too-logical minds of the mature."

"Pseudo-scientific stories whose complicated gadgetry and silly involved plots make it unsuitable for children," criticized Frank Orme, the executive vice president of the National Association for Better Broadcasting, an outfit assuming the mantle of auditor of all TV shows as they affected youngsters. Yet, separate studies by the network indicated viewers to the age of 18 enjoyed the hour-long program.

The ratings had dropped, however, according to the Nielsens, which placed *Time Tunnel* in the high 70s range out of some 100 network program. "I

An Alien curator (Michael Ansara) argues over computer equipment with Tony and Doug in "The Kidnappers."

think the shows serve two purposes," James Darren debated. "We give the youngsters lots of entertainment and at the same time pique their interest in history. We tried our best to make stories as logical as possible, but I guess this is the year of the big movies... They like to see the action first, read the real story later. I think it is a service."

It should come as a comfort for many to learn that while such programs as *Daniel Boone* and *The Time Tunnel* were twisting the facts of the past, *TV Guide* reported that 1,060,751 enrollments in history and social studies were being simultaneously serviced by closed circuit and the television spectrum. This figure originated from the Michigan State University's 13th *Compendium of Televised Education*, a fat, 488-page volume that was published months after the premiere of *The Time Tunnel*.

On March 9, 1967, *The Boston Globe* announced that the fall schedules of the TV networks, unveiling what they have for the September slate, "finally fell into place last week. Of the five ABC shows listed as doubtful of renewal, the announcement was that ABC was dumping *Rango* and *F-Troop*. Both of these were comedies. Those that will continue are *Iron Horse*, *The Time Tunnel* and *Voyage to the Bottom of the Sea*. These are all action stanzas, so the emphasis's apparently is going to get away from comedy."

"We were doing our last or next-to-last Season One episode, we were about to go on hiatus, and Irwin telephoned me on the set," recalled James Darren. "Like I said, we had a pretty special relationship. I don't think he and Bob did, to be honest with you, not that it meant anything, but Irwin and I just got on well. And so he called me on the set and told me that *Time Tunnel* had been picked up for another season. And he said, 'You can tell Bob and whoever else you wanna tell.' I was thrilled. I told Colbert, I said, 'Irwin just called me and told me that we were picked up' and blah, blah, blah. But then later, [it was announced that] *Time Tunnel* was being taken off the air."

In late June 1967, tabloids began reporting on television actors with an itch to get involved on a larger scale. Robert Vaughn, for example, had a hankering to direct an episode of *The Man From U.N.C.L.E.* for the up-coming season, while James Darren (according to a news blurb in *TV Guide* and Tom McIntyre of the *Weekend TV Editor*) wrote a plot synopsis for a second season episode, centering on Doug and Tony's encounter with Jack the Ripper.

"As I think about it, I may have suggested that to Irwin, but I really can't swear to it," recalled James Darren. "I didn't write a script because I don't consider myself a writer. It might have been just something that I talked about to him about, because that was a fascinating thing, the story of Jack the Ripper. I saw the original Laird Cregar movie [*The Lodger*, 1944], I saw the Jack Palance movie [*Man in the Attic*, 1953], and even though in a sense it's kind of sick to find him fascinating, because he was a horrible person, it is an interesting story."

"Had *The Time Tunnel* gone a second season, the possibilities would have been expanded," Darren remarked. "We could have gone into a parallel world. We could have bumped into ourselves from another travel. The possibilities were limitless. Writers often run out of ideas but with *Time Tunnel*, we would have still come up with ideas."

"I believe, had the series ran longer, by the third season there would have been more control over where we would have gone and we probably would have been in contact with the Time Tunnel [personnel] more often," remarked Robert Colbert. "There probably would have been a couple recurring characters, arch nemesis and maybe even meet up with other time travelers."

In the September 9, 1967, issue of *TV Guide*, a letter to the editor from William Cook of Orange, California, expressed his disappointment over the summer reruns. Knowing the series was not going to be renewed for a second season, pondered why the producers did not chose to film a special closer for the final telecast. "Why can't more television shows follow the fine example set by *The Fugitive*? Instead of just ending the season with another rerun, why couldn't shows like *The Time Tunnel* film a special episode and save it for the end of the season with the scientists coming out of the tunnel?"

SECOND SEASON PROPOSALS

Over 30 plot proposals were drawn up for consideration for the second season, many involving more far out plots including the destruction of the human race and major holocausts. The possibility of the stories becoming darker in nature is evident in the brief summaries reprinted below.

Lost Civilization

Tony and Doug land in the primordial ooze of a prehistoric swamp out of which come charging antediluvian dinosaurs. Running from the threat, they are stunned when they come upon the ruins of metropolitan skyscrapers. In taking refuge here from the dinosaurs, they come upon a cultivated and cultured man and woman who are under attack by the retrogressive semi-humans of this degenerate era. The man and woman are also time travelers. They are from 10,000 A.D. Tony and Doug help these two sympathetic people escape from their attackers back into the future, and themselves escape back into the limbo of time.

Note: William Welch wrote the plot titled "Prehistoric Future" as a first season episode. Contracted on April 11, 1966, this was Welch's first assignment for The Time Tunnel, *pre-dating his other contributions to the series. This was the only teleplay written and not produced as a first-season entry. Re-titled "Lost Civilization," it appears Irwin Allen planned to produce the teleplay as the premiere of the second season.*

Atlantis

In the year 6,000 B.C., Tony and Doug are drowning in the black waters of the Atlantic. With the help of the staff back at the Time Tunnel Complex, they manage to reach the island shores of a fabulous civilization. Suspected of causing strange Earth movements, they are threatened with death but are saved by Tau and Rana, a young husband and wife. In return, Tony and Doug succeed in rescuing their benefactors from the awful fate which now overtakes Atlantis. The fabled civilization explodes in volcanic fury and sinks to the bottom of the sea.

Note: It was suggested that stock footage from George Pal's Atlantis: The Lost Continent *(1961) be used should this episode be put to film.*

The Gladiators

Tony and Doug land in a chamber room leading into the Roman Coliseum during the Gladiatorial Games of 300 A.D. They are immediately seized as escaped barbarian slaves and trained as gladiators. Despite the efforts of the folks back at the Time Tunnel Complex to tranquilize the human and animal antagonists they must fight, Tony and Doug are forced to face their opponents…and finally are forced to fight each other in a display before the Roman Emperor.

*Note: Boris Sobelman's first season plot proposal, "Lions of the Coliseum,"
was never produced even though he was contracted to write a teleplay based on
his proposal. (Contract dated April 11, 1966.) The reason why this episode was
never produced remains unknown but there is speculation that a conflict of interest momentarily prevented the episode from going before the cameras. Shortly
after completing the pilot script, Shimon Wincelberg composed three possible
scenarios for future productions: "Captain Cook," "Ivanhoe Background" and
"Roman Gladiators." Arthur Weiss, the story editor, reviewed Sobelman's proposal
and attempted to clarify the difference between his story and the one created by
Wincelberg. "The only point of similarity between this story and 'Roman Gladiators'
is that our heroes go back to Rome about 350 A.D. and that a gladiatorial arena is
involved," Weiss wrote. "However, whereas the theme of 'Romans' is the developing
of 'the new religion,' the theme of our story is the escape of slave gladiators — a
public domain incident based on the historic revolt of Spartacus. In our story, there
are no sequences in catacombs; no banquets. The story, as a whole, is centered around
a rich Roman's private gladiatorial arena and involves the combat of one of our
heroes with a tiger: at no time are fights between gladiators involved except as
such stock scenes are used from the Fox picture* Demetrius and the Gladiators *in
order to set the general background of Rome."*

*"Lions of the Coliseum" was eventually re-titled "The Gladiators" and planned
to go before the cameras as a second season production.*

Inferno of Terror

In the year 2,150 A.D., Tony and Doug find themselves aboard an Alien
earth-boring vehicle, plunging at nightmare speed toward the molten core
of the Earth. In addition to the danger ahead, they face instant death from
the Aliens aboard whose mission is to extract life-forces from our world. The
scientists back at the Time Tunnel Complex vainly combat the Alien control
under which the vehicle is operating, but it is Tony and Doug who finally
succeed in defeating the Aliens and save the planet.

David and Goliath

Tony and Doug arrive in the Holy Land in time to save the life of a young
man who was about to be crushed in the mighty arms of an armed giant.
Doug becomes a prisoner of the Philistines while Tony befriends the boy,
whom he takes to the Israelite camp. Through the mechanism of the Time
Tunnel, Tony and Doug remain in contact with each other and execute the
strategy by which the youth, David, slays Goliath.

*Note: Inter-office correspondence suggests the proposal to use footage of the
David and Goliath scene from the 1951 motion picture,* David and Bathsheba.

Hannibal

Tony and Doug, in a narrow Alpine defile in the year 216 B.C., are help-lessly trapped in the path of a trumpeting charge of Hannibal's armored elephants. They are about to be executed as spies sent by the Roman enemy. Advised by the Time Tunnel, Tony and Doug make an apparently miraculous military prediction to Hannibal. Because of both ego and curiosity, he allows them to prove their innocence and good will by infiltrating the Roman lines and rescuing Hannibal's daughter, Genevre, from the brutal Roman General, Scipio. Tony and Doug accomplish the rescue during the climactic battle between Hannibal's elephant troops and the Roman legions.

Note: The plot was no doubt conceived after reviewing stock footage from the 1959 motion picture Hannibal, *starring Victor Mature, which Irwin Allen had access to courtesy of the Liber Film Company. In the movie, after making his historic crossing of the Alps with ele-phants transporting supplies and troops, Hannibal marches on Rome in a war of revenge. During his advance, he cap-tures Sylvia, the niece of Roman Senator Fabius Maximus but, instead of holding her prisoner, he shows her his power-ful army and herds of elephants, then sets her free. He is sure she will report what she has seen to his Roman enemies. Hannibal defeats the Romans at the battle of Trebbia and sends a message to Sylvia that he is marching on Rome. Sylvia succumbs to her love of Hannibal and the great war lord discovers that, in war, there can be no room for romance.*

Monster of the Snow

In 1967 (a year before Tony and Doug completed construction of the Time Tunnel and Tony entered the tunnel for the first time), Tony and Doug land on the snow-covered slopes of the Himalayas to discover that the Abominable Snowmen who attack them are in reality invading Aliens from the cold planet of a distant galaxy which is growing too warm for their continued existence. For years the Aliens have been seen in the form of Abominable Snowmen but at will can transform themselves into their real appearance resembling scantily-clad humans. When the folks back at the Time Tunnel try to help

Tony and Doug, the Tunnel itself is invaded by Snowmen, but finally Tony and Doug destroy the invaders' means of ingress to Earth.

Buried Alive with King Tut

Tony and Doug find themselves being buried alive inside the great pyramid of Cheops, together with the dead Pharaoh and his living retinue. Despite the opposing time-space-force exerted by the Time Tunnel, the huge hundred-ton granite block swings into place, sealing them forever with the embalmed mummy. The Time Tunnel makes desperate efforts to aid their escape; succeeds in electronically cutting a path toward rescue; but the way is blocked by the fanatical High Priest who is determined that all within the tomb must die. Tony and Doug ultimately succeed in rescuing themselves and all the living members of Pharaoh's court who have been entombed with them, including the Princess Tiye.

Note: After Meyer Dolinsky wrote a plot synopsis titled "Curse of the Mummy," he was contracted on May 2, 1966, to write a feasible teleplay for the first season. For reasons unknown, the episode was never produced. The story was later re-titled "Buried Alive With King Tut" (dated February 13, 1967) and planned for a second season production.

Anyone who watches "The Cave of the Wizards" and "The Ghost Planet" episodes of Lost In Space *can observe the Egyptian props and visualize what this* Time Tunnel *episode would have looked like...including the mummy.*

To verify how the information in press releases is to be taken with a grain of salt (and newspaper briefs as well since much of their information originates from these same press releases), ABC-TV produced an undated press release for this episode which never even went before the cameras:

> *At 20th Century-Fox Television studios in Hollywood, actors James Darren and Robert Colbert, portraying a pair of dedicated physicists, are starring in producer Irwin Allen's exciting new science fiction adventure series,* The Time Tunnel, *debuting in color Friday, September 9, during ABC-TV's Advance Premiere Week.*
>
> *Producer Allen's third television program (his others:* Voyage to the Bottom of the Sea *and* Lost In Space*) focuses on a remarkable machine which can project them backwards or forward through time.*
>
> *In one episode, as doctors Tony Newman and Doug Phillips (respectively, Darren and Colbert), find themselves in Egypt on the morning of November 4, 1922, at the opening of the tomb of the great Egyptian king, Tutankh-Amen, known more familiarly as King Tut. Dead since the 14th Century, B.C., the king had placed a curse over anyone desecrating his final resting place.*

The scene called for Darren and Colbert to enter the great cavern and shine their flashlights on a wall filled with hieroglyphics. The director called, "Action!" cameras turned and the actors commences the scene. Suddenly, as if it was part of the dialogue, they looked at one another and broke into controllable laughter.

"Cut!" yelled the director. "What's so funny?"

Darren and Colbert pointed to the wall, on which some wag has written: "This side of the tomb had 33 percent fewer cavities."

When Worlds Collide

Tony and Doug find themselves on a strange planet which is disintegrating all around them; great chunks of matter are being torn from its surface by the increasing, incredible magnetic attraction exerted by the approach of an immense fiery star which is steadily increasing in force. The surface of the planet splits in mile-deep fissures, mountains crack apart with their tops exploding off into space. Only the counter-magnetic force of the Time Tunnel, zeroed in on Tony and Doug, enable them to survive in order to rescue two astonishingly human-like inhabitants.

One Million B.C.

Tony and Doug find themselves in One Million B.C. when convulsions of nature shake the Earth and torrential rains drench it during exploding electrical storms. Amid the terror they find a small band of reasoning early human beings — the ancestors of today's man — in danger of being destroyed by carnivorous apes. The Time Tunnel, with its enormous molecular and atomic power, help Tony and Doug defend themselves against the awful forces of prehistoric nature. But they use their own highly sophisticated technical know-how in defeating the hordes of ape men.

Return of the Ice Age

Tony and Doug find themselves a hundred years in the future in New York City which, together with the whole Temperate Zone, is in the deadly grip of a new Ice Age. A permutation of the Earth's orbit around the Sun has resulted in immense icebergs crushing New York harbor from the sea, and in glaciers descending on the City from the North. The Time Tunnel's computer system predicts that the glaciation has reached its maximum advance and within a few days will begin to recede. Tony and Doug, inside the City's subway system, help the civic leaders fight off the attacks of roaming polar animals and to bring destructive panic under control so that the City can survive these last critical hours before the ice will begin to return to the North.

The TIME TUNNEL

ABC - TV - COLOR   FRIDAY NIGHT

EXCLUSIVE IN YOUR CITY

THE CURSE OF KING TUT'S

TOMB REVEALED: A BAD PUN

At 20th Century-Fox Television studios in Hollywood, actors James Darren and Robert Colbert, portraying a pair of dedicated physicists, are starring in producer Irwin Allen's exciting new science-fiction adventure series, "The Time Tunnel," debuting in color Friday, Sept. 9 during ABC-TV's Advance Premiere Week.

Producer Allen's third television project (his others: "Voyage to the Bottom of the Sea" and "Lost in Space") focuses on a remarkable machine which can project them backwards or forward through time.

In one episode, as doctors Tony Newman and Doug Phillips, (respectively, Darren and Colbert) find themselves in Egypt on the morning of November 4, 1922 at the opening of the tomb of the great Egyptian king, Tutankh-Amen, known more familiarly as King Tut. Dead since the 14th Century, B.C., the king had placed a curse over anyone desecrating his final resting place.

The scene called for Darren and Colbert to enter the great cavern and shine their flashlights on a wall filled with hieroglyphics.

The director called, "Action!" Cameras turned and the actors commenced the scene. Suddenly, as if it was part of the dialogue, they looked at one another and broke into uncontrollable laughter.

"Cut!" yelled the director. "What's so funny?"

Darren and Colbert pointed to the wall, on which some wag had written: "This side of the tomb had 33% fewer cavities!"

#

X

Attila the Hun

In 500 A.D., Tony and Doug stand between the barbarian hordes coming out of Asia and a defenseless Europe. With their 20th century knowledge of electricity and electronics, they harness the power of lightning, and draw on the power of the Time Tunnel in order to turn the tide of battle against Attila the Hun.

When the World Drowned

In 12,000 A.D., Tony and Doug find themselves fighting for their lives against a riptide off a rocky continental coastline. They fear they've lost each other forever when Doug is seized by savage degenerate Amphibians who are survivors of some awful cataclysm which has overtaken the Earth and apparently destroyed man and civilization. Tony is dragged under the surface of the sea to find himself in an undersea habitation, one of the underwater living complexes in which our civilization and its people have survived the cataclysm. The Time Tunnel finally succeeds in transferring Doug and the Amphibians to where Tony is under the sea. Together they lead the battle in which the people of civilization defeat the Amphibians.

The Thing in the Web

Tony and Doug are thrown back in time to 100,000 B.C., landing amid the monstrous forms of prehistoric life in the Great American Desert. Captured by the aborigines and threatened with death, they will be spared if they can destroy the Thing in the Web, which is about to destroy the local tribe. Using the power of the Time Tunnel to distract the Thing, Tony and Doug manage to reach its underground lair, but then suddenly find themselves enmeshed by the gigantic, unbreakable metallic web spun by the spider-like creature.

Note: As a cost-cutting measure, it was proposed to reuse some of the webbing and giant spider props/footage for this episode as well as "The Weird World," an episode of Land of the Giants *put before the cameras early in the season.*

World on Fire

In the year 10,000 A.D., Tony and Doug find themselves fighting along-side Earth leaders in an attempt to repel creatures from a super-hot galaxy. The creatures' purpose is to transform Earth into a burning planet so that it will be habitable to them. Tony and Doug risk their lives even though they might have safely allowed themselves to be retrieved by the Time Tunnel. They clash and outwit the burning-hot advance troops who descend to the surface of the world.

The Lost Civilization

Tony and Doug are transported into the wilds of Central America during the 15th Century to find themselves lost in a vast underground cavern which holds astonishing relics of a lost civilization. Steam engines, electrical motors, advanced forms of malleable glass greet them. But suddenly they are attacked and seized by warriors of a flourishing civilization to whom this cavern is holy. Condemned to death for violating the holy cavern, Tony and Doug prove their friendship when they use this equipment, powered remotely by the Time Tunnel, to repulse an overwhelming attack by a neighboring war-like tribe.

Beast of Evil

In the year 3,000 B.C., Tony and Doug find themselves in Ancient Greece, their lives in jeopardy. They have been thrust into the public arena to face death by sacrifice to a monster — half-man, half-bull — on orders of a pagan High Priest who has reserved the same fate for Ariadne, the daughter of a political enemy. The Time Tunnel helps turn the tables on the pagan High Priest by enabling Tony and Doug to work a few miracles. Ultimately, they have to slay the monster in order to rescue Ariadne and themselves.

Another plot proposal for "Beast of Evil" can be found in a "pitch" book Irwin Allen intended to present to executives at ABC, advertisers and Fox: In the year 3,000 B.C., Doug finds himself at the mile-deep bottom of the fabled labyrinth in Crete, unable to find his way to the surface. Suddenly, Tony and a Greek girl are brought down into the pit as sacrifices to the beast by King Minos. The Time Tunnel finds it impossible to unravel the path of the labyrinth. Tony and Doug must conquer the beast and bring the girl out of the maze against the armed might of King Minos' soldiers.

Satan in Gold

Tony and Doug find themselves hunted down and accused of murder at Sutter's Mill, California, during vigilante terror in the Gold Rush days. The Time Tunnel's computer system discovers who the real murderers are and the scientists transmit that information to Tony and Doug who will be executed by the mob which is now intent on lynching them.

The Human Magnets

When Tony and Doug arrive in the year 2,000 A.D., in the wilds of the Messabi iron range of Michigan, U.S.A., they encounter men from another dimension — men of iron rising out of the ground. These creatures from a compressed dimension between the Earth's molten core and crust move through Earth as humans move through air. All efforts of the Time Tunnel staff to protect Tony and Doug from their assaults are futile because of the magnetic field which surrounds each of these beings. Tony and Doug must stop their crushing assault on the small mining town and save their own lives.

Richard the Lion Hearted

Tony and Doug arrive in the Holy Land during the 12th Century, only to combat the challenges of the time. The climax of the situation leads to a fight to the death. Disguised by their helmets and visors, neither realizes that the other is his opponent in a battle to the death. They charge each other on horseback with leveled lances. When the shock of the clash of unhorses both of them, they continue the furious battle on foot. But when at last each discovers that he is being forced to save his own life by killing the other, they join and fight Crusader and Saracen to save both their lives.

Creatures from the Stars

Tony and Doug find themselves in a southern crossroads hamlet on a peaceful weekend in 1900 when, suddenly, Tony is snatched onto an invading spaceship from a distant galaxy. The aliens, intent on discovering whether they can change Earth human forms into their own likeness, experiment on Tony, and succeed! In a further test they program Tony to meet and destroy the man who has become the leader of the isolated embattled hamlet — Doug Phillips.

Crucible of Battle

Tony and Doug come out of the time vortex to find themselves in 1812. Washington, D.C. is being put to the torch by British soldiers. The White House itself will become a blazing furnace. President Madison, having arrived in the city incognito, will meet his death unless he is saved from the fire which could become his funeral pyre. Tony and Doug help to smuggle the President out of Washington before the British discover his identity.

This page, following pages: from the custom made "pitch" book for Irwin Allen.

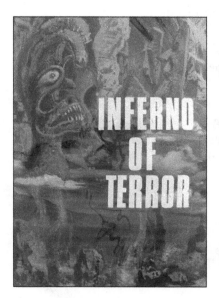

Duel of Death

Tony and Doug, hurtling out of time into 17th Century France, find tempered cold steel blades in their hands as they battle alongside the King's Musketeers against Richelieu's guards. The Time Tunnel's historical computer supplies them with secret information about the plans of Richelieu. This helps their intrigue in recovering the Queen's diamonds from the Duke of Buckingham. Finally, on the road to Calais, Doug leads the Three Musketeers in a diversionary attack while Tony, assuming the guise of D'Artagnan, saves the good name of the Queen.

Plunge to the End of Time

In December of 1969, Tony and Doug are magnetically attracted aboard an immense space vehicle whose control room alone is as big as the Time Tunnel Complex. Commanding this strange vehicle from the Andromeda Galaxy is Marek, whose purpose is to penetrate creation to the end of time. Also captured by Marek are three other strange scientist-beings, each from other Star Systems, one from Wolf 359; and a woman from Lalande 21185. Tony and Doug win the confidence of these strange beings, and organize a mutiny against Marek. They succeed in turning the space vehicle around before it runs off the end of time, and in sending their fellow prisoners and themselves back home to safety.

Note: It remains unknown who wrote the plot synopsis for this story, but "Wolf 359" was an episode of The Outer Limits, *based on a story by Richard Landau, who was also involved with story proposals for television's* Voyage to the Bottom of the Sea.

Graveyard in the Sea

Tony and Doug discover themselves alongside a dozen other 18th Century sailors in a small whaling boat, eye to eye with the greatest whale of them all — Moby Dick. A mighty flail of the giant's flukes smashes the boat and sends them all into the heaving ocean. Saving themselves from the whale only puts Tony and Doug at the mercy of the maniacal Captain Ahab, against whose cruelty Tony and Doug try to protect the weaker members of the crew. It takes the death of Ahab, dragged down to the bottom of the sea by the great white whale, to release Tony and Doug from their nightmare at sea.

Note: Stock footage from John Huston's Moby Dick *(1956), starring Gregory Peck, was going to be used should this episode go before the cameras. Irwin Allen had access to stock footage courtesy of Moulin Productions, Inc.*

No Escape from Death

In the French city of Rouen during the year 1431, Tony and Doug find themselves digging a tunnel deep beneath a castle with the help of other men. They are part of a last-minute desperate attempt to rescue Joan of Arc from her cell. Knowing the futility of this, Tony and Doug try to save the lives of some of her faithful followers. The Time Tunnel, in attempting to help them, makes Joan's enemies certain that Tony and Doug are themselves sorcerers. They are put on trial for witchcraft by the Court of Charles VII!

Note: Stock footage from Victor Fleming's Joan of Arc *(1948), starring Ingrid Bergman, was going to be used should this episode go before the cameras. Irwin Allen had access to stock footage courtesy of Sierra Pictures.*

Burial by Fire

In the year 79 A.D., Tony and Doug find themselves clinging to a rocky ledge inside the rim of Vesuvius. They are helped to safety by Claudia and Tarsus. Although they have escaped death in the fiery cauldron, Tony and Doug are trapped in Pompeii which they know will soon be buried by a river of molten lava when the volcano erupts within the next five hours. When Vesuvius erupts, Doug and Tony try to warn and rescue Claudia and Tarsis. The staff back at the Time Tunnel are certain that Tony and Doug have been buried and petrified because two of the many plaster casts (recently dug up) of Vesuvius' victims are unmistakably Tony and Doug.

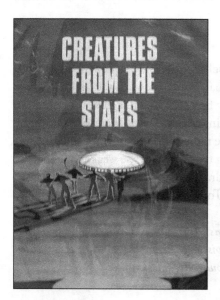

Note: Stock footage from The Last Days of Pompeii *(1959), starring Steve Reeves, was going to be used should this episode go before the cameras. Irwin Allen had access to stock footage courtesy of Cinematografica Associati Productions.*

The Golden Fleece

Tony and Doug are thrown back into legendary times and find themselves between Jason's fierce Argonauts, who believe the time travelers to be hostile, and the dragon which is guarding the Golden Fleece. Tony is forced to fight Hercules who defeats but spares him. Doug engages the dragon which is finally vanquished by lethal electrical bolts sent through time by the staff at the Time Tunnel. In return for Hercules' generous act, Tony and Doug fight a rear-guard action against King Aeetes so that Jason and his Argonauts can escape with the Golden Fleece.

Note: Stock footage from Jason and the Argonauts *(1963) was going to be used should this episode go before the cameras. Irwin Allen had access to stock footage courtesy of Columbia Pictures Corporation and Morningside Productions.*

Missile from Centauri VI

In the year 2320 A.D., a ballistic missile launched from some distant galaxy strikes a lonely desert area of Arizona, not too far from the Time Tunnel Complex. A second missile comes in on target. The Earth is under a probing attack from the unknown. Using a newly-developed technique, the staff at the Time Tunnel Complex succeeds in locating the site of the launch and transfers Tony and Doug instantaneously to that point. There they succeed in spiking the hostile fire-control apparatus until Centauri's galactic orbit swings it out of Earth's range. Centauri will not come within striking distance again for a million years.

The Doomed Brigade

In the mid-19th century, on the faraway battlefields of the Crimean War, Tony and Doug rescue Florence Nightingale from capture during an enemy bombardment. Because of her confidence in them, she adopts many of their suggestions of medical procedures which save many of the wounded. They become her "Corpsmen," but when trying to give first aid to the son of the earl of Cardigan, they are caught up in the Charge of the Light Brigade, going forward into almost certain death.

Battle in Space

In 200,000 A.D., Tony and Doug find themselves to be part of a commando patrol in a fantastic battle amid the missile platforms and guns of space. Their mission: to hunt, locate and destroy a space device from the galaxy Andromeda, which is providing the beings of that distant star system with a fix on the Milky Way in their attempt to start an intergalactic war. In their moment of triumph, Tony and Doug, a hundred thousand miles out in space, almost kill one another when they fail to recognize each other in their strange attire.

Holocaust Beneath the Sea

In 210 B.C., Tony and Doug find themselves in curiously modern deep-sea diving suits amid strangely modern depth-bombs exploding all around them in a blinding inferno at the bottom of the sea. They escape to the surface to discover themselves alongside the ancient scientist Archimedes and his two sons, who are attempting to repel the Roman sea attack on the Mediterranean island of Syracuse. Despite the efforts of Tony and Doug, father and sons are slain in the final Roman assault, and take the secret of their fantastically advanced weapons to their graves.

Battle of the Galaxies

In the year 4750 A.D., Tony and Doug are whirled out of their time vortex into a spaceship outward bound from Earth on a reconnaissance mission. They are the only humans aboard the automated vehicle. But suddenly they see, emerging from the swirling galaxies around them, a hostile fleet heading toward Earth. Beings from the invading fleet enter their space vehicle and jam the automatic devices designed to warn the Earth. Tony and Doug overcome the invaders and succeed in sending the warning which will give the world time to turn back the invasion.

The Hell Ship

Tony and Doug find themselves in the year 1790 in the midst of the conspiracy of mutiny on the Bounty. Tony is keel-hauled and Doug is trying to help him earn Bligh's enmity. Both are sentenced to be hanged from the yardarm but are saved at the last moment by the outbreak of the mutiny. They save Christian, and help the Bounty start on its voyage to Tahiti.

Note: Stock footage from Mutiny on the Bounty *(1962), starring Marlon Brando, was going to be used should this episode go before the cameras. Irwin Allen had access to stock footage courtesy of Metro-Goldwyn-Mayer and Arcola Pictures.*

Another story slated for the proposed second season was Tony and Doug's meeting with Christopher Columbus while on his way to discover America in 1492. Titled "Landfall," Theodore Apstein was originally contracted on April 11, 1966. Apstein's story proposal was originally conceived during the first season, but not used due to budgetary reasons. The boys land on Columbus' ship and soon find themselves fighting off a mutiny aboard, which temporarily impaired the famed explorer's discovery of the new world. "The story editor, Arthur Weiss, liked the idea and I developed a story outline, but later, he told me they had spent too much money on a previous show and Columbus was too expensive to do."

Artwork for the proposed first season.

THE POPULARITY

During her personal appearance tour, out of Atlanta, the plane's pilot suddenly addressed all of the passengers this way: "Welcome aboard, ladies and gentlemen. We're flying at approximately 5,000 feet. Our speed is 300 knots and the weather is perfect outside. As a matter of fact, it is doubly perfect. Our cargo today contains a lovely Hollywood actress, whose name

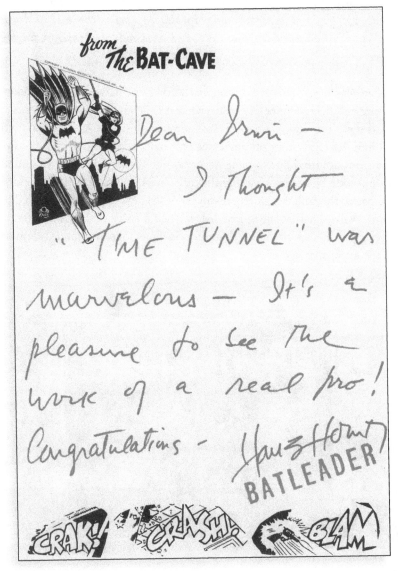

Fan letter from Howie Horwitz, producer of television's *Batman*.

is synonymous with happy flying — Mrs. Lee Merry Weather." All of the passengers then gave a round of applause and the actress was forced to stand up and take a bow. "Wouldn't you know it," she laughed, "Not five minutes later we ran into a rain squall."

The October 31, 1967, issue of *The Southern Illinoisan* featured the weekly fashion column by Florence de Santis, titled "Florence de Santis of the Fashion League." "There's a school of fashion today that lives out in the time where TV shows such as *Star Trek* and *The Time Tunnel* are situated. Designers of this school believe in nothing but the space age, now seen in a boutique in New York City called Latinas. It goes the whole space-age way in fashion. It's for gals who think about clothing in that future way. Bill Hock does all the clothes here…one outfit we really fancied looked like something to wear when working on that giant computer on *The Time Tunnel*. We have never understood why the scientists in that show, set in the 20th Century, wear smocks when they could be dressed in something smashingly space-age."

In April of 1967, *The Bucks County Courier Times* featured fiction essays by young readers. Fred Wheeler of Langhorne wrote a short story titled, "The Time Tunnel."

> *One day at The Time Tunnel, Tony and Doug were talking to General Kirk. Tony said he wanted to go into the Time Tunnel but Doug would not let him. He said it was too dangerous. But the next night Tony went into the Time Tunnel. Alarms rang out. Men came running! One of the men saw a shadow go into the Time Tunnel. The countdown was at one. Then Tony was transferred to the year 1871. He landed on Devil's Island, where men came and captured him. By the time the tunnel had a fix on him, Doug said he would go in after him, so he would be able to help Tony. Doug was transferred to 1871. He fell into a fort. Tony was tied up. Doug asked, "Tony, are you alright?" Tony said, "I'm hot. Do you know where we are?" Doug said, "Yes. Devil's Island in 1871. We must get out of here. Back at the tunnel, General Kirk was trying to get a fix on 1871. But then the animeter blew up. After that, part of the generator blew up! Somebody was controlling the Time Tunnel. A few minutes later, Tony and Doug appeared in the tunnel. They were controlling the time tunnel. Now everyone was alright. THE END.*

To encourage and educate school children in the craft of writing fiction with prose, the editor of *The Herald Statesman* agreed to print a eleven-chapter story titled, "Santa and the Fantastic Twelve." Published in November and December of 1967, each chapter was written by a different student. The eighth entry featured one student's interpretation of how Julius Caesar and George Washington met face-to-face as a result of August's (the month) violent sneezing, which in turn disturbed the mechanism of the Time Tunnel.

In December of 1967, James Darren went to Lower Bucks Hospital Bristol to visit his Uncle, Henry Ercolani. First spending an hour in the children's ward and then signing autographs for the staff, Darren found this only a temporary distraction before he had a chance to visit his Uncle.

THE CANCELLATION

The Time Tunnel and its equally-hyped lead-in that year, *The Green Hornet*, met with early ratings success but, when *The Green Hornet* suddenly turned into an unexpected ratings disaster, *Time Tunnel* became, in the words of ABC President Thomas Moore, "the unsung hero of ABC," for holding off its fierce competition: *The Man From U.N.C.L.E.*, *The Wild, Wild West*, *Tarzan* and *Hogan's Heroes*. Columnist Richard K. Shull, after comparing the time slot and the rival network competition, in the November 12, 1966, issue of the *Binghamton Press* predicted: "The odds against its success, anyone on Madison Avenue will tell you, are monumental." Late in the season, the series finally collapsed in the ratings. Irwin Allen blamed "an unfortunate time slot," but equally responsible were the increasingly careless and ludicrous storylines that drove away the much-needed adult audience. In all fairness, Allen and his crew made the best of it, putting their best foot forward. But the television viewers had the final say.

"In that time slot, there were lots of shows that were of interest to the public, we were just one of them, and you couldn't watch everything — we didn't have the ability in those days to do anything but watch one channel at a time. No VCRs, nothing," Robert Colbert points out. "So we lost a lot of audience. But the people who did watch it, they were an amazing group of people. Teachers throughout the country would build classroom assignments around the episodes because — even though we weren't historically accurate — we provoked enough interest that the kids would do reports on Robin Hood, or Krakatoa, or whatever. And it was real easy for the teachers to assign stuff, so the teachers just loved us! We had a real solid core of followers. I think if *Time Tunnel* had gone another year, we would have gone seven years. It had the appeal. Certain people just thought of it as a nighttime marvel."

"When we did *The Time Tunnel*, I think what helped the kids watch the show was, most of the Parent Teachers Associations across the country would encourage the kids to watch the historical ones," Darren explained. "I think if a new *Time Tunnel*-type series came along, kids today would be more interested in the future ones than the historical ones. They would watch the historical ones if they had a school project that would demand that they know certain things about that part of history. Not that our *Time Tunnel* was that accurate, but if a show like that was done today, it would be more accurate."

Nevertheless, ABC renewed *Time Tunnel* in March 1967 for the 1967-68 season and scheduled it to play Wednesday evenings, opposite Allen's *Lost*

Robert Colbert as Dr. Doug Phillips at the controls.

In Space, a decision which infuriated the veteran producer. "*Time Tunnel* was not cancelled because of low ratings — it did relatively well," recalled Darren to author Kyle Counts. "It was dropped because Tom Moore, head of ABC at the time, left the network. When the new regime came in, the shows that were put there under Moore were cancelled, with the exception of those that were very highly rated. Yes, we had been renewed. Irwin Allen called me on the set and told me, and I immediately told Bob Colbert the good news. Then, Irwin called me two weeks later and told me we had been dropped. I was very sad. I was hoping the show would go on for years and years."

"In the beginning the show might have been based on a good idea — perhaps H.G. Wells' *Time Machine*," remarked columnist Vernon Scott in 1967, months after the series premiered. "The promise was to have two handsome young scientists flown backwards and forwards into time from week to week involved in historic events over which they have no control. But the idea is too costly for execution, for one thing. If you are going to put a couple of

John Zaremba and Lee Meriwether at the controls.

guys back in early Rome or in the War of the Roses, you'd better have the money to make it look authentic. On this show, it never does."

"At the end of the first season, we'd had a huge party for 256 people and their families, that worked on the show," recalled Robert Colbert. "We had 256 actual people getting a salary off of the thing, and we had the biggest blast you ever saw on one of the big sound stages — I think it was the stage where we had the *Tunnel* set. We had a huge party there after we were picked up, Irwin was happier than hell, and everybody else was too; we were all happier than clams. We went home and about three months later we were told that ABC had changed their mind and cancelled it, and that was the end of that. It was a big letdown. Our ratings weren't very high; our share, whatever the hell that was, was mediocre, but, Jesus, we were up against everything in the world. There wasn't enough share to go around for that hour that we were on."

"On the final day of shooting, we had a cast and crew party," recalled Meriwether. "Instead of being sad, it was a joyous time because there was a rumor that we had been picked up. After the festivities, I was leaving the soundstage and heading to my car when an electrician yells from the back of a passing truck, 'We're gonna miss you, Lee.' I assumed he meant until next season but no. I found out that we had been canceled. No one wanted to spoil our last days together with the bad news."

"It was an exciting time," Robert Colbert looked back. "Even in the old days at, say, MGM, back in the '30s, '40s, '50s, I don't think they could have had any more fun than we did. When television came in, it was the illegitimate kid, and nobody associated with movies wanted anything to do with it. It was the little bastard child that wasn't ever going to amount to anything and was never gonna live past puberty. Well, TV just kept getting better and better and better. And, wow, I was there through that transition period and saw [TV] grow — and then of course we still had motion pictures on the side. I don't think there ever was a more exciting time in the film industry, to have been on the planet and working there, than my years. If, early on in my life, someone had predicted how wonderful it was gonna be, I would have been a doubting Thomas. I went out there trying to get a little piece of it, and I got buckets full of absolute Heaven."

When ABC was offered *Custer*, the network made a business decision that probably cost them a ratings disaster. The network chose the newly-developed *Custer* to replace the Wednesday evening time slot for the second season of *The Time Tunnel*, so it could compete head-on with NBC's *The Virginian*. *Time Tunnel*'s renewal had been rescinded and *Custer* went into the Wednesday time slot. (Ironically, *Custer* lasted all of 17 weeks, while *Time Tunnel* has been strong in syndication, DVD sales, merchandise and has since become an international cult favorite. More than half of the people reading this book probably couldn't recall who played the title role of *Custer*.)

"*Time Tunnel*'s cancellation simply had to do with the bank vault," recalled Ellis St. Joseph to author Mark Phillips. "It came down to how much money it was bringing in, and how much it wasn't. I don't want to sound bitter about the public, but sometimes you have to cater to them if you want to make it easier on yourself. *Time Tunnel* demanded something the public was unwilling to give, and that was to use their minds. Certainly, *Quantum Leap* has proved that time travel is a good idea and it has made money, although few episodes have had the excitement of *Time Tunnel*. *Tunnel* was potentially the most exciting of Irwin's TV programs. It brought stature to television and science fiction, whereas *Quantum Leap* is just jumping around."

"He loved to spend money and he would have spent more had Fox not complained to us about the budget," recalled Thomas Moore, then Vice-President of ABC. "The studio was afraid he was going to bankrupt them!"

Scott Bakula and Dean Stcokwell in *Quantum Leap*.

"*Time Tunnel* was also a very, very expensive concept," William Self told author Tom Weaver. "*Lost In Space* and *Voyage to the Bottom of the Sea* had 'the basic set'— you were on a submarine, or you were on a planet. On *Time Tunnel*, the two guys were consistent, but it was almost like an anthology. There had to be new sets every week…it was very expensive. And as a result, it was not a commercial success for Fox. We were glad to do it and all that kind of stuff, but I would be surprised if *Time Tunnel* ever showed a profit. It was a fringe show for us. It was also an enormous drain on Irwin, as I remember — he was doing all these shows at once. It wasn't really proving right for Fox or the network."

"Part of the reason it was sometimes interesting working on *Time Tunnel* was because it was like an anthology, really," Colbert seconds. "Every week we had a whole new cast and a whole new setting, new wardrobe, whatever. As an actor, it was a hoot, because you never got bored, you never knew who you were going to be working with the next week or where you were going, because you didn't have time to analyze future episodes, you just showed up, worked hard (about 14 hours a day), went home and waited for your next script, which usually came out about the night that you finished."

"Though he had line producers for all his TV shows, nobody got the title of producer but Irwin," recalled Leonard Stadd. He believed in the old Hollywood standard that 'producer' meant 'boss.' He was an oddball guy, but in a way I could understand his thinking...There were good times and bad times working with Irwin. I had disagreements with him, but underneath I thought he was a funny guy and I liked him. As a producer, he had a way of getting more for his money than anyone I knew."

"Irwin liked our scripts because we knew how to tell history by using one or two sets with a minimum of extras," explained Bob Duncan. "Irwin vigorously discouraged location filming for *Time Tunnel*. There was once a plane that flew unexpectedly over a scene that was supposedly set in the 1880s. That meant re-filming and time and money. Irwin was furious! Our conversations with him about scripts were mainly budgetary. This was disheartening since Wanda and I preferred to discuss the show's characterizations."

"The special effects were perhaps more important than story in most Irwin Allen productions but with *Time Tunnel*, we felt he had achieved a good balance between interesting characters and photographic effects," recalled Thomas Moore. But decent ratings could not help the series, even when the program followed *The Green Hornet*, starring Van Williams and Bruce Lee. A nationwide poll of high school students ranked it as their third favorite new

James Darren and Robert Colbert at the controls.

show, behind *Star Trek* and *That Girl*. Even hard-to-please UPI television critic Rick du Brow praised the fledgling series as, "Believable and interesting because the cast plays it straight. But this series looks to have cost a fortune!"

Props, sets and stock footage from *The Time Tunnel* ultimately crept into other Irwin Allen productions, including *Land of the Giants* and the third and final season of *Lost In Space*. Most notable was the episode, "Kidnapped in Space," which was filmed on Stage 18 where only half of the Time Tunnel Complex had been torn down by that time. The metal doors and the familiar control panels can clearly be seen on camera.

When James Darren appeared on *American Bandstand* in 1970, young people gathered around him, asking about his singing career. One fan suddenly exclaimed, "*Time Tunnel* was a great show. Whatever happened to it?" Darren's broad smile immediately vanished and he fixed an intense stare at the young man. "It was cancelled," Darren said solemnly.

Statistically, *The Time Tunnel* was ABC's highest rated show on Friday nights for that season (outranking *The Green Hornet* and *12 O'Clock High*), its audience declined over the season. Its seasonal average was a 14.5 rating, just shy of the 16.0 baseline needed for renewal. "*Time Tunnel* was very successful in reaching in reaching the 6-18 year olds," recalled Thomas Moore. "That audience was the most marketable group in the advertising community at

Tony and Doug join the action in "The Revenge of Robin Hood."

the time. The show's rating began very promisingly and it was well received critically. But it didn't deliver the general, national audience numbers necessary for it to continue." A persistent myth is that Moore left ABC in 1967 and this resulted in *The Time Tunnel's* cancellation. Moore denies this and confirms he remained with the network until 1968.

Part of the reason why the ratings dropped may have been evident with the scripts. In May 1967, columnist Richard K. Shull wrote: "Why does a TV series, which shows promise of good escape entertainment in its early episodes, rapidly deteriorate into silliness? Many adult viewers have asked this same question. Blame it on the system. And for a clear example of how it works, look at Irwin Allen, producer of *Voyage to the Bottom of the Sea, Lost In Space* and *Time Tunnel*. The first two of those shows will continue next fall. Allen is a modern Janus, with a faculty for presenting one face to the networks and advertisers and another to the TV audience. He is the ultimate product of television's system of buying and selling shows…It's almost superfluous to point out that *Time Tunnel* commences as a painless history lesson in which two travelers in time, weekly would step into some historical event. This idea appealed to the adults who purchased the show for TV. But again, there was the kiddie element. The little people who make the big ratings took over. When last seen, *Time Tunnel* had British General Chinese Gordon fighting for his life at Khartoum while futuristic alien beings with their brains outside their skulls were preparing to take over the earth. So it goes in the world of Irwin Allen, who has mastered the art of selling two shows under the title — one to the networks and sponsors and another to his audience."

It disturbed faithful television viewers when programs like *Maya, Coronet Blue* and *The Time Tunnel* ended without a satisfactory conclusion to the situation which had been prevalent throughout the series' tenure on the air. A wrap-up to the story arc was never considered. Many TV viewers would be left forever hanging as to whether or not Doug and Tony ever made it back home safely. Television fans would ultimately never know the identity of the amnesic on *Coronet Blue*, whether Gilligan and company would ever get off that island and whether that *Man from Shenandoah* would ever find his real name. They were about to find the same with *The Invaders* and *Run for Your Life*, and both critics and viewers questioned why programs couldn't follow the mold of *The Fugitive*, which had recently aired a satisfactory conclusion. Television producers and network executives, many times in inter-office memos, preferred a series not offer a definite outcome. Their belief was that syndication reruns would not have much meaning to viewers, and felt profits from reruns were more important than satisfying viewers who faithfully dedicated weeks of tuning in.

Continued.

438.	E. *illegible*	465.	*illegible* Oougle
439.	*illegible*	466.	Steve Civens
440.	Doreen Stapleton	467.	Candy Mike
441.	Mario Martinez	468.	*illegible* Cordle
442.	Jim Alvin	469.	David Morgan
443.	Dale Hoagland	470.	L Barkou
444.	Nancy Tuply	471.	*illegible* Pollens
445.	Peggy Severson	472.	Allison Millis
446.	*illegible*	473.	Dave Creiman
447.	*illegible* Jackson	474.	Walter Wiephart
448.	Jill Smith	475.	Jack Storm
449.	F. Fones	476.	Jorge Morse
450.	*illegible* Reagen	477.	Maria Carmena
451.	Paul Davidson	478.	Pam Woodward!
452.	Sue Anderson	479.	Lynn Impani
453.	Janet Stevenson	480.	Jim Holley
454.	Sharon Sherwood	481.	Ricki Quost
455.	Pierre Meachan	482.	Mark Spraic
456.	Laura Welch	483.	Mary Walters
457.	Florence Bapton	484.	Stephanie Boucher
458.	Debbie Meyer	485.	Debra Edwards
459.	Lisa Colson	486.	Joyce Banchieri
460.	Joe Webb	487.	*illegible* Herbert
461.	Joanie Kittrel	488.	Dick Armon
462.	Phyllis McDuff	489.	Patricia Savagini
463.	Jamie James	490.	Lu Dodworth
464.	Bonnie Lopez	491.	Bruce Moss

One page of many Irwin Allen received among petitions and letters from fans of *The Time Tunnel*, requesting the series return with a second season.

In August 1967, John Creighton of Irwin, Pennsylvania, wrote to columnist Vince Leonard at the *Pittsburg Press.* "I would like to know if *Time Tunnel* will go off the air this fall? If so, will it have an ending like *The Fugitive?*" Leonard, tongue-in-cheek, replied: "Yes, it will go off. No, it won't be resolved like *The Fugitive*. It could, though. James Darren could enter the tunnel and wind up in late August 1967 and discover that he is really David Janssen."

Above: *The Time Tunnel* board game. Right: *The Time Tunnel* coloring book.

"*The Time Tunnel* was a good show!" Allen defended to columnist Bob Mackenzie for the July 29, 1968, issue of *The Oakland Tribune*. "Irwin Allen writes all of his own stories and directs the pilots of all of his TV shows," Mackenzie wrote. "I asked him about his consciously unsuccessful opus, *The Time Tunnel*, which was unceremoniously abandoned by ABC last year after one season. This question seemed to touch a really sore spot."

Allen smarted to columnists about ABC's decision to cancel the show. "I received letters and petitions with between 400,000 and 500,000 names protesting that cancellation," he said, "so somebody out there liked it." Months later, Irwin Allen was quoted in another paper of attempting to revive the series, picking up where it left off. "We have received over 600,000 signatures from people in all walks of life protesting the shows' cancellation," he explained, "and not only were those letters unsolicited, they arrived before most viewers even knew the program was not coming back. When ABC moved us to 7:30 this summer and permitted us to start on equal terms

Above: Bumper sticker promoting *The Time Tunnel* TV series.
Left: Button promoting *The Time Tunnel* TV series.

with *Tarzan* and *Wild, Wild West*, we clobbered them. I fully expect to bring back *The Time Tunnel*. Maybe not this season…it's too late to tool up…but it'll be back."

A letter from one television viewer in the December 31, 1966, issue of *The Chicago Tribune* validated Irwin Allen's complaint. "I have a real problem," they wrote. "*The Time Tunnel* comes on at 7 p.m. and *The Man From U.N.C.L.E.* comes on at 7:30, while *Time Tunnel* is still on. I can't watch them both at the same time!"

The producers, however, made a profit courtesy of television reruns and syndication packages. Not to mention a variety of tie-in merchandise spawned by *The Time Tunnel*, including a board game (Ideal Toys), a card game, a spin-to-win game (Pressman Toys), coloring book, ViewMaster slides, and a Time Tunnel model kit. Bally Manufacturing created a pinball game called *Time Tunnel* in 1971, based loosely on the TV series, but production was stopped due to copyright infringement. The game was released with revised artwork as "Space Time."

THE COMIC BOOKS

In 1962, Gold Key was created as an imprint of Western Publishing, and featured a number of licensed properties such as *Honey West*, *The Green Hornet*, *The Man From U.N.C.L.E.*, *Star Trek*, *The Twilight Zone*, as well as two of Irwin Allen's television programs, *Voyage to the Bottom of the Sea* and *Land of the Giants*. They often used photographic montage covers for many of their

comic books, in the hopes that young children would associate the comics with the television series more clearly this way than through an artist's rendition, and licensed the use of the television properties for many comic books. In 1966 and 1967, two issues of *The Time Tunnel* were published, featuring the art of the talented Tom Gill, whose work can also be found within the comic pages of *Bonanza* and *The Lone Ranger*. George Wilson did the cover art and both issues were written by the prolific Paul S. Newman. The comic books have since been reprinted by Hermes Press.

Five individual stories were included in the two issues, all originals. In "The Assassins," Tony and Doug fail three times in their attempt to prevent Abraham Lincoln's assassination at Ford's Theater. In "The Lion or the Volcano?", the time travelers find themselves trying to escape the city of Pompeii, while Mount Vesuvius erupts. In "Mars Count-Down," Tony and Doug find themselves on board an unmanned space capsule bound for the planet Mars. After adjusting controls, and orbiting the red planet, they return to Earth moments before they vanish. In "The Conquerors,"

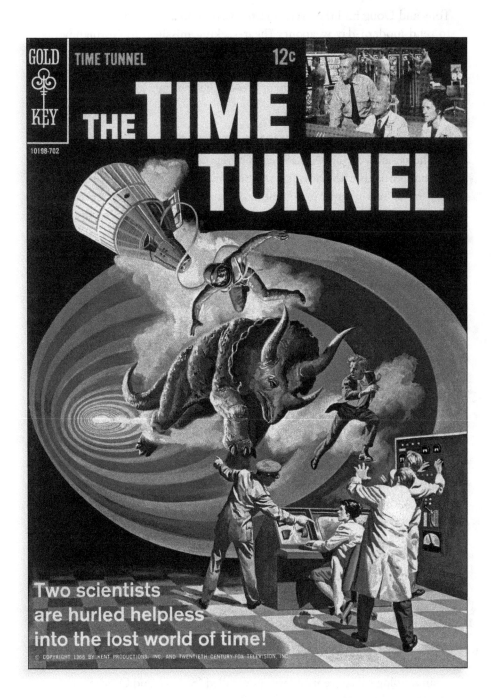

Tony and Doug find themselves in the year 2068 and discover a Nazi plot to send modern-day weaponry (heat-seeking missiles) to Normandy on D-Day to change the outcome of the war. In "The Captives," the time travelers escape from Sitting Bull and the Sioux, only to join arms with Custer's forces against the Indians…even though they know the outcome will be brutal.

FOREIGN PREMIUMS

The same two Gold Key issues were reprinted in 1967 in Mexico, with all text in Spanish. The reissue was titled, "El Tunel Del Tiempo." *The Time Tunnel* was very popular in Argentina, because a number of premiums were distributed including rings with the images of Doug and Tony on the faces; slide puzzles; a small, plastic pinball game; dominos with images of the cast printed on them; board games; collector cards; lighters; and tattoos.

In Japan, a model kit of the Time Tunnel was produced by Fujimi, with a small projector at the end of the tunnel, projecting color slides for viewing. A record album was issued in 1967 by Asahi Sonorama with a time-travel drama, "Adventure in the Lost World."

AFTERWARDS

In the summer of 1967, *The Time Tunnel* went into international syndication, courtesy of the distribution of 20th Century-Fox. In July 1967, children in Tokyo were asked to rate American TV programs broadcast in Japan. Every age group, of the 1,087 students polled, said *Bewitched* was their favorite, followed by *Flipper, The Time Tunnel, The Littlest Hobo, Disney, Jericho, The Andy Williams Show* and *The Fugitive*. Among some of the least-liked TV shows included *Popeye, Batman, The Mighty Hercules, I Dream of Jeannie* and *Gomer Pyle*. The Japanese children explained that differences in humor and customs, along with the way a show was dubbed, played a part in their decisions.

In April of 1967, *Billboard* magazine reported that Gary McFarland, composer, conductor and arranger, was preparing a new album for Verve Records in which "he'll make the electronic and 'freak out' sounds of contemporary music. The album will be titled 'Time Tunnel'." Months later, the same magazine reported the jazz album would have an astrological concept and was now called "Scorpio and Other Signs." Apparently the intention of using "Time Tunnel" was dropped.

Above: Model kit of the Time Tunnel Complex. Below: *The Time Tunnel* View-Master disks offered photos from "Rendezvous With Yesterday," including scenes not featured in the finished pilot. A 16-page booklet was included with the circular slides.

Japanese record album, "Adventure in the Lost World," from 1967.
The package came with a colorful 12-page booklet which showcases
original storybook artwork of the record's episode with the intrepid
time travelers being terrorized by rampaging dinosaurs and angry
cavemen.

On the evening of July 9, 1968, *The Time Tunnel* debuted on the BBC. That same summer, *The Time Tunnel* began telecast in Australia. One newspaper columnist down under remarked: "*Dr. Who* was there first with TV time travel and for some, the new American *Time Tunnel* will only confirm the limits of man's imagination. Though its scope is seemingly endless, the series can be best described as shriveled Cecil B. DeMille."

James Darren in *The Man from the 25th Century.*

THE MAN FROM THE 25TH CENTURY

Columnist Howard Pearson, in the April 19, 1967, issue of the Utah *Deseret News*, reported: "James Darren's *Time Tunnel* series has been cancelled but he has enough confidence in his ability to move into another TV series that he just bought two expensive cars after *Time Tunnel* got the ax."

In 1968, a short time following *The Time Tunnel*'s cancellation, James Darren starred in a short presentation film for an Irwin Allen television pilot, *The Man from the 25th Century*, which ultimately never sold. Darren played the role of Tomo (Earth name: Robert Prentice), an alien sent to Earth to help make preparations for an invasion. His mission is to destroy Project Delphi, a top-secret complex similar to the Time Tunnel, which will shield the entire planet of Earth from attacks from outer space. After foiling the alien scheme, Tomo chooses to join a secret Government organization to fight the intruders.

The pilot film used numerous props (including the time tunnel badges) and stock footage from prior Irwin Allen productions. Employees in the Project Delphi Complex are wearing the same Tic Toc radiation badges seen on *The Time Tunnel.* Computer tape drives, control panels and other set pieces from *The Time Tunnel* were also featured in the pilot. John Napier, Patrick Culliton, Joey Tata, John Crawford and Ford Rainey also appear in the cast.

T.J. Hooker (1982-1986 TV series)

All five had appeared in past episodes of *The Time Tunnel.**

After *The Time Tunnel*, James Darren and comedian Buddy Hackett formed a successful act that toured the country for year. Darren continued his acting career as Officer Jim Corrigan on *T.J. Hooker* from 1982 to 1986. The series was a success and Darren soon found a new calling. "Once when I was on *Hooker*, I noticed there was one sequence coming up and there was no director listed," Darren recalled. "So I asked if I could give it a try, and they let me. When it was shown, I got several offers to direct, and soon I was getting so many jobs as a director, I kind of gave up acting and singing." A

---

* In 1967, Irwin Allen produced another presentation reel, *City Beneath the Sea*. Props and stock footage from *The Time Tunnel* was also used. The pilot, scripted by Harold Jack Bloom, never sold to the networks. John M. Lucas later wrote a two-hour 1971 movie of the same name (which reunited Darren and Colbert).

short time later, Darren was offered an acting job on *Star Trek: Deep Space Nine*. "I almost turned it down. I read the script and I loved it. It called for me to sing again, this time as a sort of Vegas Rat Pack-type singer named Vic Fontaine. A lounge singer — a hologram. I really didn't want to sing again, but I took the job and it worked out well. They had me in eight episodes."

"It was such a great opportunity to do the show. I look back on it, it was just fun," remarked James Darren. "When you're doing things at the present moment, it can all seem [mundane] sometimes…you may be tired one day, you may have had a bad night the night before…but you look back on the good fortune of doing *Time Tunnel* and I wish I could do it again. I had that experience with all three series that I did [*The Time Tunnel*, *T.J. Hooker*, *Star Trek: Deep Space Nine*]. I don't look back on any of them and think, 'My God, I'm so thrilled that that thing is over,' because I just had a good time. I had an especially good time on *Time Tunnel* and also on *Star Trek: Deep Space Nine*. I loved doing that show, that was Heaven." According to Joan Crosby, of the nationally syndicated *TV Scout* columns in 1969, Robert Colbert was offered the role of Bolgar for further *Land of the Giants* episodes but he turned it down. Robert Colbert went on to a number of motion pictures, such as *Amazon Women on the Moon* (1987) and *Timescape* (1992). Colbert even had a guest spot on *Land of the Giants*, playing the role of Security Chief O. Bolgar in the episode, "Sabotage." In 1971, he found himself working with Irwin Allen again in *The City Beneath the Sea*, where he was briefly reunited with James Darren and Whit Bissell. Harold Jack Bloom, who scripted the pilot for *The Time Tunnel*, wrote the script for *City* and recalled: "I had to write it simultaneously with another two-hour pilot for Fox, *Farewell, My Lovely*. Irwin Allen was furious."

"I was one of the leads, and Jimmy did a little cameo in it. It had a pretty good cast of 'outsiders' [actors not associated with Irwin Allen] who came in and worked with us, like Stuart Whitman and Robert Wagner," recalled Robert Colbert. "Stu Whitman didn't want to do it, I think he'd heard some horror stories about Irwin. He called me and asked me what I thought, and I said, 'Come on, suit up and get in here, you'll have fun.' Somehow or other, between when I talked to him and when he showed up on the set, he injured his shoulder badly — really tore it up doing something, I forget what. He could hardly move that arm, so we shot the whole show with him with one side of his body immobilized. Robert Wagner, to me, was always very aloof. He came from a very wealthy family, and he had a high opinion of himself as I recall — there was just something arrogant and different about Bob. I'd meet him some place and say hi, and he wouldn't know me from Adam no matter how many times he met me. He was that kind of a fellow, just from a different breed than I was. Then Bob's daughter Natasha, his youngest daughter, had a horrible crush on my boy Clayton. Oh, she wouldn't let him out of her sight, and he finally had to set things straight, because he didn't feel the same way she did. But, boy, she had her sights set on my son, I remember that. I thought, 'Gee, it'd be funny if I end up being related to Robert Wagner!' [Laughs]"

Robert Colbert has the quick draw on "Billy the Kid."

From 1973 to 1983, Colbert played the role of Stuart Brooks on *The Young and the Restless*, which kept him busy for a number of years. Colbert also made recurring roles on *Dallas, Hunter, Reasonable Doubts*, and *Baywatch*.

"I went to Roadtown, in Tortola, down in the British Virgins," Colbert recalled. "I was at the Moorings, sailing one of those big 60-foot Morgans [a yacht], and one day I happened to walk from the Moorings into Roadtown. I started at one end of town and by the time I got to the other end of this small town, there were all these people following me—I looked like the Pied Piper of the Saloon Set! *The Time Tunnel* was the biggest hit on the island. I found out later that, throughout the British Virgins and so forth, that little puppy was big-time television. In England they still show it, apparently, because I get fan mail and different things from England, from people who are just nuts about it. You'd think it was in prime time and just released. Out here [in California], on my lineup of TV stations, it's shown six days a week, every morning except Sunday. So it's had a 'shelf life' bar none—I don't know of any other show with such a limited original viewing audience that still runs with the frequency of *Time Tunnel*."

"I've had 100 fan letters from people saying that their careers were dictated by and based on their interest in *Time Tunnel* when they were kids," Colbert continued. "This one gal is a scientist, she designs aircraft over in London, and she said that she got interested in becoming a scientist because of *The Time Tunnel*. There've been lots of people like that. So it was an interesting show, it had a lot of merit. Sure, it was crude in some ways but, God, it's still something that stands up today in many ways, which is hard to believe."

"I must have answered, a day or two ago, about 250 or 300 letters for photographs," Darren confirmed. "And a lot of [fan letters] were *Time Tunnel*. From all over — I said to my wife, 'Look where all these things are from!' They were from all over the United States and some were from Germany, some were from South America — it was incredible. I'd say I get maybe two, three hundred letters a month, believe it or not. I'm thankful that they still care and remember."

Lee Meriwether continued acting on television beyond *The Time Tunnel*. In the summer of 1969, she was hired to play the role of an IMF agent named Tracey, on television's *Mission: Impossible*. Barbara Bain and Paramount Studios were locked in a legal battle and until the issue was resolved, Meriwether was one of several actresses to play IMF agents for the 1969-1970 season. It was speculated at the time that Meriwether might become the permanent replacement for the departed Barbara Bain, but her stint lasted a mere six episodes. She continued to do guest spots on television programs and recurring roles such as Lee Sawyer on *The New Andy Griffith Show* (1971), Betty Jones on *Barnaby Jones* (1973-1980) and Lily Munster on *The Munsters Today* (1988-1991). Over the past two decades, Meriwether, Darren and Colbert have made frequent appearances at autograph shows and pop culture conventions to sign autographs for fans, answer their questions and pose for photographs.

James Darren and Lee Meriwether.

"I always loved working with Jimmy," Robert Colbert recalled to author Kyle Counts. "I just thought he was dynamite. I didn't socialize with him. We put in long hours and after you spend a few hundred hours a month with somebody, you're not thinking about getting together for dinner. I always felt bad about that, because I would have liked to have known him better."

After his four weekly television programs concluded, Irwin Allen continued producing theatrical motion pictures including *The Poseidon Adventure* (1972) and *The Towering Inferno* (1974), both of which were box office successes and Allen was labeled "The Master of Disaster" films. He produced a number of made-for-television movies including *City Beneath the Sea* (1971) and *The Time Travelers* (1976), both of which were inspired by his prior television success, and he hoped would launch a television series of the same names. "I did the part of the professor," recalled Booth Colman, one of the two leads on *The Time Travelers*. "It didn't sell, for what reason I don't know; it was as good as any of the other junk made at the time [laughs]! I would have been a regular on the show if it had taken off."

"I'm a big believer in time travel and hope to still do a program based on it," Irwin Allen told columnist Kay Gardella for the May 9, 1977, issue of the New York *Daily News*. *The Time Travelers* was scripted by Rod Serling, recycling unused material from *The Twilight Zone*. In the mid-sixties, Rod Serling considered producing a *Twilight Zone* movie, and wrote a story about two researchers who travel back in time to 1871, in the hopes of discovering the cure to a modern-day epidemic that plagued the city of Chicago a hundred years previous. Irwin Allen purchased Serling's story and produced the Friday Night Movie, in what *Variety* magazine reviewed: "If the plot and the script seemed the product of a feverish 12-year-old with a smattering of scientific interest and, maybe, even a little knowledge, so what? The mind of the creator was talking to his peers. Groom and Hallick were perfectly cast as iron men for the wooden dialog."

The made-for-TV movie starred Sam Groom and Tom Hallick as two scientists who travel back to Chicago, 1871, to solve a medical mystery.

A third attempt at a time travel series was on the drawing board in 1982, *Time Project*, which Allen referred to as "the Godson of Time Tunnel." In it, Lt. Col. Casey Redman and Dr. Lucas Royce use a time capsule called Kronos to travel one million years into the future, to learn how humanity solved the energy crisis. They meet Omega, a strange being who is master of the time stream. They also travel back to 1896, a trip that gives Redman the creeps. "We're walking into a world of ghosts!" he bristles. A memo from Allen noted: "We want to evoke the spirit of *Time Tunnel* yet must acknowledge the sophistication of today's audiences." This included something Tony and

Doug never had: a time travelers' Prime Directive that, "under no condition may you tamper with the past." *Time Project* ended on the storyboard stage after a similar show on NBC, *Voyagers!*, failed during the 1982-83 season.

In the May 14, 1980, issue of *The Post News and Courier*, TV talk columnist Fred L. Smith wrote for the South Carolina paper: "There's an amusing book out now called *The Golden Turkey Awards*, recalling the worst in American

Sam Groom and Tom Hallick in *The Time Travelers* (1977).

cinema. That's a great idea but the authors forgot worst television shows. I didn't, so without further ado, here are the worst ideas ever for a TV series, the nominees being *Longstreet*, *The Time Tunnel* and *Three's A Crowd*. And the winner is: *The Time Tunnel*. It's not that a show about two guys lost in time is such a bad idea but it became a bad idea due to 20th Century-Fox's short-sightedness. The studio, which produced many TV series in the 1960s for ABC, used stock footage from various old movies as a backdrop. But there is only so much old film footage available and the show was forced to cancel when all of the old footage was used up."

A few days before Christmas 1986, John Zaremba died of a heart attack at the age of 77. Following his tenure at the Tic Toc Complex, Zaremba made numerous guest appearances on television programs including *Mission: Impossible* and *Land of the Giants*. He played the recurring role of a judge on *Owen Marshall: Counselor at Law*, Judge Adams on *Little*

House on the Prairie and Dr. Harlen Danvers on *Dallas*. Regrettably, his obituary in newspapers across the country focused more on his television commercials than his acting career. Zaremba played the white-haired coffee bean buyer in the Hills Brothers Coffee commercials for 14 years, and had been filming a new TV commercial for the Hills Brothers coffee line called Gold Label just days before his death. He appeared in more than 100 Hills

Gunnar Hellstrom learns about the camera technique courtesy of director Sobey Martin during filming of "The Ghost of Nero."

Brothers commercials and was one of a handful of actors who found that TV commercials did not interfere with his acting employment. Six months before his death, Zaremba was interviewed for *The Los Angeles Times*: "In Hollywood, I am viewed as a lawyer, judge or doctor and so that's what I've concentrated on playing."

Irwin Allen died of a heart attack on November 2, 1991, at his home in Malibu. Among the pallbearers were Robert Colbert. "Well, I liked him, I had no reason not to," the actor recalled. "And I respected the fact that he had 250-something people working [on his series], and that's a lot of families, a lot of food, a lot of bread. I've always respected the guy who put the knife and the fork on the table. He wasn't anybody that I would wanna hang with, because he came from a whole different mindset than I did. But to dislike Irwin Allen would be pretty picky, because he didn't really interfere much in what you did. He didn't have the most gregarious personality in the world, he wasn't a "hail fellow well met" kind of guy, but, Jesus, he was busier than a cranberry merchant.

"He was a great guy, I loved Irwin Allen," remarked Darren. "He was a terrific man and he was very good to me, and very fair. I do miss him, I'll be honest with ya, I really miss him."

REVISITING *THE TIME TUNNEL*

In 1982, five feature length television movies were put together from 10 complete episodes with portions of the first episode as introductory material. *Raiders from Outer Space* consisted of two stories set in outer space: "One Way to the Moon" and "The Kidnappers." *Revenge of the Gods* consisted of two stories of Biblical proportions: "Revenge of the Gods" and "The Walls of Jericho." *Kill or Be Killed* consisted of two episodes concerning World War II: "The Day the Sky Fell In" and "Kill Two by Two." *Old Legends Never Die* consisted of two episodes from the swashbuckling era: "The Revenge of Robin Hood" and "Merlin

Timothy Edwards, a voice artist for commercials and radio in Canada, grew up watching *The Time Tunnel* on ABC when he was a teenager. In 2006, he recalled the following experience to author Mark Phillips: "In 1975, I wrote to the Governor of Arizona and told him there were rumors that there was an underground complex in Arizona that was designed for time travel. I actually got a reply from the Governor weeks later. I guess somebody on his staff must have found my letter amusing. I'm sure he didn't have time to open his own mail, so my letter must have caught his staff's attention. His response to me was written on official government letterhead paper and said, 'Dear Mr. Edwards, regarding the rumors you have heard of an underground time travel complex under the desert of Arizona, I can assure you that such rumors are totally unfounded. Sincerely, Raul H. Castro, Governor of Arizona.' I was absolutely amazed that I even got such a letter back from him. Nowhere in my original letter did I actually mention *The Time Tunnel* television series to him, nor did he mention it to me in response. It was just a fun thing I did and never dreamed that I would get that kind of interesting reply."

the Magician." *Aliens from Another Planet* consisted of two episodes involving extra-terrestrials: "Chase Through Time" and "Visitors from Beyond the Stars."

In 2002, the Fox Broadcasting Company expressed an interest in a remake of *The Time Tunnel*. An hour-long television pilot was produced by Twentieth Century Fox Television, Synthesis Entertainment and Regency Television, in association with Irwin Allen Properties. Todd Holland, Andrew Lazar, Rand Ravich, Kevin Burns and Jon Jashni were executive producers. Paul Rabwin and Sheila Allen were the producers. The remake was designed to give the characters a purpose for traveling through time, rather than be whisked to various eras with no purpose. Tony Newman was now Toni Newman, a female character.

Set in the 21st Century, the Department of Energy's research project into "cold fusion" causes an unintended "time storm." For four hours, the time storm was uncontrollably whipping about in the past and changing history. A specially-trained team (including Doug and Toni) must go back to 1944, to the Battle of Hürtgen Forest in Germany. They are to retrieve a person who was moved there by the time storm from 1546. They find out that the displaced person is a medieval monk who is carrying bubonic plague. During the mission, Doug Phillips meets his grandfather, a soldier who will be killed in this battle. Doug knows this, but cannot tell him and save his life because it would change history. Toni Newman tells him that she used to have three brothers and two sisters before the time storm accident, but is now an only child. Everyone who came in contact with the monk is given an antibiotic injection and the time ripples stop. When a member of the team has been fatally stabbed, he reveals that Doug was a bitter man before the "incident," but he now has a family and suggests making the necessary corrections might benefit the world, but not Doug. The title of the pilot was "The 240"—based on the number of minutes the cold fusion project developed a tear in time and changed the past.

In 2005, executives representing the Sci-Fi Channel announced the possible future for a remake series of *The Time Tunnel*. Irwin Allen's wife, Sheila, and two producers of the 2002 FOX remake (Kevin Burns and Jon Jashni) began work on the new pilot. The series never materialized.

EPISODE GUIDE

Small note about the episode guide: while the author had access to many archives across the country, many of the production files were incomplete. As a result, some of the episodes may be lacking details that others feature extensively. The information contained herein is complete as possible.

SERIES CAST
Whit Bissell as Lt. Gen. Heywood Kirk
Robert Colbert as Doug Phillips
James Darren as Tony Newman
Lee Meriwether as Dr. Ann MacGregor
John Zaremba as Dr. Raymond Swain

SERIES PRODUCTION CREDITS
CREATOR AND PRODUCER: Irwin Allen
ART DIRECTOR: Jack Martin Smith and Rodger E. Maus
ASSISTANT TO THE PRODUCER: Paul Zastupnevich
ASSOCIATE PRODUCER: Jerry Briskin
DIRECTOR OF PHOTOGRAPHY: Winton Hoch, A.S.C.
HAIR STYLING SUPERVISION: Margaret Donovan
MAKE-UP SUPERVISION: Ben Nye
MUSIC EDITOR: Sam E. Levin
MUSIC SUPERVISION: Lionel Newman
MUSIC THEME: Johnny Williams
PRODUCTION ASSOCIATE: Hal Herman
PRODUCTION COORDINATOR: Les Warner
PRODUCTION SUPERVISOR: Jack Sonntag
POST PRODUCTION COORDINATOR: Robert Mintz
POST PRODUCTION SUPERVISOR: George E. Swink
SET DECORATION: Walter M. Scott and Norman Rockett
SOUND EFFECTS EDITOR: Robert Cornett
SPECIAL PHOTOGRAPHIC EFFECTS: L.B. Abbott, A.S.C.
STORY EDITOR: Arthur Weiss
SUPERVISING MUSIC EDITOR: Leonard A. Engel
SUPERVISING SOUND EFFECTS EDITOR: Don Hall Jr.
UNIT PRODUCTION MANAGER: Bob Anderson

PILOT EPISODE
PRODUCER AND DIRECTOR: Irwin Allen
PRODUCTION MANAGER: Jack Sonntag
ASSOCIATE PRODUCER: Jerry Briskin

UNIT PRODUCTION MANAGER: Eric Stacey
FIRST ASSISTANT DIRECTOR: Les Warner
SECOND ASSISTANT DIRECTOR: Al Murphy
ASSISTANT TO PRODUCER: Paul Zastupnevich
PRODUCTION ASSISTANT: Timothy Sims
ART DIRECTOR: William J. Creber
POST PRODUCTION SUPERVISOR: George E. Swink
SCRIPT SUPERVISOR: Teresa Brachetto
CAMERAMAN: Winton Hoch, A.S.C.
CAMERA OPERATORS: Paul Lockwood and Irving Rosenberg
ASSISTANT CAMERAMEN: Lee Crawford and Al Baerthelein
STILL MAN: Jim Mitchell
SOUND MIXER: Clarence Peterson
RECORDER: Al Cuesta
BOOM OPERATOR: Victor Goode
CABLE MAN: Roger Smedley
KEY GRIP: Henry Gerzen
SECOND GRIP: Wayne Johnson
GAFFER: Kenny Lang
BEST BOY: William Hoffman III
PROPERTY MASTER: Bob McLaughlin
ASSISTANT PROPERTY MANAGER: Robert Boettcher
SET DECORATOR: Norman Rockett
MEN'S COSTUMES: Bruce Walkup and Jerry Sklar
WOMEN'S COSTUMES: Marjorie Fletcher
MAKEUP: Marvin Westmore
HAIR STYLIST: Helen Gruzik
PHOTO EFFECTS: Bill Abbott and Babe Lydecker
MECHANICAL EFFECTS MAN: Verne Archer
CRAFT SERVICE MAN: Jack Lambakian
FILM EDITOR: Jim Baiotto
ASSISTANT FILM EDITOR: Irving Greenberg
CASTING (CAST): Joe D'Agosta
CASTING (EXTRAS): Lee Traver
TRANSPORTATION CAPTAIN: Jim White
ASSOCIATE STORY EDITOR: Al Gail
SPECIAL PHOTOGRAPHIC EFFECTS: L.B. Abbott, A.S.C.,
   and Howard Lydecker
STORY EDITOR: William Welch
UNIT PRODUCTION MANAGER: Eric Stacey

PRODUCTION #6034
RENDEZVOUS WITH YESTERDAY

INITIAL TELECAST: September 9, 1966
SHOOTING SCRIPT DATED: December 28, 1965, with revised pages dated
January 3, 10, 17 and 18, 1966
DATES OF PRODUCTION: December 22, 23 and 28, 1965, and January 3
to 7, 10 to 14, 17 to 21 and 24 to 26, 1966.
GUEST CAST: Nadine Arlyn (Jeanine Corbeau); William Beckley (loading
crewman, British); Ann Dore (the woman); Gerald Carter (the radio offi-
cer); Susan Hampshire (Althea Hall); Michael Haynes (the young soldier);
Dennis Hopper (Tabor); Don Knight (Grainger, the first mate); Bart La
Rue (Tic Toc control voice *and* Lear Jet Pilot's voice); Wesley Lau (Master
Sgt. Jiggs); Donald Lawton (the chief Steward); Wayne Lundy (soldier,
A-7, American); Ivan Markota (the range officer); Gary Merrill (Senator
Leroy Clark); Eric Michelwood (second loading crewman, British); Gerard
Michenaud (Marcel Corbeau); John Neris (Robert Corbeau); Pat O'Hara
(the radio operator); Bret Parker (the countdown technician); George Pelling
(Steward on *Titanic*); Dinny Powell (stoker in boiler room); Michael Rennie
(Capt. Malcolm Smith); Paul Stader (sailor on the *Titanic*); Peter Tannan
(Sentry L-7, American); and John Winston (the guard).

ART DIRECTORS: Jack Martin Smith and William J. Creber
ASSISTANT DIRECTOR: Ted Butcher
DIRECTOR: Irwin Allen
FILM EDITOR: James Baiotto
MUSIC EDITOR: Joseph Ruby
Teleplay by Harold Jack Bloom and Shimon Wincelberg
Story by Irwin Allen, Shimon Wincelberg and Harold Jack Bloom.

STORY: In 1968, Senator Clark visits the secret underground Tic-Toc project,
concerned about tax payer dollars being wasted on a dream. Questioning the
validity and importance of the Time Tunnel's ability to transport and recover
a human being, Senator Clark suggests shutting down the project — until
Tony Newman, a young physicist, acting on his own, switches the controls
and runs into the Time Tunnel. Tony soon discovers he is an unlisted passenger on board the *Titanic*, the day before the fateful sinking. His warnings
to the Captain go unheeded and the scientist, mistaken as a stowaway, is
locked up on one of the lower decks. Hoping to rescue his friend and associate,
Doug Phillips goes into the Time Tunnel and together the two manage to

make a minor difference to one passenger, Althea Hall, who believes she has no right to board the lifeboats because of a growth in her head. Convinced there is a chance of survival, she agrees to board a lifeboat. Tony and Doug are transferred from the ship before it sinks, but their destination is yet to be determined — the Time Tunnel was never perfected and the personnel in the Complex cannot bring their men back home. All they can do is randomly

Michael Rennie as the Captain of the Titanic.

drop them into another time, hoping it will be a better place than the horrible fate that awaits them should they say on board.

MUSIC SCORE BY JOHNNY WILLIAMS *(dated February 22, 1966):* Bumper (:03); Disappearing Act (:13 and :23); Main Title (:36); To the Tunnel (3:24); This Way Senator (:23); Tony's Tall Tale (:23); Tony Enters Machine (1:47); Tony's First Trip (1:40); The Titanic Trot (1:40); Disappearing Act (:03); The Titanic (:16); Tony's Tall Tale (1:11); State Room (:23); Althea's Attack (:45); Making Contact (:42); Doug's Count Down (1:10); The Jungle (:05); Bumper #2 (:03); The Boiler Room (:36); Doug's Arrival (1:13); Hose Nose (:04); The Telegraph (:32); Approaching the Berg (1:34); Be My Little Baby Bumble Bee (by Stanley Murphy and Henry I. Marshall, 1:34); The Ice Berg Cometh (1:34); The Jungle (:05); Time Transfer (:41 and :41); The Jungle (:11); Time Transfer (:45); The Jungle (:45); End Credits (:48); Fox I.D. (by Alfred Newman, :05).

EPISODE BUDGET:

Story Rights & Expense $29,986	Makeup & Hairdressing $3,910
Scenario $15,000	Process $2,583
Producer $11,000	Re-Recording $6,480
Direction $10,300	Special Camera Effects $14,130
Extras $23,542	Production Film & Lab Charges $30,144
Staff $8,112	Stills $3,000
Music $8,112	Transportation $12,800
Art Costs $33,094	Opticals, Fades & Dissolves $2,600
Sets $74,956	Titles $4,100
Operating Labor & Material $12,190	Post Production & Lab Charges $14,304
Miniatures $10,250	Projectionists $2,000
Camera $11,859	Editorial $9,396
Sound $4,113	Fringe Benefits $62,600
Electrical $13,137	Location Expense $5,000
Mechanical Effects $8,760	Miscellaneous $2,750
Set Dressing $34,634	General Overhead $75,120
Women's Wardrobe $4,110	*Total Picture Cost $575,920**
Men's Wardrobe $11,848	

* The estimated cost of the pilot on November 30, 1965, was $535,190. The actual cost was $575,920. For comparison, the cost of Irwin Allen's other television pilots was $292,639 for *Voyage to the Bottom of the Sea* and $395,170 for *Lost In Space*.

SET PRODUCTION COSTS

Exterior Desert and Tunnel $2,800

Interior Underground Auto Tunnel (a.k.a. Century City) $100

Interior Tile Tunnel (airport) $200

Interior Second Door, sign needed, $100

Interior Security Lock, podium and security device $2,400

Interior Elevator and express shaft $1,800

Exterior Bridge Complex for matte #1 and #2 $800

Interior Tunnel Control and Time Tunnel $22,500

Interior Canteen $150

Exterior Titanic Deck $5,200

Exterior Upper Deck $2,225

Interior Main Salon and Stairway $1,150

Interior Crew Cabin and Passageway $425

Interior Steerage $3,275

Interior Boiler Room $1,800

Interior Marconi Room and Passageway $1,325

Exterior Tropical Jungle (to match the prehistoric footage) $2,000

Miscellaneous Backings $1,200

Miscellaneous Purchases $1,000

Exterior Titanic Deck for Process $250

Construction Foreman $7,605

Scaffold and Material $7,981

Strike $3,500

Manufacture and rig action device, 2 men to fly with wires, lifeboat lowering, and miniature sets (elevator shaft and power shaft) $2,180

Total $71,966

ABC CENSORSHIP CONCERNS

After reviewing the final draft of the teleplay, ABC sent a list of suggestions and recommendations to Irwin Allen, covering every aspect that would protect the network from complaints and potential lawsuits. "We urgently suggest you make this a later date than 1968 to avoid impersonating real people such as senators, chiefs of staff, foreign dignitaries, etc. as the series runs for years and years," the network suggested. "Be sure U.S. Senator Clark bears no resemblance to anyone in the senate or public political life today." Ironically, the initial story date in the first draft of the script was 1999, but during the earliest meeting (November 10), it was decided to change the story date to the near-present time, but still with a futuristic look. Allen never commissioned any changes ABC made, and retained 1968 in the script and the final film.

Regarding the Titanic story, ABC cautioned Allen to "be sure your legal department has cleared the idea of impersonating Captain Smith and any others actually a part of the real story of the Titanic, particularly if they

In order to capture the crane shot from within the tunnel, for Tony's first vanishing act, the back of the tunnel was removed for the camera operator.

appear in a poor light." This may explain why the Captain of the Titanic was a fictional Malcolm Smith, instead of the historically accurate Edward John Smith. None of the crew on board the Titanic was historically accurate either. While fans of the program today consider this a lack of historical accuracy, and claim the script writers and production crew failed to do any historical research beforehand, the fact remains that research was conducted and the name change was more than likely to please the ABC network, fearing a potential lawsuit from families who lost a loved one on the Titanic as a result of the unauthorized use of names.

Other suggestions from ABC included:

Delete the spitting (referring to the stoker).

Please do not portray the stoker in a derogatory fashion.

Do not portray the S.O.S. or C.Q.D. signal by sound effect.

Be cautious about the shots of the frantic people and that they are not too grim.

Caution that the prehistoric reptile won't produce nightmares.

This last suggestion was in reference to the prehistoric footage at end of the pilot film, unused stock footage which originated from the production of Irwin Allen's *The Lost World.* (Notice how Doug and Tony are staring up towards the left side of the screen but the giant lizard is on the right side!) That footage was to explain to the network and potential sponsors how each episode would end with a cliffhanger, leaving Tony and Doug in a different time and place. Ultimately, this footage would not be seen by the television audience at the end of the broadcast version of "Rendezvous With Yesterday," being replaced with the first few minutes of the second broadcast, "One Way to the Moon." Only the network and the potential sponsors saw the footage of Doug and Tony encountering a giant reptile in a prehistoric land. While filming the tropical jungle sequence, and in the event that the network would not purchase the series, an alternate ending was filmed, Production #6034, at a cost of $8,344. Tony and Doug discover that the folks at the Time Tunnel Complex have found a way to bring them back and it concludes with the time travelers hurrying toward the light at the end of the tunnel. (See Appendix A.) This happy ending would suffice should the footage be edited into a theatrical motion picture.

LOGISTICS

The scenes of the barren desert were shot at Coyote Dry Lake near Barstow, California.

Shot on location, the military driver was William Graeff, and the soldiers were Dick Elmore, Jim Ellsgood, Bruce Merman, Joe Schaplain and Bob Todd.

Irwin Allen directs Susan Hampshire and Dennis Hopper in "Rendezvous With Yesterday."

The driver of the black 65 Imperial convertible was A. Bullock. Wesley Lau played the role of Jiggs. The young soldier was Michael Haynes.

The helicopter pilot for aerial shots was Harry Hause, and the cameraman in the helicopter was Carl (Brick) Marquard. This was a combined operation from Tyler Camera Systems and Mercury General American (Helicopter Division). Aerial shots were filmed on January 25, 1966.

James Darren and Dennis Hopper in "Rendezvous With Yesterday."

The "William Lear" Jet landed on location from the California Airmotive Corp., Van Nuys Airport.

NOTES

On the afternoon of February 7, 1966, days before the music score was composed and sound effects added to the movie, Bill Self screened the rough cut of the unaired pilot in the projection room. A number of changes were made after Self shared his opinions with Irwin Allen. It was unanimously decided not to use narration on the opening of the show. It was proposed to try and put in a shot of the ship hitting the iceberg as the captain is sipping brandy. (The cost factor of having Michael Rennie return to the set ultimately overruled such a shot being made.) It was also decided to eliminate the subplot involving Tabor, which meant eliminating a number of shots and scenes from the picture. A scene with Dennis

Hopper on the deck of the ship ended up on the cutting room floor, as well as a ballroom sequence on the deck with Tabor talking to the captain, and a scene in which Tabor was dressed as a woman, attempting to sneak on board one of the lifeboats.

To add an aura of mystery to the Time Tunnel Complex, the Senator was on a pilot-less plane (though no shots are in both pilots (aired and unaired)

Albert Salmi visits the set during filming. Salmi is in the same costume he wore for an episode of *Voyage to the Bottom of the Sea* which was being filmed at the studio.

to suggest this more clearly to the television audience) and the scene with Gary Merrill putting his seat belt on was removed from the film. The opening and closing credits became the next step in finishing the pilot film, in late March. During the closing credits, Lear Siegler, Inc. was acknowledged for supplying the airplane seen in this episode. An inter-office memo at Fox dated March 31, 1966 remarks: "It appears that the FCC regulations require a credit somewhere on *The Time Tunnel* pilot as follows: 'Airplane furnished by Lear Siegler, Inc.' ABC may have some objections to this [because Siegler was not among the sponsors of the program] but if we limit it to the pilot and do not use the jet in the series we should be able to meet ABC's objections." Naturally, the problem was resolved and both parties agreed that there were no sponsorship conflicts.

Robert Colbert and Gary Merrill prepare for the optical effects used to simulate the elevator shaft.

Irwin Allen insisted on directing the pilot episode, and supervised the remainder of the episodes he produced. "He didn't come down much when he didn't have reason to; he monitored it from afar," recalled Robert Colbert. "It was a rare visit by him, and when he did come, he usually brought somebody [a set visitor]. If he was showin' someone around the lot, why, he'd bring 'em to *The Time Tunnel*. Irwin was as big a fan as any of us, and, hell,

he'd bring people like Joseph Cotton, Edward G. Robinson, Victor Mature... one time I met Bill Lear, of the Lear Jet, and his family. We used a Lear jet in the pilot, and Irwin and Bill knew each other, and I got to meet Bill Lear, which I thought was really cool. Bill brought four of his daughters along, and one of 'em was named Shanda. Shanda Lear [laughs]. I thought that was cool, too. The four daughters were cute as hell, but I was a happily married man, so all I could do was look. So you never knew who was gonna come wander around the set with Irwin, and it was always fun to have all these people that you were just a fan of, coming around to visit with you and wanting to meet you and sit and talk to you and take you to lunch. I was havin' a lot of fun."

In the Marconi room, there is a dime novel on the counter, "The Life Adventures of Captain Billy Whipple Privateer by Tobias Wentworth Finch," a prop which was originally created for an episode *Bonanza*, "A Dime's Worth of Glory" (November 1, 1964), and which played an important part in that particular episode. (The fictional author, Tobias Finch, was also a fictional character for that *Bonanza* episode.) That same prop would be featured in a later *Bonanza* episode, "New Man" (October 10, 1972).

The September 12, 1966, issue of *Daily Variety* reviewed: "Merrill did an excellent job orienting the audience…Miss Hampshire and Rennie also were excellent, and Colbert impresses as a rational, but appealing, character. Darren is the weakest of the principals, relying too much on pained expression and one-note acting." Michael Rennie worked with Irwin Allen five years prior in *The Lost World* (1960) and, like many of the cast, never performed a screen test for his role.

According to an ABC-TV press release, one of Rennie's closest boyhood friends was lost when the vessel slid in the icy North Atlantic. One has to question the validity of this claim when you consider the fact that the actor was only 2 ½ years old at the time the Titanic sunk. Ironically, Rennie was also the narrator for the 1953 black and white production of *Titanic*, which was the same movie which stock footage was lifted from for this episode. The black and white footage was color tinted to blend in on the viewing screen.

Susan Hampshire was flown to the U.S. from England to play the role of Althea. She had been to the U.S. in 1961 for guest appearances on *Armstrong Theatre* and *Adventures in Paradise*, so this wasn't her first visit to the States. When asked what she thought about Hollywood, she remarked: "All the men have crocodile wives and ulcers and gold-and-diamond rings they twist around their hairy fingers. The big shots also had arms they kept putting around me that managed to be long enough to reach my left breast. I told them, 'I don't have to do that. I can act.'" Her experience was not without distaste and she returned to England until Irwin Allen called. "Irwin Allen was always very enthusiastic and hands on and seemed so American," Susan Hampshire recalled. "On the first day of filming or maybe signing for the part, Mr. Allen gave all the cast a beautiful leather-bound script which was so generous and luxurious and something that had never happened before on other productions. The filming days were long and hot. Makeup was thick in those days and I don't know if there was air conditioning on the set on not, but the period costumes seemed very warm. Coming from England, I wasn't used to the California heat."

Columnist Hedda Hopper, in her January 15, 1966, column, began promoting Irwin Allen's new program even before filming was completed for the pilot. "Susan Hampshire, here in Hollywood from England to do a pilot for Irwin Allen's *Time Tunnel* series for 20th Century-Fox, puts other screen heroines in Hollywood to shame when it comes to real-life adventure and competition. Travel and adventure have always lured this young actress. A year ago she flew from London to Africa alone and went on a safari!"

The opening titles credits Harold Jack Bloom and Shimon Wincelberg for the teleplay, and Bloom, Wincelberg and Irwin Allen for story credit. In the unaired pilot, story and teleplay credits are different: Wincelberg is not

James Darren during the rehearsals.

mentioned at all and Harold Jack Bloom receives a solo teleplay credit, based on a story by Irwin Allen.

This is the only episode of the series where someone other than Paul Zastupnevich is credited as an assistant to the producer: Timothy Sims.

Having played the role of a German Sergeant on *Combat!*, Don Knight accepted the role of Grainger in the pilot of *The Time Tunnel*, his second acting job in Hollywood following his studies for the Ordained Ministry in Maryland. A friend of Robert Mitchum, Knight did not get his acting career started as a result of asking for any favors. "I am a professional actor and a Christian," Knight was quoted in a press release. "The two are not opposites of each other. As an Englishman I am bending all of my efforts to establish characters that will utilize my dialects in character-type roles."

TRIVIA

In "Rendezvous With Yesterday", Tony states he was born in 1938. Yet in "The Day The Sky Fell In", he is portrayed as a seven-year-old at the time of the attack on Pearl Harbor. James Darren was actually born in 1936, coincidentally consistent with Tony being 30 at the start of the show.

PRODUCTION #9603
ONE WAY TO THE MOON

INITIAL TELECAST: September 16, 1966
SHOOTING SCRIPT DATED: June 20, 1966, with revised pages dated July 5 and 8, 1966
DATES OF PRODUCTION: July 6, 7, 8, 11, 12, 13, 14 and 15, 1966
FILMING LOCATIONS: Stage 2, Stage 18 and Stage 19
GUEST CAST: James T. Callahan (Ensign Beard); Ben Cooper (Nazarro); Ross Elliott (Dr. Brandon); Barry Kelley (Admiral Killian); Wesley Lau (Master Sgt. Jiggs); Warren Stevens (Harlow); Dick Tufeld (the countdown voice); and Larry Ward (Kane).

PRODUCTION CREDITS
ART DIRECTORS: Jack Martin Smith and William J. Creber
ASSISTANT DIRECTOR: Ted Butcher
DIRECTOR: Harry Harris
FILM EDITOR: Dick Wormell
MUSIC: Lyn Murray
MUSIC EDITOR: Sam E. Levin
Teleplay by William Welch.

STORY: In the year 1978, Tony and Doug alight in the Mars Excursion Module — a project they had known of in their own time ten years earlier. Commander Kane, learning from flight engineer Beard that they are carrying 300 pounds extra weight, is forced to jettison the service module so they can reach escape velocity. Instead, Beard fires the boosters, losing fuel that will have to be replenished by a stop on the surface of the moon. When the reluctant stowaways are discovered, they are thought to be saboteurs by everyone except Harlow. Cut off from radio communication, Beard insists that the saboteurs be ejected into space, while Kane calls for a calculation to see if their added weight will prevent a safe landing on the moon. The latter is proposed and Tony and Doug are held under guard while Beard and Harlow, wandering the lunar surface, go for fuel. Beard kills Harlow at the fuel pumps, then takes explosives to blow up the spaceship — his purpose being to keep the U.S. from getting to Mars first. Meanwhile, the real saboteur is revealed in the Time Tunnel Complex and Dr. Brandon, in desperation, draws a gun. Attempting to avoid the armed guards at the complex, Brandon runs through the Complex and is shot by the younger Beard, a spy who outranks him, placing him in good standing with the future Mars project. Back on the surface of the moon, Tony and Doug manage to get spacesuits and close in on the older Beard and blow him up with the fuel depot. Kane blasts off, leaving them in space suits that won't last longer than two hours. But control of the Time Tunnel is regained and the time travelers are once again caught up in the vortex of time.

MUSIC SCORE BY LYN MURRAY *(dated August 17, 1966):* Color Bumper (by Johnny Williams, :03); Shimmer (by Williams, :09); Take Off (2:48); Jettison (:52); Main Title (by Williams, :35); H.Q. (:26); Escape Velocity (1:00); Hatch (:32); This Way, Senator (by Williams, :16); The Jungle (by Williams, :07); Rocket launch (:22); No Word (:43); Meteor (1:56); Space Beauty (1:20); Space Work (1:10); Moon Approach (:57); Bumper (by Williams, :03); Impact (:13); Impact #2 (1:15); Moon Walk (1:24); Plastic Device (:30); Moon Fuel (1:35); Break Out (:45); Beard and Doug (2:17); Brandon Take Over (:47); Control and Stalk (1:01); Tony Suits Up (1:08); Tony Suits Up #2 (1:28); Tony Missing (1:51); Brandon Search (:21); Moon Walk (1:51); Brandon Stalked (1:33); Brandon Death (:33); Moon Survival (:43); Time Lock (:13); Tony's First Trip (by Williams, :13); The Mine (:50); Mine Trap (1:26); Mine Trap #2 (:08); End Credits (by Williams, :49); and Fox I.D. (by Alfred Newman, :05).

EPISODE BUDGET

Story Rights & Expense $1,500	Process $285
Scenario $5,808	Production Film & Lab Charges $9,513
Producer $8,215	Stills $150
Direction $3,000	Transportation $2,900
Cast $16,890	Re-recording $1,784
Extras $2,380	Photo Effects $2,754
Music $3,500	Opticals, Fades & Dissolves $2,150
Staff $3,121	Titles $745
Art $1,900	Post Production & Lab Charges $14,304
Sets $11,685	Projectionists $205
Operating Labor $5,208	Editorial $5,874
Miniatures $3,000	Fringe Benefits $16,180
Camera $2,580	Miscellaneous $630
Sound $1,625	Amortizations $1,002
Electrical $3,949	Contract Overhead $15,000
Mechanical Effects $1,815	General Overhead $6,866
Set Dressing $5,933	*Total Picture Cost* $167,640
Women's Wardrobe $929	
Men's Wardrobe $3,154	
Makeup & Hairdressing $1,106	

Series Budget $168,907
Pre-Production Budget $167,640
Under Budget $1,267

ORIGINAL STORY TREATMENT

Space age drama was frowned upon on *The Time Tunnel*, with Irwin Allen already cornering the market with *Lost In Space*, but to feature the second episode set in the near future introduced the television audience to the wide range of story possibilities the series could explore. The cost involved, however, in renting space suits and stock footage of intelligence science-fiction proved too challenging when 20th Century-Fox offered a wide variety of period costumes and props. William Welch, who wrote the teleplay, was lucky enough to have his original 15-page story treatment purchased. First submitted to Irwin Allen circa May 20, 1966, Welch was paid $3,970 for his teleplay: $600 for his story "Missile to the Moon," $1,870 upon delivery of the first draft, and $1,500 upon delivery of the final draft (contract dated May 17, 1966). Very little differed from the initial story proposal when compared to the teleplay. The following, however, are differences contained within the proposal that are not evident in the finished film we see today.

Tony discovers the space ship is sealed shut.

Ensign Beard tenders his resignation on the spot after witnessing his future self deliver the orders to jettison Doug and Tony from the space craft. His resignation is promptly rejected by the Admiral. After all, who are they to condemn him for future behavior, when his decision may be the very thing that will save the expedition from total disaster?

In the Time Tunnel Complex, during the third act, while the attention of

Robert Colbert shares a laugh on set.

the others is fixed on the viewing screen, Beard uses the time to make a few furtive adjustments to the Tunnel controls. When Swain attempts to shift Tony and Doug in time, there is an explosion in the Complex which wrecks the elaborate control equipment.

The conclusion of the episode, inside the Time Tunnel Complex, is completely different from what appears on the film we see today. Beard's guilt in the Time Tunnel Complex is revealed when they hear Beard's admission, and his real purpose, on the viewing screen. Beard admits to Doug that he has been in the pay of the other government for more than ten years. He joined NASA as an Ensign and served as an Aide to Admiral Killian, all the time planning to work himself into a position where he could sabotage the U.S. space effort. Beard, taking advantage of the astonishment of the others, suddenly disarms the security guard and confronts them with the weapon. He switches off the image area and forces them, at gun point, to enter the mouth of the tunnel. He plans to switch on full power and disintegrate them all. Beard theorizes that there is no question of his success. They have seen him, ten years from now, carrying out the final phase of his plan. What they all didn't realize as they were watching is that the Time Tunnel and its

Actor Ben Cooper in "One Way to the Moon."

personnel were no longer in existence, which explains Swain's inability to switch the time travelers again. His plan doesn't work when he discovers that Sergeant Jiggs and his security guards responded to a secret alarm sounded by General Kirk, and they switched the power off.

Beard, realizing his plan has been frustrated, exchanges shots with the converging security guards. A chase begins through the elaborate Time Tunnel Complex with Beard acting like a desperate, hunted animal fighting for his life. After a while, Beard, trying to elude his pursuers, works his way back to the control area. Ducking the security guards, he heads into the tunnel itself just as Sergeant Jiggs, in another area, pulls the switch that restores full power. There is an enormous flash and Beard is disintegrated before their eyes at the tunnel mouth.

No explanation is offered as to why Beard would be featured on the viewing screen, ten years in the future, alive and well. This error in time travel physics is probably why the ending was revised before it was typed into a feasible teleplay for production.

HISTORICAL FACTS AND FIGURES

Weeks before William Welch wrote the final shooting script, the unmanned American Surveyor 1 craft landed on the moon and transmitted photographs and other data back to Earth. The Soviet Union had already lunched the Luna 10, an unmanned probe that achieved lunar orbit — the first object to do so. It was clear to television viewers that the foreign country attempting to sabotage the space mission were Russian agents, even though no reference to the country was made during this broadcast. Ironically, four months after the initial telecast, President Lyndon Johnson and counterparts in London and Moscow signed the "Treaty on Principals Governing the Activities and States in the Exploration and Use of Outer Space." Signatories agreed, among other points, that outer space would remain demilitarized, no territorial claims on Earth orbit or any planetary bodies will be made and that astronauts or cosmonauts who find themselves landing off course would be returned to their home countries. Three years before this fictional account took place, on July 15, 1975, the last Apollo mission, in orbit, docked with a Soviet Soyuz spacecraft. The mission proved the compatibility of the two space programs and paved the way for future collaborations and rescue missions.

NOTES

The colored costumes used on this episode were the same created for George Pal's *Destination Moon* (1950). This was because Allen wanted to make sure they matched the stock footage from the same movie used in this episode. The same costumes were used on other television programs such as *Tom Corbett, Space Cadet* (1950-55), *Space Patrol* (1950-55), and Ib Melchior's motion picture, *Robinson Crusoe on Mars* (1964). Stock footage of the lunar landing originated from *Destination Moon* (1950), and to ensure the footage of spacemen on the lunar landscape matched that of *The Time Tunnel* production, each actor was assigned a specific color so that it would match the footage they intended to use.

Stock footage of the astronauts walking on the outside of the space ship during flight from *Destination Moon* was carefully edited to make sure the actors from the 1950 movie were not visibly seen through the glass pane on the helmets. This means that while John Archer and the rest of the cast of *Destination Moon* are not seen or heard on this *Time Tunnel* episode, they appear courtesy of stock footage.

Ensign Beard's badge number is 11378, the same one technician Jerry wears in the handful of episodes.

The stock footage of the rocket launch in the beginning of this episode was the same footage seen in two episodes of *Voyage to the Bottom of the Sea*. The compartment where Tony and Doug land is the same set used for the sail on top of the dorsal of the Seaview on *Voyage to the Bottom of the Sea*. The hatch between the commander center of the space vessel and the compartment is the same used in many *Voyage* episodes.

BLOOPERS!

During the fight between Beard and Harlow in the supply house on the surface of the moon, the metal canisters strapped to the back of the actors are replaced with square foam disguised as rounded canisters. This was so the stunt men would not be injured when falling onto their backs. During the fight, the canisters switch back and forth from round metal cans to painted square foam.

The air hoses on the spacesuit helmets switch from left to right during the walk on the lunar surface.

There can be no fires burning on the moon since fire requires oxygen. The crew shouldn't be able to hear sound, either, but they certainly react to the noise.

PRODUCTION #9602
END OF THE WORLD

INITIAL TELECAST: September 23, 1966
SHOOTING SCRIPT DATED: May 31, 1966, with revised pages dated June 2, June 6 and July 1, 1966
DATES OF PRODUCTION: June 27, 28, 29, 30, July 1, 4, 5 and 6, 1966
FILMING LOCATIONS: Stage 18, Stage 19 and Western Street
GUEST CAST: Robert Adler (the man); Paul Carr (Blaine); Glen Colbert (townsperson); Dave Dunlap (miner); Paul Fix (Henderson); Sam Groom (Jerry); Orwin C. Harvey (townsperson); Gregory Morton (Professor Ainsley); and James Westerfield (the sheriff).

PRODUCTION CREDITS
ART DIRECTORS: Jack Martin Smith and William J. Creber
ASSISTANT DIRECTOR: Fred R. Simpson
DIRECTOR: Sobey Martin
FILM EDITOR: James Baiotto
MUSIC: Lyn Murray
MUSIC EDITOR: Sam E. Levin
Teleplay by William Welch, based on a story by Peter Germano and William Welch.

STORY: Tony and Doug arrive in a mine shaft just at the moment when an explosion collapses part of the mine — the year is 1910. Tony, caught between cave-ins, is sealed into a short length of the tunnel while dirt and debris trap 200 miners beyond. Doug rushes to the mining superintendent for help, only to be greeted by a dour Mr. Henderson who says it doesn't matter anyway, because a giant comet is seemingly headed straight for the Earth. Back at the Time Tunnel, Ann and Dr. Swain confirm the object as being Halley's Comet, but that means nothing to Henderson who's convinced the world is coming to an end. Doug digs Tony out himself as a rumbling shake announces further collapse inside. None of the surviving miners outside can be shaken from the doomed forecast, because the famed astronomer, Ainsley, has predicted the comet will hit. While Tony goes into town to round up men, Doug visits Professor Ainsley. Using a primitive radioscope, Doug is able to show the astronomer the otherwise invisible object that will draw the comet away from its collision course with Earth. As the townspeople gather on the hillside to pray, Tony, Doug and Professor Ainsley convince them that hope is not lost and everyone runs to help dig out the miners.

MUSIC CUES: Color Bumper (by Johnny Williams, :03); Falling (by Williams, :17); The Mine (by Lyn Murray, :51); Krueger Comes Back (by Lennie Hayton (:37); Hold #4 (by Alexander Courage, :37); Mine Trap (by Murray, :37); Meteor (by Murray, :37); Dinner Chimes (by Williams, :37); Main Title (a.k.a. Time Tunnel Theme, by Williams, :37); End of the World Title (by Murray, :32); Destroying the Complex (by Hayton, :42); Falling (by Williams, :42); Space Beauty (by Murray, :42 and :13); Take Off (by Murray, :13); Falling (by Williams, :13); Hold #4 (by Courage, :31); The Big Whew (by Courage, :22); Episode Titles (by Courage, :09); No Exit (by Courage, :25); Crafty (by Courage, :25); Destroying the Complex (by Hayton, :50); Receding Quake (by Leith Stevens, :13); Torches (by Murray, :13); The Big Whew (by Courage, :13); The Iceberg Cometh (by Williams, :13); Episode Titles (by Courage, :13); Hot Sun Ralston (by Courage, :37); Between Heaven and Hell (by Hugo Friedhofer, :20); Cave In to City Mob (by Murray, :20); Receding Quake (by Stevens, :20); Tunnel Lights (by Murray, :39); Hold #4 (:58); Mine to Asia Mob (by Murray, :09); Radiometer to Mine (by Murray, :48); Bumper (by Williams, :03); Nicholas Micrometer* (by Murray, 1:03); Episode Titles (by Courage, :09); Receding Quake (by Stevens, :09); Comet Tail to Explosion (by Murray, 1:01); Hot Sun Ralston (by Courage, 1:01); The Big Whew (by Courage, 1:01); Clear the Complex (by Murray, :30); The Wind Roars (by Murray, :12); More Wind (by Murray, :13); The Underground Complex (by Hayton, :45); Destroying the Complex (by Hayton, :45); Tony's Tall Tale (by Williams, :59); Saved and Disappear (by Murray, 3:22); Desert Act Out (by Murray, :04); Falling (by Williams, :10); Jap Perfidy (by Murray, 1:50); Next Week (by Murray, :13); End Credits (a.k.a. Time Tunnel Theme, by Williams, :48); and Fox I.D. (by Newman, :05).

EPISODE BUDGET

Story Rights & Expense $1,500	Operating Labor $4,583
Scenario $5,808	Miniatures $3,000
Producer $8,215	Camera $2,640
Direction $3,000	Sound $1,625
Cast $16,965	Electrical $3,944
Extras $6,075	Mechanical Effects $2,485
Music $3,500	Set Dressing $5,399
Staff $3,121	Women's Wardrobe $854
Art $1,900	Men's Wardrobe $1,504
Sets $11,055	Makeup & Hairdressing $1,111
	Process $285

* This title originates from the music cue sheets and may have been a typo for "Nichols."

Production Film & Lab Charges
   $9,513
Stills $150
Transportation $2,900
Re-recording $1,784
Photo Effects $4,202
Opticals, Fades & Dissolves $2,150
Titles $745
Post Production & Lab Charges
   $13,679

Projectionists $205
Editorial $5,875
Fringe Benefits $16,880
Miscellaneous $855
Amortizations $1,002
Contract Overhead $15,000
General Overhead $7,430
Total Picture Cost $170,939

Series Budget $168,907
Pre-Production Estimate $170,939
Over Budget $2,032

SET PRODUCTION COSTS
Mine Entrance and Street $720
Mine — Upper Shaft $2,175
Mine — Debris $260
Mine — Office $1,030
Sheriff's Office $640
Observatory $1,065
Mine (falling rocks) $150
Mine (blocked passage) $150
Construction Foreman $825
Total $7,015

PROPOSED SALARIES
The initial salary sheets for the first draft of the script verify an English Lord, two hilltop men, someone to voice the Senator (just the voice), three stunt doubles and the preacher.

HISTORICAL FACTS AND FIGURES

Professor Ainsley and Doug use a Radiometer, which, according to Ainsley, was one of only six in existence. Luckily, he had access to one of them. The Nichols Radiometer was created in 1901 but there were more than six available by 1910. But then again, who's counting?

In this episode, the tail of the comet disappeared on the evening of May

21, 1910. The calendar in the mine office says May 22. While some historians debate whether this was a historical inaccuracy or not, it is historical fact that the comet would have still been visible on May 22 in certain parts of the world.

On May 19, the Earth actually passed through the tail of the comet. One of the substances discovered in the tail by spectroscopic analysis was the toxic gas cyanogen, which led French astronomer Camille Flammarion to claim that when Earth passed through the tail the gas "would impregnate the atmosphere and possibly snuff out all life on the planet." His pronouncement led to panicked buying of gas masks and quack "anti-comet pills" and "anti-comet umbrellas" by the public. In reality, as other astronomers were quick to point out, the gas is so diffuse that the world suffered no ill effects from the passage through the tail. Ironically, Camille Flammarion was the author of *La Fin du Monde* (a.k.a. *The End of the World*, 1893-1894), a science fiction novel about a comet colliding with the Earth, followed by several million years leading up to the gradual death of the planet.

ORIGINAL STORY TREATMENT

Peter Germano's story treatment, "End of the World," formed the basis of this episode. Originally contracted on April 11, 1966, Germano was to receive a total of $3,370 at completion; $1,870 payable upon delivery of the first draft and $1,500 upon delivery of the final draft. His treatment, dated April 25, 1966, reveals a number of initial concepts that never made it to

teleplay form. The mine office was referred to as "Henderson Mine No. 2" and Henderson's original name was Halstead Davenport.

For reasons unknown, Germano was cut off at the story and walked away from the series. The teleplay was assigned to William Welch and, since Germano's agent, Mark Lichtman of General Artists Corporation, requested it, Germano was entitled under the Guild rules to a twenty percent (20%) penalty payment in the amount of $125.99.

William Welch was then hired to write a feasible teleplay based on Germano's story, with the same payment plan and amounts. Welch was contracted on May 3, 1966, to write the teleplay. Under Welch's treatment, adapted from Germano's, the subplot involved a woman named Susan Prudholm, who frantically tries to convince the miners to go into the tunnel and rescue her husband, Roger, but finds her pleas ignored and brushed aside. "Ain't nobody going back in there, Miss Prudholm," one of them mutters.

Susan has been married less than a year and her father, Halstead, opposed the marriage. She throws wild accusations at the old man, blaming him for sending Roger down into the mine hoping something like this would happen. It is true he didn't like Roger, an outsider, a newly graduated mine engineer. (Perhaps there is a bit of bitterness between the older, experienced man feeling the push of competition from the younger man, plus the loss of

a daughter whom he had to depend upon after his wife died.) But Halstead argues that Roger went down into the mine because he wanted to. It is his job. There had been a report of a possible gas leakage, which caused the explosion.

"You could have stopped him!" Susan throws back at him. Then, bitterly, forlornly: "It's all going to end, anyway, in three more days. But we could have spent them together...we could have crowded a lifetime in those 72 hours."

While Doug attempts to persuade Professor Ainsley to retract his statement about Halley's Comet hitting Earth in the hope that it will convince the miners to start a rescue, Tony and Sam (a rational miner) investigate the mine and start digging. A cave-in injures Sam and Tony emerges, carrying him into the office. Distracted with the new emergency, Susan tends to Sam's medical needs. Meanwhile, a large group of miners and their women have come to the mine. In mob-like fashion, they have come to burn Halstead out, blaming him for sending employees down into the mine.

At the local College Observatory, using a Nichols Radiometer, Doug convinces Professor Ainsley that he is wrong and he retracts his statement.

Tony, meanwhile, has spliced the wires together and the mob hears Roger's voice over a speaker. Shamed by their own women, when Susan makes a plea to spend her remaining time with her husband, the miners pick up their shovels and pick axes.

In the closing tag, Tony and Doug watch the comet with Roger, Susan and Halstead. It is now the night after it was predicted to hit, and it is no longer a threat. The tail is gone, it is a small light in the sky, speeding away. "You knew," Susan murmurs. "How?" Tony shrugs. Roger offers a cigarette to Doug. He takes it, reaches in his pocket and brings out a matchbook. He lights it up, then offers the light to Roger. Susan is staring at the matchbook. It reads: World's Fair, 1968. Who is he? And Doug? But Tony only smiles. It doesn't matter...as he joins Doug and they fade away.

DELETED SCENE

At the Time Tunnel Complex, the scientists try to send Doug a modern-day radarscope to help him convince Ainsley, but the Comet blasts the radarscope out of the Tunnel. Doug is forced instead to use a primitive radioscope. The only scene at the Time Tunnel Complex that remains is Jerry's prediction that the magnetic force of the comet will start to meddle with the controls of the Time Tunnel, reminding all who work at the complex that they only have marginal control of the situation.

The scene with actor Nelson Leigh as a preacher ultimately ended up on the cutting room floor, but Leigh received credit on the studio press release, which was used for such periodicals as *TV Guide*, which accidentally credited the actor in the role.

ABC CENSORSHIP CONCERNS

In mine shaft and cave-in scenes: Your usual good care in seeing that shots of debris, etc. falling on the men and shots of the group trapped in the shaft are in no way shocking to view.

Accompanying shouts and yells o.k. but please be sure that piercing cries of pain or such are not added. Also caution on how the "torn hands" are indicated — Blood, etc. to minimum." (The crew ultimately featured close ups of dirty hands, not torn hands.)

The whiskey bottle should not be identifiable as to actual trade/brand names.

NOTES

The footage of military troops running through the complex was originally created and used for the pilot episode.

The footage of the comet in this episode was also used in four *Lost In Space* episodes: "Blast Off Into Space," "Wild Adventure," "Flight into the Future" and "The Condemned of Space," also with the same music cues featured. The same footage can be seen in "The Lobster Man," an episode of *Voyage to the Bottom of the Sea*.

This episode marked William J. Creber's third and final contribution to the series as an art director. Beginning with the next broadcast, Rodger E. Maus assisted Jack Martin Smith.

Whether it was the Flammarion prediction or newspaper accounts from other "authorities" that formed the basis of this episode, "End of the World" helped establish two points of interest to the television viewers. One, Dr. Ann MacGregor and Dr. Raymond Swain point out that they had only "marginal control" over the controls of the Time Tunnel, and the results of their efforts were only fifty percent predictable. Second, Doug and Tony could not alter the course of events that already happened (also evident with the failed warnings of the Titanic sinking), but could in fact participate in events and make a difference, even if their involvement was minor on a local front. But their next visit in "The Day the Sky Fell In," would play against a historic event too large for them to alter, no matter how much effort they applied.

The TV Previews columnist for *The Milwaukee Journal* reviewed this episode as "suspenseful" and "convincing."

COMMENTARY

In this episode, Lee Meriwether's character shows a pre-feminist attitude by saving Jerry's life after he suffers a heart attack. General Kirk and Dr. Swain stand helpless as Jerry dies, so Ann pushes them aside, tears open a control panel, pulls out some electrical wires, rips open Jerry's shirt and jams the wires into Jerry's chest. This surges him back to life as all the men watch the results, dumbfounded.

BLOOPER!

When Tony grabs the sheriff as the lawman gets ready to answer the telephone, the shadow of the boom mike can be seen on the wall.

> *"So far we've learned more from failure than success."*
> Dr. Ann MacGregor to General Kirk

> *"The H-Bomb is nothing but a toy balloon compared to the forces we're using here."*
> Dr. Raymond Swain to Dr. Ann MacGregor

PRODUCTION #9606
THE DAY THE SKY FELL IN

INITIAL TELECAST: September 30, 1966
REVISED FINAL SHOOTING SCRIPT DATED: July 25, 1966
DATES OF PRODUCTION: July 26, 27, 28, 29, and August 1 and 2, 1966
FILMING LOCATIONS: Stage 18, Stage 19 and Street
GUEST CAST: Linden Chiles (Commander Newman); Pat Culliton (radio operator); Susan Flannery (Louise); Jerry Fujikawa (Okuno); Lew Gallo (Lt. Anderson); Sheldon Golomb (young Tony Newman); Sam Groom (Jerry); Frankie Kabott (Billy); Caroline Kido (Yuko); Shuji Nozawa, a.k.a. Fuji (Sumida); Bob Okazaki (Tasaka); and Robert Riordan (Admiral Brandt).

Japanese stunt doubles: H.B. Haggerty, Yoneo Iguchi and Bill Saito
Stand-ins and extras during the panic at Pearl Harbor: Glen Colbert, Bill Graeff, Pat Murphy, Virginia Semon and Gene Silvani.

While H.B. Haggerty is seen in this episode doubling for one of the actors, Bill Saito replaced him in mid-shooting. "On the 20th Century-Fox lot, I had just finished shooting a fight scene with Steve McQueen in *The Sand Pebbles*, and was finished for the day," recalled Saito. "I went to *The Time Tunnel* sound stage to visit my judo friend, Fuji. They were setting up a fight with the stars, Fuji and another soldier, played by a former pro wrestler, Hard Boiled Haggerty (H.B. Haggerty). The director yelled, 'that man (H.B.) isn't Japanese!' Someone pointed me out and they asked me to get into H.B.'s uniform, paying him off and giving me the job."

PRODUCTION CREDITS
ART DIRECTORS: Jack Martin Smith and Rodger E. Maus
ASSISTANT DIRECTOR: Ted Butcher
DIRECTOR: William Hale
FILM EDITOR: James Baiotto
MUSIC: Paul Sawtell
MUSIC EDITOR: Sam E. Levin
Teleplay by Ellis St. Joseph.

STORY: Tony and Doug find themselves in the Japanese Consulate in Honolulu and witness Chief of Espionage Tosaka, his aide Okuno, and agent Sumida burning files. It doesn't take long for them to discover the date: December 6, 1941. Tony reveals to Doug that he was born in Pearl Harbor and his father, a communications officer, was lost in the sneak attack; now, perhaps he can discover what happened to him. The two go to Mrs. Neal's house, find Tony's father, and warn him that the Japanese are going to attack tomorrow. When Tony and Doug leave Mrs. Neal's house, Sumida and his goons overtake the boys and ship them off to a warehouse, where Tasaka and Okuno wait to sweat the truth out of them, but they are unable to do so. The time travelers solve the problem by breaking out of the warehouse, then racing to Mrs. Neal's where they persuade her to take little Tony and her son up to the mountains for safety. By now the attack has started but they race to the Naval Yard where Tony's father is at the radio. A barrage hits and Newman is struck, now lying wounded and dying. After alerting the Enterprise to turn back and avoid Pearl Harbor, Commander Newman dies — but not before accepting the fact that Tony is his son. At this time, those in the Time Tunnel see an unexploded bomb in the Naval Office. They can hold it long enough for Tony and Doug to escape. An explosion destroys the building, leaving no trace of Tony's father. Tony now knows why his father was never found, and the boys move back into the vortex of time.

MUSIC SCORE BY PAUL SAWTELL *(dated September 8, 1966):* Color Bumper (by Johnny Williams, :03); The Boiler Room (by Williams, :34); The Japanese Consulate (1:34); Tony Remembers (:56); Main Title (a.k.a. Time Tunnel Theme, :37); The Neal Mansion (1:36); A Strange Meeting (1:29); Tony's Frustration (1:42); The Japanese Fleet (:16); To the Hide Out (:46); The Admiral (:11); Drugged Interrogation (2:02); Tony Talks (1:59); Louise's Discovery (2:38); The Take Off (:58); Too Late (:10); Bumper (by Williams, :03); Time is Short (:28); Boys Escape (2:25); Sky Full of Planes (:47); Trying to Remember (2:24); The Bombing (:56); Complete Destruction (1:47); Tony rescued (2:05); The Time Lock (3:12); The Recognition (3:45); Nothing Left (1:41); Falling (by Williams, :17); Next Week (by Lyn Murray, :33); Exit Ullrich (by Alexander Courage, :33); Tony's Tall Tale (by Williams, :33); Destroying the Complex (by Lennie Hayton, :33); Crafty (by Courage, :33); End Credits (a.k.a. Time Tunnel Theme, by Williams, :48); Fox I.D. (by Alfred Newman, :05).

EPISODE BUDGET

Story Rights & Expense $500	Extras $2,111
Scenario $5,808	Music $3,500
Producer $8,215	Staff $3,259
Direction $3,000	Art $1,900
Cast $17,440	Sets $12,470
	Operating Labor $5,311

Miniatures $3,000

Camera $2,663

Sound $1,625

Electrical $3,949

Mechanical Effects $1,305

Set Dressing $5,093

Animals & Action Devices $0

Women's Wardrobe $729

Men's Wardrobe $1,399

Makeup & Hairdressing $1,256

Process $285

Production Film & Lab Charges
    $9,242

Stills $150

Transportation $3,000

Re-recording $1,784

Photo Effects $2,210

Opticals, Fades & Dissolves $2,150

Titles $745

Post Production & Lab Charges
    $15,054

Projectionists $205

Editorial $5,875

Fringe Benefits $15,632

Miscellaneous $630

Amortizations $1,002

Contract Overhead $15,000

General Overhead $6,375

Total Picture Cost $163,872

Series Budget $168,907

Pre-Production Estimate: $163,872

Under budget: $5,035

SET PRODUCTION COSTS

Tasaka's Office $965

Japanese Consulate $30

Exterior Neal Villa $4,370

Warehouse $60

Warehouse $445

Communications Office $240

Communications Office $60

Warehouse Street $60

Communications Office (bombed) $80

Allowance for Night Work $155

Foremen $970

Total $7,435

STORY DEVELOPMENT

The first draft of the script, dated July 5, 1966, was titled "The Day the Zeroes Came," based on a story proposal by Ellis St. Joseph, who was paid $630 for the story and $1,870 upon delivery of the first draft and $1,500 upon delivery of the final draft.

After reviewing the first draft of the script, Jerry Briskin suggested, "To help reduce set cost, change kitchen to dining room," which was done for this episode. Another suggestion from Briskin was Tasaka's final speech after Doug and Tony are discovered in the Japanese Consulate. "He should express the thought that Doug and Tony are too stupid to be spies," Briskin wrote. "They are probably what they say they are but should be followed in any event. If he thought they were spies and had seen them burning their documents, he would certainly not let them go even at the risk of creating an incident." Briskin's comment was logical, but for the sake of setting the stage, for dramatics, the scene was never changed.

While fans know Tony was unable to remember the events of Pearl Harbor, or what happened to his father, the memory loss was not a practical plot device in the initial draft of the teleplay. Instead, Tony remarked that he was able to live on the island without the help of his father, and bore a grudge against him for not being there in time of need. Briskin, however,

Doug and Tony catch up to his seven-year-old self in "The Day the Sky Fell In."

suggested a better device that was used for the revised teleplay. "Wouldn't it be better to say that Tony had once told Kirk that he had suffered a memory blackout from the attack and has never been able to recall much of his childhood because of it? This is his chance to fill in the blanks and he thinks Tony should be given every possible chance to do so. So they will stay with them as long as possible."

John Zaremba checks his facts on the clipboard.

As for the final act, Briskin felt the end was unsatisfactory. On August 1, Arthur Weiss wrote to Irwin Allen, regarding the revised final shooting draft. "There is a lack of excitement in this story," Weiss wrote. "The one major point is that our Tunnel does not play an important enough part here. The Time Tunnel's first introduction in this script is on page 19 and that scene is approximately one page only. The next time we see the tunnel group is on pages 31, 32 and 33 and half of this is them watching stock footage of planes and the Japanese fleet. Our next meeting with the tunnel group is page 60, which is the very end of the story. Shouldn't there be a scene that illustrates the tunnel group's concern for Tony and Doug? Have them make some sort of effort to get the boys out of this difficult situation?"

For practical purposes, Weiss believed there were too many sets and locations for this episode. "We have a street near the harbor, an alley and Navy yard indicated in the script. But if this is going to be shot in the backlot, I don't know how we can control the smoke that we want put into this scene. How do we prevent the smoke from blowing away and exposing the backlot background?" Concern for the budget also involved cutting back the cast, which Weiss believed was too large. "Why can't we eliminate the butler in the Neal home, Jerry at the Tunnel, some of the Japanese and possibly some of the American servicemen?" Thankfully, the cast was not cut out of the final draft.

The original concept was to have Commander Newman, hot-headed like his son, pulling a gun on the time travelers when he suspects them of being foreign spies. Later in the script, there was a planned car chase, with the Japanese chasing Newman right up to the gates of the U.S. navy yard. Instead, it was decided to focus on Doug and Tony combating the Japanese spies, and leaving little exploration of the father-son relationship until the attack on Pearl Harbor, which is when the story ends. Weiss suggested: "Is it possible to open with Tony and Doug landing in Japanese Consulate hallway and not in Tasaka's office which might give us a chase sequence to open the show with? After the boys are caught it might be good to have them escape and then make the script an exciting chase story with the Japanese attempting to locate and kill our leading men while our heroes in turn are trying to convince one and all of what is about to take place."

After reviewing the teleplay, Weiss also made a suggestion that helped with the teleplay. "The Time Tunnel group does nothing in the script as it now stands. I am not suggesting that a Japanese solder appear in the Tunnel but I do believe that something of similar importance take place. Maybe the Tunnel group tries to prevent the Japanese from sending in their planes on Pearl Harbor…maybe the Tunnel bunch attempts to send photos, etc. of Pearl Harbor bombing to the Fleet Commander…maybe the Tunnel group attempts to bring back a top military leader to prove to him that the Japanese are going to attack the Islands." As a result, the character of Jerry gets desperate and calls in the bomb to the Complex, in the hopes of de-activating the device. It was also suggested to have the bomb floating in the viewing area, but when it was revealed to be cost effective simply to have the bomb on the floor inside the Tunnel, the script was revised again.

Even with all of the revisions made to the script, many fans of the series regard "The Day the Sky Fell In" as the best episode of the series. Even *Time* magazine singled it out as the week's television highlight, calling the story "chilling." Those who choose to debate, however, will admit it is one of the best episodes of the series. And if Doug and Tony ever thought it was possible to change the course of history to save human lives, their theory is shot down for good with the death of Tony's father. Taking a page from Shimon Wincelberg's initial plot proposal for the pilot, that of the attempt to save a family relative from a historic disaster, Ellis St. Joseph's teleplay went through a number of revisions before it was polished for production. The end result is perhaps one of the best episodes of the series.

"I was deeply moved while writing that scene," recalled Ellis St. Joseph to author Mark Phillips. "My own father died when I was young, and

SCENE 7   TOWARD IMAGE AREA
(CONT. SUPER 5) (1ST UNIT)

THE SCIENTISTS WATCH THE ACTION....
ON THE SCREEN.....

SCENE 8

P.O.V. OF DOUG & TONY... FEATURING
WALL CALENDAR....

Storyboard for the opening scene of "The Day the Zeroes Came."

while writing this story, I realized that I loved him more than I knew. That scene in 'Sky' is absolutely foolproof. I watched the episode with playwright William Inge, who wrote *Splendor in the Grass*, and he was teary-eyed at the end. 'That's good…that's really good,' and that reaction is invariably the same from whomever watches it. That show can still make people cry."

"There were a couple of weak moments," the writer continued. "The Japanese agent hiding behind the tree, spying on the time travelers, was done for melodrama and it doesn't hold up. When they're tied up in chairs and interrogated by the Japanese, it's done too easy and fast. On the whole, however, I'm very proud of the episode and it was a big success with Irwin."

NOTES

Robert Colbert believes the pilot episode and "The Day the Sky Fell In" were the best episodes of the series. "I thought Jimmy was great in it. I loved the whole premise. Susan Flannery, a young, attractive actress, was in that. We had this scene where we're running across a grassy field. She fell down, and her dress came clear up over her head, exposing her. Like Sir Galahad, I rushed over and covered her. I felt so proud of myself."

This page, next page: storyboard for a suggested ending that was never filmed for "The Day the Sky Fell In."

...THEN SUPERIMPOSE a MEDIUM CLOSE-UP of
LITTLE TONY, SLEEPING IN BED....

SUGGESTION... USE THE CIRCLE FORM OF THE RISING
SUN...ON THE JAPANESE FLAG TO
PAN IN ON....OR SUPERIMPOSE THE
SHOT OF TONY SLEEPING.....

SCENE 71 CONTINUES....

SCENE (I) FADES OUT,
LEAVING ONLY SHOT OF LITTLE TONY ASLEEP
IN BED... ROAR OF JAPANESE BOMBER
PLANE CONTINUES OVER SLEEPING CHILD....

"The one that I like most is the Pearl Harbor one, because it was a very nice role for me to play," recalled James Darren. "Tony Newman going back to Pearl Harbor in 1941 and meeting his dad [Linden Chiles], who was killed when Tony was seven or eight. As Tony, I try to warn him to not stay there, to leave, so that he will not have died. I try to alter history. It was just a nice role for me, so I liked that. I liked 'Billy the Kid' too, because of the story. Robert Walker Jr. played Billy the Kid and he was quite good — he was a good actor, and he's still working. So those are a couple that I really had a particular love for, so to speak."

Actor Linden Chiles is appreciative that while he was considered for a role in "Rendezvous With Yesterday," he never got the job, else he would not have played the role of Commander Newman in this episode. "It was a terrific script and a very nice role," Chiles recalled. "It also has a wonderfully historic storyline. We had an excellent director, Bill Hale. He gave us plenty of time to work through our scenes. One day, producer Irwin Allen came on the set and suddenly took over the directing. He was not a good director, and we were all relieved when Bill was allowed to return and finish the show."

Lew Gallo, reporting to 20th Century-Fox for a role in this episode, found out he would be wearing the same uniform he wore in the movie *Pork Chop Hill* in 1956. And the terrible thing was (according to Gallo) that the uniform still fit him. The actor had been going to a health club to build up his body and evidently there was no improvement!

Most of the episode was filmed on Stage 18 and 19, except for the street scenes on the afternoon of Friday, July 29. For that day, a call was placed for stand-ins and extras for four people driving their own 1935 to 1941 cars, who could also double for sailors running through the streets as well. On the same day, two civilians were needed, both of whom drove their own cars, circa 1935 to 1941.

The inspiration for the film *The Final Countdown* (1980), where the U.S.S. Nimitz was thrown back in time to Pearl Harbor, was taken from this episode. "It really was my story, but since 20th Century-Fox owned my script, I received no pay or credit," Ellis explained. "*The Final Countdown* didn't work because you didn't feel anything for the characters. It left you cold."

CRITICS HAVE THEIR SAY

While fans consider this among the best episodes of the series, critics from various trade columns varied. The columnist for the *TV Scout* column in the *Utica Observer-Dispatch* remarked: "Let's remember Pearl Harbor, but surely not the way *Time Tunnel* does."

In the summer of 1968, *The Time Tunnel* began running in Australia. Columnist Bill Law of *The Evening Times* reviewed this episode in the July 31, 1968, issue. "I said a few weeks ago that I'd try to get used to *The Time Tunnel* in time. But not if it is over-burdened with that sloppy American sentimentality that spewed out of last night's episode, 'The Day the Sky Fell In.' The travelers in time, Tony Newman (James Darren) and Doug Phillips (Robert Colbert) dropped in on Pearl Harbor the night before the 1941 Japanese attack. As one would expect, we got all of the old news reels and a few studio attack shots for realism. But when realism gave way to fantasy it was stretching things too far, such as having young Tony living in the past at Pearl Harbor as well as having the one here from the tunnel. This meant there were two Tony Newmans on the loose, if you see what I mean. The present-day Tony's father, a U.S. Navy officer, was reported missing after the Pearl Harbor bombing and Tony set out to warn his father of the impending catastrophe. Dad does not believe him and the usual complications ensue, ending with Dad dying in the 'now' Tony's arms while the 'there' Tony stands safely on a hill just outside town. All of this was told with the usual background of dramatic, heart-pulling music. If all this sounds confusing, it was that kind of program."

HISTORICAL FIGURES

The *Enterprise* was returning to Oahu on the morning of December 7, 1941. In the wake of the attack, *Enterprise*, though surprised, immediately went into action in defense of the naval base. They even launched F4F Wildcats of Fighting Squadron Six. No one in the communications department, including the fictional Commander Newman, gave warning for *Enterprise* to turn back and avoid the island. A framed photo of the *U.S.S. Enterprise* can be seen on the living room table in the Neal living room, and the same prop can be seen in the communications room.

ABC CENSORSHIP CONCERNS

Please substitute Japanese for "Jap."

Deletion of "into this hell" in Commander's line.

Of course, all names of Navy personnel and Japanese, connected with the Pearl Harbor event, must remain fictitious.

The stabbing of the butler must be off camera.

Standard caution on the bruises of the man in death. Keep blood to a minimum.

Hypodermic injections to be done off-camera or covered from view.

Use your usual special care to see that fights are not unnecessarily brutal or prolonged. No close ups or graphic demonstrations of the various chops in the jujitsu scene. Particular caution showing Nojiri because we must not see him choking.

Note that the fall on the sword scene happens off camera. Tasaka's death here must not be grotesque or bloody, and his eyes must be closed.

TRIVIA

In "The Day The Sky Fell In", Tony's father is referred to as a Lieutenant Commander (O-4) in rank, yet his shoulder boards are three full stripes (and silver collar insignia), indicating the rank of Commander (O-5).

The Novikov self-consistency principle was anticipated by the tacit understanding of the Time Tunnel scientists that recorded history could not be altered although in this episode, the time travelers make it their concern to see to it that young Tony Newman escapes being killed in the Pearl Harbor bombing in order to prevent the adult Tony from ceasing to exist.

> *"Someday you'll realize that all men have to learn to live with their past.*
> *It can't be changed."*
> General Kirk to Jerry, a technician

BLOOPERS!

During the Japanese attack in the street, Tony is momentarily knocked unconscious by falling debris from an explosion, and lands on his back. After the commercial break, Tony is found by Doug, lying on his chest.

Bad editing: During one sequence, when the Time Tunnel personnel are watching little Tony asleep in his bed, Jerry is seen standing next to the console and seconds later, sitting next to another console.

The back door accidentally opens when the Red Cross ambulance pulls away.

If Tony Newman was seven years old in this episode, which took place in 1941, why was it revealed in the pilot episode that he was born in 1938?

PRODUCTION #9607
THE LAST PATROL

INITIAL TELECAST: October 7, 1966
REVISED FINAL SHOOTING SCRIPT DATED: August 1, 1966
DATES OF PRODUCTION: August 1, 2, 3, 4, 5, 8, 9 and 10, 1966
FILMING LOCATIONS: Stage 18, Stage 4, Stage 5, Stage 6, and Western
GUEST CAST: John Burns (the American Scout); Marshal Carter (the British Soldier); Chris King (the U.S. Sergeant); John Napier (Capt. Jenkins); Carroll O'Connor (General Southall *and* Colonel Southall); Michael Pate (Capt. Hotchkiss); David Watson (Lt. Rynerson); and John Winston (the British sentry).

PRODUCTION CREDITS
ART DIRECTORS: Jack Martin Smith and Rodger E. Maus
ASSISTANT DIRECTOR: Fred R. Simpson
DIRECTOR: Sobey Martin
FILM EDITOR: Dick Wormell
MUSIC: Lyn Murray
MUSIC EDITOR: Sam E. Levin
Teleplay by Bob and Wanda Duncan.

STORY: Landing in the middle of the last battle of the War of 1812 (January 6, 1815, to be exact), Tony and Doug are captured by a patrol and brought before Colonel Southall, who orders them to be tried as spies. The harried Colonel is engaged in a battle at New Orleans against Andrew Jackson's forces, despite a treaty that has been signed by Ghent two weeks before, and is desperately in need of information as to whether Jackson is concentrating his strength to the East or to the West. Meanwhile, in the Time Tunnel Complex, the crew has brought in expert General Southall, descendent of the Colonel, to help pinpoint the exact time and placement of Tony and Doug. Having made a career of studying his ancestor's fatal blunder at this battle, the General asks to be transported to the scene. With Doug facing a firing squad, and with permission from the highest authority, the scientists see no other choice but to send the General back in time. Materializing at the execution scene, the General saves Doug and then concentrates his efforts on convincing his ancestor that he has knowledge of how this battle is going to turn out. He knows the Colonel will attack to the East, yet the signal will tell him to attack to the West. What he wants to know is why. Doug and Tony, meanwhile, escape from Hotchkiss and manage to alter the signal so

Southall is told to attack West. The General, realizing his ancestor wasn't fooling him, dies happily in the disastrous battle, while the time travelers are whirled back into the vortex.

MUSIC SCORE BY LYN MURRAY *(dated September 13, 1966):* Color Bumper (by Johnny Williams, :03); Falling (by Williams, :24); Next Week (:28); No Exit (by Alexander Courage, :28); Tony's Tall Tale (:28); Destroying the Complex (by Lennie Hayton, :28); Crafty (by Courage, :28); To the Stockade (:37); Trial Curtain (:08); Main Title (a.k.a. Time Tunnel Theme, :37); The Last Patrol (:28); Court Martial (:13); New Orleans — 1812 (:25 and :23); Geni Southall (:29); No Chance (:09); Firing Squad (:16); Honor (:27); Wilderness (:13); Percussive (:01); The Take Off (by Paul Sawtell, :15); Drugged Interrogation (by Sawtell, :28); Tony Rescued (by Sawtell, :32); A Strange Meeting (by Sawtell, :32); Tony Talks (by Sawtell, :32 and :33); Two Sentries (:33); Tony Rescued (by Sawtell, :33); The Rifle (:18); Too Late (by Sawtell, :18); Bumper (a.k.a. Time Tunnel Theme, by Williams, :03); A Strange Meeting (by Sawtell, :31); Col. Southall (:45); Sword in Belly (:30); Gen. to Tunnel (:28); Count Down General (1:29); Falling (by Williams, :13); Firing Squad A.O. (:22); Gun Squad to Swamp (1:52); Gun Squad to Swamp #2 (1:16); Col. Laugh (:14); Log Entry (:25); 1812 Rocket (2:10); Artillery (:32); Cock O' the North (by Urban Thielmann, 1:15); The General Dies (2:14); Clothes and Disappear (:10); Falling (by Williams, :23); Krakatoa (:15); Krakatoa #2 (:08); Next Week (:08); End Credits (a.k.a. Time Tunnel Theme, by Williams, :48); and Fox I.D. (by Alfred Newman, :05).

EPISODE BUDGET

Story Rights & Expense $500	Sound $1,625
Scenario $5,808	Electrical $3,949
Producer $8,215	Mechanical Effects $2,455
Direction $3,000	Set Dressing $4,591
Cast $17,440	Animals & Action Devices $0
Extras $5,932	Women's Wardrobe $654
Music $3,500	Men's Wardrobe $4,204
Staff $3,121	Makeup & Hairdressing $1,436
Art $1,900	Process $285
Sets $9,490	Production Film & Lab Charges $8,500
Operating Labor $4,943	Stills $150
Miniatures $3,000	Transportation $2,900
Camera $3,045	Re-recording $1,784

Photo Effects $1,690
Opticals, Fades & Dissolves $2,150
Titles $745
Post Production & Lab Charges
    $15,054
Projectionists $205
Editorial $5,875

Fringe Benefits $15,018
Miscellaneous $630
Amortizations $1,002
Contract Overhead $15,000
General Overhead $6,719
Total Picture Cost $166,515

Series Budget $167,757
Pre-Production Estimate: $166,515
Under $1,242

SET PRODUCTION COSTS
Wooded Area $110
Clearing & Campsite $400
British camp $300
Colonel Southall's Cabin $100
American Camp $500
Bog Area $1,500
Signaling Area Station $450
Battlefield $250
Construction Foreman $690
Total $4,300

Stunt Doubles

Frank Graham (double for Tony)
Paul Stader (double for Doug *and* Lt. Rynerson)
Eddie Saenz or Tom Steele (double for Lt. Rynerson on August 10)
Chris King (double for American Sgt. on August 4)

HISTORICAL NOTES

A British invasion of Louisiana (unknowingly launched after the Treaty of Ghent was negotiated to end the war) was defeated with very heavy British losses by General Andrew Jackson at the Battle of New Orleans in January 1815. This episode takes place the day before the invasion, but everything else appears to be pure fiction. There was no Colonel Southall, or a Seventh Royal Regiment. Most television viewers knew of the War of 1812, but very few of them knew when the war ended in 1815, let alone the true names of the British Generals and the Regiments.

ABC CENSORSHIP CONCERNS

Please modify scene 140 shot so that muskets are not pointed directly into camera.

STORY DEVELOPMENT

This episode was based on not one, but two original short stories by Bob and Wanda Duncan, which were purchased for a total of $630, and an additional $1,870 upon delivery of the first draft of the teleplay, and $1,500 for delivery of the final draft. The revised shooting script was reviewed by Jerry Briskin on July 27, and it appears Briskin was being pressured to cut the budget down by trimming the number of actors in the script. In a lengthy inter-office memo, Briskin questioned, "I don't see why we need the two extra soldiers when Tony and Doug are first captured. It seems to me that Hotchkiss and one soldier with guns could capture our two men who have no arms." Another comment by Briskin, "I would like to eliminate any reference to the firing squad as I would like to lose the six soldiers in the script. I believe this could be done by officers taking the men out to execute them in the two instances that the boys' lives are threatened. This would save not only the cost of the soldiers but the cost of the uniforms, which is approximately $100 per uniform." And yet another comment by Briskin: "If firing squad eliminated and Rynerson is alone with Doug,

Cover of the shooting script for "The Last Patrol."

we could eliminate the British officer who appears in this scene but who says nothing."

"If the American Sergeant and Corporal could make mention of turning Tony and Hotchkiss over to someone at the camp, at the time they capture the men, we could avoid carrying these two actors for five days due to the shooting schedule," Briskin also commented. "Another solution to this

problem might be to use two actors under contract to the studio and buy them at a small weekly price." In the same inter-office memo, Briskin wrote: "Again I would like to recommend our losing Major Sutherland from the script as he does little and says less and we would save an estimated $900 for the cost of the actor."

NOTES

An average of nine pages were shot each day. The interior and exterior of the cabin where Colonel Southall resides is on the 20th Century-Fox lot, and was the same used for a number of *Daniel Boone* television episodes. The difference between the two cabins is evident when the amount of mud packed between the logs varies from interior shots versus exterior shots. The same cabin sets are used in "The Death Merchant."

Carroll O'Connor plays two roles, General Southall and Colonel Southall. It was originally proposed to have two different actors play the roles, but it was Jerry Briskin's cost-cutting suggestion that resulted in the dual role. "If General Southall and Colonel Southall could be played by the same actor, we would save the cost of one additional actor which at this time is estimated at approximately $2,000, due to the fact he works five or six days. The two characters only have one scene together of any consequence (INT. COLONEL

James Darren and Michael Pate in "The Last Patrol."

SOUTHALL'S CABIN) and I believe we could get away with one or two split screens at the most," Briskin remarked. To help with timing, Howard Culver was on the set, providing the voice double for the split screen discussions between O'Connor's two selves.

Against Briskin's judgment, General Southall did travel through the vortex, courtesy of the special effects department, at an optical cost most episodes

Lee Meriwether and a V.I.P. visit the set.

did not acquire. Like James Darren in the pilot episode, Carroll O'Connor is seen bending down as he reached the far end of the tunnel, before the sparks and smoke disguised his disappearance. This scene was shot a number of times because the special effects for the tunnel scene was not on cue that day, and the cast and crew were forced to re-shoot the scene. Production lost 60 minutes that day as a result of the technical complications and timing.

BLOOPER!

It's mentioned that the Battle of New Orleans began on January 7. It really began January 8.

CRACK OF DOOM

INITIAL TELECAST: October 14, 1966

REVISED FINAL SHOOTING SCRIPTS DATED: August 5, 1966, and August 16, 1966

DATES OF PRODUCTION: August 11, 12, 15, 16, 17 and 18, 1966

FILMING LOCATIONS: Stage 18 and Stage B

GUEST CAST: Sam Groom (Jerry); Kim Kahana (one of the natives); Vic Lundin (Karnosu); George Matsui (Young Native); Ellen McRae (Eve Holland); and Torin Thatcher (Dr. Holland).

Stand-ins for Crack of Doom: Glen Colbert, Gene Silvani, William H. Graeff, Pat Murphy and Virginia Semon.

Stunt Doubles

Frank Graham (double for Tony)

Paul Stader (double for Doug)

PRODUCTION CREDITS

ART DIRECTORS: Jack Martin Smith and Rodger E. Maus

ASSISTANT DIRECTOR: Ted Butcher

DIRECTOR: William Hale

FILM EDITOR: Axel Hubert

MUSIC: Robert Drasnin

MUSIC EDITOR: Sam E. Levin

Teleplay by William Welch.

STORY: Doug and Tony materialize in a tropical jungle in the year 1883, in the midst of a volcanic eruption. There they meet Dr. Howland, a middle-aged explorer sent by the Royal Society to study the volcanic island of Krakatoa. Knowing Krakatoa blew up on the morning of August 27, 1883, Doug consults Dr. Howland's daughter's diary to discover the date is August 26. Neither Howland nor Eve believe Doug's insistence that an eruption is imminent. After Dr. Howland admits that he knows full well the volcano will explode soon and wanted the chance to measure the volcanic activity up to the moment of explosion and promises to leave with them in the afternoon when his instrument readings will be completed, Doug discovers that Eve forgot about the International Date Line — today is August 27. Meanwhile, Karnosu, a tribal leader, mistakes Doug and Tony as devils and believes a human sacrifice will appease the volcano. Karnosu and his natives swarm over them, determined to make a sacrifice. Thanks to the heroic efforts of the Time Tunnel personnel, Tony creates shock and awe, convincing the superstitious natives to leave him and Doug alone. Karnosu, however, falls to his death and the others subside. Thanks to General Kirk making voice contact with Tony, the scientists are convinced of the truth and Dr. Howland and his daughter make an immediate departure for Sumatra. Doug and Tony cannot board the boat because of the weight, but remain on the beach in the hopes they will be relocated…again.

MUSIC SCORE BY ROBERT DRASNIN *(dated September 20, 1966):* Color Bumper (by Johnny Williams, :03); The Boiler Room (:31); Volcanic Island (1:15); Native Danger (:39); Native Grabbers (:23); Main Title (a.k.a. Time Tunnel Theme, by Williams, :37); Krakatoa Greetings (:34); Name Dropper (:12); Volcano Talk (:26); Daughter Danger (:24); Eve of Suspicion (:39); Eve's Bridge (:14); Me Worry? (1:20); Tidal Wave (1:40); Storm Signals (:20); He Won't Budge (:16); Back to Work (:14); Leave Us Alone (:25); Time To Go (:22); Volcano Biz (:52); Feed Back (:16); Shock Wave (:28); Bumper #1 (a.k.a. Time Tunnel Theme, by Williams, :06); More Volcano Biz (:24); Paternal Squeeze (1:17); To Cook a Goose (1:22); Disappearance (:08); Falling (by Williams, :05); Tunnel Return (:19); Chilling Reception (:29); A Stitch in Time (4:17); Falling (by Williams, :09); Fats in the Fire (1:23); Voice in the Sky (1:40); Good-Byes (:27); Complex Problem (:50); Volcanic Panic (1:26); Falling (by Williams, :07); Flying Chord (:04); The Boiler Room (by Williams, :21); Pursuit (by Hugo Friedhofer, :21); Someone Moved (by Alfred Newman, :21); Urgent Detergent (by Newman, :21); Trouble for Us (by Newman, :21); What Now? (by Friedhofer, :21); Bleeker St. East (:21); End Credits (a.k.a. Time Tunnel Theme, by Williams, :48); and Fox I.D. (by Newman, :05).

EPISODE BUDGET

Story Rights & Expense $1,500	Sets $4,825
Scenario $5,808	Operating Labor $4,819
Producer $7,215	Miniatures $3,000
Direction $3,000	Camera $2,814
Cast $17,440	Sound $1,625
Extras $6,726	Electrical $3,949
Music $3,500	Mechanical Effects $2,030
Staff $3,121	Set Dressing $4,301
Art $2,642	Animals & Action Devices $350
	Women's Wardrobe $829

Men's Wardrobe $1,354

Makeup & Hairdressing $1,368

Process $285

Production Film & Lab Charges
$8,500

Stills $150

Transportation $2,900

Re-recording $1,784

Photo Effects $1,820

Opticals, Fades & Dissolves $2,150

Titles $745

Post Production & Lab Charges
$14,229

Projectionists $205

Editorial $5,875

Fringe Benefits $14,463

Miscellaneous $630

Amortizations $1,002

Contract Overhead $15,000

General Overhead $5,543

Total Picture Cost $157,497

Series Budget $167,757

Pre-Production Estimate $157,497

Under Budget $10,260

SET PRODUCTION COSTS

Steam Fissure, Jungle $2,260

Construction Foreman $295

Amortized $2,000

Total $4,555

Proposed Casting

Dr. Holland: Brian Aherne, Sidney Blackmer, Joseph Cotton, James Donald, Maurice Evans, Edward Mulhare, Walter Pidgeon, Donald Pleasance, Clive Revill, Wilfrid Hyde White and Michael Wilding.

Eve Holland: Juliet Mills

NOTES

Writer William Welch was paid a total of $4,000 for his original story and the first and final draft of a shooting script. After receiving the first draft, Arthur Weiss sent the author a number of notes, hoping they could be addressed for the final draft. Doug and Tony's initial observation of their surroundings was questioned. "Don't tropical plants grow in other areas than near the equator? What has Doug seen to make him say, 'There's a 100 percent chance this volcano is going to erupt?'"

"Dr. Holland appears to be a stiff, proper, dull Englishman based on his manner of speech," Weiss questioned. "Why doesn't Dr. Holland notice Tony and Doug's attire? Having been on the island for only a week, wouldn't the Hollands know the dates on which they departed from the mainland?

Wouldn't Tony and Doug have to account for not even having a boat? I realize we have to identify this as Krakatoa island to the boys and the Time Tunnel but couldn't our boys fake some other reason for being on the island and maneuver their whereabouts in speaking with Holland, as they have done in other episodes? Would not Holland, being British himself, ask the boys, 'You're not British, are you?' after he hears them talk?"

Eve Holland and Tony Newman feel the ground shake underneath them.

Welch, however, did not address most of these questions and the dialog as he had it in the script remained, for the most part, untouched.

In the October 14, 1966, issue of Johnny Robinson's syndicated TV column, the columnist remarked this was "one of tonight's best TV highlights." Joan Crosby's syndicated "TV Scout" column, dated the same day, remarked: "*Time Tunnel* blasts away tonight with another explosive situation for its scientists…They are on the edge of a volcano, which for dramatic purposes is conveniently spitting fire. If you know your history, the year is 1883, the island is Krakatoa, near Java and you also know they are in for big trouble. The bit here is that the local natives think that the time-traveling scientists are white faces who had prompted the eruption. The sight and sound effects in this episode are excellent!"

In her autobiography, actress Ellen Burstyn recalled how production on the final day was running behind and the special effects were anything but excellent. "By lunchtime word came down that we absolutely could not go over," she explained. "We had to shoot everything we could and stop on time. Anything that wasn't shot wouldn't be in the show. But how would the show make sense? No one knew. With ten minutes left in the shooting day,

Torin Thatcher as Dr. Holland.

we'd gotten everything but the eruption of the volcano. The scene was set up, but there was no way to get a master shot and coverage. What were they thinking? With five minutes to go, Irwin Allen appeared on the set with a pot and a wooden spoon. He placed all the actors and extras at the foot of the volcano, then shouted, 'Okay! When I hit the pot with the spoon, you all jump to the right. When I hit it again, you jump to the left.' And that was the climax of the story of the largest volcanic eruption ever heard or witnessed on the planet Earth."

"Our director, Bill Hale, was a nice young guy, an actor's director," Vic Lundin verified. "Apparently he was taking too long because Irwin Allen came down and reamed Bill out in front of everyone. Irwin took over and almost kicked Bill off the set. Irwin was a very petulant guy. If you crossed him, that was it."

"When we cast the Krakatoa episode of *The Time Tunnel*, Irwin's first choice as the scientist was Walter Pidgeon," recalled Larry Stewart, the casting director. "He was interested but he was way out of our price range. We also tried for Donald Pleasance and Edward Mulhare. We almost got Joseph Cotton, another of Irwin's friends. We ended up signing Torin Thatcher, someone who was not famous but someone we could afford and he did a fine job. We got a lot of wonderful actors on *Time Tunnel* because actors loved to play people from history. The show wasn't perceived as science fiction and that helped because the genre had a real stigma at the time. And unlike *Lost In Space* and *Voyage to the Bottom of the Sea*, we didn't have to convince them to act with monsters!"

In a few episodes, people observed Tony and Doug disappear before their eyes. This episode, however, is the only time someone witnesses the arrival of Doug and Tony. Superstitious natives observe the time travelers landing on the ground. One of the natives was played by Vic Lundin. "Jimmy Darren and I were going to have a fight scene, I said to Jimmy. 'Jimmy, I know you like doing your own stunts, but I'll use a stunt double.' Well, Jimmy was really swinging, and he splattered the stunt guy's nose all over the set. That could have been me! I had just had my nose broken on another show."

"Actors love doing action stuff," Darren explained. "I mean, most actors — I can't speak for every one of them. But most actors love doing their own stunts. When I did a movie called *Gunman's Walk* (1958) with Van Heflin and Tab Hunter, we had to actually herd cattle. I had ridden before, but I had not ever herded cattle before. Cutting cattle, that's a big job! And it's a big responsibility: If the horse gets spooked, you're in trouble, because if it throws you, then you're under the hooves of all the steers. So it was kind of exciting. My point is that many actors, including myself — especially myself — love to do my own stunts. When I did *T.J. Hooker*, God Almighty, I was doing every car stunt I possibly could, that they would allow me to do. 'cause I enjoyed it. It takes you back to being a kid. I think that's really where it lies: It takes you back to your childhood. Only you're playing with big toys now!

Clay Gowran of *The Chicago Tribune* paid a visit to the set during the filming of this episode. In the August 17, 1966, issue he described the production as "one of the most uncomfortable places in California…That's because it houses an island complete with a smoking volcano. In this make-believe world, the volcano smoke is made with steam. The island is a sound stage model only 30 foot squared, which will seem larger when it is seen on TV. As we watched there was a sudden hissing sound and steam began to rise from a crack running across the 'island.' We saw lots of fake coconuts, trees and lava, although the stage smelled more like a Chinese laundry show…

Victor Lundin, an actor who looks a lot like Elliot Ness, was a native chief who wanted to feed Darren and Colbert to the volcano. He was saying to another actor, Torin Thatcher, 'When the Earth grows angry, there must be a sacrifice to the fires!' It was a speech that took Lundin several takes to get it right and the same number of times Thatcher told Lundin, 'I want no more of that talk, I warn you!' Finally, everybody seemed satisfied with the scene and a bored-looking fellow, who has been studying the sports page out of a newspaper, climbed up into a camera rig and they shot the scene, which was worth about 75 seconds of film."

BLOOPERS!

The back of Doug's shirt is covered with dirt throughout the second fight sequence with Karnosu and his men. After Karnosu falls to his death into the boiling lava, everyone leaves the scene to make a steady escape off the island. After which, the back of Doug's shirt does not have the dirt stain anymore. Tony's sweater switches back and forth from dirty to clean in this episode.

In the beginning of this episode, when Tony Newman falls to the ground, the shadow of the rope is visible, which was used by the stunt double.

REVENGE OF THE GODS

INITIAL TELECAST: October 21, 1966
REVISED FINAL SHOOTING SCRIPTS DATED: August 17, 1966
DATES OF PRODUCTION: August 19, 22, 23, 24, 25 and 26, 1966
FILMING LOCATIONS: Stage 6, Stage 18 and Stage 19
GUEST CAST: Tony Brand (the Trojan Captain); Paul Carr (Paris); Pat Culliton (sentry); John Doucette (Ulysses); Kevin Hagen (Greek Sword Leader); Dee Hartford (Helen); Wesley Lau (Master Sgt. Jiggs); Joseph Ruskin (Sardis); Paul Stader (silent bit part as a Greek); and Abraham Sofaer (Epeios).

Stunt Doubles
Frank Graham (double for Tony)
Victor Paul (also a double for Tony)
Paul Stader (double for Doug, Sardis and Trojan Captain)
Gil Perkins (double for Ulysses)

PRODUCTION CREDITS
ART DIRECTORS: Jack Martin Smith and Rodger E. Maus
ASSISTANT DIRECTOR: Fred R. Simpson
DIRECTOR: Sobey Martin
FILM EDITOR: James Baiotto
MUSIC: Leith Stevens
MUSIC EDITOR: Sam E. Levin
Teleplay by William Read Woodfield and Allan Balter.

STORY: Somewhere on the Mediterranean, before 500 B.C., battle trumpets blow and Tony and Doug discover they are in no-man's land between the converging armies of the Greeks and the Trojans, outside of Troy. Captured immediately, they are taken to Ulysses, leader of the Greek Army, and his aide, Sardis. When Doug and Tony predict that the Greeks will win this ten year conflict, Ulysses takes them for gods and the boys masquerade as such. Sardis, disgruntled after losing physical combat against Tony, sneaks off to Troy to join forces with Paris, the Trojan prince, who holds Helen prisoner against her will. Doug is captured by Sardis and taken behind the Trojan walls, where he predicts a quarrel between Paris and Helen. Helen warns Paris that to kill one god is to offend them all, so Paris orders that Doug is not to be harmed. Late the next night, a large wooden horse is finished and Ulysses pretends to depart. The horse is left outside the city gates as a supposed tribute to the victors, so Paris brings it inside for all to see. During the night, Greek soldiers slip out of the horse and open the city gates, letting in more Greek troops. Tony, one of the stowaways in the horse, manages to rescue Doug while Sardis sounds the alarm. The Trojans are taken by surprise. Sardis is killed; Ulysses cuts Paris down; Helen is rescued; and Troy is burned. Ulysses and Helen thank the mythical Gods for their assistance, then watch as Doug and Tony vanish before their eyes.

MUSIC SCORE BY LEITH STEVENS *(dated October 4, 1966)*: Color Bumper (by Johnny Williams, :03); Boiler Room (by Williams, :25); 1,200 B.C. (1:57); Main Title (a.k.a. Time Tunnel Theme, :37); Episode Titles (1:19); Who Are You? (:50); First Test, Part One (:33); First Test, Part Two (1:19); First Test, Part Three (:33); Helen (1:02); Go Ahead (:13); Don't Let Him Keep You (:25); Fire the Camp (:54); One of Ulysses' Gods (:20); Take Him Away (1:10); Fight With Us (2:37); There's Tony (1:34); Bumper (by Williams, :03); Return to Battle (2:30); Reverse Polarity, Part One (2:17); Good Night (:24); Act Out (:07); Act Opening (:08); Bring the Horse Into the City (1:58); The Horse (1:05); Coda (1:06); It's Happening (1:11); Paris Dead (:51); Torturak (1:08); No Name (:10); Boiler Room (by Williams, :12); Bomber is Destroyed (by Alfred Newman, 1:07); Next Week (by Lyn Murray, 1:07); End Credits (a.k.a. Time Tunnel Theme, by Williams, :49); and Fox I.D. (by Newman, :05).

EPISODE BUDGET

Story Rights & Expense $1,500	Electrical $3,949
Scenario $5,808	Mechanical Effects $1,945
Producer $8,215	Set Dressing $5,358
Direction $3,000	Animals & Action Devices $0
Cast $17,600	Women's Wardrobe $979
Extras $7,142	Men's Wardrobe $5,054
Music $3,500	Makeup & Hairdressing $1,642
Staff $3,121	Process $285
Art $1,900	Production Film & Lab Charges $9,513
Sets $7,595	Stills $150
Operating Labor $4,752	Transportation $2,900
Miniatures $3,000	Re-recording $1,784
Camera $2,580	Photo Effects $1,893
Sound $1,625	Opticals, Fades & Dissolves $2,150

Titles $745
Post Production & Lab Charges
    $14,304
Projectionists $205
Editorial $5,875
Fringe Benefits $15,100

Miscellaneous $630
Amortizations $1,002
Contract Overhead $15,000
General Overhead $7,020
Total Picture Cost $168,821

Series Budget $167,757
Pre-Production Budget $168,821
Over Budget: $864

SET PRODUCTION COSTS
City Wall $150
Tony and Doug's Tent $500
Throne Room Parapet $50
Dungeon and Pit $1,230
Belly of Horse $125
Parapet $50
Foremen $315
Ulysses' Tent $1,470
Paris' Throne Room $4,800
Foremen $945
Total $9,635

HISTORICAL NOTES

A mixture of mythology, science fiction and good old-fashioned action made this episode unique, but mixing mythology proved a challenge. Ann makes reference that the time is about 1,200 B.C. Most historians believe the actual events depicted in this episode occurred in 1,250 B.C. But the Siege of Troy is difficult to write about from a historical perspective because much of it lies in Greek mythology, which Tony himself recounts to Ulysses. In Homer's *Odyssey*, it was Odysseus, one of the Achaean leaders, who rescued Helen. Since this episode was designed to establish a real time line for a mythical peace of world history, great liberties were applied as a result.

Not all television viewers were impressed. Betsy Brown of Mt. Lebanon, Pennsylvania, wrote to *The Pittsburg Press*, complaining about the tunnel out of time: "On the October 21 *Time Tunnel* episode dealing with the Trojan War, they were greatly mistaken about the Gods' names. They were Juno and Minerva. These are Roman names. The Trojan War took place between the

Greeks and Trojans. Hera and Pallas Athena are the correct names. I think TV writers could be a great deal more careful, especially on such obvious things." The television editor's reply: "It is something to get 'Thor' about, at that!"

ABC CENSORSHIP CONCERNS

Delete shot of screaming driver dragging man in the dust.

Paris can push Helen away but please cut the "vicious slap."

Please be sure we do not see the sword blades at moment of contact with the bodies.

Delete shot of guards screaming through the flames and running with clothes on fire.

PROPS

The iron maiden in the dungeon reappears in the dungeon scene of "The Walls of Jericho" and "The Revenge of Robin Hood." The torture rack is the same featured in "The Walls of Jericho." The same dungeon and torture racks can be seen in the *Lost In Space* episode, "The Astral Traveler."

ORIGINAL STORY CONCEPT

In the original April 29, 1966, story proposal, Doug and Tony find themselves caught in the middle of a raging battle on the plains outside Troy as the armies of the outraged King Menalaus pour ashore from their "thousand ships," to do battle with the Trojans, and restore Helen to the side of her

The November 12, 1966, issue of *TV Guide* featured a letter to the editor, written by John M. Patrick of Utah State University. "I'm willing to accept a few yards of old movie footage in the battle sequences, even the substitution of Persians for Trojans, and Thermopylae for Troy, but why in the name of Zeus were the ancient Greeks and Trojans speaking perfect present-day English? How come the Greek gods and goddesses had Roman names — as did Ulysses (who was Odysseus to the Greeks)? Was Agamemnon a private in the rear ranks, or did Ulysses simply supersede him as leader of the Greeks because today's TV viewers wouldn't know the difference anyhow? Our time-travelers knew that Paris died by the sword of Ulysses the night Troy fell — but since this never happened in the Homeric epics, how could they know it?"

husband. The raging armies come together. In the melee Doug and Tony are separated. Doug is taken into Troy where he is flung at the feet of Paris who kidnapped and is now holding Helen captive. Tony is captured by the Spartans and taken before Menalaus' general of the armies — Ulysses. As the endless battles between the two armies turn the plains to red, Tony proves his valor to Ulysses and is allowed to enter Troy with the handful of men

Doug and Tony in conference with Ulysses.

secreted in the famed "Trojan Horse." His objective — to save not only Doug but Helen as well. Tony finds Doug about to be cast into a pit of half-starved jackals and rescues him. Together, they outwit the cunning and evil Paris and take Helen out of the city as gates are opened and the Greeks pour into the city to reduce it to ashes.

The May 3 revision offers more details, and is closer to the version that was filmed a few months later, but there were still a few noticeable differences. Ulysses banishes Sardis for disgracing his sword and sets the boys up in a tent with food, clothes and slave girls. Tony and Doug are living it up in their tent — wine, slave girls, but no song. Tony and his girl decide to go for a walk. The Time Tunnel decides to wait until the boys are together before snatching them back. As Doug lolls with his girl, Sardis and his men silently knife the guards outside Doug's tent, slip in, overpower Doug and drag him out. For obvious reasons, the slave girls were never featured in the shooting script and never filmed.

While captive, Doug, enraged, grabs a sword and goes for Paris. A guard steps in and protects Paris. Doug fights and kills the guard. Paris is about to have Doug killed when Helen reminds him that he may be killing a God —

Doug offers words of comfort to Helen.

and sealing his own doom. He has them both flung into cells. This scene was not included in the shooting script — probably to eliminate Doug's needless killing.

In order to send the crazed Trojan back into the tunnel, security guards finally subdue and tranquilize the Trojan. Quickly, while the tunnel is zeroed in, they send him back. In the actual production, security simply outnumbers the Trojan and forces him back into the tunnel without needing to subdue or tranquilize him.

Paris, out of his mind at his latest defeat in battle, devises a diabolically clever plan. He has Doug brought to him, has his wrists lashed to a chariot. Paris says he will now lead the assault — in this chariot. Sardis is against this move for fear of Godly reprisals. Paris will hear no argument against this. He leads his army again into battle. As the armies clash, the lead element of the Greek army see what Paris has done. They refuse to fire on the lead chariot. Before Ulysses can help them, they are surrounded. The Trojan army closes in from all sides and beats them to the ground. Finally, with Doug still at his side, Paris orders the archers to fire into the huddled circle of Greeks until the last man is dead. Paris returns to Troy. He is informed that after

Dee Hartford as Helen of Troy.

this crushing defeat, the Greeks are leaving. They are getting into their ships and sailing away. Paris is jubilant. He says Doug has served him well — but now must die so that there can be no Greek return to battle. He has Doug lashed over the pit of half-starved jackals. As the crazed animals leap and growl below him, a candle slowly burns towards the single rope that holds him above the slavering jaws. This scene was never in the teleplay, nor was it ever filmed. Instead, Doug is simply put on a rack and tortured.

SCRIPT NOTES

Script writing duties for this episode were in the hands of William Read Woodfield and Allan Balter, the former of whom scripted episodes of *Lost In Space* and *Voyage to the Bottom of the Sea*. The writers were paid $2,500 for both the original story concept and the first draft of the teleplay, which was completed on May 17, 1966, and $1,500 for the final draft dated June 2, 1966. It was first titled "Gift of Death," then re-titled "The Jackals of Troy."

"I liked *Time Tunnel*," Woodfield told author Mark Phillips. "It was an interesting idea. That series was the 'stock footage' show. We decided to do Helen of Troy primarily because there was an Italian movie that spent a fortune on this horse, which must have been 40 stories tall. It was great footage. We got that [stock footage] for $20 a foot, and it was gorgeous film. Then, there was *The 300 Spartans* made at Fox, about the Greek war, with guys with brushes on their heads fighting, so we said, 'Okay, we have the battle here, we'll drop [Tony and Doug] into the battle.' But we didn't know anything about Helen of Troy. We had the horse in mind, looked up who was who and constructed the story so that these guys would end up in the horse. That was the trick: to make them wind up in the horse."

Script writer William Read Woodfield was also an accomplished artist and photographer. His first professional photo assignment was a picture of Elizabeth Taylor and her new baby, which appeared in *Life* magazine. The issue of *Playboy* magazine that included his pictures of Jayne Mansfield sold more than one million copies. He also photographed Marilyn Monroe in the nude, on the set of her uncompleted 1962 film, *Something's Got To Give*, with Monroe shedding her bathing suit by the swimming pool.

After reading the revised teleplay, Jerry Briskin submitted notes (dated June 6, 1966) to the writer in the hopes that revisions could be made that would cut away a fraction of the production costs.

Eliminate fires breaking out in Tunnel Complex.
Eliminate fire in the pit area.
Eliminate any wire shots, i.e. Soldier and Sardis being shot with arrows.

*Would like to submit a torture of some kind to Doug in place of pit and burn-
ing rope as this trick requires a harness and wire work in order to be shot properly.*

*If we can eliminate Sardis and soldiers crossing river to capture Doug, we
would not require double wardrobe as actors would not be seen in water and
therefore would not come into Doug's tent soaking wet.*

*We would probably have to have one stuntman commence work at least one
week in advance of shooting to stage fights, and work with Sobey Martin.*

NOTES

Stock footage of the Trojan Horse scenes originate from *Helen of Troy*
(1955). Stock footage of the battle sequences originate from *The 300 Spartans*
(1962). Much of the stock footage from *Helen of Troy* was directed by Yakima
Canutt, but because it was stock footage, Canutt received no screen credit
in this episode. Costumes worn by the actors in this episode were created to
resemble the ones seen in the stock footage from *The 300 Spartans*.

Dee Hartford, who played the role of Helen in this episode, may have
been cast simply because she was a good friend of the producer. Hartford
was married to director Howard Hawks and was signed for the role because
she was a neighbor of Irwin Allen's in Bel-Air.

Paul Carr recalled in an interview for *Starlog* magazine how embarrassed he
was playing the role of Paris, "in the most outlandish costume you've ever seen."
Carr also recalled: "I walked into the commissary wearing these flowing robes
with all this make-up and a head full of curls. I mean, you could have scraped
the make-up off with a shovel, and I ran into an old friend who was producing
a picture at Fox. He looked up at me very casually and said, 'Hi, Paul. Workin'?'"

In an issue of *Epilog*, Pat Culliton recalled a scene involving James Darren
and Joseph Ruskin dueling with swords. Doug offered to take on Sardis, but
Tony replies that since the sword was thrown at him, he'll take the challenge.
During the first take, the sword was thrown in between the actors and the
two ad-libbed lines as to who the sword was thrown to until Sobey Martin,
the director, realized the actors were not taking the scene seriously and had
to call a "cut" and redo the scene.

The footage of security personnel placing weapons into the Time Tunnel
to send back to help Doug and Tony would later be reused in "Attack of the
Barbarians." Just like the latter episode, Tony and Doug never make use of
them, nor is any mention ever made later in the episode. The careless editing
would have made observant television viewers wonder whatever became of
the modern-day weaponry that was sent back in time.

The Hartford Courant in Connecticut remarked, "It's an intriguing
installment."

RENDEZVOUS WITH DEATH

In the summer of 1966, William Read Woodfield and Allan Balter submitted a three-page plot proposal titled "The Brave Die Once," concerning Tony and Doug's arrival behind the German lines during WWI, being taken captive, and assisting the Allies in making and improving gas masks to defend themselves against the new chemical warfare the Germans were planning to use. On June 6, 1966, they wrote a plot synopsis now titled, "Rendezvous With Death," concerning Tony and Doug's arrival at the Battle of Ypres. After being mistaken for spies and jailed, the time travelers meet a Canadian, Jack Langdon, who proves to be a coward in the face of danger. After escaping jail and finding their way back to Allied headquarters, all three of them report on General Kronendorf, and how he and his men have perfected a new gas mask that will be used in the next attack. To prove their story, Langdon is ordered to go back behind enemy lines and retrieve such a mask. With the assistance of Doug and Tony, Langdon succeeds and the Allies begin burning wood so that charcoal can be placed into their masks, just like the Germans.

Kronendorf, meanwhile, is accidentally picked up and brought to the Time Tunnel Complex in 1968. General Kirk attempts to convince Kronendorf that a gas attack is not feasible and, while the German attempts to avoid any form of brainwashing, he eventually relents and is sent back to 1915. Kirk, however, having been exposed to the radiation of the tunnel, has aged to the appearance of a 100-year-old man. Using the Tunnel, Ann and Swain manage to reverse the aging process and save Kirk from a horrible fate. Kronendorf, back in his own time, calls off the gas attack. Field Marshall Von Steiner demands to know why the attack was called off and when Kronendorf, brainwashed, cannot explain why, Von Steiner orders the attack to commence. Langdon, fearful for his life during the attack, attempts to flee and is shot and killed. Hundreds of other lives, however, were saved courtesy of the bravery of Doug and Tony.

The time travelers soon find themselves back in the vortex, and presumably landing in "The Exploding City," a plot proposal written by Rik Sherman, which also never went into production.

PRODUCTION #9609
MASSACRE

INITIAL TELECAST: October 28, 1966

SHOOTING SCRIPT DATED: August 25, 1966, with revised pages dated August 26, 1966

DATES OF PRODUCTION: August 29, 30, 31, September 1, 2 and 6, 1966

FILMING LOCATIONS: Ranch Location, Stage 18, Stage 19 and Western Avenue

GUEST CAST: Paul Comi (Captain Frederick Benteen); Christopher Dark (Crazy Horse); Jim Halferty (Tim McGinnis); Perry Lopez (Dr. Charles Whitebird); Joe Maross (General Custer); Bruce Mars (Thomas Custer); George Mitchell (Sitting Bull); Lawrence Montaigne (Yellow Elk); and John Pickard (Major Marcus Reno).

Stunt Doubles
Paul Stader (double for Yellow Elk)
Eddie Saenz (stunt Indian with knife fighting Tony)
Denver Mattson (stunt double for Tony)
Reggie Parton (Indian during opening scene in woods)
Eddie Seikes (Indian during opening scene in woods)

PRODUCTION CREDITS
ART DIRECTORS: Jack Martin Smith and Rodger E. Maus
ASSISTANT DIRECTOR: Ted Butcher
DIRECTOR: Murray Golden
FILM EDITOR: Dick Wormell
MUSIC: Joseph Mullendore
MUSIC EDITOR: Sam E. Levin
Teleplay by Carey Wilber.

STORY: Doug and Tony, landing on the edge of a prairie in Eastern Montana Territory, amidst a half-dozen dead Cavalry soldiers, are threatened by a trio of knife-wielding Indians, which includes Crazy Horse and Yellow Elk. At the Time Tunnel, the crew has called in an expert from the Indian Bureau to help fix the time and place where the time travelers have landed. Dr. Charles Whitebird, a Sioux, reports that his early-day relatives were brewing trouble and helps calm down Yellow Elk when the scientists accidentally yank the native out of his own time and into theirs. Meanwhile, Doug and Tony are rescued by 15-year-old Tim McGinnis, the sole survivor of the dead detail. During the harrowing escape, Doug is rescued but Tony remains captured. Tony is brought before Chief Sitting Bull and learns that he is at Little Big Horn, June 24, 1876. Tony tells Sitting Bull that though he will win the forthcoming battle, his people will suffer for it for years to come. Sitting Bull, impressed by his courage, agrees to let Tony seek out General George Armstrong Custer and talk peace. Meanwhile, Doug, a prisoner of Custer, witnesses the General planning the greatest coup of his military career. Custer wants to take the gathered Indians by surprise. Tony arrives with his plea for peace; he too is imprisoned. Custer mounts his attack, at the last minute assigning Tim to a new battalion leader, Major Reno. As Custer marches toward battle, Tony and Doug distract their guards and escape, meeting Tim and delaying his joining Reno until the battle moves on toward Custer. Yellow Elk, on the fringe of the massacre, warns the trio to flee for their lives, but not before he delivers a message to Doug and Tony. Doug and Tony ultimately witness the massacre and the field of dead bodies and dematerialize into the time vortex.

MUSIC SCORE BY JOSEPH MULLENDORE *(dated October 11, 1966):* Color Bumper (by Johnny Williams, :03); Boiler Room (by Williams, :24); Indian Vengeance (3:06); Main Title (a.k.a. Time Tunnel Theme, by Williams, :37); Episode Titles (:27); Gary Owen (public domain, adapted by Lionel Newman, :17 and :06); I'm a Crazy Horse (:23); Bugle Boy (1:02); Steal Horses (1:45); War Drums (1:22); Die Brave (1:09); You Call Me Brother! (:43); Custer's H.Q. (:28); Take Him Away (:09); Doug Escapes (1:24); You Must Fight (1:14); Bumper (by Williams, :03); Tomahawk Fight (1:38); Cavalry (1:12); Custer's Tent (:21); How Did It Go? (:22); War Drums (2:32); Crazy Horse to Yellow Elk (:06); Yellow Elk 1966 (1:06); Yellow Elk Goes Back (1:06); Custer's Troops (:48); Officer's call (:10); Custer's Premonition (:20); What About McGinnis? (:28); Indians Amass (1:00); Boots and Saddles (1:13); Custer's Troops (:47); War Drums (:33); Indians to Battle (:38); Battle (2:43); Retreat (:12); Final Curtain (1:07); Boiler Room (by Williams, :17); The Paperhanger is Still Alive (by Daniele Amfitheatrof, :31); Boy Attempts to Escape (by Paul Sawtell, :31); Someone Moved (by Lionel Newman, :31); Pursuit (by Hugo Friedhofer, :31); Next Week (by Lyn Murray, :09); End Credits (a.k.a. Time Tunnel Theme, by Williams, :49); and Fox I.D. (by Alfred Newman, :05).

EPISODE BUDGET
Story Rights & Expense $1,500
Scenario $5,808
Producer $7,215
Direction $3,000
Cast $17,700
Extras $6,083
Music $3,500
Staff $3,256
Art $2,642
Sets $5,540
Operating Labor $5,086
Miniatures $3,000
Camera $2,701
Sound $1,625
Electrical $4,001
Mechanical Effects $1,320
Set Dressing $4,437
Animals & Action Devices $935
Women's Wardrobe $929
Men's Wardrobe $3,709

Makeup & Hairdressing $1,656
Process $285
Production Film & Lab Charges
    $8,500
Stills $150
Transportation $4,800
Re-recording $1,784
Photo Effects $3,350
Opticals, Fades & Dissolves $2,150
Titles $745
Post Production & Lab Charges
    $14,679
Projectionists $205
Editorial $5,875
Fringe Benefits $14,974
Miscellaneous $900
Amortizations $1,002
Contract Overhead $15,000
General Overhead $6,756
Total Picture Cost $166,798

SET PRODUCTION COSTS
Edge of Woods $150
Woods $550
Indian Camp $75
Tepee, Custer's Tent $670
Indian Village $330
Cavalry Bivouac $150
Landmark Rock $500
Total $2,425

MUSIC NOTES

Joseph Mullendore, credited only as "Mullendore" during the closing credits, made his only contribution for *The Time Tunnel* with this episode. Yet, his music cues would appear in multiple episodes following "Massacre."

Only after Mullendore completed the music did the Music Department at Fox take a few moments to confirm the fact that the song "Garry Owen" was in public domain and, therefore, could be used in this show. "Garry Owen" was the unofficial marching song of the Seventh Cavalry. However, "Boots and Saddles" cost the studio an additional $750 and, in addition, the Music Department recommended that the latter song not be used to avoid copyright problems. As a result, "Boots and Saddles" was replaced with music cues in the Fox library.

HISTORICAL MISTAKE

It was mentioned that George Armstrong Custer reached brigadier status at the age of 21. Custer was made brigadier, but at the age of 23.

A number of television columnists were not impressed. Joan Crosby of TV Scout (a syndicated column) wrote of this episode for her October 2, 1966, column: "*Time Tunnel* is preposterous but entertaining tonight. 'Massacre' takes considerable liberties with history in retelling Custer's last stand at the Little Big Horn. Yet this segment does manage to convey the strong ego of Custer (Joe Maross), who had hoped to one day become the President of the United States. The episode also shows the savagery and yet curious warmth of Chief Sitting Bull." The columnist for the St. Joseph, Missouri, *News Press* reviewed differently: "There is no denying it, the western boom on television is on…It is pretty accurate and fairly suspenseful as usual, bearing the same old tendency to futilely attempt to avert history."

Actors position themselves to play dead men from a massacre while Darren and Colbert stand where instructed.

Just a week prior, the *Bob Hope* anthology series presented their own take on the same subject, "Massacre at Fort Phil Kearny," which was placed before the Custer debacle, laying the groundwork of what really happened at the battle of Little Big Horn. Between these two television programs was a fair assessment of the behind-the-scenes that led to the final rebellion of the Sioux and their Allies.

Darren and Colbert discuss the next scene with script in hand.

A columnist for *The Evening Independent* wrote: "Youngsters will enjoy this science fiction thriller as it turns to the action of a cowboy and Indian yarn. There is plenty of riding, shooting and narrow escapes for the western-adventure fans."

ABC CENSORSHIP CONCERNS

Please be sure Tim's reference here to tobacco is acceptable to program's tobacco sponsors.

Particular caution here that all material, indicated as historical fact, is accurate — especially those parts of the script that deal with General Custer.

Usual caution that all material, indicated as historical fact, is accurate. Standard caution on your choice of stock shots of battle sequences. Can only be approved on film.

Men are pulled but not dragged behind horses. The brand-iron torch does not touch the men.

Please do not feature a close up blow with the tomahawk; Tony being jabbed with stick; the Karate chops. Also caution that shrieks are not over-done.

Of course, Gall's spitting must be a 'dry' one.

Just a caution that Tony's hitting the boy comes off as an act of necessity and not one of brutality.

NOTES

August 5, 1966, memo: "Richard Zanuck and William Self have approved the following. Please amend by deal memo dated June 3, 1966, to provide that Murray Golden is to direct Episode 9 of *The Time Tunnel* in lieu of Episode 9 of *Voyage to the Bottom of the Sea*."

PAUL COMI

Actor Paul Comi played the role of Captain Frederick Benteen, who served under George Armstrong Custer. Comi had worked with Irwin Allen before on an episode of *Voyage to the Bottom of the Sea*. "The incident on *Time Tunnel* that remains with me happened in the first day of shooting," recalled Comi. "I, along with others, had been assigned a horse to ride. As we were in the process of mounting and were being told where we would proceed to in a gallop, suddenly the area was loaded with swarms of bees or hornets that the horses probably stepped on and the bees were attacking both horses and riders. In an instant there was a mass scattering of horses and riders which led to a fairly long passage of time re-gathering everyone. In my case, although I had done a lot of riding in the film *Warlock*, where I played the part of Luke Friendly, one of the gang of 'bad guys' that ultimately were beaten by Henry Fonda and his sidekick. Anthony Quinn had been hired by the town to rid the threat of our gang. In spite of my having had experience with horseback riding, the added problem with hornets led to me simply hanging on for dear life and fortunately maintaining myself in the saddle."

ORIGINAL STORY TREATMENT

Writer Carey Wilber was paid $630 for his story, "The Massacre," and an option of $3,370 to write the teleplay ($1,870 for the first draft, $1,500 for delivery of the final draft). Wilber admitted that he wanted to tell the epic of Custer's Last Stand from a different viewpoint. "It is the story of Captain Benteen's feud with General George Armstrong Custer; Benteen arguing for humanity; Custer for war and glory. It is also the story of Sitting Bull's effort to maintain peace despite an egocentric's provocations," Wilber explained.

Caught up in this turmoil of war and politics, Doug and Tony struggle to avert total disaster on the Little Big Horn. They succeed in warning a single soldier of Major Reno's battalion. The soldier carries the warning back to Reno, who withdraws in time to save his men. Then, Tony and Doug barely save their own lives. The above is historically correct: there was a Captain Benteen, and there was a Major Reno whose battalion was saved. But the

General Custer (Joe Maross) makes his last stand.

facts behind the acrimonious relationship between the two are shrouded in mystery. Historians have painted the two in various lights, leaving Americans to assume what kind of role they played in the decision making.

Wilber's original story treatment was a bit different from what was captured on celluloid. In the original story, Doug and Tony were taken captive and thanks to a brave trumpeter named Sol Wiseman (name changed to Tim McGinnis before the final draft was completed), a boy of about 15 years, Tony gets away, leaving Doug to face the Indians as their captive. In a three-man council with Sitting Bull and the bitterly hostile Gall (Yellow Elk in the revised teleplay), Doug foretells the future. If the Indians fight Custer they will win a great victory but in the end it will bring about their downfall as a nation. In the end Doug persuades Sitting Bull not to make the first hostile move. "If Yellowhair comes to talk then we will talk with him," Sitting Bull says. "But if he comes to fight we will kill him and all his men."

In Custer's camp, Tony predicts the next day's disaster to Sol. An interested listener is Captain Benteen. Later he comes to where Tony is held under guard to ask a personal question. Will he be among those killed next day? Tony assures him that he will not, that he will live, suffer through the controversy of Custer's defeat and retire. Benteen then fondly reminisces about his wife and child. Doug arrives, bringing a message of peace from

Doug and Tony decide not to stay around any longer.

Sitting Bull. Custer calls a council of war. He is strangely exuberant as he questions Doug before his brother, Tom Custer; a newspaper man, Brouard; his chief of scouts, Major Reno; and Captain Benteen. He dismisses Doug and then reveals his plan. They will hit the Sioux villages as they hit the Cheyenne on the Washita with a divided command. Reno will attack the lower end of the village, Custer the upper. Benteen, with three companies of cavalry, will furnish the reserve and guard the packs. This action will violate Sitting Bull's peace offer. Custer brushes this aside. He has come to settle the Indian question for once and for all and out of this, by God, he will win nomination for the Presidency of the United States. Benteen points out that this very plan will end in Tony's predicted disaster. Custer scornfully brushes aside Benteen's argument.

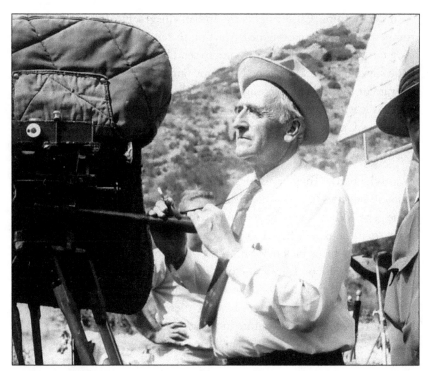

The cameraman sets up the frame.

In the morning, Custer sights the Indian villages. He dispatches another trumpeter, an older man named Martini, to tell Benteen to come on and bring the packs. Tony pleads with him to send Sol instead but Custer refuses. To do so would indicate that he had some faith in Tony's story. They ride on, unaware of the Indians massing under Gall. But Sol is uneasy. He doesn't want to die with an Indian arrow in him. He manages to get Doug and Tony free just as Custer orders his charge on the village. Together the three ride away from the battle.

The story ends when the three of them encounter Benteen riding hard toward the battle. Tony urges him to turn back and support Reno. Benteen, although he hates Custer, feels his honor requires that he ride to the sound of the guns. What guns? There is silence from the field beside the Little Big Horn, then the faintly heard, exultant cries of the Indians as they loot the dead. Benteen turns his horse and rides off as sound of heavy firing breaks out on a nearby ridge. Tony and Doug are left to themselves. They start after Benteen, are surprised by a body of Indians and face certain death when the Time Tunnel Complex manages to yank them out of the period and send them hurtling to a new adventure in some other time.[*]

BLOOPER!

During the fight between Tony and Yellow Elk, in an attempt to be adopted by the Sioux, Yellow Elk's knife in his left hand vanishes and then reappears between cuts.

George Armstrong Custer was referred to as a General in this episode. In reality, he was a Lieutenant Colonel, a rank he held up to the day he died.

---

[*] In the initial story proposal, Dr. Charles Whiteowl, a distinguished anthropologist, arrives at the Time Tunnel Complex in response to a call for help. His name would be changed to Dr. Charles Whitebird before the final teleplay was drafted.

DEVIL'S ISLAND

INITIAL TELECAST: November 11, 1966

REVISED SHOOTING FINAL SCRIPT DATED: September 16, 1966, revised September 19, 1966

SECOND REVISED (FINAL) SHOOTING SCRIPT DATED: September 22, 1966

DATES OF PRODUCTION: September 20, 21, 22, 23, 26 and 27, 1966

FILMING LOCATIONS: Stage B, Stage 18 and Stage 19

GUEST CAST: Bob Adler (Gaunt Man); Peter Balakoff* (Capt. Dreyfuss); Oscar Beregi (Commandant Rubidoux); Fred Carson (the first guard); Steven Geray (Perrault); Marcel Hillaire (Boudaire); Theodore Marcuse** (Lescaux); Alain Patrick*** (Claude); and George Sawaya (the French sailor).

Stunt Doubles
Frank Graham (double for Tony, Claude and Boudaire)
Paul Stader (double for Doug)

PRODUCTION CREDITS
ART DIRECTORS: Jack Martin Smith and Rodger E. Maus
ASSISTANT DIRECTOR: Ted Butcher
DIRECTOR: Jerry Hopper
FILM EDITOR: James Baiotto
MUSIC: stock
MUSIC EDITOR: Sam E. Levin
Teleplay by Bob and Wanda Duncan.

STORY: Tony and Doug land on Devil's Island, a French penal colony housing political prisoners, in January 1895. Devil's Island is run with an iron fist by the notorious Lescaux and is superintended by the Commandant of the camp, a bored bureaucrat named Rubidoux. Tony and Doug are mistaken for two political prisoners and are each assigned a number and case file. A recent visitor to the Island, Alfred Dreyfuss, a famous French artillery officer who was placed on trial and found guilty on charges of treason,

---

* Peter Balakoff is billed during the closing credits as "Ted Roter."
** Actor Theodore Marcuse is billed during the closing credits as "Theo Marcuse."
*** Actor Alain Patrick is billed during the closing credits as "Alain Patrice."

makes his acquaintance with the inmates. The prisoners are spurred by the
arrival of the heroic Dreyfuss to plan an escape for themselves and him.
One of the prisoners, Boudaire, is accidentally transported to the present
via the Time Tunnel Complex. At first, Boudaire prefers not to return…
until he learns that Lescaux and the Commandant have arranged a death
trap for Dreyfuss. The escape attempt is foiled and the prisoners escape —
except for Dreyfuss who chooses to remain until his innocence is proved. It
is his duty to stay and stand up for his principles. With the Commandant
all but urging him to escape, Doug suddenly sees what Boudaire has not
been able to tell them — it's a plot to kill Dreyfuss. Assuring Dreyfuss
that he will be taken off the island soon and acquitted, Doug and Tony
sprint out…and the two scientists once again find themselves traveling
through time.

MUSIC CUES: Color Bumper (by Johnny Williams, :03); Falling (by
Williams, :23); Pursuit (by Hugo Friedhofer, :33); A Dark Night (by
Lionel Newman, :33); Boy Attempts to Escape (by Paul Sawtell, :33); The
Paperhanger is Still Alive (by Daniele Amfitheatrof, :33 and :04); The Boys'
Introduction (by Sawtell, :30); Main Title (a.k.a. Time Tunnel Theme, by
Williams, :37); Volcanic Island (by Robert Drasnin, 1:08); U.S. Intelligence
(by Sawtell, :14); Louis Discovery (by Sawtell, :48); The Boys' Escape (by
Sawtell, :48); Louis Discovery (by Sawtell, :19); Pursuit (by Friedhofer,
:31); The Death Seats (by Sawtell, :31); Krueger Comes Back* (by Lennie
Hayton, :27); The Boys' Introduction (by Sawtell, :27); Trying to Signal (by
Sawtell, :36); Trying to Remember (by Sawtell, :36); Tony Talks (by Sawtell,
1:21); The Paperhanger is Still Alive (by Amfitheatrof, 1:21); The Long
Count Down (by Sawtell, 1:04); A Dark Night (by Lionel Newman, 1:04
and :07); U.S. Intelligence (by Sawtell, :17); Volcanic Island (by Drasnin,
:35); Complex Problem (by Drasnin, :35); Bleeker St. East (by Drasnin,
:35); Time Transfer (by Williams, :13); The Iceberg Cometh (by Williams,
:13); Disappearing Act (by Williams, :13); Bumper (by Williams, :03);
First Test Part Three (by Leith Stevens, :20); Time Transfer (by Williams,
1:09); Take Him Away (by Joseph Mullendore, 1:09); The Boys Survived
(by Sawtell, :28); Jettison (by Lyn Murray, :27); The Death Seats (by
Sawtell, :15); Deceitful Alexis (by Sawtell, :15); A Fool (by Sawtell, 15);
Louise's Discovery (by Sawtell, :31); The Boys' Escape (by Sawtell, :31);

*The music cue titled "Krueger Comes Back" was originally composed and scored for "The Phantom
Strikes" episode of *Voyage to the Bottom of the Sea*.

Tony Talks (by Sawtell, :31); Time Transfer (by Williams, :14); The Boys' Escape (by Sawtell, :14); Tony Talks (by Sawtell, :21); Footsteps in the Dark (by Sawtell, :21); Two Sentries (by Murray, :19); The Boys' Escape (by Sawtell, :19); The Bombing (by Sawtell, :19); U.S. Intelligence (by Sawtell, :07); Saved and Disappear (by Murray, :07); The Jungle (by Williams, :07); The Boiler Room (by Williams, :18); Bleeker St. East (by Drasnin, :23); The Japanese Consulate (by Sawtell, :21); A Strange Meeting (by Sawtell, :21); Complete Destruction (by Sawtell, :21); Volcanic Island (by Drasnin, :21); Mine Trap #2 (by Murray, :21); End Credits (a.k.a. Time Tunnel Theme, by Williams, :48); and Fox I.D. (by Alfred Newman, :05).

EPISODE BUDGET
Story Rights & Expense $1,500
Scenario $5,808
Producer $7,215
Direction $3,000
Cast $18,500
Extras $5,330
Music $3,500
Staff $3,121
Art $2,642
Sets $11,495
Operating Labor $5,025
Miniatures $3,000
Camera $2,701
Sound $1,625
Electrical $3,949
Mechanical Effects $1,265
Set Dressing $4,560
Animals & Action Devices $200
Women's Wardrobe $404
Men's Wardrobe $1,579

Makeup & Hairdressing $1,436
Process $285
Production Film & Lab Charges
    $9,017
Stills $150
Transportation $2,900
Re-recording $1,784
Photo Effects $2,996
Opticals, Fades & Dissolves $2,150
Titles $745
Post Production & Lab Charges
    $13,679
Projectionists $205
Editorial $5,875
Fringe Benefits $16,050
Miscellaneous $630
Amortizations $1,002
Contract Overhead $15,000
General Overhead $6,798
Total Picture Cost $167,121

Series Budget $167,757
Pre-Production Estimate: $167,121
Under Budget: $636

SET PRODUCTION COSTS
Barracks $1,550
Commandant's Office $1,065
Dreyfuss Hut $550
Sweatbox $375
Prison Compound $2,660
Beach $75
Various Jungle $200
Total $6,475

ORIGINAL STORY TREATMENT

Writers Bob and Wanda Duncan received a total of $3,345 for writing this episode. $2,100 paid upon the delivery of the first draft of the teleplay, and $1,245 upon delivery of the final draft. Their script was adapted from an original (untitled) story treatment, dated August 31, 1966. The story treatment, for the most part, is the same as the finished film, but what isn't revealed in the finished film, but is explained in the treatment, was the construction job that Tony and Doug are sent out to with the convicts: they are working on the infamous Road Zero, a stretch of road in the jungle that leads from nowhere to nowhere and is designed just to keep the men busy.

The script originally called for actor George Sawaya to play a man exiting the torture box when Doug is forced to enter and take his place. ABC had a concern about this scene, noting: "Just a caution that the 'emaciated man' is not too unpleasantly shocking for home viewers." As a result, the initial salary fee schedule was revised to remove George Sawaya from the list and production was saved $250.

NOTES

The beach scene with the boat used for the inmates' escape was the same set used for a prior episode, "Crack of Doom."

"Thank God we had the stock footage, because the sets were 'Puke City' many times," Robert Colbert recalled to author Kyle Counts. "We would be out on the [20th] back lot, running around trying to pretend we were on the shores of some thriving tropical island, when all that was there was a pool of water and some dead plants that were painted green. We did the best we could with what we had, but it was depressing at times. I don't want to get into naming names or downgrading anybody involved with the show, because there were many wonderful people there. But they weren't what I call top-quality people. Irwin just seemed to come in a little under class all the time. He would downgrade things and cheapen the show. With just a few more dollars, he could have made the show marvelous."

Carl Michael Galli, columnist for "The Eye Television" column in November 23, 1966 issue of *The Miami News*, was harshly critical of *The Time Tunnel* in general. He did not hold back his opinion after watching this episode. "In last Fridays' program, Tony and Doug were on Devil's

Marcel Hillaire as Boudaire.

Island in 1895. However, and follow this closely, in order to get a fix on the two time voyagers, the tunnel scientists had to know the exact date. They fed the Devil's Island prisoners' ID numbers into the tunnel's history computer and lo and behold, nothing! Yet thirty seconds later, Whit Bissell, as General Kirk, had put a call through to France requesting the dates on which the prisoners were originally issued their uniform numbers. Funny, when you realize that he announced only seconds before that these files were incomplete. The director could be forgiven such minor sins, however, and his inordinate use of old movie film and his confusing the Greek and

Roman names of Odysseus and numerous other things in other episodes, if it were not for certain details: notorious bad acting, especially on the part of Whit Bissell, who in an effort to make the most of his meager role, often throws his shoulders back and yells, 'Clear the tunnel area!' Two dimensional characters are another fault, plus scripts turned out by the same assembly belt that is turning out Fords."

Alain Patrick as Claude.

The November 10, 1966, issue of the Connecticut *Meriden Journal* reviewed this episode in their TV Key Previews column: "It's another slam-bang adventure that the youngsters will enjoy."

An inter-office memo stated "Jerry Hopper will direct Episode 12 of *Voyage to the Bottom of the Sea* in lieu of his assignment to direct Episode 12 of *Time Tunnel*." (For the sum of $3,000).

BLOOPERS!

Immediately after the struggle on the sandy beach, sand and dirt stick to the back of Tony's uniform. In the next scene and the scenes that follow, the dirt and sand are no longer there.

For the viewers at the time with color television sets, it might be noted that the prisoners originally wore red and white striped uniforms in real fact but the producers thought they looked silly on screen and the outfits were changed for television purposes.

During a fight on the beach, Doug backs against a large rock that actually moves!

Tony gets tough before he realizes where he's landed.

RECURRING THEME

At the end of every episode, Doug and Tony always somehow reverted to the same cleaned, pressed clothes, as evident when landing in a new time. Once in a great while their clothes would revert back before transport. For Tony, a green turtleneck sweater and a pair of gray slacks. For Doug, a conservative Norfolk suit. Doug never takes off his tie (although he loosens it occasionally). Doug's clothes were originally meant for the 1912 Titanic, but the suit somehow changes to being contemporary style in future episodes.

PRODUCTION #9612
REIGN OF TERROR

INITIAL TELECAST: November 18, 1966
GUEST CAST: Whit Bissell (Querque); Howard Culver (the voice); Monique Lemaire (Marie Antoinette); Tiger Joe Marsh (the executioner); Louis Mercier (Antione Simon); Patrick Michenaud (Louis Joseph Xavier Francois, a.k.a. Dauphin); David Opatoshu (the shopkeeper); and Joey Tata (Napoleon Bonaparte).

PRODUCTION CREDITS
ART DIRECTORS: Jack Martin Smith and Rodger E. Maus
ASSISTANT DIRECTOR: Fred R. Simpson
DIRECTOR: Sobey Martin
FILM EDITOR: Dick Wormell
MUSIC: Leith Stevens
MUSIC EDITOR: Sam E. Levin
Teleplay by William Welch.

STORY: Tony and Doug find themselves stranded in 1793 Paris, towards the conclusion of the French Revolution. They meet a shopkeeper whose motive in hiding them is that since they're obviously foreigners, they must be here to help his Queen, Marie Antoinette, in whose service he is deeply involved. But while he is having them exchange their conspicuous apparel for citizen's sans-culottes, General Querque arrests him and takes him off to prison. Back at the Time Tunnel Complex, General Kirk allows a family heirloom, a ring, to receive the Radiation Bath and be sent back in time so the Time Tunnel staff can place a fix on Tony and Doug and bring them back. The ring, however, falls into the hands of Querque. As a result, the General, who bears a striking resemblance to General Kirk, is transported to the present. The mistake is soon corrected, after General Kirk receives his ring back. Doug and Tony, meanwhile, meet Marie Antoinette and agree to help her young son, Louis Francois, escape Paris and avoid the fate she is about to receive. Tony and Doug succeed and happen to brush past Napoleon Bonaparte, standing guard on the docks. After keeping the Corsican lieutenant spellbound with an account of his great destiny, and avoiding capture, Tony and Doug find themselves trapped, about to be shot when they quickly vanish into the vortex. Back at the Time Tunnel Complex, research reveals that a branch of General Kirk's family did live in France.

MUSIC SCORE BY LEITH STEVENS *(dated November 1, 1966):* Color Bumper (by Johnny Williams, :03); The Boiler Room (by Williams, :25); Opening (:29); Opening II (:29); Careful Citizen (2:12); Fight (:31); Main Title (a.k.a. Time Tunnel Theme, :37); Episode Titles (:27); Field Drums (:14); This Way (:27); The Way to Help (:36); This House (1:43); Try It (:25); King is Ready (1:56); It's Kirk (2:02); Temple of Justice (:37); The National

Whit Bissell in the dual role of General Querque.

Razor (1:04); Starling Resemblance (:20); No Pursuit (1:09); Come On (1:17); Escape (:29); Another Wagon Load (1:24); Bon Jour (:47); Bonaparte (2:37); Shoot Them (:26); The Boiler Room (by Williams, :18); Bleeker St. East (by Robert Drasnin, 2:13); End Credits (a.k.a. Time Tunnel Theme, by Williams, :48); and Fox I.D. (by Alfred Newman, :05).

HISTORICAL MISTAKES

It was mentioned in this episode that Marie Antoinette was executed on October 15, 1793. She was really executed on October 16.

By 1793, Napoleon Bonaparte was already a commander of artillery and was famously engaged in the siege of Toulon, and would not have been in Paris.

Young Louis was referred to as Dauphin, a title he no longer had after 1791.

NOTES

The back story about Kirk's ring was never fully explained — even in the original shooting script. Where did he originally get the ring from?

Patrick Michenaud is the older brother of Gerald Michenaud, the young boy who befriended Doug on board the *Titanic* in the pilot episode. Patrick was the young child who picked up the "Spindrift" in the pilot episode of *Land of the Giants*.

Ex-wrestling champion Tiger Joe Marsh appears in this episode in silhouette only, as the executioner of Marie Antoinette.

"Irwin put a big ad in the trade papers that read, 'Irwin Allen is looking for Napoleon!'," recalled actor Joey Tata. "I'm thinking, 'I gotta get a chance at this.' I asked Larry Stewart, the casting director, for the role but Larry and Irwin didn't feel I was right for it. So I called up Larry using a French accent. He told me to come in. When he saw me, he said, 'Joey! It's you!' Larry called up Irwin and gave me the phone. I pretended I was an actor named Pierre and did my French accent for Irwin. He invited me to his office. When I walked in, he looked up from his desk and said, 'Tat? You were the actor doing the accent? You conned me! You crazy actor. Get outta here. You've got the part.'"

If the European streets in this episode look familiar, it's because they were used for a number of other episodes, including the next one, "Secret Weapon." The same street at the Fox Studio was also used for the all the evening stock shots of the Black Beauty on *The Green Hornet*.

"It was fun being in both the present and the past," recalled Whit Bissell. "The director knew what he was doing. I remember they put white tape on the floor to mark my spot. I stood in the spot and promised not to move about and someone read the lines to me and I responded. Then I changed costumes and hair and stood in the other spot and the same fellow — I cannot recall who it was — read the lines I just spoke and I delivered the lines he spoke to me a moment before. And that's how I was able to play two roles in the lab."

Howard Culver was on the set, providing the voice double for the split screen discussions between Whit Bissell's two selves.

Stock footage originates from *The Purple Mask* (1955), starring Tony Curtis, a Napoleonic adventure.

THE CRITICS HAVE THEIR SAY

The Milwaukee Journal reviewed, "the period's sense of terror is nicely captured in this segment." (The same critic for the *Journal* made an error and claimed Whit Bissell doubled for the role of the shop keeper who helps Doug and Tony.) *The Pittsburg Press* remarked: "*Time Tunnel* is much bloodier this week than usual."

General Querque watches the past displayed in front of him.

BLOOPER!

The lamp post during the fight sequence after Doug and Tony help Dauphin escape, is apparently not stationary. It moves and wobbles freely when the actors are fighting in the street.

The muzzle loaders require reloading before firing a second shot but for the sake of speeding up the action, have a repeating feature.

Whit Bissell in the dual role of General Querque.

PRODUCTION #9605
SECRET WEAPON

INITIAL TELECAST: November 25, 1966
REVISED FINAL SHOOTING SCRIPT DATED: July 13, 1966 with revised pages dated July 18.
DATES OF PRODUCTION: July 18, 19, 20, 21, 22 and 25, 1966
FILMING LOCATIONS: Stage 5, Stage 6, Stage 8, Stage 18, Stage 19 and Stage 20
GUEST CAST: Michael Ansara (Hruda); Russell Conway (General Parker); Gregory Gay (Alexis); Sam Groom (Jerry); Kevin Hagen (McDonnell); and Nehemiah Persoff (Biraki).

Stunt Doubles
Frank Graham (double for Tony)
Paul Stader (double for Doug)
Buddy Vanhorn (security guard and double for Alexis)
Dale Van Sickel (security guard)

PRODUCTION CREDITS
ART DIRECTORS: Jack Martin Smith and Rodger E. Maus
ASSISTANT DIRECTOR: Fred R. Simpson
DIRECTOR: Sobey Martin
FILM EDITOR: Axel Hubert
MUSIC: Paul Sawtell
MUSIC EDITOR: Sam E. Levin
Teleplay by Theodore Apstein.

STORY: In his interview with General Parker, Dr. Biraki offers his services as a Time Tunnel expert to the U.S. He claims to have built a machine in his country but did not realize he was serving the wrong political cause. General Parker, hoping to establish the validity of Biraki's claim, requests the time travelers check the background of the doctor when they land in Russia in June of 1956. Meeting a man named Alexis, they are mistaken for a pair of scientists who are to be escorted in the morning to Project A-13. Arriving there the next day, the project turns out to be a primitive replica of a time tunnel, presided over by a Dr. Biraki, some ten years younger than the one who spoke to General Parker. Dr. Biraki, expecting spies Smith and Williams, takes Doug and Tony as compatriots and urges them to have a good look at the tunnel. They learn that Biraki means to send the travelers through the time capsule, a technique which means certain death, and they have been chosen to make the test flight. The result is disastrous — Tony and Doug are nearly killed as the forces from the two tunnels tear at them. Later, Biraki and Hruda overhear the boys talking about the lack of a radiation bath and hold them prisoner until they construct one. The two get to work, but instead make the tunnel explode. Biraki thinks they are dead, but in effect they have just ejected themselves into the time vortex, while back in 1968, Biraki's scheme to learn how far the United States has come with their own time travel device is foiled and Central Intelligence puts a trace on their unwanted visitor.

MUSIC SCORE BY PAUL SAWTELL *(dated September 27, 1966):* Color Bumper (by Johnny Williams, :03); Falling (by Williams, :23); Unfriendly Atmosphere (2:29); Main Title (a.k.a. Time Tunnel Theme, :36); Secret Weapon (:49); Message Received (2:25); Footsteps in the Dark (:10); The Boy's Introduction (1:23); An Impressive Creation (:35); They Will Do (:19); Total Surprise (:10); U.S. Intelligence (:18); Very Extra Ordinary (:34); The Death Seats (1:10); Boy Attempts to Escape (1:05); Bumper (a.k.a. Time Tunnel Theme, by Williams, :03); A Fool (:07); Trying to Signal (1:05); Traitor Alexis (:25); The Fade Out (:36); Deceitful Alexis (:29); The Name (:07); Baraki is Lying (:32); The Long Count Down (2:59); Between Time (1:44); Survival in Limbo (1:30); Place is Bugged (:43); Try it Again (:13); Count Down (2:46); Boys Survived (:33); Falling (:04); Act Out (:04); End Credits (a.k.a. Time Tunnel Theme, by Williams, :48); and Fox I.D. (by Alfred Newman, :05).

EPISODE BUDGET

Story Rights & Expense $1,500	Sound $1,625
Scenario $5,808	Electrical $3,949
Producer $8,215	Mechanical Effects $1,745
Direction $3,000	Set Dressing $5,204
Cast $14,390	Animals & Action Devices $0
Extras $4,841	Women's Wardrobe $829
Music $450	Men's Wardrobe $1,529
Staff $3,121	Makeup & Hairdressing $1,161
Art $1,900	Process $285
Sets $8,430	Production Film & Lab Charges
Operating Labor $5,158	$9,738
Miniatures $3,000	Stills $150
Camera $2,640	Transportation $2,900
	Re-recording $1,784

Photo Effects $1,893
Opticals, Fades & Dissolves $2,150
Titles $745
Post Production & Lab Charges
    $13,029
Projectionists $205
Editorial $5,875

Fringe Benefits $15,640
Miscellaneous $630
Amortizations $1,002
Contract Overhead $15,000
General Overhead $5,636
Total Picture Cost $155,157

Series Budget $168,907
Pre-Production Estimate $155,157
Under Budget $13,750

SET PRODUCTION COSTS
Foreign Street $1,200
Parker's Office and Outer Office $80
1956 Complex $305
Time Capsule $2,200
Time Capsule in Space $240
A-13 Room $715
Foremen $715
Amortization $2,000
Total $7,455

NOTES

After being turned down for a story proposal involving Christopher Columbus and his discovery of America in 1492, script writer Theodore Apstein realized how a cost-effective method would convince the story editor to purchase his plot proposal. "I drove home wondering how I could do a simple story for the series, and the idea of the travelers going to another time tunnel, using the same sets, was born," recalled Apstein to author Mark Phillips. "It was a quaint idea to use the time tunnel set-up in another country. America didn't have the exclusivity for building a time machine, and that has been true of other discoveries. I developed a simple story, but the producers were very noncommittal at first, with a 'Yes, that might be an interesting notion' to 'We'll go ahead with it.' I don't remember any particular enthusiasm, but they needed a script fast!"

Apstein was disappointed in the episode when he saw the finished product. Some things in the script had been cut out. "The basic concept of *Time Tunnel* was interesting, but they didn't always use the most exciting material. Their budgetary concerns got in the way."

The glass time capsule in this episode was reused as a possible time travel device in the episode, "Chase Through Time," and as the frog-alien's means of transport in the *Lost In Space* episode, "The Golden Man."

Michael Ansara really had his head shaved in this episode. No fake makeup. Ansara was playing the role of King Mongkut of Siam in *The King and I* on stage, a part which required his head to be shaved.

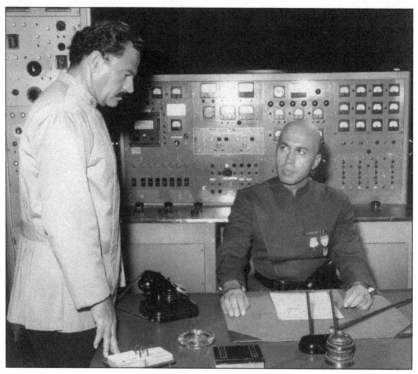

Biraki (Nehemiah Persoff) takes his orders from Hruda (Michael Ansara).

Theodore Apstein was paid $630 for his short story of the same name and $1,870 upon delivery of the first draft of the teleplay, and $1,500 upon delivery of the final draft of the teleplay (contract dated May 26, 1966). In the initial story proposal, Kirk communicates with the Government and is told that Doug and Tony could perform a great service if they can verify the scientist's pro-democratic views and ascertain whether the country really has an atomic weapon. The people in the Tunnel succeed in sending something of a message to Tony and Doug — enough to alert them to continue participating in the escape plans of the group of people they've been with. It turns out that the scientist is, indeed, one of the group. It is his invention which has given the atomic weapon to his country, but when he realizes that such proliferation will lead to an all-out war, he wants to destroy his own creation. After innumerable barriers are gradually removed, and after going through considerable jeopardy, Tony and Doug help the scientist destroy the atomic weapon and get out of the country. These actions prove the scientist's trustworthiness and the fact that his country lacks the atomic weapon it claims (and can make no others without his presence, since he was the only expert on nuclear fission in the country).

Michael Ansara during a break between scenes.

The premise was then revised on June 3, 1966, when Apstein expanded and revised his plot proposal. Tony and Doug are relaxing on a beach. No sooner have they learned that they're now in 1956 than a glowing silver bar materializes next to them on the sand. In the same manner as the filmed episode, Tony lets out a cry of pain, and Doug sees that Tony can't disengage himself from the bar. Thanks to Doug, Tony is saved and a few seconds later, the bar disintegrates. A second bar appears on the same beach, and explodes in front of Doug and Tony. On a street in a foreign city, Tony and Doug hesitate when they see a third glowing silver bar. But they can't ignore it either, realizing by now that the Tunnel must be very anxious to get in touch with them. This time the bar begins to smoke and burn, but it does leave a half-burned message behind. Tony and Doug learn they're supposed to take the place of defecting scientists from the West, and the message briefs them of their mission. In the complex, Biraki explains how the Russians are trying to create their own time machine, and wants to know the extent of their knowledge. Biraki's two associates — a military man named Hruda and a woman scientist (Clara) — are in conflict with Biraki over these two defectors. Hruda wants to use native talent, but Biraki insists that none of his countrymen are qualified for the special assignment he has in mind for the boys. Clara questions Tony and Doug, attempting to confuse them, but

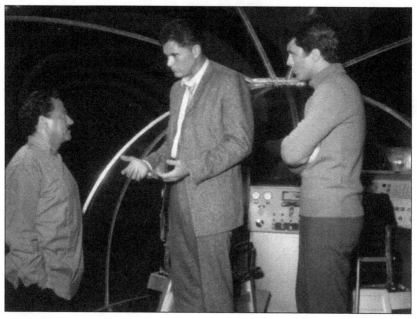

Doug and Tony try to convince Biraki that his time travel scheme won't work.

they manage to put her down. The remainder of the story pretty much goes the way of the filmed version.

Naturally, the character of Clara was eliminated, no doubt to cut salary costs. Jerry Briskin's notes after reading the first draft, dated June 13, 1966, suggested another cost cutting measure: "The idea of them landing in the Time Tunnel Complex (1956) could be very exciting and would solve many problems script wise. Especially if Washington had requested that an attempt be made to send the boys back to this particular time and place. This would make it possible to eliminate the beach and foreign street and café sets entirely."

"Working for Irwin Allen was no different than working for any producer," recalled Nehemiah Persoff. "I got the call to play a role on *Voyage to the Bottom of the Sea* which, as you know, was his first television series. I recall playing the role over the top and the episode involved a two-headed monster. The

director wanted over the top. Somehow Irwin must have loved it because the next thing I knew, I was being asked to play a role on his new series, *The Time Tunnel*. I do not recall what the reason was, or if there was a problem on the set, but Irwin Allen replaced the director for a brief spell. I think word reached his office that we were behind in filming and one scene was taking too long to film. He directed that sequence within…I guess it was 15

James Darren prepares for the shot.

minutes. Then he handed the reigns over to the director and went back to his office. I never saw him again. I was hoping it was not something I did wrong. Sometime after that I was asked to appear on *Land of the Giants* so it must have been the director."

The Daily Reporter, a newspaper in Ohio, reviewed this episode as "an exciting but pretty far-fetched episode…it's a wild, confusing and suspenseful episode, with a fine acting job by Mr. Persoff."

ABC CENSORSHIP CONCERNS

Delete business of burning palms with live cigarette.

The scene can go out with idea that Tony and Doug are going to be "worked over" for the information, but please no "torture device" in the scene.

BLOOPERS!

While Doug and Tony are talking to Alexis, receiving their assignment, James Darren's voice is dubbed but his mouth is not moving!

Doug ponders what century they are in, but fails to observe an electric lamp on the outside of the building.

In the opening scene, television viewers can look in the glass with the Slav words in the background and for nearly 40 seconds, observe the figure of an extra cast member wearing the cap of a soldier. The actor was simply positioned to walk past Doug and Tony when he saw his cue, and the reflection is of the same actor.

When Doug and Tony first land in Russia, one of the signs is not in Russian or Slav, but rather "Noichi," the name of a town in Japan. The sign, however, is reversed and hung on the wall to confuse the viewers into believing they were in Russia. Why they thought this could be substituted for a European sign is beyond anyone's rational thinking.

If Project A-13 is supposed to be a top secret project, why are there signs outside the building stating "Project A-13"?

Doug searches for the "Secret Weapon."

PRODUCTION #9613
THE DEATH TRAP

INITIAL TELECAST: December 2, 1966
SHOOTING SCRIPT DATED: October 4, 1966, with revised pages dated October 6, 1966
DATES OF PRODUCTION: October 6, 7, 10, 11, 12 and 13, 1966
FILMING LOCATIONS: Desilu 40 Acres, Stage 18 and Stage 19
GUEST CAST: R. G. Armstrong (Allan Pinkerton); Dick Geary (Carver, a Pinkerton agent); Bill Graeff (conspirator #2 in night warehouse); Christopher Harris (David); Scott Marlowe (Jeremiah); Pat Murphy (conspirator #3 in night warehouse); Ford Rainey (Abraham Lincoln); George Robotham (Scot, a Pinkerton agent); Mark Russell (third Pinkerton man); Gene Silvani (conspirator #1 in night warehouse); and Tom Skerritt (Matthew).

Stunt Doubles
Paul Stader (double as Doug)
Frank Graham (double as Tony)
Denver Mattson (double as Jeremiah)

Stand-Ins
Sandy Lee Gimpel was the female stand-in for Tom Skerritt in this episode. Gimpel would later become the un-credited stunt woman for Lindsay Wagner on television's *The Bionic Woman*. Skip Burnham, Bill Graeff, Pat Murphy and Gene Silvani were the male stand-ins for the depot and street scenes.

PRODUCTION CREDITS
ART DIRECTORS: Jack Martin Smith and Rodger E. Maus
ASSISTANT DIRECTOR: Ted Butcher
DIRECTOR: William Hale
FILM EDITOR: Axel Hubert
MUSIC: Robert Drasnin
MUSIC EDITOR: Sam E. Levin
Teleplay by Leonard Stadd.

STORY: February 22, 1861. Tony and Doug whirl out of the time vortex into a dimly-lit barn where armed men, led by fanatic Jeremiah, are holding a meeting. Jeremiah means to kill Abraham Lincoln as he travels through Baltimore on the way to his Inauguration. Jeremiah's fear is that Lincoln will make peace with the seceding states in the South. His assassination will be blamed on Southern Secessionists, and the North will then attack the South, abolishing slavery. When the meeting is raided by Allan Pinkerton and his men, who have been tipped to the plot, Tony is knocked out by a raider and dragged off by Jeremiah and his brother Matthew, while Doug is captured by Pinkerton and interrogated at the railway depot nearby. Tony, meanwhile, unintentionally joins the group led by Jeremiah, a sympathizer of John Brown's gang at Harper's Ferry. Jeremiah reveals the time bomb created to blow up President-elect Abraham Lincoln, and Tony frees himself and runs to the station to give warning. In an attempt to pick up the bomb, the staff at the Time Tunnel Complex inadvertently pick up little David, Jeremiah's younger brother, and gives the young man a tool to jam the device. Young David is returned to his own time. After Tony and Doug convince Pinkerton of the real threat, the lawman allows the time travelers to help find the bomb and they succeed. Lincoln's train continues en route, pulling away from the depot and the time travelers vanish back into the vortex.

MUSIC SCORE BY ROBERT DRASNIN *(dated November 14, 1966):* Color Bumper (by Johnny Williams, :03); Falling (by Williams, :23); Two Drop In (1:11); The Assassins (:59); Fright, Flight, Fight (:45); Main Title (a.k.a. Time Tunnel Theme, by Williams, :37); Chapter and Verse (:58); Seeds of Doubt-Sounds (:49); Plea of Innocence (:57); Yellow Liver (:13); Frat Spat (1:12); Hat Bridge (:26); The Nation's Future (:40); Rabbit Rouser (:58); To Plant a Bomb (1:17); Under Guard (:17); Bumper (by Williams, :03); Here and There (2:17); That's Bomb Biz (1:28); Tunnel Trip (1:02); Saved and Disappear (by Lyn Murray, :33); Fear Will Out (:16); Tunnel of Slow Return (2:09); Brothers Apart (2:17); Key Bridge (:24); Bomb Steer (:27); Search and Find (:50); Sir Valence (:21); Bomb Warp (2:26); Bumper (by Williams, :03); Bleeker St. East (:17); What Now? (by Friedhofer, :17); Trouble For Us (by Lionel Newman, :17); First Test Part Two (by Leith Stevens, :17); No Pursuit (by Stevens, :17); Fight (by Stevens, :17); Someone Moved (by Newman, :17); Mine Trap #2 (by Murray, :08); End Credits (a.k.a. Time Tunnel Theme, by Williams, :38); and Fox I.D. (by Alfred Newman, :05).

EPISODE BUDGET

Story Rights and Expense $1,500	Cast $17,440
Scenario $5,808	Extras $3,054
Producer $7,215	Music $3,500
Direction $3,000	Staff $3,397
	Art $2,642

Sets $10,880
Operating Labor $5,089
Miniatures $3,000
Camera $3,044
Sound $1,625
Electrical $3,949
Mechanical Effects $1,272
Set Dressing $4,885
Animals and Action Devices $75
Women's Wardrobe $404
Men's Wardrobe $2,224
Makeup and hairdressing $1,751
Process $285
Production Film & Lab Charges
    $9,017
Stills $150

Transportation $3,261
Re-Recording $1,784
Photo Effects $1,900
Opticals, fades and Dissolves $2,150
Titles $745
Post production Film & Lab
    Charges $13,679
Projectionists $205
Editorial $5,875
Fringe Benefits $15,480
Miscellaneous $960
Amortizations $1,002
Contract Overhead $15,000
General Overhead $6,338
Total Picture Cost $163,585

Series Budget $167,757
Pre-Production Estimate $163,585
Under $4,172

SET PRODUCTION COSTS
Time Tunnel Control (they had to coat the lacquer floor) $225
Barn $500
Kitchen $1,300
Train Depot $350
Depot with Pot Bellied Stove $1,300
Dirt Streets and Shacks $350
Construction Foreman $605
Amortized $2,000
Total $6,630

HISTORICAL ERRORS

When Joan Crosby of *TV Scout* reviewed this episode, it was evident she was aware of the numerous historical errors in this episode. "There is more history and hokum to please series fans," she wrote. Among the errors it was mentioned that the train carrying President-elect Abraham Lincoln was en route to Washington, D.C., stopping momentarily in Northern Baltimore, having come direct from Philadelphia. The train actually came from Harrisburg, not Philadelphia.

The real threat to Lincoln has never been discovered, and Pinkerton himself swore a number of assassins armed with knives hoped to get close enough to Lincoln to stab him. There is nothing in the history books to verify a time bomb was ever created.

While Jeremiah's last name was never disclosed in this episode, John Brown had a number of sympathizers, including Jeremiah Goldsmith

Ford Rainey getting makeup applied to look like Abraham Lincoln.

Anderson, who was killed during the storming of John Brown's Fort.

It was pointed out (in the script) that dynamite was not used in 1861. Research shows the U.S. patent was granted in 1868. Black powder was used before dynamite. During pre-production, there was a careful attempt to make sure the clock (the timing device) not have any wires, which would have indicated electricity.

ABC CENSORSHIP CONCERNS

Usual caution that any material indicated as historical fact is accurate. Please be sure that there is any needed legal clearance for the representation of Pinkerton and his men, particularly if they appear in rather a poor light.

The rifles can be close to, but not pressed against, the head or chin.

Delete slap on pages 16, 17 and 18, and modify "Trying to beat it out of me"; "I'm considering beating the truth out of you" and "get to work on him."

Since Jeremiah has frantically plotted assassination and advocated killing throughout, please indicate "change" or retribution more clearly.

Ford Rainey takes his place for the camera.

STORY DEVELOPMENT

Amidst the censorship concerns, one scene was never altered but ultimately ended up on the cutting room floor. "Irwin Allen was always surrounded by his mafia," script writer Leonard Stadd recalled to Mark Phillips. "There was his cousin, Al Gail, who was a very nice man, and associate producer Frank La Tourette, who taught at UCLA, and Jerry Briskin, another associate producer.

Jerry's father had been a big name in the early days of film, and Jerry has remained the son of an old-time producer. Jerry was basically a functionary. I would give him a script to read and he would give me 78 notes on my script like, 'This should be a comma on page 36 and you've used a colon.' I'm not exaggerating. It was all kinds of crap, mainly production notes of no consequence to me. He never cared whether you used his input or not."

Part of Briskin's job was to ensure the scripts did not lack continuity or implausible details the audience might find offbeat. On September 27, 1966, for example, Jerry Briskin addressed a number of concerns in an inter-office memo to Irwin Allen. "For a person who is attempting to kill the President of the United States with either a bomb or a rifle, Jeremiah certainly appears to be running a lot in broad daylight. I don't think he is particularly clever in his approach to murder...Page 15, scene 45. This is the first time Pinkerton's name is mentioned and, therefore, how did Doug know Pinkerton's name? It seems to me that Pinkerton should have more of an introduction in this script."

"In 'Death Trap,' you had a President who was ultimately going to be assassinated," continued Stadd, "and these kids [Tony and Doug] knew it. So after they're captured at the railroad station, there was a bit in my script where Lincoln is told that these boys contend they're from the future, a couple of nuts. To tweak them, Lincoln says, 'Well, if you're from the future, then you must know what will happen to me.' Naturally, that's the first thing you would ask. Tony and Doug can't tell him that he's going to be killed because that would be tampering with history. So, there was a marvelous page-and-a-half of dialogue where you see their hearts breaking because they can't tell him. It was good drama. That scene was crossed out."

In the same inter-office memo, Briskin wrote: "Pages 27 to 31, Doug-Lincoln scenes read like an old history lesson. They are not, in my opinion, very entertaining scenes…When the re-write is done, I would like to see all of the dialogue sharpened."

"During the filming, the director, Billy Hale, asked me down to the set to discuss the script," continued Stadd, "and he said, 'Look, there was a great scene between Lincoln and the boys. What happened to it?' I laughed and said it was probably cut for time. 'But it belongs here!' Bill said, 'For God's sake, it makes the script do something!' So, Bill called up Irwin and minutes later, Irwin and a couple of guys came running down the hall saying, 'What's happening? What's this all about?' Bill explained the missing scene to Irwin and Irwin passed a copy of the script to me and said, 'Read the scene to me, Len.' So I did and Irwin said, 'Jesus! That's just quibbling, Bill. This is a running-and-jumping show!' Then, he and his guys ran back down the hall. That's how Irwin operated. He didn't give a crap about the content of a scene. To him, it was a running-and-jumping show and he didn't go for quibbling. It's really too bad, because Irwin has many opportunities to do more thematic scripts and if he had, *Time Tunnel* might still be on today."

As a result, Lincoln's concern for the future was dismissed after his initial talk with Doug and Tony. Toward the end of the episode, after Lincoln has been saved and Jeremiah arrested, Pinkerton commented something about how maybe Lincoln was right. It was a line not featured in the original script and remains a mystery to this day whether the actor ad-libbed or if the director wrote the line himself. "It was out of tone with my style," recalled Stadd, " and it was absolutely ridiculous in terms of character and the story itself."

"Everyone has done the 1865 Ford Theater thing," recalled Stadd to author Mark Phillips. "It was more interesting to do a story on the little-known assassination attempt in 1861. I'd written a play in New York, *The Trial of Mary Todd Lincoln*, so I had done research on him. Lincoln wasn't the way people always remember him, in his black suit and top hat. I've seen pictures of him in white suits with gambling hats on. He was an interesting man, and I had a great deal of respect for him. But in *Time Tunnel*, there wasn't room for deep characterization. I mean, the stories were about Tony and Doug lost in time, they weren't about Lincoln. So, there he was, in his black suit and top hat."

When the Time Tunnel Complex personnel transported the old-fashioned bomb to 1968, they accidentally picked up young David by mistake. "I worked that out with Arthur Weiss," Stadd continued. "You had to do

something with the tunnel. You were always so static with it, and the characters were always saying, 'Lock in the coordinates,' and all this gibberish.
So we came up with the idea of this kid who picks up the bomb and he's
brought into the tunnel. I saw another episode where the tunnel accidentally
brought back some guy with a big sword, and he ran out trying to slaughter
everybody!"

Leonard Stadd was paid $3,345 for his story and teleplay. $655 for his
original story, $2,100 upon completion of the first draft of the teleplay and
$1,245 for the final draft.

Cast Suggestions
Lincoln: John Anderson and Ford Rainey
Pinkerton: Charles Aidman, Henry Beckman, De Forest Kelley and
Larry D. Mann
Jeremiah: John Drew Barrymore, James Broderick, John Crawford,
Scott Marlowe and Fritz Weaver
Matthew: Geoffrey Horne and Wayne Rogers

NOTES

When David is sent back to 1861 with the time bomb, the tool kit still
remains in the tunnel. Why didn't the tool kit travel through time?

Ford Rainey had previously played the role of a U.S. President in the pilot
episode of *Lost In Space* and on two episodes of *Voyage to the Bottom of the Sea.*

Jerry Briskin did not approve of the assassination scene on the Time
Tunnel viewing screen, early in the episode. Briskin wrote to Allen on
September 27, 1966: "I believe the stock footage of Lincoln's assassination
should be introduced deeper into the script. Furthermore, as now written,
if the stock is used as presently written, I think the viewers are going to be
confused because the action following the stock film is written as a continu-
ous scene. Personally, I would like to see the assassination used later on in
the story and at a time when the Tunnel group might be attempting to take
action to save Tony or Doug."

Ironically, Jerry Briskin, best known for removing characters from scripts
before they went to production so salary costs could be cut down, wrote to
Irwin Allen in the same letter, after reviewing the script. "I feel that Pinkerton
is a stupid, arrogant man. He is not even smart enough to have the required
number of security guards around to protect Lincoln at the train, the exterior
of the depot or the interior of the depot. If Pinkerton didn't have enough
guards of his own, it seems to me he would have brought in local police for
added protection."

Supposedly this script was based on material found in the book, *Reader's Digest Best Loved Books, Volume* 4. The hardcover was published in 1966 and featured abridged versions of four novels: *The Hunchback of Notre Dame*, *Lost Horizon, Great Cases of Sherlock Holmes* and *Abe Lincoln Grows Up*. Carl Sandburg's book, however, does not feature any reference to the attempted assassination.

Veteran actor Ford Rainey played the role of Abraham Lincoln in this episode. Rainey was fast becoming the country's leading portrayer of Lincoln in television and film, and this Time Tunnel segment was supposedly his 13th appearance before the cameras as the beloved President. But the role almost didn't come about, recalled Rainey. "I had just finished a western feature at another studio, *Gunpoint*, which required that I have long hair, which coincidentally, would have been just right for the part of Lincoln. The comparatively long hair Lincoln had is a real necessity for an actor to convincingly fill the role. But before I got the role on *Time Tunnel*, I was on my way to the barber shop to get my long hair cut when the phone rang. It was producer Irwin Allen, with the offer to play Lincoln on his *Time Tunnel* series. Irwin called me just in time! So I ended having just the right length of hair to portray Lincoln. That was important, because the makeup men in Hollywood can do wonderful things but they have never been able to fit me with any kind of a wig convincingly and have it look like Lincoln's hair. I have always had to rely on my own hair. So things worked out well for *Time Tunnel*." The behind-the-scenes photographs, included in this book, suggest otherwise. Ford Rainey's comments in the studio press release may not have been accurate (as in the case of the "King Tut" episode).

WILLIAM HALE

When William Hale signed on as director on June 2, 1966, he signed on for three episodes, this being one of them. He ultimately directed four episodes. After reviewing the dailies, Jerry Briskin wrote to director William Hale on October 11, 1966, suggesting a few shots that would make this episode fresh and inventive. "The following are the shots that I spoke to you about yesterday and which I feel are necessary for 'The Death Trap.' Scenes 160 and 161 — This is the shot through the spokes of a wheel. We should have a close-up of Matthew speaking to Jeremiah and a close up of Jeremiah reacting and debating to what Matthew has to say. For scenes 169 and 170, we need a close up of Matthew telling Jeremiah to kill him (Matthew) and a tight two-shot of Tony and Doug reacting to the situation between the two brothers. For scenes 154 and 155, we need a close-up of Doug to cover his dialogue. For scene 141, we should have a close-up reaction of David Watching Jeremiah and Matthew fighting.

BLOOPERS!

When Jeremiah introduces to Tony the bomb he created, and places it on the table, the small hand on the timing device points to XII. Seconds later, the needle reads IX, before Jeremiah moves it to XII.

While being tied up by Matthew, Tony is arguing with Jeremiah, who backhands him across the face. But Jeremiah raises his right hand, then the camera angle changes to show him hitting Tony with his left hand.

When Ford Rainey makes his initial appearance as Abraham Lincoln in this episode, stepping down off the train, the reflection of a microphone can be seen on the window of the box car.

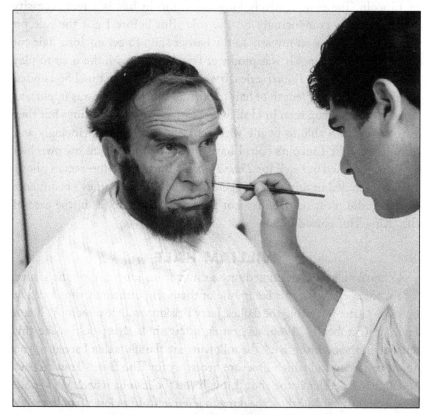

Ford Rainey getting makeup applied to look like Abraham Lincoln.

THE ALAMO

INITIAL TELECAST: December 9, 1966
SHOOTING SCRIPT DATED: October 13, 1966
DATES OF PRODUCTION: October 14, 17, 18, 19, 20 and 21, 1966
FILMING LOCATIONS: Desilu 40 Acres, Stage 18 and Stage 19
GUEST CAST: Edward Colmans (Dr. Armandez); Jim Davis (Colonel James Bowie); Orwin C. Harvey (a sentry); Rodolfo Hoyos (Captain Rodriguez); John Lupton (Captain Reynerson); Alberto Monte (Sergeant Garcia); Rhodes Reason (Colonel William B. Travis); Elizabeth Rogers (Mrs. Reynerson); Virginia Semon (female in the Alamo); and Fred Stromsoe (a sentry).

Stunt Doubles
Paul Stader (double for Doug)
Chuck Waters (stunt Sentry and double for Bowie)
Eddie Saenz (stunt Sentry)
Frank Graham (double for Tony)

PRODUCTION CREDITS
ART DIRECTORS: Jack Martin Smith and Rodger E. Maus
ASSISTANT DIRECTOR: Fred R. Simpson
DIRECTOR: Sobey Martin
FILM EDITOR: James Baiotto
MUSIC: stock
MUSIC EDITOR: Sam E. Levin
Teleplay by Bob and Wanda Duncan.

STORY: March 6, 1836. Tony and Doug find themselves taking refuge from Mexican snipers, and manage to get to the shelter of a nearby fort, being let in by Captain Reynerson, who thinks they are bringing word of reinforcements to come. Under the same impression is the current commander of the fort, Colonel Travis, who comes to question them. Recognizing the names mentioned, the boys discover they are at The Alamo, just hours before it will fall to Santa Anna. Colonel Travis, ignoring Tony's pleas to let the wounded escape before the impending attack, places Doug and Tony under arrest. Tony escapes to seek a doctor to treat Doug, who has been injured during a scuffle, since the fort surgeon is dead. At the Time Tunnel Complex, Colonel Travis is accidentally transported to the present and General Kirk explains the scenario. Faced with the scientists and flashing consoles, he doubts all that is told him until he's shown the actual outcome of the battle for the Alamo — and his own death. Then he insists on going back to meet his fate. With his promise to free Doug, he is returned to the fort. Tony arrives with a doctor, who begins treating the wounded, and manages to save the life of Mrs. Reynerson, a nurse. Just as the Mexicans are storming the fort, Doug and Tony vanish.

STOCK MUSIC: Color Bumper (by Johnny Williams, :03); The Boiler Room (by Williams, :27); Fight (by Leith Stevens, :19); No Pursuit (by Stevens, :19); First Test Part Two (by Stevens, :19); Trouble for Us (by Lionel Newman, :19); What Now? (by Friedhofer, :19); A Dark Night (by Newman, :19); Urgent Detergent (by Newman, :19); Another Wagon Load (by Stevens, :47); Die Brave (by Joseph Mullendore, :32); Main Title (a.k.a. Time Tunnel Theme, by Williams, :37); Alternate Drums (by Newman, 1:02); Complex Problem (by Robert Drasnin, :12); The Take Off (by Paul Sawtell, :12); The Death Seats (by Sawtell, :37); Trying to Remember (by Sawtell, :37); The Boys' Escape (by Sawtell, :57); The Long Count Down (by Sawtell, 1:22 and :13); The Boys' Escape (by Sawtell, :13); The Bombing (by Sawtell, :13); Paternal Squeeze (by Drasnin, :23); Me Worry? (by Drasnin, :23); Tidal Wave (by Drasnin, :23); The Boys Survived (by Sawtell, :21); The Death Seats (by Sawtell, :23); Sky Full of Planes (by Sawtell, :23); Two Sentries (by Lyn Murray, :09); U.S. Intelligence (by Sawtell, ::09); The Long Count Down (by Sawtell, :49); Jerry Collapse (by Murray, :49); Tony Remembers (by Sawtell, :05); Bumper (by Williams, :03); Lee in Action (by Hugo Friedhofer, :29); Rescue (by Friedhofer, :29); It's Kirk (by Stevens, :29); Escape (by Stevens, :31); Lee In Action (by Friedhofer, :31); First Test Part Two (by Stevens, :28); Fight (by Stevens, :28); The Paperhanger is Still Alive (by Daniele Amfitheatrof, :28); Coda (by Stevens, :28); Rescue (by Friedhofer, :28); Baraki is Lying (by Sawtell, :34); Voice in the Sky (by Drasnin, :34); Louise's Discovery (by Sawtell, :34); Voice in the Sky (by Drasnin, :29); Complex Problem (by Drasnin, :29); Bring Him Back (by Stevens, :06); Death of Christian (by Friedhofer, 1:01); The Paperhanger is Still Alive (by Amfitheatrof, :12); What Now? (by Friedhofer, :12); No Exit (by Alexander Courage, :12); Count Down General (by Murray, :09); Yellow Elk 96 (by Mullendore, :09); A Dark Night (by Newman, :09); Field Drums (by Newman, :03); One of Ulysses' Guards (by Stevens, :07); Field Drums (by Newman, :05); A Dark Night (by Newman, :23); Saved and Disappear (by Lyn Murray, :04); Battle (by Mullendore, :39); Someone Moved (by Newman, :39); Battle (by Mullendore, :39); Death of Christian (by Friedhofer, :23); A Dark Night (by

Newman, :23); More Trouble (by Newman, :23); Time Transfer (by Williams, :03); The Boiler Room (by Williams, :13); The Paperhanger is Still Alive (by Amfitheatrof, :45); Rescue (by Friedhofer, :45); Next Week (by Murray, :45); End Credits (a.k.a. Time Tunnel Theme, by Williams, :48); and Fox I.D. (by Alfred Newman, :05).

EPISODE BUDGET
Story Rights and Expense $1,500
Scenario $5,808
Producer $7,215
Direction $3,000
Cast $17,925
Extras $7,256
Music $3,500
Staff $3,121
Art $2,642
Sets $11,013
Operating Labor $5,019
Miniatures $3,000
Camera $3,306
Sound $1,625
Electrical $3,949
Mechanical Effects $1,375
Set Dressing $4,906
Animals and Action Devices $340
Women's Wardrobe $404
Men's Wardrobe $4,244

Makeup and Hairdressing $1,581
Process $285
Production Film & Lab Charges
$9,017
Stills $150
Transportation $3,622
Re-Recording $1,784
Photo Effects $1,560
Opticals, Fades and Dissolves
$2,150
Titles $745
Post Production Film & Lab
Charges $14,729
Projectionists $205
Editorial $5,875
Fringe Benefits $15,390
Miscellaneous $1,770
Amortizations $1,002
Contract Overhead $15,000
General Overhead $7,652
Total Picture Cost $173,665

Series Budget $167,757
Pre-Production Estimate $173,665
Over $5,908

SET PRODUCTION COSTS
Exterior of Alamo Compound $2,815*
Interior Storeroom $1,320
Exterior Western Street $400
Interior Rodriguez Room $1,385

---

* Includes wood gates, rough boards, fire and kettle, platforms, flatbed wagon, stairs, doors and cannon.

Exterior Campfire Area $500
Stove and Scaffold $1,630
Construction Foreman $963
Amortized $2,000
Total $11,013

NOTES

A good view of the Time Tunnel Control panels are presented in this episode, revealing the fact that the panels changed from one episode to another throughout the series.

Contrary to written books and websites, footage from John Wayne's *The Alamo* was not used for this episode. Stock footage originates from *The Last Command*, a Republic Pictures production shot in TruColor. Footage of actor Arthur Hunnicutt as Davy Crockett, blowing up the gunpowder so the Mexicans did not get it, is seen in this episode — footage that never made it to the final cut of the movie.

Once Tony is outside the Alamo, location shots were filmed in the same Western Street used for the prior episode, "The Death Trap." The light green barn with the shrubbery remains in the background as the Mexican rides his cart into town, with Tony in the back. The alley where Tony hides behind wooden crates and bales of cotton is the same place Doug and Tony met up with David and a wounded Matthew in the same episode.

This episode fails to explain exactly how Tony and the doctor arrived back at the Alamo after his departure, especially since the fort was being stormed by thousands of Mexicans at the time.

Playing the role of Colonel James Bowie was actor Jim Davis, the epitome of the Old West. Of the more than 150 Westerns in which Davis appeared, 14 of them had a Jim Bowie character and 11 of those Bowies were played by Davis himself. "I should have learned something from playing Bowie so often; but I'm afraid I haven't," he told a reporter for the *Schenectady Gazette*. "At home I'm so unprofessional with a knife that my wife doesn't let me anywhere near the table until the roast is carved. In fact, I arrived at the studio 10 minutes late for my first day as Bowie on *The Time Tunnel*. I had cut myself shaving."

"My wife and I visited San Antonio last year and seeing the real-life Alamo was quite an experience," Rhodes Reason recalled to Mark Phillips. "I wanted to find the exact location where Col. Travis has been killed in battle. I located it at the northeast corner and said to my wife, in a rather loud voice, 'This is where I was killed!' That brought a few surprised stares from people. People thought I had gone around the bend."

"Going back in time and depicting historical events accurately was both educational and entertaining," Reason continued. "That juxtaposition of history and how it might be changed by people from the future was interesting to watch. The scene where Colonel Travis is bought into the future and witnesses his own demise on the time tunnel's screen is such an occurrence. Before the scene began, I had to stand in the tunnel with my eyes closed and

Tony tries to speak reason to Colonel Travis.

my hands covering my ears. After the tunnel's explosions went off behind me, with the giant arc lights flashing. I walked through the smoke, into the tunnel's laboratory, where I expressed Travis' bewilderment of being in the future."

Critics had mixed feelings about this episode, which avoided the use of the Davy Crockett character (possibly because Fess Parker's portrayal had already been well-accepted by television viewers). Joan Crosby of *TV Scout* reviewed: "There is a lot of exciting action in this one, with stalwart performances by the actors playing Texas heroes like Colonel Travis (Rhodes Reason) and Col. Bowie (Jim Davis)." A columnist for *The Modesto Bee*, a California newspaper, recommended this episode for viewing.

COST CUTTING MEASURES

Bob and Wanda Duncan were paid $4,000 for their story and the first and final draft of the teleplay. Utilizing stock footage from one of four movies depicting the Alamo, shot in color, would have made this episode easy to produce. But production ran over more than $3,000 and, plot-wise, network concerns over violence and Jerry Briskin's concern over the number of actors required to pull it off (not to mention limited use of sets) hampered the production. What could have been one of the more exciting episodes of the series ultimately finished with plot holes and mistakes that even the casual viewer could not have overlooked.

On October 11, 1966, Jerry Briskin wrote to Irwin Allen proposing changes to the first draft. "In scenes 43-45, eliminate sentry falling off platform. Also eliminate other fights in these scenes and just have soldiers stop Tony from doing anything further by pointing their guns at him and threatening his life...Scene 282. Soldiers don't fall off of platform, they collapse on platform. At the same time, Reynerson does not get blown off of platform but staggers down the stairs and finally collapses."

To cut further costs, Les Warner suggested in a memo to Irwin Allen a number of other script revisions. "The three Mexicans that Bowie fights are now reduced to one Mexican who is shot by Bowie, but fires and kills Bowie before he drops. The wounded man tripping Tony with his crutch is deleted. Tony now just stumbles...As Reynerson comes down off the wall and heads toward Tony and Doug he passes Mrs. Reynerson, who is emergency bandaging a man. He says to her, 'Have him taken to the infirmary area,' plays rest of scene as is — but leaving her still bandaging the man, and crosses to Tony and Doug. In other words, play down the injured man's business and delete the other two men...Scenes 71-83. Cut the three men with Bowie to two men and have only one of the men mount the wall to fire after Tony... Scene B-162. Delete the guard's coming into the room. The timing should still be logical that Tony could get out before the guard could enter, and we don't want to tie him in with a location exterior set and a stage interior set... Scenes 163, 164. Re-write to cut Tony's fight with the guard down to a single blow that kayo's him. This will reduce the guard from an S.A.G. fighter to an adjusted extra — and we have certainly had enough preceding action to justify this...Scene 203. In this and various other preceding scenes, Mexican horsemen are referred to. I would have no more than two Mexican riders on this set and double them over, by changing appearance with moustaches, etc."

Warner summed it up nicely when he remarked, "There are very few final battle scenes now left in the script that we have to shoot as most of the action is now stock, and I believe that any further deletions would materially hurt the climax. If we are still in trouble, and we very well may be, then I would suggest completely eliminating Tony and Doug's fight that prompts Travis to have them jailed in the storeroom (scenes 43-45) and have this motivated through dialogue conflict between Travis and our boys."

Production was still technical, with the company loading the trucks with equipment on Thursday night, so they would be ready on Friday morning.

General Kirk has a better time speaking reason to Colonel Travis.

Generators were needed to power the cameras and lights on location at Desilu 40 Acres. Seventeen stand-ins were needed for the first day of filming, including 12 Texans, four Mexicans and one woman. Two Mexican stuntmen were needed. For the second day of filming, 12 Texans and three Sentries were needed. On the third day, 12 Texans and 12 Mexicans were required. Nineteen stand-ins were required on day six alone.

Regardless of the efforts to maintain budget control, the budget for salaries was $17,440; the salaries for this episode ran over $785. The series budget allowed for $10,675 maximum for set costs; it ran over $338.

ABC CENSORSHIP CONCERNS

Violence on television is always a concern, especially when production is set at the Alamo. This was the first episode in which Doug actually kills a person. During the attack on the fort, Doug picks up a rifle and shoots two

Mexicans dead. ABC, reviewing the first draft of the script, sent a lengthy list of suggestions to tame the violence factor. A few of their concerns are listed below.

Caution that fights are not overly brutal or unnecessarily prolonged. Please telescope where possible. Of course, no close up of blows with rifles, log, etc.

The knife cuts only clothing.

In the interest of not putting the Mexican people in a seeming unfair light: clarification of the idea of the American-Mexican territorial war, per our discussion, as opposed to "slaughter."

Generally, caution that the Mexican men are not portrayed in "stereotype."

Liquor, wine bottle not identifiable as to actual trade/brand names.

HISTORICAL ERRORS

The final assault came before daybreak on the morning of March 6, 1836, as Mexican soldiers emerged from the predawn darkness and headed for the Alamo's walls. In this version of "The Alamo," the final attack doesn't begin in late afternoon.

Captain Reynerson and his wife were, in real life, the Dickinsons.

Because the Alamo set was not constructed for this episode, but rather a left-over fort on the Desilu 40 Acres lot, it features what is considered by historians as the most inaccurate Alamo featured in a film or TV production. The Alamo defenders' weapons and costumes were, ironically, a little futuristic and not the style of weapons and costumes of the time period.

Colonel Travis states he has a 12-year-old son. Travis' son Charles Edward was actually seven at the time of the battle. Travis was 26 years old at the time of his death, but he is portrayed by an actor who appears to be (at the least) in his mid-thirties.

BLOOPERS!

When Tony meets up with Doug when he returns to the Alamo, his sweater is not dirty as it has been for most of the episode. A moment later, the sweater is dirty again.

Just after Tony and Doug arrive, an officer tells them that Davy Crockett was killed "yesterday," but during the climactic battle, we see him twice (courtesy of stock footage).

During the siege of the Alamo, shortly after Col. Travis returns to his own time, an exterior shot of the riflemen taking shots at the Mexicans clearly features someone's head on the bottom right of the screen, obviously one of the camera crew or technicians.

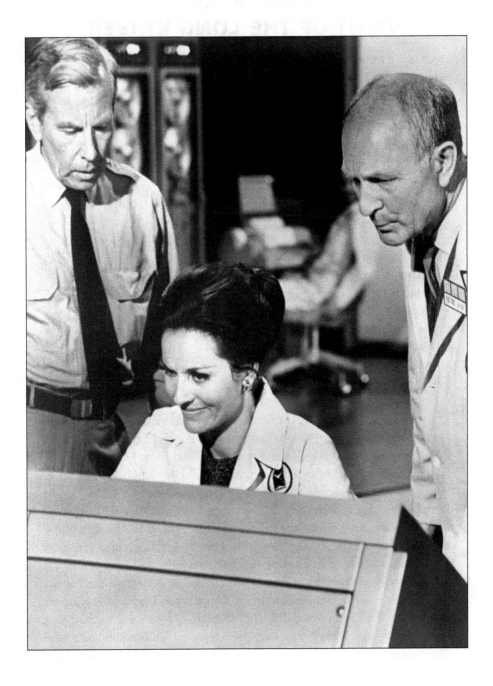

PRODUCTION #9615
NIGHT OF THE LONG KNIVES

INITIAL TELECAST: December 16, 1966
SHOOTING SCRIPT DATED: October 21, 1966, with revised pages dated
October 24 and 31, 1966
DATES OF PRODUCTION: October 24, 25, 26, 27, 28 and 31, 1966
FILMING LOCATIONS: Lone Pine, Stage 18 and Stage 19
GUEST CAST: Peter Brocco (Kashi, the blind man); Brendan Dillon (Col.
Fettretch); Bill Graeff (a guard); Sam Groom (Jerry); George Keymas (Ali);
Perry Lopez (Major Kabir); Dayton Lummis (Gladstone); Pat Murphy (a
sentry); Malachi Throne (Hira Singh); David Watson (Rudyard Kipling);
and Ben Wright (Cabinet Minister).

PRODUCTION CREDITS
ART DIRECTORS: Jack Martin Smith and Rodger E. Maus
ASSISTANT DIRECTOR: Ted Butcher
DIRECTOR: Paul Stanley
FILM EDITOR: Dick Wormell
MUSIC: stock
MUSIC EDITOR: Sam E. Levin
Teleplay by William Welch.

STORY: British India, 1886. The time travelers land in an Asian desert where
Doug is carried off by tribesmen and Tony is rescued from the scorching
sands by an adventurous and inquisitive young Englishman named Rudyard
Kipling. In the hands of an Afghan tribal chief, Hira Singh, Doug is questioned for his knowledge of the nearby English outpost. Meanwhile, in
London this area is occupying the attention of Prime Minister Gladstone,
who tells his cabinet that if the tribes ever unite against the English at the
border, Indian will be lost. At the tent of Hira Singh, Doug discovers he is
to be made a martyr for the cause — he will be killed and strapped to the
back of a horse. When the occupying British at Fort Albert get riled up, an
Arab uprising will begin. Meanwhile, at the garrison, Tony and Kipling try
to convince the commander, Colonel Fettretch, that he must rescue Doug
from the Afghans. Doug, meanwhile, is released by Kashi, a blind man who
directs him to the fort. Kashi makes it to the fort, eventually, but not before
he is attacked and, dying, lives just long enough to warn that tomorrow is
the night of the planned uprising. Rudyard Kipling is kidnapped by Hira
Singh, so Tony and Doug lead the attack against Hira Singh's camp. The

result is that the pair join the attack on the border chieftain, while those in the Time Tunnel watch. The maneuver is successful — Kipling is rescued, Singh is contained and the plan to start an uprising against the British has been foiled.

STOCK MUSIC: Color Bumper (by Johnny Williams, :03); The Boiler Room (by Williams, :26); The Paperhanger is Still Alive (by Daniele Amfitheatrof, :39); Booby Trap (by Hugo Friedhofer, :39); The National Razor (by Leith Stevens, :39); Urgent Detergent (by Lionel Newman, :39); It's Kirk (by Stevens, :39); Main Title (a.k.a. Time Tunnel Theme, by Williams, :37); Hammer of God (by Bernard Herrmann, :27); Volcanic Island (by Robert Drasnin, :11); Temple of Justice (by Stevens, :35); Key Bridge (by Drasnin, :09); The Spearmen (by Herrmann, :27); First Test Part Two (by Stevens, :13); The Khan's Rage (by Herrmann, :13); Let's Go (by Stevens, :13); Try It Again (by Sawtell, :13); He Won't Budge (by Drasnin, :15); Tunnel of Slow Return (by Drasnin, :05); Search and Find (by Drasnin, :05); You Call Me Brother? (by Joseph Mullendore, :07); Take Him Away (by Mullendore, :07); Hammer of God (by Herrmann, :07); Highland Laddie (by Lionel Newman, :36); The Sentries (by Herrmann, :25); Two Sentries (by Lyn Murray, :15); Name Dropper (by Drasnin, :04); On the Double (public domain, adapted by Newman, :10); Prelude (by Herrmann, 1:05); The Pass (by Herrmann, 1:05); The Fight (by Herrmann, 1:05); Bumper (by Williams, :03); The Name (by Sawtell, :07); First Test Part Two (by Stevens, :19); First Test Part Three (by Stevens, :19); First Test Part One (by Stevens, :19); What Now? (by Friedhofer, :19); Take Him Away (by Mullendore, :13); The Knife (by Herrmann, :13); The Message (by Herrmann, :13); How Did It Go? (by Mullendore, :21); Custer's Premonition (by Mullendore, :11); Jettison (by Lyn Murray, :12); First Test Part Three (by Stevens, :11); The Sentries (by Herrmann, :17); The Letter (by Herrmann, 1:27); Death of Christian (by Friedhofer, :27); Lee in Action (by Friedhofer, :27); Two Sentries (by Murray, :16); The Sentries (by Herrmann, :03); Prelude (by Herrmann, :09); The Mirror (by Herrmann, :33); Booby Trap (by Friedhofer, :33); The Awakening (by Herrmann, :18); The Message (by Herrmann, :18): The Pass (by Herrmann, :18); The Storm (by Herrmann, :18); Someone Moved (by Newman, :18); Urgent Detergent (by Newman, :18); The Spearmen (by Herrmann, :18); Tomahawk Fight (by Mullendore, :18); Urgent Detergent (by Newman, :18); The Quarrel (by Herrmann, :18); Terror Stinger (by Fred Steiner, :18); Fright, Flight, Fight (by Drasnin, :18); House of Bamboo (by Leigh Harline, :18); Prelude (by Herrmann, :17); Time Transfer (by Williams, :21); The Jungle (by Williams, :04); Bumper (by Williams, :03); The Paperhanger is Still Alive (by Amfitheatrof, 1:27); Booby Trap (by Friedhofer, 1:27); Next Week (by Murray, :09); End Credits (a.k.a. Time Tunnel Theme, by Williams, :49); and Fox I.D. (by Alfred Newman, :05).

EPISODE BUDGET

Story Rights and Expense $1,500	Process $285
Scenario $5,808	Production Film & Lab Charges $9,017
Producer $7,215	Stills $150
Direction $3,000	Transportation $3,837
Cast $15,800	Location Expenses $2,367
Extras $3,802	Re-Recording $1,784
Music $3,500	Photo Effects $805
Staff $3,313	Opticals , Fades and Dissolves $2,150
Art $2,642	Titles $745
Sets $7,910	Post Production Film & Lab Charges $14,679
Operating Labor $4,166	Projectionists $205
Miniatures $3,000	Editorial $5,875
Camera $3,488	Fringe Benefits $13,785
Sound $1,625	Miscellaneous $780
Electrical $3,253	Amortizations $1,002
Mechanical Effects $815	Contract Overhead $15,000
Set Dressing $3,839	General Overhead $5,625
Animals and Action Devices $790	*Total Picture Cost* $158,124
Women's Wardrobe $529	
Men's Wardrobe $2,534	
Makeup and hairdressing $1,504	

Series Budget $167,757
Pre-Production Estimate $158,124
Under $9,633

SET PRODUCTION COSTS
Colonel's Office $1,300
Fort Building $850
Post Infirmary $450
Cabinet Room $600
Construction Foreman $600
Amortized $2,000
Scaffold $1,310
Total $7,110

NOTES

The tent in which Hira Singh resides is nothing more than a few drapes used to simulate a tent during production. The same drapes were again used to simulate a tent in "Attack of the Barbarians" and "The Walls of Jericho."

William Welch was paid $4,000 for his story and the first and final draft of the teleplay (contact dated June 1, 1966). Formerly titled "Khyber Rifles," and originally assigned production #9666, the name of Welch's original story treatment was obviously inspired by the movie, *King of the Khyber Rifles* (1953), from which stock footage used in this episode originated.

The opinions of newspaper columnists were divided. "Oh, what a romantic adventure this one is!" was quoted in the Lively Arts TV Column in the December 16, 1966, issue of the *St. Petersburg Times*. On the same date, TV Key Previews in the California *Modesto Bee* suggested this episode as

Malachi Throne as Hira Singh.

"recommended viewing." The December 16 issue of *The Hartford Courant* remarked: "It's as far-fetched as any of the other episodes of this series but as usual, it does make history come alive and it is interesting."

The December 22, 1966, issue of the Virginia *Free-Lance Star* was perhaps the harshest critic. "Between all of the contrived plots here, and if you take into consideration the occasional history bending for dramatic purposes by *Time Tunnel*'s script writers, a youngster can get some insight into some of history's noted personalities…" The ratings should not be used to judge the success of the series when you consider the stiff competition ABC faced from the other networks in that time slot. One has to admit that it was difficult to compete with a series that was now routinely using extra-terrestrials for time travel plots when a rival network was offering Joan Crawford as a guest on the popular rival program *The Man From U.N.C.L.E.*

James Darren in costume.

ABC CENSORSHIP CONCERNS

Modify so that rifle is not pointed directly into camera (early scene on page 3).

No close up of hilt of knife protruding from back.

Blood to minimum, no more than slight trickle, as indicated.

Please be sure that there is no buildup of Singh knocking old man down. Delete direction "he continues to strike" and have Doug stop Singh before he strikes a second time.

LONE PINE: SHOOTING ON LOCATION

After reviewing the first draft of the teleplay, dated October 4, 1966, Bob Anderson wrote to Irwin Allen on October 10: "After viewing stock film for 'Long Knives,' and discussing the locations with Rodger Maus and Jerry Briskin, it is my feeling that in order to give you the value you expect to see for this show, we'll need two days location in the Lone Pine area. After breaking

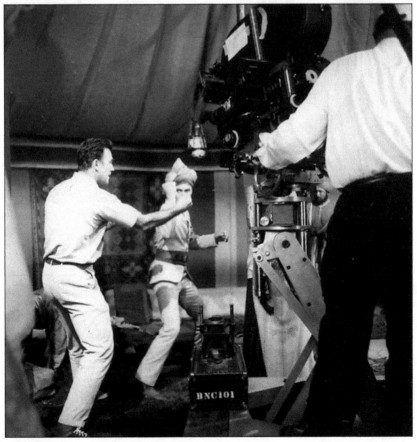

The actors receive fight instructions.

" NIGHT OF THE LONG KNIVES"

SCENE 142   ANGLE ON TUNNEL

KIRK   ANN   SWAIN

* TUNNEL FLASHES BRILLIANTLY AND
  SMOKE ENVELOPES JERRY'S FIGURE....

"We have to take chances," said Jerry, who proposes to bypass the breaker system. Not much goes on in the Time Tunnel Complex in this episode except for the Tunnel personnel losing contact of Doug and Tony and spend the entire time trying to regain contact. Because of this rationale, it remains unclear why Irwin Allen's production company even bothered to film scenes at the Time Tunnel Complex for this episode. In the original draft of the script, Jerry makes a more desperate "chance" as you can see in these storyboards.

JERRY'S FIGURE SPINNING AND
TURNING IN THE LIMBO OF TIME....

KIRK   ANN   SWAIN

AS _ THROUGH THE SMOKE _ A BODY
BECOMES VISIBLE _ LYING ON THE FLOOR
OF THE TUNNEL....

down the first draft script which I did over the weekend, I feel without such a location, we would hurt our story. Extras are low in this story and cast should not be very expensive. Also, sets are few — three to be exact. Therefore, we could handle the expense of two days location. I also feel this would open up the story to a great advantage which we haven't had the opportunity to do before except in stock footage."

This was one of the few episodes of *The Time Tunnel* to feature location shooting. Irwin Allen hated shooting television episodes on location because of the numerous costs involved that weren't assumed until the paperwork was totaled and the breakdown revealed. Tom Nolan was the contact man for the location scouting trip, paid $250 for his services. Most of the cast and crew left for the Fox Hills on Sunday evening, others arrived early Monday morning. All of the materials (including generators to power the camera) were loaded on trucks Friday night, and transportation left from the casting office. Four horses were needed for shooting at Lone Pine, involving additional costs. Filming on location was not completed until 2:30 in the afternoon of Tuesday, October 25, so many of the cast and crew stayed over Sunday and Monday night. The cost of lodging totaled $476. Breakfast, lunch and dinners cost a total of $1,466, which included coffee and donuts. A permit for shooting film and a clean-up fee amounted to $175.

BLOOPER!

Stock footage is used to simulate Doug jumping an Arab during the offensive, but the costume Doug wears does not match that in the stock footage.

PRODUCTION #9616
INVASION

INITIAL TELECAST: December 23, 1966

SECOND REVISED SHOOTING (FINAL) SCRIPT DATED: October 31, 1966

REVISED SHOOTING SCRIPT DATED: November 1, 1966

DATES OF PRODUCTION: November 1, 2, 3, 4, 7 and 8, 1966

FILMING LOCATIONS: French Street, Stage 18, Stage 19 and Studio near Grip Dept.

GUEST CAST: Lyle Bettger (Major Hoffman); Robert Carricart (Mirabeau); Francis De Sales (Dr. Shumate); Dick Dial (the soldier); Michael St. Clair (Duchamps); Joey Tata (Verlaine); and John Wengraf (Dr. Hans Kleinemann).

Stunt Doubles
Frank Graham (double for Tony)
Reggie Parton (double for Doug)
Denver Mattson (stunt driver)
Vince Dedrick (double for Hoffman)
Orwin Harvey (stunt guard)
Paul Stader (double for Doug *and* Mirabeau)
George Robotham (stuntman)

PRODUCTION CREDITS
ART DIRECTORS: Jack Martin Smith and Rodger E. Maus
ASSISTANT DIRECTOR: Fred R. Simpson
DIRECTOR: Sobey Martin
FILM EDITOR: Alex Hubert
MUSIC: stock
MUSIC EDITOR: Sam E. Levin
Teleplay by Bob and Wanda Duncan.

STORY: The date is June 4, 1944, forty-eight hours before D-Day along the Cherbourg Peninsula of Normandy. Tony is picked up by the French Underground, while Doug is taken captive by Major Hoffman of the Gestapo. Dr. Kleinemann is doing research in brainwashing and experiments on Doug, skillfully transforming him through effective use of drugs and hypnosis. Tony tries to get three saboteurs to help him rescue his friend from the Gestapo headquarters. As an electrician, Tony agrees to aid their cause, knowing it will help aid in Doug's rescue. Believing he is Heinrich

Krieger,* a Nazi Captain, the reconditioned Doug sets out in full German regalia to hunt down and murder Tony, whom he believes is an enemy. Doug tries to kill Tony on sight, but he, with others, manages to escape to a new hideout and there plan their last coup before the scheduled invasion. When the French Underground captures Doug, the brainwashed victim gives away the name of the traitor amongst their group. The French resistance blows up the Gestapo headquarters, crippling German communications while the Americans move in, but not before Tony rushes in and kidnaps the evil doctor. The scientist, no warrior, comes along peaceably and gives Doug the needed antidote. Morning arrives and the invasion begins, whereupon Tony and Doug, restored, are caught up in the vortex of time.

STOCK MUSIC: Color Bumper (by Johnny Williams, :03); The Boiler Room (by Williams, :23); The Paperhanger is Still Alive (by Daniele Amfitheatrof, :32 and :32); Pursuit (by Hugo Friedhofer, :32); The Underground Complex (by Lennie Hayton, :32); The Boys' Introduction (by Sawtell, :29); Main Title (a.k.a. Time Tunnel Theme, by Williams, :37); Lee in Action (by Friedhofer, :29); A Dark Night (by Lionel Newman, 3:45); Drugged Interrogation (by Sawtell, 1:44); U.S. Intelligence (by Sawtell, :17); Under Guard (by Drasnin, :48); A Dark Night (by Newman, :48); The Paperhanger is Still Alive (by Amfitheatrof, :48); Pursuit (by Friedhofer, :48); The Assassins (by Robert Drasnin, :16); Rescue (by Friedhofer, :16); Search and Find (by Drasnin, :16); Bumper (by Williams, :03); The Name (by Sawtell, :08); Fright, Flight, Fight (by Drasnin, :17); Bomb Warp (by Drasnin, :17); The Assassins (by Drasnin, :17); A Fool (by Sawtell, :17); Rabbit Rouser (by Drasnin, :17); Pursuit (by Friedhofer, :17); Bomber is Destroyed (by Alfred Newman, :17); How About You? (by Burton Lane and Ralph Freed, :12); The Spearmen (by Bernard Herrmann, :22); The Bombing (by Sawtell, :22); Death of Christian (by Friedhofer, :55); A Dark Night (by Newman, :23); The Underground Complex (by Hayton, :23); Lee in Action (by Friedhofer, :23); Careful Citizen (by Leith Stevens, :37); Pursuit (by Friedhofer, :37); Destroying the Complex (by Hayton, :27); Urgent Detergent (by Newman, :27); Complex Problem (by Drasnin, :27); Pursuit (by Friedhofer, :27); Tony Talks (by Sawtell, :57); Louise's Discovery (by Sawtell, :57 and :16); Mine Trap (by Joseph Mullendore, :10); Time Transfer (by Williams, :09); The Bombing (by Sawtell, :09); The Boiler Room (by Williams, :19); Opening (by Stevens, :24); Opening #11

---

*The script gives the name as "Krieger." Fans who turn on the subtitles on the DVD will notice the name given is "Kreuger."

(by Stevens, :24); Fight (by Stevens, :24); The Awakening (by Herrmann, :24); The Quarrel (by Herrmann, :24); Next Week (by Murray, :09); End Credits (a.k.a. Time Tunnel Theme, by Williams, :48); and Fox I.D. (by Alfred Newman, :05).

EPISODE BUDGET
Story Rights & Expense $1,500
Scenario $5,808
Producer $7,215
Direction $3,000
Cast $17,440
Extras $4,491
Music $3,500
Staff $3,121
Art $2,642
Sets $11,658
Operating Labor $4,932
Miniatures $3,000
Camera $3,568
Sound $1,625
Electrical $3,949
Mechanical Effects $1,805
Set Dressing $4,669
Animals & Action Devices $0
Women's Wardrobe $269
Men's Wardrobe $3,004

Makeup & Hairdressing $1,401
Process $285
Production Film & Lab Charges $9,017
Stills $150
Transportation $2,900
Re-recording $1,784
Photo Effects $2,150
Opticals, Fades & Dissolves $2,150
Titles $745
Post Production & Lab Charges $13,829
Projectionists $205
Editorial $5,875
Fringe Benefits $15,430
Miscellaneous $630
Amortizations $1,002
Contract Overhead $15,000
General Overhead $6,718
Total Picture Cost $166,467

Series Budget $167,757
Pre-Production Estimate $166,467
Under Budget $1,290

SET PRODUCTION COSTS
Warehouse and Deserted Street $200
Gestapo Headquarters and Street $250
Gestapo Headquarters $2,050
Underground HQ $200
Underground HQ $1,050
Truck $100
Powerhouse $100
2nd Underground Headquarters $50

2nd Underground Headquarters $650
Motor Pool $1,075
Total $5,725

HISTORICAL ERROR

Towards the beginning of this episode, pictures of Adolph Hitler, Heinrich Himmler and Rudolph Hess are seen hanging on the wall at Gestapo Headquarters. This proved to be a historical error because Hess escaped from Germany in 1941, and the events in this episode occurred in 1944. The director realized this and ordered Hess' picture removed and Heinrich Hammler's picture moved two feet lower on the wall.

ABC CENSORSHIP CONCERNS

Standard caution that these fights are not unnecessarily brutal or prolonged. No close up of blows with weapons or the choking.

Knife contact must be off camera or completely covered.

We can see the guard being hit but there must be no effect of body being stitched or splattered with bullets. Noted that in other scenes no one is hit with machine gun fire.

NOTES

A great number of Austrian and German actors were forced to flee their homeland during the rise of Adolf Hitler and the Nazis in the late 1930s only to find themselves smack dab in Hollywood pictures playing thoroughly nefarious Gestapo commanders. Viennese performer John Wengraf was one such actor. He plays a member of the Nazi party in this episode, his final screen appearance before retiring days after production was completed.

"Producer Irwin Allen was the toughest S.O.B. in the world," recalled actor Joey Tata. "Ninety-nine percent of people were intimidated by him, but we hit it off. Whenever an actor went in for wardrobe, you had to walk across the Fox lot and let Irwin approve you."

This episode is a wonderful example of how everyone manages to speak English no matter if they are German or French.

Where did the Germans get a photograph of Tony so quickly for the slide show, and the life-size cutout plastered on plywood?

On one of the days during production, James Darren was sent for a visit to his physician, on an extended lunch hour.

This was supposed to be Jerry Briskin's directorial debut, but for reasons unknown, he did not take up the directing chair.

This is the first episode in which Tony deliberately commits murder. He picks up a gun and shoots two Germans while entering the headquarters to find the doctor who can restore his friend back to normal.

At the secret rendezvous of the French resistance, the purple bottle and burning candle is the same prop seen in other episodes of *The Time Tunnel*.

Writers Bob and Wanda Duncan were paid $4,000 for their short story and the first and final draft of their teleplay.

CRITICS HAVE THEIR SAY

The December 23, 1966, issue of *The Milwaukee Journal* remarked: "This show has all of the inventiveness of a standard old WWII drama." Joan Crosby of *TV Scout* felt this episode made "for a clean, wholesome and dull adventure." *The Free Lance Press*, a Virginia newspaper, joked: "The home TV viewers were not brainwashed by this series."

Robert Colbert gets ready for his big scene.

Charles Witbeck, columnist for *TV Key* remarked, "A rugged adventure, dealing as it does with the D-Day invasion, but the kids will be absorbed by the heroic exploits of our era-hopping travelers. In addition to the usual quota of two-fisted action and breathless escapes, there's the menace of the Gestapo in pursuit to hold their attention here."

BLOOPER!

When Doug, strapped to the table, is suffering under the effects of the truth serum, he reveals the date of the Allied invasion as June 6, 1945. He should have said 1944.

TRIVIA

Dick Tufeld was not only the announcer for the opening narration of the series, he is perhaps best known as the voice of the Robot in the TV series *Lost in Space*, a role he reprised for the 1998 feature film. He also provided the narration voice-over for *Voyage to the Bottom of the Sea*. He did voice work for the 1978 animated television series, *Fantastic Four*. He narrated several episodes of *Thundarr the Barbarian* (1980). The main title narrator on the 1979 DePatie-Freleng series *Spider-Woman*, he was also the main title announcer on the 1981 Marvel Productions show *Spider-Man and His Amazing Friends*.

THE REVENGE OF ROBIN HOOD

INITIAL TELECAST: December 30, 1966
SHOOTING SCRIPT DATED: November 7, 1966
DATES OF PRODUCTION: November 9, 10, 11, 14, 15 and 16, 1966
FILMING LOCATIONS: Stage 16, Stage 18, Stage 19 and Sherwood Forest (Ward Ranch at Thousand Oaks)
GUEST CAST: John Alderson (Little John); John Crawford (King John); Donald Harron (Earl of Huntingdon, a.k.a. Robin Hood); James Lanphier (Dubois); Ronald Long (Friar Tuck); Denver Mattson (stunt guard #1); Erin O'Brien-Moore (Baroness Elmont); John Orchard (Engelard de Cigogne); and Eddie Saenz (stunt guard #2).

Stunt Doubles
Pete Kellett (double for King John)
Paul Stader (double for Doug *and* Huntingdon)
Dave Sharpe (double for Tony)
Frank Graham (double for Tony)

Five stand-ins (Interior Corridor and Dungeon, Interior Corridor and Throne Room) were Skip Burnham, John Drake, Bill Graeff, John Moio and Gene Silvani. Stuntmen and stand-ins included: Lyle Bettger, Robert Carricart, George Robotham, Michael St. Clair, and John Wengraf. Virginia Semon was the female stand-in.

PRODUCTION CREDITS
ART DIRECTORS: Jack Martin Smith and Rodger E. Maus
ASSISTANT DIRECTOR: Steve Bernhardt
DIRECTOR: William Hale
FILM EDITOR: James Baiotto
MUSIC: stock
MUSIC EDITOR: Sam E. Levin
Teleplay by Leonard Stadd.

STORY: June, 1215. The Earl of Huntingdon (a.k.a. Robin Hood) is taken prisoner when King John refuses to sign the Articles of the Barons, a.k.a. the Magna Carta, and denounces Huntingdon as a traitor for spearheading a movement among his Barons to get him to sign the document guaranteeing freedom to his subjects. Tony and Doug fail in their attempt to rescue

Robin Hood from the dungeon, but flee to the forest where they learn their whereabouts when they meet up with Friar Tuck and Little John and find that the captured Huntingdon is none other than Robin Hood. Back at the Time Tunnel, the scientists decide to send a homing post to the pair as a means of extracting them from danger. But the metal post falls into the dungeon where no one will see it. Out in Sherwood Forest, Little John is struck with an arrow from King John's men and Tuck guides them to the nearby Kirkley Hall where Baroness Elmont offers sanctuary. None of the men are aware that the Baroness was seduced by an offer from King John for gold in exchange for information. Using the Baroness' chemicals, meanwhile, Doug heals Little John and then creates smoke bombs. Meanwhile, Tuck and Tony pose as friars sent to administer last rights to Huntingdon and thus get inside his cell and free him. The three escape, join Doug and Little John and all quickly plan to capture the King to prevent the disaster he plans for Runnymede. With an assist from the chemical cupboard, Doug combines 1968 chemistry with alchemy of 1215, creating nerve gas that is used to give Robin Hood's men the leverage they need to overpower the guards at the castle. As a result, Robin Hood is rescued and King John furiously affixes his seal to the Magna Carta. Tony and Doug finally reach the homing post, only to discover the power has been drained and it does not work. They quickly vanish back into the vortex.

STOCK MUSIC: Color Bumper (by Johnny Williams, :03); The Boiler Room (by Williams, :25); The Fens (by Franz Waxman, :42); Fight (by Leith Stevens, :26); The Japanese Consulate (by Paul Sawtell, :27); Main Title (a.k.a. Time Tunnel Theme, by Williams, :37); Main Title (by Waxman, :32): The Fens (by Waxman, :37); Trapped (by Waxman, :37); The First Chase (by Waxman, :37); The Fens (by Waxman, :16); The First Chase (by Waxman, :16); Derry's Death (by Waxman, :16); Sir Valence (by Robert Drasnin, :16); A Rainy Night (by Waxman, :12); Bomber is Destroyed (by Alfred Newman, :12); The First Chase (by Waxman, :12); Derry's Death (by Waxman, :12); Sir Valence (by Drasnin, :12); Death of Christian (by Hugo Friedhofer, :58); Death of Christian (by Friedhofer, :12); The Return (by Leith Stevens, :12); Derry's Death (by Waxman, :10); Val Escape (by Waxman, :17); Raleigh's Secret (by Waxman, :17); Pursuit (by Friedhofer, :45); The Boys' Escape (by Sawtell, :45); Let's Go (by Stevens, :03); Derry's Death (by Waxman, :24 and :23); Bomber is Destroyed (by Newman, :23); The Ring (by Waxman, :23); First Test Part Three (by Stevens, :34); The Paperhanger is Still Alive (by Daniele Amfitheatrof, :34); Bomber is Destroyed (by Newman, :34); Escape (by Waxman, :34); Bomber is Destroyed (by Newman, :09); Raleigh's Secret (by Waxman, :09); Bomber is Destroyed (by Newman, :17); The Spearmen (by Bernard Herrmann, :17); Val Escape (by Waxman, :17); Sir Brack (by Waxman, :37); Escape (by Waxman, :23); Bomber is Destroyed (by Newman, :17); Raleigh's Secret (by Waxman, :17); Two Drop In (by Drasnin, :10); Sir Brack (by Waxman, :10); The Fens (by Waxman, :10); Terror Stinger (by Fred Steiner, :10); Bumper (by Williams, :03); Sir Brack (by Waxman, :38); Trapped (by Waxman, :38); Val Escapes (by Waxman, :38); Escape (by Waxman, :38); Sir Gawain (by Waxman, :38); The Spearmen (by Herrmann, :38); Bomber is Destroyed (by Newman, :38); The First Chase (by Waxman, 1:51); Escape (by Waxman, :29); Bomber is Destroyed (by Newman, :19 and :19); Derry's Death (by Waxman, :47); Escape (by Waxman, :47); Main Title (by Waxman, :19); The First Chase (by Waxman, :19); Sir Gawain (by Waxman, :11); The First Chase (by Waxman, :31); Derry's Death (by Waxman, :31); A Rainy Night (by Waxman, :31); Bomber is Destroyed (by Newman, :05); Escape (by Waxman, :31); The Fens (by Waxman, :31); The First Chase (by Waxman, :31); Derry's Death (by Waxman, :31); A Rainy Night (by Waxman, :31); The Ring (by Waxman, :31); Bomber is Destroyed (by Newman, :31); Trapped (by Waxman, :11); Raleigh's Secret (by Waxman, :11); Bomber is Destroyed (by Newman, :11); Time Transfer (by Williams, :02); Flying Chord (by Drasnin, :02); End Credits (a.k.a. Time Tunnel Theme, by Williams, :38); and Fox I.D. (by Alfred Newman, :05).

INITIAL EPISODE BUDGET

Story Rights and Expense $1,900
Scenario $5,908
Producer $6,461
Direction $3,000
Cast $18,200
Extras $4,945
Music $3,675
Staff $3,121
Art $2,642
Sets $11,508
Operating Labor $4,841
Miniatures $1,500
Camera $3,164
Sound $1,625
Electrical $3,949
Mechanical Effects $1,395
Set Dressing $5,105
Animals and Action Devices $195
Women's Wardrobe $929
Men's Wardrobe $3,779
Makeup and Hairdressing $1,586
Process $40
Production Film & Lab Charges $8,809
Stills $150
Transportation $4,800
Location Expenses $200
Re-Recording $3,610
Photo Effects $910
Opticals, Fades and Dissolves $3,150
Titles $585
Post Production Film & Lab Charges $14,859
Projectionists $205

Editorial $7,426
Fringe Benefits $15,790
Miscellaneous $1,055
Amortizations $2,753

Series Budget $167,757
Pre-prod $176,835
Over $9,078

Contract Overhead $15,000
General Overhead $8,065
Total Picture Cost $176,835

REVISED EPISODE BUDGET
Story Rights and Expense $1,500
Scenario $5,808
Producer $7,215
Direction $3,000
Cast $18,200
Extras $4,945
Music $3,500
Staff $3,121
Art $2,642
Sets $12,008
Operating Labor $4,841
Miniatures $3,000
Camera $3,164
Sound $1,625
Electrical $3,949
Mechanical Effects $1,395
Set Dressing $5,105
Animals and Action Devices $195
Women's Wardrobe $929
Men's Wardrobe $3,779
Makeup and Hairdressing $1,586

Process $285
Production Film & Lab Charges
   $9,017
Stills $150
Transportation $4,800
Location Expenses $200
Re-Recording $1,784
Photo Effects $910
Opticals, Fades and Dissolves
   $2,150
Titles $785
Post Production Film & Lab
   Charges $13,979
Projectionists $205
Editorial $5,875
Fringe Benefits $15,500
Miscellaneous $1,055
Amortizations $1,021
Contract Overhead $15,000
General Overhead $7,375
Total Picture Cost $171,598

Series Budget $167,757
Pre-prod $171,598
Over $3,841

SET PRODUCTION COSTS
Interior Dungeon and Corridor (with torture props, heavy oak door and bars to bend) $2,580
Interior Throne Room (corridor and parapet) $2,050

Interior Kirkley Hall $570
Exterior Parapet $500
Exterior Forest and Broken Castle Wall $900
Exterior Forest Campsite $100
Exterior Kirkley Hall $150
Construction Foreman $1,028
Amortized $2,000
Total $9,878

PHOTOGRAPHIC EFFECTS
Doug, Tony & Huntingdon in Dungeon $260
Huntingdon in Chains in Dungeon $130
Abbess talking to Doug and Tony $130
Homing Post in Dungeon $130
Huntingdon in Chains and Homing Post Glows $130
Huntingdon Chains Engelard to Wall in Dungeon $130
Total $910

STORY DEVELOPMENT

The initial story proposal, dated October 19, 1966, was sold without a title to Irwin Allen. Later, Leonard Stadd assigned a title of "The Tyrant," for an expanded and more detailed plot synopsis. The original plot proposal reveals very few differences when compared to the finished film. The sheriff, Engelard, is originally the sadistic bastard in the torture chamber, not the captain of the guards. The door of the torture chamber is discovered to be locked — Tony didn't lock it to protect his friends. In the Time Tunnel, they tune in the image area and find our boys. They propose to get a message to them regarding the whereabouts of the homing post. By coordinating their fix, the Time Tunnel people send back a tube containing a message. The tube lands in the fireplace and is not seen. Through this scene they also try voice contact and fail. The attempt to contact the boys is not in the filmed episode. Later, in the dungeon, Tony and Friar Tuck overpower the sheriff and a couple of guards. The old window has been mended with a grate of steel, so they make the sheriff and his men strip and don their costumes. As other guards come charging down the corridor, our men get out, shove the guards into the cell, and lock the door after them. This scene was modified for the film and they never masquerade in the guards' costumes.

Before storming the castle towards the end of the episode, there is a scene involving a witch that was never filmed for this episode. In a shack in the woods, we see an old crone sprinkling a substance on a fire. Doug and Friar

Tuck stand over her and watch green sparks fly up from the fire. Doug tells the old hag that all she used to create that effect was a handful of salt. Friar Tuck has told Doug that she has the stuff which would create bigger effects. Under the prodding of Friar Tuck, Witch Maude finally opens her bag of tricks and allows Doug to examine the raw chemicals. At last he finds the substance he wants and gets Witch Maude to give him a large quantity of it.

Robert Colbert discusses the set-up for the next scene.

In the episode that was filmed, Doug instead uses chemicals the Baroness Elmont had in her medicine cabinet. When the rockets are launched, panic reigns as guards rush in the throne room, yelling about fire hailing from the skies. (This scene was also not filmed).

At the end, when Tony and Doug catch up to the homing post, DuBois enters the dungeon with sword in hand and swings it, trying to take off two heads at once. Doug and Tony drop the post and scramble for possible weapons. DuBois has his foot on the post as he's about to run Tony through. Pan to Robin Hood in the doorway, letting an arrow fly at DuBois. DuBois dematerializes with the homing post. Dubois appears in the Time Tunnel with an arrow sticking out of his chest. Kirk orders him returned immediately. He goes, leaving the post in the tunnel.

After reading the plot synopsis, Briskin suggested a number of changes to the plot summary, which were implemented when the initial teleplay was written. Briskin wanted to delete the witch character, a.k.a. "Old Crone" and

Ronald Long as Friar Tuck.

"Witch Maude." Briskin questioned why have the guard who was shot with an arrow materialize in the Tunnel? "It doesn't pay off," he explained. Briskin was also concerned about the large number of wardrobes needed, the large cast and the number of horses and requested the number of roles be trimmed.

After the teleplay was written, Irwin Allen expressed criticism in an inter-office memo. "I feel that the dialogue throughout the script could be

sharpened considerably," he wrote. "Some of it at the present time reads like a little theater costume production. The torture of Huntingdon is drawn out too long. It goes on and on and on. I don't think King John would let it continue for such a long time and I don't believe any man could take it without at least losing consciousness."

Jerry Briskin, however, did not like the script at all. On November 1, he wrote to Allen: "Personally, I do not feel this is an exciting, suspenseful or dramatic script. I have no likes or dislikes for any of the characters in the story. Most of the physical action involving Tony and Doug takes place in the first 23 pages. On page 11, the guard outside the dungeon is still pounding on the door and hasn't called for help three pages after he first found out there was trouble in the dungeon. On page 12, rather than worry about the cell bars being hot, why doesn't Tony or Doug pick up a bucket of water and throw it on the bars and cool them off immediately so they can make their escape? On page 13, if Tony and Doug know so much about King John's era, and the Magna Carta, and the Barons of Runnymede, how come they don't know the Earl of Huntingdon is also known as Robin Hood? On page 21, rather than having to do a wire rigging just to have Littlejohn shot, I suggest that we get a cut of an archer firing a crossbow and then a cut of Littlejohn with the arrow already in his shoulder."

ABC CENSORSHIP CONCERNS

If skull and bones used, please no close up.

Please be sure that Huntingdon is not suspended off the ground with the chains.

Blood to minimum, no close up of wound. Pulling out the arrow and the cauterizing of the wound, off camera, please.

Caution on indications of torture. Huntingdon must in no way be shocking to look at. Also, please be sure that Engelhard does not cut him with the dagger during the scene.

NOTES

This episode was not meant to be historically accurate, especially since the Earl of Huntingdon was not involved with the signing of the Magna Carta. "A month after that show aired, I was at a party with a CPA friend of mine and I was introduced to an attorney," recalled Leonard Stadd. "When he heard I was a TV writer, he asked, 'What show do you write for?' I said *Time Tunnel* and he said, 'Oh my God, I saw a show a few weeks ago about how the Magna Carta came into existence.' I said, 'You're kidding! I wrote that!' He said, 'Man, that was fantastic history!' 'History?' I cried, 'Robin Hood gets King John to sign the Magna Carta and that's history?' It shows you how much education this lawyer had!'

The teleplay and story proposal and all other paperwork misspells the name as Huntington. It has been corrected to Huntingdon throughout this book for accuracy.

The throne King John sits in, the candle holders and the yellow flags with red dragon symbols are props from the movie, *Prince Valiant* (1954). Even the table in front of King John's throne is a piece of King Arthur's Round Table from the same movie. Stock footage of King John's Castle was Camelot in *Prince Valiant*, and a number of music cues originated from the same movie, which were composed and conducted by Franz Waxman (who obviously gets

John Crawford as King John.

no screen credit like Bernard Herrmann, whose scores were also used). The knights approaching the camp in Sherwood Forest do not wear costumes that match the stock footage from the movie. The throne and candle holders would also be reused for the episode "The Attack of the Barbarians."

It is mentioned that the Time Tunnel Complex has used the homing post before, but this is the first time it is featured on the series. According to General Kirk, a homing post was tried before to return Doug and Tony to the present, and we can only assume it was without success.

The iron maiden in the dungeon reappears in the dungeon scene of "The Walls of Jericho" and "Revenge of the Gods."

Actor John Crawford (not to be confused with actor Johnny Crawford of TV's *The Rifleman*) made his first of four appearances on *The Time Tunnel* in this episode. During the filming of this episode, Crawford was enjoying his role of King John. When he paused in between delivering lines, someone from behind shouted "cut!" Irritated that he had been interrupted while in the middle of a scene, Crawford continued the scene, delivering every line

Robert Colbert in full costume.

as written in the script. The actor soon discovered, upon finishing his acting chops, that the man who called "cut" was none other than Irwin Allen himself, who happened to be on the set at the time.

Actor John Orchard, who played the role of Engelard de Cigogne, strained his ankle on Friday, November 11, and the studio sent him to the emergency hospital. On Monday morning, he reported for work with a cast on his right

foot. This explains why he limps slightly when leaving King John's chambers after being told to go saddle the horses. The character of Engelard was supposed to be the sheriff in the original concept, but in this episode he wears a guard's uniform instead. Even in an earlier scene, when instructed to get information out of Robin Hood, it is evident that his right leg is thicker than the left as a result of the cast.

Donald Harron, who played the title role of Robin Hood, recalled: "It was refreshing to play a character who could smile. I has been cast in grim roles because I have a naturally worried-looking face. But as Robin Hood, I didn't have to frown. My strongest memory was going to lunch on Sunset Boulevard and I had this big, bloody gash on my forehead. It was fake but it looked very realistic. People were pointing and staring at me. I was tutored in the sword-fighting scenes by a man [Paul Stader] who had served as Errol Flynn's stand-in for all of those swashbuckling movies and we used one of the old castle sets from the 1930s. It really was like stepping back into time. James Darren was one of the wittiest people I have ever met. It's too bad he didn't get a chance to play more comedy. He was terrific to work with."

CRITICS HAVE THEIR SAY

Joan Crosby of *TV Scout* reviewed this episode as "A treat for the kids and all adventure fans…There is plenty of swordplay and all kinds of derring-do, with King John's horsemen in hot pursuit." The TV Previews column in the December 30, 1966, issue of the *St. Petersburg Times* remarked: "Now it's Time Tunnel's turn to speculate on the wonder of Robin Hood and his merry men." *The St. Joseph News-Press* of Missouri was more harsh in their December 30 column: "This series has evidently abandoned all pretenses of doing sincere science fiction and has delivered itself up to the early 1940s movie historical extravaganzas…Basil Rathbone and Errol Flynn did it all a lot better than this. And here, on *Time Tunnel*, the merry men's long johns don't even fit too well. And over on NBC tonight, *The Man from U.N.C.L.E.* episode, "Take Me To Your Leader Affair," shows that that series has also taken a leave of its senses!"

BLOOPER!

When Little John is shot with an arrow, no blood is seen (no doubt at the request of ABC Censors) but later, Doug makes the comment that Little John "has lost too much blood already."

One of Robin Hood's archers drops an arrow instead of shooting it.

KILL TWO BY TWO

INITIAL TELECAST: January 6, 1967

SHOOTING SCRIPT DATED: November 22, 1966, with revised pages dated November 28, 1966

DATES OF PRODUCTION: November 28, 29, 30, December 1, 2 and 5, 1966

FILMING LOCATIONS: Moat, Stage 18, Stage 19 and Stage 21

GUEST CAST: Philip Ahn (Dr. Nakamura); Brent Davis (the marine sergeant who spoke); John Drake (the first marine); Vince Howard (the medic); Mako Iwamatsu* (Lieutenant Nakamura); and Kam Tong (Sergeant Itsugi).

Stunt Doubles
Paul Stader (double for Doug)
Yoneo Iguchi (double for Nakamura)
Roy Agato (double for Itsugi)
Frank Graham (double for Tony)

PRODUCTION CREDITS
ART DIRECTORS: Jack Martin Smith and Rodger E. Maus
ASSISTANT DIRECTOR: Steve Bernhardt
DIRECTOR: Herschel Daugherty
FILM EDITOR: Alex Hubert
MUSIC: stock
MUSIC EDITOR: Sam E. Levin
Teleplay by Bob and Wanda Duncan.

STORY: February 17, 1945. Tony and Doug land on a South Pacific island that, moments before, the Japanese abandoned as the invading U.S. Marines are within sight. Tony sprains his ankle and soon discovers this is the least of his concerns. Lt. Nakamura, a psychopath filled with so much bitterness that it is eating him up inside, finds the two Americans and decides to humiliate them before killing them. They are numbered two and two, and they will stalk each other through the jungle, he handicapped by a partner who is an old man. Back at the Time Tunnel Complex, Dr. Nakamura is brought in to identify landmarks on the island only to discover his son was still on the island. He collapses from shock. Lt. Nakamura, he later explains, was a kamikaze pilot who failed in his mission. Disgraced, Lt. Nakamura

---

* Billed simply as Mako on the opening credits.

forgot the teachings of his childhood and is determined to die in action as an honorable Japanese solider in the Imperial Japanese Army. Back on the island, Doug manages to slip into the shack storehouse and gets away with five grenades, a theft soon discovered by Nakamura. Doug melts into the jungle and the time travelers find themselves playing a deadly game of cat and mouse with the Japanese men, unwilling to murder their torturer. For Nakamura, his request is granted when he decides to fulfill his sacred obligation: he offers himself to Doug to kill. Doug can't do it, but a landing Marine takes care of it for him. Nakamura is shot dead. As the island is being taken by the U.S. Marines, Doug and Tony are swept up into the vortex of time.

STOCK MUSIC: Color Bumper (by Johnny Williams, :03); The Boiler Room (by Williams, :26); Tony Rescued (by Paul Sawtell, :25); The Japanese Consulate (by Sawtell, :25); The Quarrel (by Bernard Herrmann, :02); A Dark Night (by Lionel Newman, :45); Tony Talks (by Sawtell, :23); The Boys' Escape (by Sawtell, :23); Louise's Discovery (by Sawtell, :23); The Neal Mansion (by Sawtell, :23); A Strange Meeting (by Sawtell, :23); Drugged Interrogation (by Sawtell, :23); Footsteps in the Dark (by Sawtell, :23); Tony Talks (by Sawtell, :23); Too Late (by Sawtell, :23); Main Title (a.k.a. Time Tunnel Theme, by Williams, :37); Total Surprise (by Sawtell, :10); Act Out (by Leslie Stevens, :14); Episode Titles (by Stevens, :14); Take Him Away (by Joseph Mullendore, :27); Steal Horses (by Mullendore, :27); Tomahawk Fight (by Mullendore, :27); The Wind Roars (by Lyn Murray, :07); Under Guard (by Robert Drasnin, :07); To Plant A Bomb (by Drasnin, :21); Tony Talks (by Sawtell, :45); The Paperhanger is Still Alive (by Daniele Amfitheatrof, :45); Tunnel of Slow Return (by Drasnin, :45); To Plant a Bomb (by Drasnin, :45); The Long Countdown (by Sawtell, :45); Two Drop In (by Drasnin, :45); The Assassins (by Drasnin, :45); Booby Trap (by Hugo Friedhofer, :45); To Plant a Bomb (by Drasnin, :20); That's Bomb Biz (by Drasnin, :21); Tony Remembers (by Sawtell, :30); Bumper (by Williams, :03); Tony Remembers (by Sawtell, :13); Louise's Discovery (by Sawtell, :57); Pursuit (by Friedhofer, :57); A Dark Night (by Lionel Newman, :57); Volcanic Island (by Drasnin, :10); Time is Short (by Sawtell, :28); Nothing Left (by Sawtell, 1:20); The First Chase (by Waxman, :10); Sky Full of Planes (by Sawtell, :10); Volcanic Island (by Drasnin, :25); Native Danger (by Drasnin, :25); Mock Mysterioso (by Newman, :25); Take Him Away (by Mullendore, :25); The Take Off (by Sawtell, :25); Urgent Detergent (by Newman, :25); The Bombing (by Sawtell, :25); Cry For Fun (by Newman, :20); Trap (by Herman Stein, :33); Millard's Death (by Friedhofer, :33); Tony's Frustration (by Sawtell, :33); The Pledge (by Waxman, :33); The Paperhanger is Still Alive (by Amfitheatrof, :33); Firing Squad A.O. (by Murray, :33); The Neal Mansion (by Sawtell, :33); Time Transfer (by Williams, :01); Flying Chord (by Drasnin, :03); The Boiler Room (by Williams, :16); Tony's Tall Tale (by Williams, :08); Saved and Disappear (by Murray, :02); The Quarrel (by Herrmann, :37); The Mine (by Herrmann, :37); Tony Enters Machine (by Williams, :37); Next Week (by Murray, :09); End Credits (a.k.a. Time Tunnel Theme, by Williams, :49); and Fox I.D. (by Alfred Newman, :05).

EPISODE BUDGET
Story Rights and Expense $1,500
Scenario $5,808
Producer $6,461
Direction $3,000
Cast $12,500
Extras $2,633
Music $3,675
Staff $3,121
Art $2,642
Sets $7,085
Operating Labor $5,166
Miniatures $1,500
Camera $2,843
Sound $1,625
Electrical $4,806
Mechanical Effects $2,472
Set Dressing $4,496
Animals and Action Devices $170
Women's Wardrobe $404
Men's Wardrobe $1,509

Makeup and Hairdressing $1,086
Process $40
Production Film & Lab Charges
    $8,809
Stills $150
Transportation $2,900
Re-Recording $3,610
Photo Effects $1,485
Opticals, Fades and Dissolves
    $3,150
Titles $585
Post Production Film & Lab
    Charges $14,859
Projectionists $205
Editorial $7,426
Fringe Benefits $14,540
Miscellaneous $630
Amortizations $2,753
Contract Overhead $15,000
General Overhead $5,347
Total Picture Cost $155,991

Series Budget $167,757
Pre-prod $155,991
Under $11,766

ORIGINAL TREATMENT

The first draft of the script varies from the final draft (the version put before the cameras). Nakamura offers Doug and Tony some information and a prize, should they win the deadly cat-and-mouse game. Knowing the Americans will be landing today, thinking the island abandoned, the Japanese really have a mass air attack planned. The prize is the shack itself — in it

is a radio transmitter they could use to warn their side. This, of course, was discarded so the story could center on the character study of Nakamura.

The closing of the episode was originally different as well. After witnessing the events unfold, and realizing what Nakamura is trying to do, the father offers an impossible alternative — no information on the island's location unless the Time Tunnel will pick up his son and bring him to the present. Reluctantly, Kirk orders a fix on Nakamura. But they never get the chance to fulfill the request because the Americans arrive on the island and Nakamura is shot and killed before he can be transported.

STORY DEVELOPMENT

Bob and Wanda Duncan were paid $4,000 total for their original story, plus the first and final draft of the teleplay. The original title was "Kill Two" when they submitted their story proposal, which was assigned production number 9616. After reading the first draft of the teleplay, Jerry Briskin wrote to Irwin Allen: "I had a feeling that the story bogged down a little somewhere in the third act. I believe I might have felt this way due to the fact that some of the action seems repetitious in parts." Other comments by Jerry Briskin reveal some variations contained in the first draft.

"I wonder if Lieutenant Nakamura's crying scene comes too early in the

Mako as Lt. Nakamura.

story. I wonder if it would play better for his characterization towards the end of the script."

"I would like to see some more suspense built out of some of the action scenes and I believe this could possibly be done if we don't expose the idea that the Lieutenant wants to be killed quite so early in the story."

"Should Tony possibly be the one who fights the Lieutenant at the cave-rocky area? Up to now, Doug has set up all the plans."

"Nakamura challenges Tony to "Kendo" and in my opinion this fight is going to be a duplication of the Littlejohn "Staff" fight in Robin Hood."

"Nakamura runs out of the supply room without any caution although he has just learned that someone has taken grenades out of the supply room."

"In the description of the shack, I am not sure they had glass windows in this type of building."

Les Warner, concerned for budget, wrote to Allen on the same day with the following proposals: "Consider the possibility of one actor playing both of the Nakamura parts (father and son)…The set operation of machine guns and their bullet hit effects is costly. Machine guns are indicated extensively throughout this story, and I feel that in several sequences they could be replaced with rifles. I suggest that this should definitely be the case in the cliff-and-cave scenes for the following reasons: (a) The machine gun bullet hits could very well be needed at a high elevation of the set where we would be using a camera crane, and the time-consumption and cost to rig these 'hits' would be exorbitant. (b) It is very possible that the cliff-face construction would not accommodate to the simulation of these 'hits.'"

HISTORICAL ERROR

General Kirk declares that both the Illinois and the Missouri were together for the up-coming invasion of Iwo Jima, because of the stock footage, but this is a historical inaccuracy. Only the Missouri was present. The Illinois was never fully built and never commissioned. There was a previous Illinois, but it was renamed Prairie State in 1941. The new one was never fully completed due to a shift in building carriers instead of battleships.

ABC CENSORSHIP CONCERNS

Indications of wound and blood kept to a minimum.
Standard caution, the gun is not fired directly into camera.
Your usual care in seeing that bodies in death are not grotesque or shocking to view.

TRIVIA

The name of the island is verified in the Time Tunnel Complex as Minami Iwo.

One Japanese soldier extra was needed on set on the last day of filming.

NOTES

This episode is one of the better adventures of the series, probably because it functions on an emotional rather than a pseudo-historical level. When a World War II type story came along involving two time traveling scientists, Newman and Phillips, and a pair of isolated Japanese soldiers on Iwo Jima in 1945, the producers cast one of the movies' all-time favorite bad guys, Philip Ahn. Philip was a little too old to play one of the soldiers but he played a scientist back at the Time Tunnel who gets caught up in a weird experience. "There is never time to develop a character," sighed Philip Ahn. "I played a

Storyboards for the episode "Kill Two By Two."

"KILL TWO BY TWO"

SCENE 31   P.O.V. SHOT   SUPPLY ROOM

A ROOM AS LARGE AS THE MAIN ROOM - WITH
BAGS OF RICE STACKED ALONG ONE SIDE -
BOXES OF GRENADES AND ORDINANCE - A
TABLE AND A COUPLE OF CHAIRS . . .

FADE IN -   "KILL TWO BY TWO"

SCENE 41   INT. TIME TUNNEL (NEW SUPER)
            (1ST UNIT)

doctor in the United States who was called to the tunnel. I look at a Pacific island 20 years ago and I supposedly see my son, a Japanese soldier, still fighting the war. And I had the weird feeling that was looking back at me, 20 years before. It was as if I was playing father and son."

"I wasn't ever badly injured on *Time Tunnel* in spite of all of the rolling and tumbling and swordfights and fistfights and rifle fire," recalled Robert Colbert. "God Almighty, I fought everything but a camel on that show!" This episode, however, featured more injuries than any other. At 3:15 p.m. on December 2, James Darren hurt the big toe of his left foot while working without a shoe during production, temporarily halting filming for a short time while a doctor was called in to look at it. Three days later, on December 5, Robert Colbert wrenched his back in a sequence involving a chase through the jungle.

Actor Brent Davis played the role of the Marine who shoots Lieutenant Nakamura at the conclusion of the adventure. "I was living in Studio City and had a very small role in a play directed by Larry Stewart, a casting director at 20th Century-Fox," Davis recalled. "Larry was married to actress Sue England. Sue was in the play's cast along with movie and TV bad guys Ken Mayer and Paul Carr. Subsequently, Larry asked me to do a scene with an actress Fox was interested in for their New Talent Program. She didn't make it. I did. While under contract, I did a *Voyage to the Bottom of the Sea* and then a *Time Tunnel*. And a couple more *Voyages* and *Lost In Space* before I was dropped from the program. Later, I worked for Fox many times and Larry and his wife were always very good to me socially and professionally and I valued their friendship. As for *Time Tunnel*, I only worked one day on it. James Darren and Robert Colbert were both nice guys. I actually had run into Bob Colbert a few times before as he used to come into a bar/restaurant where I parked cars, bartended, etc. He was friends with the owners. James Darren was very quiet and reserved…maybe shy. Colbert was a little more out-going. Both were very pleasant to me and I can only speak positively about them. My scenes in *Time Tunnel* were done at the end of the day and went pretty quickly…maybe 1-2 takes per shot."

BLOOPERS!

In the beginning of the episode, a small white jar is on the shelf located above the radio, but is not there when Tony later returns to the hut.

In some scenes the image is left-right reversed as in a mirror image.

Brent Davis is listed in the closing credits as "Marine Sargeant" instead of "Marine Sergeant."

PRODUCTION #9618
VISITORS FROM BEYOND THE STARS

INITIAL TELECAST: January 13, 1967

SHOOTING SCRIPT DATED: November 15, 1966, with revised pages dated November 21, 1966

DATES OF PRODUCTION: November 17, 18, 21, 22, 23 and 25, 1966

FILMING LOCATIONS: Fox Ranch, Stage 18, Stage 19 and Western Street

GUEST CAST: Fred Beir (Taureg); Dusty Cadis (cowboy #1 in saloon); Tris Coffin (Jess Crawford, the rancher); Ann Doree* (female Time Tunnel technician); Dave Dunlap (Johnson); Ross Elliott (the sheriff); Byron Foulger (Williams, the saloon keeper); Gary Haynes (Deputy Sam Colt); John Hoyt (Alien Leader); Jan Merlin (Centauri); Dave Sharpe (cowboy #2 in saloon); and Paul Stader (cowboy #3 in saloon).

Stunt Doubles
Dave Sharpe (double for Tony)
Paul Stader (double for Doug)
Interior of Sheriff's Office: Chuck Waters
Crawford Ranch, Road and Hill Country: Tom Steele, Dave Sharpe, Eddie Saenz

PRODUCTION CREDITS
ART DIRECTORS: Jack Martin Smith and Rodger E. Maus
ASSISTANT DIRECTOR: Fred R. Simpson
DIRECTOR: Sobey Martin
FILM EDITOR: Dick Wormell
MUSIC: stock
MUSIC EDITOR: Sam E. Levin
Teleplay by Bob and Wanda Duncan.

STORY: Space aliens from Alpha-1 land outside Mullins, Arizona, in the year 1885, an advance scouting party with the intention of depleting Earth's protein resources. The aliens do not care about human life; their only morality is their survival. They have been raiding other planets throughout the universe because their home planet is completely depleted. They land at the

---

* Ann Doree was an un-billed female Time Tunnel technician in a number of episodes. While listed for this episode and "The Walls of Jericho" and others in this book, it remains possible that she appears in other episodes. The spelling of her name has not been verified.

farm of a truculent farmer, Crawford, and Tony is dispatched to the nearby town to round up all available food. Doug then conspires with Crawford to try to blast the machine, the source of the Aliens' power. But they miss, and Crawford is struck dead while Doug is converted through their mind-control device. Back in town, Tony is unable to convince the delegation of leaders to visit the outer space visitors for negotiations. The citizens, including the sheriff, assume Tony is off his rocker — until the Aliens burn down part of the town and put in a personal appearance. While Doug and the Aliens organize the gathering of food and protein to be picked up, Tony seeks the now-willing sheriff's assistance. Tony acquires their "projector" and smashes it, rendering the Aliens defenseless and releasing control of all who the Aliens have brainwashed, including Doug. The Aliens return home and Doug and Tony vanish back into the vortex. Back at the Time Tunnel Complex, an Alien leader appears, threatening to destroy the Earth unless the Time Tunnel personnel can verify the mysterious disappearance of an Alien space craft was not of our doing. After witnessing the proof on the viewing screen, the Aliens retreat back home…but not without a warning that they would return again one day soon.

STOCK MUSIC: Color Bumper (by Johnny Williams, :03); The Boiler Room (by Williams, :24); Tony's Tall Tale (by Williams, 1:18); Time Transfer (by Williams, :09); Main Title (a.k.a. Time Tunnel Theme, by Williams, :37); Outer Space (by Bernard Herrmann, :21); Booby Trap (by Hugo Friedhofer, :48); The Quarrel (by Herrmann, :48); The Mine (by Herrmann, :48); Tony Enters Machine (by Williams, :48); The Reef (by Herrmann, :41); Tony Suits Up #2 (by Lyn Murray); Plastic Device (by Murray, :16); Impact (by Murray, :50); Take Off (by Murray, :50); Brandon Take Over (by Murray, :23); Moon Walk (by Murray, :23); Steal Horses (by Joseph Mullendore, :38); U.S. Intelligence (by Sawtell, :19); The Quarrel (by Herrmann, 1:01); The Mine (by Herrmann, :43); The Quarrel (by Herrmann, :43); Brandon Stalked (by Murray, :43); Meteor (by Murray, :43); The National Razor (by Leith Stevens, :32); Booby Trap (by Friedhofer, :32); The Paperhanger is Still Alive (by Daniele Amfitheatrof, :32); Battle (by Mullendore, :32); Lots of It (by Lionel Newman, :32); Indian Revenge (by Mullendore, :32); Fright, Flight, Fight (by Robert Drasnin, :07); Search and Find (by Drasnin, :07); Bumper (by Williams, :03); Brothers Apart (by Drasnin, :31); Doug's Count Down (by Williams, :31); Doug's Arrival (by Williams, :17); The Telegraph (by Williams, :17); Appear Sting (by Herrmann, :02); The Jungle (by Herrmann, :13); Time Transfer (by Williams, :51); Hatch (by Murray, :23); Brandon Take Over (by Murray, :09); Episode Titles (by Alexander

Courage, :18); Doug's Arrival (by Williams, :18); Derry's Death (by Waxman, :18); Mock Mysterioso (by Newman, :18); Someone Moved (by Newman, :18); Tunnel of Slow Return (by Drasnin, :18); Plastic Device (by Murray, 1:17); Control and Stalk (by Murray, 1:17); First Test Part Two (by Stevens, 1:17); The Quarrel (by Herrmann, 1:17); Hot Sun Ralston (by Courage, :04); Take Off (by Murray, :49); Wild Anxiety (by Alfred Newman, :49); Goodbyes (by Drasnin, :11); Time Transfer (by Williams, :02); Flying Chord (by Drasnin, :03); Boiler Room (by Williams, :26); The Quarrel (by Herrmann, :29); Terror (by Herrmann, :30); Next Week (by Murray, :09); End Credits (a.k.a. Time Tunnel Theme, by Williams, :49); and Fox I.D. (by Alfred Newman, :05).

EPISODE BUDGET

Story Rights and Expense $1,900
Scenario $5,908
Producer $6,461
Direction $3,000
Cast $16,100
Extras $4,096
Music $3,675
Staff $3,165
Art $2,642
Sets $9,725
Operating Labor $4,866
Miniatures $1,500
Camera $3,306
Sound $1,625
Electrical $3,949
Mechanical Effects $1,450
Set Dressing $4,453
Animals and Action Devices $270
Women's Wardrobe $404
Men's Wardrobe $1,454
Makeup and Hairdressing $1,206

Process $40
Production Film & Lab Charges
    $8,809
Stills $150
Transportation $4,800
Location Expenses $1,000
Re-Recording $3,610
Photo Effects $1,560
Opticals, Fades and Dissolves
    $3,150
Titles $585
Post Production Film & Lab
    Charges $14,809
Projectionists $205
Editorial $7,426
Fringe Benefits $15,260
Miscellaneous $885
Amortizations $2,753
Contract Overhead $15,000
General Overhead $6,930
Total Picture Cost $168,127

Series Budget $167,757
Pre-prod $168,127
Over $370

SET PRODUCTION COSTS

Interior Alien Spaceship, light control area, viewing screen, control box and colored panels, $1,200

Exterior Ranch House and Barn, Barrel to explode, bushes, flat rock for action $50

Exterior Open Country, road and rocky area $50

Exterior Western Street, Exterior Sheriff's office and Exterior saloon $150

Interior Sheriff's office $1,380

Interior Saloon $1,800

Interior Farmhouse Kitchen built, clock and shotgun rack $870

Construction Foreman $825

Amortized $2,000

Total $8,325

STORY DEVELOPMENT

Bob and Wanda Duncan were the first to propose aliens from outer space for an episode set in the near future. Their initial concept was titled "Outer Space," which was followed by a revised plot titled "The Attack of Alfa-One," both a single paragraph in length.

"The Attack of Alfa-One"
by The Duncans

Tony and Doug are snatched out of time by an invading space ship from an over-populated planet that is sending a colony to take over the Earth. The Air Force picks up the UFO on radar but can't identify it. The invaders intend to use the Time Tunnel as a means of getting their party onto Earth, and Doug and Tony are forced to cooperate. With their extra-sensory powers, the invaders move into the Time Tunnel and take it over as their base headquarters from which they issue an ultimatum to the Earth: unless room is made for the colony from outer space, the aliens will destroy the planet. But an android servant brought here by the aliens escapes and it is up to Doug to track him down in an American town and bring him back before a crisis destroys the negotiations and leads to war. Doug captures the android, but the American people have been so panicked by him that the decision is made to destroy the Time Tunnel and the aliens in it — an act which will prevent the aliens from using it as a means of getting to Earth. It is only through an extreme act of heroism on the part of Doug and Tony that the aliens are sent back through space, and Doug and Tony are once again lost in time.

On October 30, 1966, they wrote a third version of their plot proposal, two to three pages in length, and now titled "The Alien Raid." It was here that they were paid $4,000 for their story, and the first and final draft of the teleplay. In this version, Tony and Doug materialize on an incoming Alien spaceship operated by two cruel and insensitive creatures from Alfa One who have come to make a raid on Earth to gather protein to send back to their starving planet. They take Doug and Tony captive and arrive on a small Arizona ranch in the year 1885. The ranch is run by a man and his wife named Crawford and the aliens take it over, intending to use it as a base from which they will transport the cattle herds they collect back to their own planet. On Earth, the creatures take on human form and are distinguishable from other humans only by a triangulation of blue dots behind the right ear. Crawford resists and is vaporized by the aliens who then use Doug to carry an ultimatum to the town.

All of the cattle herds in the vicinity are to be rounded up and turned over to the Aliens, plus all of the grains and food supplies in the town. Doug is to deliver the message and bring back one of the leaders of the town within three hours or the creatures will wreak terrible destruction. Back in the Time Tunnel, Swain and Ann establish the date and the fact that creatures from other planets have been raiding Earth for thousands of years. In town, Doug

Deputy Sam Colt (Gary Haynes) holds Tony Newman at gunpoint.

goes to see the sheriff who is a hard, practical man who scoffs at the ultimatum and doesn't have time to listen to stories about Aliens. The Apaches are on the warpath and his town is in the grip of a real Indian scare. He warns Doug not to try to profit on the panic of a town that will pay any price for peace. Meanwhile, Tony tries to escape and save Mrs. Crawford, but he is recaptured by the Aliens. Doug escapes from the jail and tries to force the sheriff to go

Gary Haynes takes a quick break between scenes.

to the ranch with him, but they run across an Indian fight with the Cavalry and the sheriff escapes. Doug is forced to go back to the ranch alone.

When Doug reports to the Alien creatures, they decide that since the sheriff will not come to them, they will go to him, and they materialize in the saloon. The Aliens take over the town and make their demands. If the town will comply, the Aliens will protect the town from the Indians. One of the Aliens takes

Deputy Sam Colt (Gary Haynes) and the sheriff (Ross Elliott).

the sheriff to the edge of town, waves his hand, and immediately the plains are full of charging Indians (a hallucination, of course). The sheriff panics. The Aliens wave their hands and the Indians disappear. Now the Aliens begin the progressive looting of the town. They direct whole herds of cattle into a stampede by ESP and direct them, and when the cattle reach a certain area, they are dematerialized and sent through space. The Aliens only have one weakness. After a certain time away from their ship, they change back to the form they assume on Alfa One and must return to the ship to recharge their powers.

In the end, Tony, Doug, the Sheriff and Mrs. Crawford fight against the Aliens, blocking the Aliens' route to their spaceship. The sheriff uses bullets against them, which are ineffective, and Tony uses fire to hold them back. It works. The Aliens are destroyed and their spaceship disappears. When the Aliens die, the Indians massed on the hill also dematerialize.

After reviewing the first draft of the script, Jerry Briskin wrote to Irwin Allen: "The one major story point that I do not understand, and this covers several situations in the script, is why the aliens don't simply change every-

The cast prepares for filming.

one in the town that they come in contact with, collect what they want and depart? Isn't this what the aliens would have done if Tony and Doug had not appeared on the scene?" The Duncans understood and, when they wrote the teleplay, put Doug under the influence with the same three triangular markings behind the ear.

Briskin was also concerned about production cost and time, and proposed removing the radioactive glow of the space suits. "The makeup required for the aliens will be a time-consuming item unless the so-called 'normal' alien makeup and their human appearance can be scheduled in such a way as not to hold up production. The only other solution might possibly the use of photographic doubles." Because the spaceship did not resemble the spaceship described in the story, the description in the teleplay was altered to fit the one in storage, and avoid huge construction costs.

It was initially considered to utilize the Indian-Cavalry stock footage from "Massacre" again, but Briskin ruled it out. "That fighting took place at the river bed and is very easy to identify," he explained.

On November 5, Les Warner wrote to Irwin Allen, regarding production factors: "I suggest we indicate in the script that our two aliens are wearing gauntlet-type gloves in their spaceship; otherwise, we might have to do things

Even Aliens from outer space need to take a break.

with their hands before they change to human forms…Would the Desilu-Culver Western Street be suitable for an 1885 Arizona town? However, I don't believe there is now a full day's work indicated on the street and it might behoove us to try to plot this somewhere where we could also shoot our countryside exteriors…I believe there is no particular problem with the spaceship interiors as I understand we are going to use our 'One Way to the

Moon' sets…What about reusing the kitchen set in 'The Death Trap'?" The kitchen set was used as proposed, but only some of the interiors from "One Way to the Moon" were reused — with new designs to prevent the audience from recognizing the same controls and computers.

"Aliens look like a 'pulsing mass' and Warner considered doubling Centauri's and Taureg's 'masks' instead, and use only one mask since they do not appear on the screen at the same time," Warner continued. "There are no miniatures; however, it is extremely doubtful that the exterior shots of the alien spaceship now indicated as Stock can be found. Considering the cost we are already faced with on this production, it is obvious that new miniatures could not even be considered. My only suggestion would be to explore the cost of painting a spaceship onto a desert shot and not have it set down or take off, and delete the spaceship the Time Tunnel sees and just have them hear its signals or something."

Jerry Briskin wrote to Irwin Allen on November 10, remarking: "Doug's speech about the aliens having a hard time taking over the earth — doesn't

it seem stranger that the aliens would have a hard time taking over the earth in 1885 when with just the wave of a hand or the pointing of a finger they can control or destroy whomever they desire?"

For the final version of the teleplay, the roles of Doug and Tony were reversed. It was originally intended for Tony to be brainwashed and Doug who comes to the rescue.

ABC CENSORSHIP CONCERNS

Please be sure that the quotes from Look *and* Life *magazines are accurate and that clearance is obtained from publishers for use.*

If definitely mentally ill, please sub for "raving lunatic."

Caution that there is no close up of choking and that fight is not unnecessarily prolonged.

CRITICS HAVE THEIR SAY

Days after this episode was telecast, columnist Howard Pearson expressed his disappointment in alien infiltration on *The Time Tunnel* in his January 16, 1967, issue of the Utah *Deseret News*. "When the names of busy men in the entertainment world are mentioned, the name of Irwin Allen is at or near the top," Pearson wrote. "He has also been dubbed 'The Jules Verne of television.' From his fertile mind has come ideas for such shows as *The Time Tunnel, Voyage to the Bottom of the Sea* and *Lost In Space*. All of them are successful programs on television this season and all three take a great deal of imagination, like on *Time Tunnel* last week. Allen had alien space men from another planet land on Earth in 1885. That's where most of the drama took place, yet he also had these spacemen from the past, who knew more about electronics than we do today, step into the future."

"I feel everyone is interested in fantasy," Allen said during one of those rare times he settled down for an interview. "I have tried to keep everything believable. On *Time Tunnel*, we research every episode. I do want to add a little sugar-coating to education. I think our viewers, especially the young ones, will then scurry back for more information on things that they see on our show. We have programs dealing with Nero, the Walls of Jericho, the Aztecs, Billy the Kid and we have one episode that has Tony and Doug [the show's heroes] participate in a chase from One Million A.D. to One Million B.C."

When we were able to get a word in, we asked about the recent criticism of *Voyage to the Bottom of the Sea*. "You started out with an entrancing underwater adventure series and now you've been introducing so many monsters, until it seems like they have taken over the show," we noted. Allen replied,

"Well, the viewers who write in to us seem to like the monsters so we just decided to give them more of the same. If there are many in your area who object, have them write to us at ABC in Hollywood. We would like to hear from them."

Six months later on June 30, Joan Crosby wrote in her syndicated column: "If *The Time Tunnel* had stayed with this kind of full hour science fiction nonsense every week, instead of going historical, they might have made it to another season."

The Hartford Courant remarked, "The main trouble with *The Time Tunnel* series has always been that it can't get out of the past and into the future… It's an interesting combination of several things — joining a Western-type setting (they land in a small town out west) with science fiction and just plain mystery. Doug is electronically brainwashed and sent to work for the space enemies. Incidentally, the Deputy here is played by Gary Haynes, a *Peyton Place* regular."

"It's the first chance I've had to look at the people I'm talking to and it's a whole new experience," remarked Gary Haynes. The actor was not blind, but he played the role of a blind youth on television's *Peyton Place*. This episode marked his first guest spot on another television program since he signed on to play Chris Webber on *Peyton Place*, also filmed on the 20th Century Studio back lot. "At this point I've completed 50 episodes of *Peyton Place*, and before that a role in *Ben Casey* had been the only film experience I had. I've gotten away from acting with my eyes. I have to concentrate on not over-acting. The task is all the more difficult since I'm playing a 19th century westerner reacting to spacemen who are completely silver from head to foot."

"They had me wear this silver paint for makeup and I the script called for me to speak like a robot," recalled Jan Merlin. "Consider that a departure from the kiddie fare I had done on *Tom Corbett*. This was not live television but it was certainly fun to do. I do not recall how silly the episode was with cowboys and aliens fighting against each other…I do know they later took the film and edited it into a movie which still airs on television from time to time."

NOTES

Props from prior *Lost In Space* episodes were used as the décor of the interior of the space ship. Notice the glass homing post from "The Revenge of Robin Hood" hanging vertically on the wall in the alien space craft as part of the alien décor.

The space suits the aliens wear are modified from the Robinson family's attire, from the second season of *Lost In Space*.

To create an atmosphere of an outer space menace, many of the music cues in this episode originate from Bernard Herrmann's motion picture soundtrack for *The Day the Earth Stood Still* (1951).

Stock footage of the stampeding cattle was the same used in the episode "Massacre" and the two-part *Batman* production "Come Back, Shame" and "It's the Way You Play the Game."

The interior of the house where Doug and the farmer are held captive is the same set used for the interior of Jeremiah's residence in "The Death Trap." Picture frames have been replaced and tins have been replaced by a clock, but the towel and the coffee pot from the former episode are still featured on the stove in this episode!

If Doug's mind has been taken over by the aliens, why is he bulletproof like the aliens? Doug is shot at twice with no sign of injury.

To accomplish the alien's foreign language, two different audio recordings from other scenes in this episode were combined and then played in reverse. The shooting script says the aliens are to "babble" but thanks to today's technology, it has been verified that the alien dialogue was a soundtrack played backwards. What the aliens were really saying was "From this moment on, you exist only in vulnerable point." (The last two from an audio track separate from the rest.) The closing lines delivered by the aliens were "that there are three alternatives," "primary test objective," "we have studied Earth from a," "has been located," "know its vulnerable points" and "you exist only as a convenience."

"I had never heard of a science fiction western before," recalled actor Jan Merlin. "It was weird to be out west as a silver-skinned alien. After they dabbed the makeup on me and Fred Beir, we noticed our eyeballs had changed to yellow-pink. I didn't care for the way we were told to play the aliens. It was the same tired version of aliens we've seen since the Saturday matinee days."

The alien commander makes a reference at the Time Tunnel Complex that we recently landed on the moon, though the series takes place in 1968 and we didn't land on the moon until 1969. The writers were close in their prediction, but no cigar.

Robert Colbert remembers that at the time this episode was being filmed, it was not one of his favorites.

To shoot on location at the Western Street, on November 18, police/security roped off a sufficient area north of Western Street for 10 dressing room trailers. Some of the stores outside the saloon are nothing but paint on large sheets of plywood and an observant watcher might notice how the actors as they leave the saloon cast their smooth shadows on the storefronts.

BLOOPER!

When Doug uses a crow bar and breaks the lock of the weapons shack so he can sneak inside and steal some weapons, he tosses the crowbar on the ground outside the door. When he opens the door and steps inside, he is holding the crowbar in his hand and places it on wooden crates.

One of the boulders moves when Tony pushes against it.

RECURRING THEME

Almost all of the non-regular characters, even characters from sides that oppose each other, and in particular all of the aliens, are hostile to Doug and Tony and to Time Tunnel personnel, to one extent or another.

THE GHOST OF NERO

INITIAL TELECAST: January 20, 1967

SHOOTING SCRIPT DATED: November 28, 1966, with revised pages dated November 30, December 2 and 5.

DATES OF PRODUCTION: December 6, 7, 8, 9, 12 and 13, 1966

FILMING LOCATIONS: Stage 18 and Stage 19

GUEST CAST: Nino Candido (Italian Corporal, a.k.a. Mussolini); Eduardo Ciannelli (Count Galba); Orwin Harvey (German soldier #4); Gunnar Hellstrom (Neistadt); John Hoyt (Dr. Steinholtz); Gregg Jacobson (German soldier #1); Richard Jaeckel (Sgt. Mueller); Ed Jahnke (German soldier #3); Seymour Koenig (Italian soldier #1); Denver Mattson (German soldier #5); Louis Paul (Italian soldier #2); George Robotham (German Corporal); Miriam Schelber (a technician at Time Tunnel); and Stephen Smith (German soldier #2).

Stunt Doubles
Bill Graeff (double for Galba)
Glen Colbert (double for Doug)
Frank Graham (double for Tony)
Paul Stader (double for Doug)
Stand-Ins: Skip Burnham, John Drake, Steve Howell and Gene Silvani

Stand-Ins
Interior Cellar and Corridor: Glen Colbert, Bill Graeff, Frank Graham, Orwin Harvey, Tony Mancuso, Denver Mattson and Paul Stader
Interior Time Tunnel Complex and Interior Galba's Room: Glen Colbert, Frank Graham, Denver Mattson, Paul Stader and Chuck Waters

PRODUCTION CREDITS
ART DIRECTORS: Jack Martin Smith and Rodger E. Maus
ASSISTANT DIRECTOR: Fred R. Simpson
DIRECTOR: Sobey Martin
FILM EDITOR: James Baiotto
MUSIC: stock
MUSIC EDITOR: Sam E. Levin
Teleplay by Leonard Stadd.

STORY: October 23, 1915. Tony and Doug find themselves near the Italian-Austrian Alps during World War I, about two months after Italy declared war against Germany. Confined in the villa of Count Galba, under the scrutiny of the German military, under the leadership of Major Neistadt and Sergeant Mueller, Tony and Doug struggle against three odds: how to escape, how to alert the Italians that the Germans are using the villa as a spotter's post for all roads through, and how to assist Count Galba with his struggle against the ghost of Nero, the Roman Emperor. Galba discovers his ancestral home secretly housed catacombs containing the coffin and remains of Nero, and the ghost of Nero seeks vengeance on the man who got his throne — Galba, the present Count's ancestor. The ghost enters the body of Mueller and attacks Galba, who is saved by Doug and Tony. Back at the Time Tunnel Complex, the ghost is accidentally transported to the present and the scientists and security combat the specter until it retreats back to the tunnel. By this time, the battle outside is escalating. The Italians are fighting back and Neistadt gives orders to abandon the villa and blow it up. But the Italians swarm the place, led by a stocky Corporal. The Corporal then encounters Neistadt and Mueller, who are both killed. The ghost thereupon enters the body of the Corporal and Tony and Doug finally see that he is Benito Mussolini, moments before they are swept into the vortex of time.

STOCK MUSIC: Color Bumper (by Johnny Williams, :03); The Boiler Room (by Williams, :31); The Quarrel (by Bernard Herrmann, :15); The Glowing (by Herrmann, :15); Danger (by Herrmann, :15); Main Title (a.k.a. Time Tunnel Theme, by Williams, :37); The Glowing (by Herrmann, 1:04); The Paperhanger is Still Alive (by Daniele Amfitheatrof, :15); Mock Mysterioso (by Lionel Newman, :15); The Paperhanger is Still Alive (by Amfitheatrof, 1:27); The Glowing (by Herrmann, 1:27); Tony Rescued (by Sawtell, :30); Take Him Away (by Joseph Mullendore, :30); U.S. Intelligence (by Sawtell, :18); Tony and Comet (by Lyn Murray, :10); The Glowing (by Herrmann, :10 and :23); The Crater (by Herrmann, :23); Terror (by Herrmann, :23); The Quarrel (by Herrmann, :23); Bomb Warp (by Robert Drasnin, :23); Fright, Flight, Fight (by Drasnin, :23 and :23); Time Travel (by Murray, :14); The Crater (by Herrmann, :14); Panic (by Herrmann, :14); The Visor (by Herrmann, :31); Terror Stinger (by Fred Steiner, :34); It's Last Approach (by Murray, :34); Wild Anxiety (by Alfred Newman, :34); The Crater (by Herrmann, :34); Gort (by Herrmann, :34); Bumper (by Williams, :03); The Flashlight (by Herrmann, :32); The Glowing (by Herrmann, :32); Comet #7 (by Murray, :32); Tony's Tall Tale (by Williams, :20); To the Tunnel (by

Williams, :20); The Crater (by Herrmann, :42); Escape (by Herrmann, :42); The Quarrel (by Herrmann, :42); Wild Anxiety (by Alfred Newman, :42); The Jungle (by Williams, :42); Tony Enters Machine (by Williams, :27); Flying Chord (by Drasnin, :27); The Crater (by Herrmann, :53); Wild Anxiety (by Alfred Newman, :12); The Paperhanger is Still Alive (by Amfitheatrof, :12); A Dark Night (by Lionel Newman, :23); First Test Part Two (by Leith Stevens, :37); Urgent Detergent (by Lionel Newman, :37); The Bombing (by Sawtell, :05); Someone Moved (by Lionel Newman, :29); The Crater (by Herrmann, :29); The Glowing (by Herrmann, :29); Time Transfer (by Williams, :02); Flying Chord (by Drasnin, :02); The Boiler Room (by Williams, :21); First Test Part Two (by Stevens, :22); Coda (by Stevens, :22); Next Week (by Murray, :09); End Credits (a.k.a. Time Tunnel Theme, by Williams, :38); and Fox I.D. (by Alfred Newman, :05).

EPISODE BUDGET

Story Rights and Expense $1,900
Scenario $5,908
Producer $6,461
Direction $3,000
Cast $17,440
Extras $5,005
Music $3,675
Staff $3,121
Art $2,642
Sets $11,475
Operating Labor $4,501
Miniatures $1,500
Camera $3,044
Sound $1,625
Electrical $3,949
Mechanical Effects $1,695
Set Dressing $5,632
Women's Wardrobe $404
Men's Wardrobe $2,289
Makeup and Hairdressing $1,086

Process $40
Production Film & Lab Charges $8,809
Stills $150
Transportation $2,900
Re-Recording $3,610
Photo Effects $1,470
Opticals, Fades and Dissolves $3,150
Titles $585
Post Production Film & Lab Charges $14,509
Projectionists $205
Editorial $7,426
Fringe Benefits $15,770
Miscellaneous $630
Amortizations $2,753
Contract Overhead $15,000
General Overhead $7,253
Total Picture Cost $170,612

Series Budget $167,757
Pre-prod $170,612
Over $2,855

SET PRODUCTION COSTS
Exterior Wall of Villa $200
Cellar-Crypt $1,530
Catacombs $1,440
Galba's Room $2,200
Observation Room $1,030
Roman Throne $100
Construction Foreman $975
Amortized $1,500
Total $8,975

NOTES

This episode came about when Leonard Stadd was inspired by old war-movie footage. When questioned about whether the supernatural element might have made faithful viewers into harsh critics, Stadd remarked, "*Time Tunnel* was a comic strip. It had nothing to do with science, so why not introduce a ghost into the concept? For crying out loud, you could have brought in Frankenstein's monster. In 'Nero,' I got away with combining science fiction with metaphysical stuff like poltergeists and possession. It was great melodrama and lots of fun."

Stadd was a good friend of William Welch, who scripted more than 50 episodes for Irwin Allen's television productions. Welch wrote a play, *How to Make a Man*, a comedy about robots. The play wasn't doing badly on Broadway, but it got bumped for Neil Simon's first play, *Come Blow Your Horn*. For Welch, it was a disaster. When Irwin Allen wanted to buy the screen rights to the stage play, he was introduced to William Welch. Welch incorporated a number of ghosts in his scripts for *Voyage to the Bottom of the Sea*, because he was fascinated by the spirit world. Stadd figured if Welch could inject the supernatural in a *Voyage* episode, he could do the same for *The Time Tunnel*.

"Eduardo Ciannelli, now there was a class act. A total gentleman," recalled Robert Colbert. "He treated me like a prince. Somehow or other, he almost kinda adopted me. He couldn't have been kinder. And I was like a fan of his. Boy, he just stood out to me. I wish I could have spent a lot more time with that man. He was quite a bit older than I was and all, but my experience with him, working with him, was one of the best I ever had."

Eduardo Ciannelli, whose grim mouth and expressive eyes were rooted in a craggy visage, was familiar to millions of people through his hundreds of roles in movies and TV. But he had a rule of never seeing himself perform on screen, except once. "I was horrified when I first saw myself on film," he recalled grimly. "I never went to the movie theater to see myself again!" So even if Ciannelli wasn't watching, millions of TV viewers saw his performance in "The Ghost of Nero." Ciannelli played an Italian count who helped Doug and Tony escape from a WW1 predicament in Italy, which included the very active ghost of the Emperor Nero and a cocky, barrel-chested Italian Army Corporal named Benito Mussolini, played by

Nino Candido as the Italian Corporal known as Mussolini.

Nino Candido. Explaining his abhorrence of watching himself on screen, Ciannelli remarked, "I worry too much about the way I am acting and once my performance is on film, it is too late to change what has been done. It isn't necessary for an actor to see his own work anyway. He learns by doing and by watching others."

STORY DEVELOPMENT

The November 8, 1966, plot proposal by Leonard Stadd, titled "The Ghost of Black Castle," was a bit different from what you see in the film, with a few minor differences such as the boys being threatened with a large beam, not a sword. Tony retraces the possible exit through the secret corridor, while the Germans find Doug and Count Galba in the room and the Count alibis for Doug. The Germans are unaware of Tony's presence. Back in the cellar, Tony fights for his life with a German soldier and after escaping, it's assumed by the Germans that Tony is an Italian partisan.

While Doug and Galba are in the locked room, in action as it's happening, we get the full story of the ghost of Nero and his curse on the Galbas. Galba, the General who succeeded Nero as Emperor, had declared Nero a public enemy and the tyrant was forced to flee from Rome. For centuries, various

Actor Gunnar Hellstrom and director Sobey Martin.

descendants of Galba were strangled by the ghost. But about a hundred years ago, the menace was put to rest by sealing his stone casket in the crypt in the cellar. When the ghost pounds at the door, Galba sees Nero's face through the window. (Doug cannot see him as the ghost can be seen only by descendants of Galba.)

A subplot in the proposal that was never filmed (probably to eliminate the cost of more actors, costumes and creating another set or filming on the backlot) involved Tony's temporary escape from the catacombs and his attempt to convince the Italian force that the Germans have arrived a day and a half early. He tells the Italian Corporal that the Germans are using the Villa as a spotting post. Tony is disbelieved and ultimately dragged before a military court with the Colonel presiding. The Colonel reads the charges against him, gets a couple of nods from two fellow officers, and pronounces the death sentence on Tony. Tony kicks over the lamp on the table and gets away in the dark as he's being fired at. There is a chase scene to the bridge and Tony jumps off bridge, hitting water. Guards fire at him in water. Instead, a subplot involving the Time Tunnel Complex and their temporary complication with the ghost of Nero was written into the teleplay.

Eduardo Ciannelli as Count Galba.

Another notable scene in the plot proposal was Doug and Galba observing the Italians' advance from their window. With the Germans stationed at the mountain outpost, they could create a problem and they need to do something to stop the slaughter of wounded. Doug can't stand by and let this happen. He decides to knock out the radio if he can. He goes through the secret exit behind the closet which the Count locks behind him. Doug comes out of the secret exit in the basement. He is caught by German guards and is about to be shot as Tony leaps in through the window. Between them, they knock out the Germans and gather up weapons and go off intending to knock out radio. A squad of Italian soldiers come in through window. A

Corporal barks orders to his men, but we don't see his face. He moves toward the crypt. Tony and Doug crash into the German's observation room and get the drop on the Major and his men. They destroy the radio room. Doug and Tony leave the Germans in the hands of the Italian soldiers and then head back to Galba's room.

Outside Galba's room the Italian Corporal demands that the door be

Count Galba explains a ghost of a problem to Doug Phillips.

opened. The Count fearfully asks who it is. The Corporal says that he has arrived to save the Count. Galba opens the door. The Corporal enters the room, and attacks the Count. He is killing him when Doug and Tony rush in and counter-attack, finally pulling the Corporal off the Count. We see the Corporal's face for the first time — it is Benito Mussolini. As he leaves the room, he egomaniacally says that he will be back to fulfill his destiny! Nero's ghost has entered him. Tony and Doug dematerialize.

"Initial script provides for no villain. There really is no threat or anything to put the boys into the jeopardy required of television heroes in an action-adventure series. They contribute nothing," Jerry Briskin remarked in an inter-office memo to Irwin Allen on November 10. "As presented, Tony and Doug appear to be on the outside looking in rather than being an integral part of the story. Also, I would like to see more threat to Tony and Doug in the script. I suggest that Galba and the German officer be strengthened in characterization and made more menacing. I wonder, if we are going to do a ghost story, if we shouldn't go all out and do as great ghost stories have been done — great suspense — tense, taut scenes with characters believing they hear or see ghosts at every turn…and seeing same."

After reading the first draft of the teleplay, Irwin Allen, upon reading the plot proposal, pointed out in scene 48, the old Bible, the crucifix, the books, and the matches are completely out of place in the catacombs, which were mainly underground burial and hiding places during the early Christian days. This was, naturally, adjusted before the final draft of the teleplay was completed. "The idea of having the ghost of Nero come into the Time Tunnel Complex is good," Allen added. "However, as it is now written, I think the scene will get a laugh. I would hate to be the director who had to stage the action where the ghost expert, Steinholtz, is talking to an unseen ghost in an attempt to get the ghost to go back to his own time."

Les Warner, after reviewing the November 14 revision, now titled "Ghost Story," considered any possibility of scaling back production costs. In an inter-office memo dated the same, Warner asked that the Sentry's sub-machine gun be replaced with a rifle. "Too many effects involved," he explained. He also suggested deleting the wounded soldier that Tony is helping in scene 92, and "we could be in trouble with the number now suggested in the script, plus the quantity of silent bit adjustments now indicated. I earnestly suggest deleting the 'crowd' in scenes 157 and 158 and playing this business on a comparatively deserted street area." Warner suggested introducing the Italian Corporal (Mussolini) earlier in the episode, by using him instead of Carboneri at Tony's trail, and that it is he who leads the chase after Tony.

A final revision of the plot proposal was drafted on November 16, now titled "The Ghost of Nero," followed by a first draft of the teleplay, dated November 28. This time the script called for an eerie voice of the ghost. On December 1, Briskin wrote to Allen, questioning why the voice was even included. "Why does the eerie voice of the Ghost, who is now in the Complex, call out for Galba? Galba isn't in the Complex and I was under the impression that the Ghost was in the Complex to stop the Complex Group from aiding Tony, Doug and Galba."

Eliminating the scene with Tony trying to convince the Italian Corporal that the Germans are using the Villa as a spotting post, the entire episode was shot on Stage 18 and Stage 19.

The first draft of the script also features noticeable differences from what we see today in the final production. As Doug and Tony run through the basement corridors in flight from the Germans, shortly after their arrival, the ghost follows, leaving a sword stuck through a soldier along the way. Another noticeable difference was the ghost possessing the body of Tony. Steinholtz, an expert on the supernatural, recommends shock treatment and the Tunnel directs a momentary current of electricity at him. But as he falls unconscious, the mad spirit descends on the Tunnel instead.

DELETED SCENE

This episode was originally going to feature a flashback scene, told by Count Galba to Doug and Tony, of his ancestors and their encounter with the Roman Emperor. The scene was shot on the afternoon of December 9, 1966. Chuck Waters was hired to double for Galba during the brief action. Production cost $1,470 for special photographic effects for the Ghost of Nero, including an animated glow for scene 159 (breakdown listed below). Due to time constraints, it can be understandable if the back-story, told in flashback, was never used. But after considerable expense to create the special effects, it remains unknown why the producers decided to dismiss the special effects and use the old "invisible force" trick, cheapening the production.

SPECIAL PHOTOGRAPHIC EFFECTS FOR THE GHOST OF NERO
First scene (scene 30) $260
Remaining seven scenes at $130 each
Animated glow (scene 159) $300
Total $1,470

ABC CENSORSHIP CONCERNS

Caution that there are no "full skeleton" shots and that, generally, these skull and bones shots are not too frightening for family viewing.
Sword not pressed against the throat.

CRITICS HAVE THEIR SAY

This very episode caused UP-International writer Vernon Scott to mea-sure the worth of a television program, weighing the merits, if any, on the basis of the audience it was attempting to reach. "Recently it wasn't enough that the heroes found themselves in an Italian nobleman's villa during World War I where they are badgered by the Kaiser's troops and — get this — the ghost of Nero. A spoof you ask? No. A bit of satire perhaps? No. It was pure tedium. A mature mind must ask itself why on earth this particular hour-long episode was filmed and aired, and for whom it was intended. At best it was comic book nonsense for adolescents. But it cannot be written off so lightly. In reality it is typical of the effrontery of television executives determining what the public is offered for viewing. But this isn't to single out *The Time Tunnel*. It is no better nor much worse than the common fare American viewers have been slapped in the face with for too many years to count…it is pitiful that a great and powerful medium, indeed America's mass medium, cannot or will not do better."

The January 20, 1967, issue of *The Free Lance Star* reviewed this episode: "Scientists Newman and Phillips, like the bouncing ball seen in Mitch Miller's sing-along show, bounce into the year 1915. They become caught between warring factions of Italians and Germans as WWI progresses. Into this science fiction plot they have added a touch of fantasy, as the ghost of Nero appears. It is no place for the discriminating television viewer."

The visitor's badge on Dr. Steinholtz is number 4134, the same being worn by Dr. Raymond Swain in the same episode!

The effect of books flying off the shelf is accomplished with a black cloth backing where a member of the shooting crew pushed the books off the shelves. In one shot, the cloth and force to push the books are evident on camera.

Music cues for this episode originated from Bernard Herrmann's composition for *The Day the Earth Stood Still* (1951) and *Journey to the Center of the Earth* (1959).

Stock footage from the 1957 David O. Selznick production of *A Farewell to Arms* is featured in this episode. The footage was licensed from Associated Producers, Inc.

TRIVIA

Italy declared war on Austria-Hungary in May 1915, but it was not until August 1916 that Italy declared war on Germany. Count Galba also appeals to Nero for help against the "Huns," a common nickname for the Germans in WWI. But the real Huns invaded Italy four centuries after Nero's demise.

PRODUCTION #9621
THE WALLS OF JERICHO

INITIAL TELECAST: January 27, 1967
SHOOTING SCRIPT DATED: December 6, 1966, with revised pages dated
December 12 and 13, 1966
DATES OF PRODUCTION: December 14, 15, 16, 19, 20 and 21, 1966
FILMING LOCATIONS: Stage B, Stage 18 and Stage 19
GUEST CAST: Ann Doree (a technician at the Time Tunnel); Myrna Fahey
(Rahab); Lisa Gaye (Ahza); B. Glennie (a technician at the Time Tunnel);
Orwin Harvey (the first soldier); Cynthia Lane (Shala, Rahab's sister);
Tiger Joe Marsh (Torturer); Arnold Moss (Malek); Michael Pate (Captain);
Rhodes Reason (Joshua); Virginia Semon (a technician at the Time Tunnel);
and Abraham Sofaer (Father of Rahab).

Stunt Doubles
Glen Colbert (double for Doug)
Denver Mattson (double for Tony)
Eddie Saenz (double for Captain)

Four male stand-ins and stuntmen were needed for the fight scenes in the
street and the exterior of Rahab's roof: Skip Burnham, John Drake, Bill
Graeff and Gene Silvani.

PRODUCTION CREDITS
ART DIRECTORS: Jack Martin Smith and Rodger E. Maus
ASSISTANT DIRECTOR: Steve Bernhardt
DIRECTOR: Nathan Juran
FILM EDITOR: Dick Wormell
MUSIC: stock
MUSIC EDITOR: Sam E. Levin
Teleplay by Ellis St. Joseph.

STORY: Joshua, the warrior prophet who will bring down the walls of Jericho,
sends Tony and Doug over the wall into the city as his spies. In suitable dress,
they reach the city only to find its leadership upset and sacrifices about to be
made. Doug and Tony watch as a procession of virgins are marched up to the
Temple and one of them, Shala, is to be killed by High Priest Malek. They
quickly intervene, surprising everyone so that Shala is able to run to her sister,
Rahab, and the two disappear. Doug, however, is captured and momentarily

tortured as Malek demands to know the reason why the Israelites have been marching around the city. Tony hides in the house of Rahab, who tells them she can get them back to the Israelites through a back window at night and sends for her father to tell Tony how to get into the dungeon to save Doug. Tony succeeds in rescuing Doug, thanks to Rahab distracting the soldiers. Back at the Time Tunnel Complex, Ann will not accept the images projected on the screen. As a scientist, she will not permit the belief of Biblical miracles, and makes rash judgment calls in her efforts to rescue Doug and Tony, jeopardizing their lives and putting them at risk. By now Joshua's marching is incessant, and as he orders all the horns blown, a tornado bears down on the frightened city, and the walls indeed begin to tumble. Tony and Rahab, recently captured for her betrayal, are freed by Doug during all the commotion. The Temple totters, the altar falls, and the Israelites sweep in. Rahab is reunited with her family and the time travelers dematerialize into the vortex.

STOCK MUSIC: Color Bumper (by Johnny Williams, :03); The Boiler Room (by Williams, :34); First Test Part Two (by Leith Stevens, :23); Coda (by Leith Stevens, :23); Down in the Mine (by Lyn Murray, :19); Trapped Underground (by Murray, :19); Down in the Mine (by Murray, :43); Main Title (a.k.a. Time Tunnel Theme, by Williams, :37); Twelve Hundred B.C. (by Stevens, :36); Episode Titles (by Stevens, :36); Fire the Camp (by Stevens, :36); Careful Citizen (by Stevens, :36); Egyptian Dancers (by Franz Waxman, :36); The Rescue (by Lionel Newman, 1:14); Bomb Warp (by Robert Drasnin, :38); That's Bomb Biz (by Drasnin, :38); Wild Anxiety (by Alfred Newman, :45); The Rescue (by Lionel Newman, :45); Escape (by Waxman, :45); Shalimar (by Lionel Newman, :29); The Boys Survived (by Sawtell, :29); Complex Problem (by Drasnin, :18); Bleaker Street East (by Drasnin, :18); Two Drop In (by Drasnin, :18); Paternal Squeeze (by Drasnin, :19); The Message (by Herrmann, :40); Complex Problem (by Drasnin, :40); Bleaker Street East (by Drasnin, :40); Two Drop In (by Drasnin, :40); Search and Find (by Drasnin, :40); Opening II (by Stevens, :40); U.S. Intelligence (by Sawtell, :20); Who Are You? (by Stevens, :31); Reverse Polarity (by Stevens, :31); Act Out (by Stevens, :07); Bumper (by Williams, :03); Eve's Bridge (by Drasnin, :15); Pursuit (by Hugo Friedhofer, :53); Mock Mysterioso (by Lionel Newman, :53); The Quarrel (by Herrmann, :53); Escape (by Waxman, :53); Leave Us Alone (by Drasnin, :53); The Rescue (by Lionel Newman, :53); Tony Talks (by Sawtell, :53); The Paperhanger is Still Alive (by Daniele Amfitheatrof, :53); Boy Attempts to Escape (by Sawtell, :43); Bomb Warp (by Drasnin, :15); A Fool (by Sawtell, :07); Death of Christian (by Friedhofer, :35); Tidal Wave (by Drasnin, :16); The Rescue (by Lionel Newman, :15); Pursuit (by Friedhofer,

:15); Time Transfer (by Williams, :04); Shalimar (by Lionel Newman, :04); The Boiler Room (by Williams, :17); The Bomber is Destroyed (by Alfred Newman, :41); Mock Mysterioso (by Lionel Newman, :41); Deceitful Alexis (by Sawtell, :41); Next Week (by Murray, 09); End Credits (a.k.a. Time Tunnel Theme, by Williams, :48); and Fox I.D. (by Alfred Newman, :05).

EPISODE BUDGET

Story Rights and Expense $1,900
Scenario $5,908
Producer $6,461
Direction $3,000
Cast $17,440
Extras $4,686
Music $3,675
Staff $3,121
Art $2,642
Sets $11,675
Operating Labor $4,672
Miniatures $1,500
Camera $3,306
Sound $1,625
Electrical $3,949
Mechanical Effects $1,405
Set Dressing $4,202
Women's Wardrobe $929
Men's Wardrobe $3,094

Makeup and Hairdressing $1,526
Process $40
Production Film & Lab Charges
    $8,809
Stills $150
Transportation $2,900
Re-Recording $3,610
Photo Effects $1,170
Opticals, Fades and Dissolves $3,150
Titles $585
Post Production Film & Lab
    Charges $14,409
Projectionists $205
Editorial $7,426
Fringe Benefits $15,620
Miscellaneous $630
Amortizations $2,753
Contract Overhead $15,000
General Overhead $7,226
Total Picture Cost $170,399

Series Budget $167,757
Pre-prod $170,339
Over $2,642

SET PRODUCTION COSTS

Joshua's Tent (exterior and interior) $525
Exterior Top of Wall $500
Interior Open Temple $1,530
Int and Ext Rahab's Quarters and Alley $2,370
Interior Dungeon $250
Rahab's Roof $1,325
Construction Foreman $975
Amortized $1,500
Total $8,975

ORIGINAL STORY TREATMENT

The entire teleplay was adapted from an original 23-page story treatment by Ellis St. Joseph, submitted to Irwin Allen circa November 11, 1966. Very little differed from the initial story proposal versus the teleplay. The following are differences contained within the proposal that are not evident in the finished film we see today.

When Doug and Tony arrive, they are accused of being sorcerers more than once.

Dagon, King of Jericho, was described as wearing "a great horned crown," and sat on a throne. Malek, his High Priest, wore a horned headdress. All of the soldiers of Jericho wore helmets with long curved horns representing the head of their monster god, Chemosh. The soldiers' faces were described as "barely glimpsed between the open ferocious jaws of the monster. The omnipresence of these horns are a constant reminder that the whole city is evil and monstrous, and must be destroyed."

The large statue of the horned monster god, Chemosh, dominated a raised stone platform. Malek, not King Dagon, stood before the sacrificial block, holding the triangular-shaped stone knife that would be used for the human sacrifice.

Shala was described as a 12-year-old, and was among a procession of young girls, and chosen as the one for the sacrifice.

It was suggested to use stock footage of the market place from *The Story of Ruth*, as well as the procession of the young virgins from the same movie.

After Doug and Tony defile the sacrificial virgin by the touch of their hands, making her no longer acceptable to Chemosh, a second young girl mounts the steps, and the sacrifice proceeds. "Malek places her on the stone block and raises his knife aloft. Doug, unable to move, can only close his horrified eyes."

There were two torturers in the dungeon, wearing iron circlets with monster horns. Obviously, the need to keep the talent fees low called for only one torturer.

It was suggested that a panoramic view of the City of Jericho could originate from long shots of the walled city from *The Golden Horde* (1951).

The initial plot proposal did not have Tony hiding next to Doug while the soldiers plunged their swords into the flax to make sure no one was hidden under it. Instead, Doug and Tony hid behind the wooden lid of a water trough used for soaking the stalks. The lid protected them from the swords.

It was suggested to feature an enormous dark tornado funneling across the desert as the figure of God who appeared in a cloud of dust, and the footage be lifted from *David and Bathsheba*. It was also proposed to use stock shots from *The Golden Horde* for the hand-to-hand combat after to convey the impression of Joshua's troops destroying the enemy, and stock shots from *David and Bathsheba* of the city being consumed by tornado and fire.

The end of the episode was to feature Malek's attempt to plunge his triangular-shaped stone knife into the bosom of Rahab, until Doug appears through the smoke and impales him on his sword. This scene was never written into the teleplay and was never filmed.

Rahab's father (Abraham Sofaer) introduces himself to Tony Newman.

TITLE CHANGES

On November 11, 1966, Ellis St. Joseph wrote a 23-page plot synopsis titled "Joshua and the Walls of Jericho." The original title of the first draft of the script dated December 6, 1966, was "Joshua." On December 7, Les Warner wrote to Irwin Allen, raising a red flag. "The actual sacrifice of the young virgin (a child), will be highly objectionable, no matter how it is photographed. Among the concerns: the network, the censors, the need of adding another child into the cast, plus costume cost and restricted work hours, etc." Warner also added, "Although we deleted all of the scenes with people involved in the city's collapse [and a storm] that would have created intolerable adjustment costs, there is still a cost item with the number of people we still must use, but this will have to be controlled at the Budget Meeting."

The title had changed to "The Walls of Jericho" by January 19, when submitted to ABC for review. Ellis St. Joseph was paid $4,000 for his story, and the first and final draft of the teleplay.

Tony's escape is assisted by Rahab (Myrna Fahey).

ABC CENSORSHIP CONCERNS

In relation to second storyline inside the city of Jericho: Delete "blood stains" on sacrificial block.

Please ensure groans and head thrashing not overdone. Move away from this shot to scientists as quickly as possible.

Caution to make-up on how wounds and bruises are indicated: blood, etc. to a minimum. These men must not be horrible to look at.

Caution that Rahab's scenes with the soldiers are not played overly suggestively.

Delete "Captain reaches to tear the rest of it off her" with Tony's line coming in sooner. Please be sure that no more than the shoulder be exposed.

NOTES

For Doug and Tony to play the role of the two spies was not a problem, because the names of the spies were not revealed in The Bible. This did not alter what had already been recorded history. Irwin Allen offered his explanation earlier in the season: "Our boys will not change history, but help create it. There are moments in history that are unexplained mysteries. We offer our own explanations of what happened."

The complication of dramatizing a Biblical event is to avoid disturbing the purists, and losing a percentage of the audience. Covering any subject from The Bible is risky business and, told through a science fiction mold, often generated a number of letters to the studio and the network expressing disappointment. To allow for character development, Ann MacGregor was described as a scientist with a scientific mind, unable to accept the reality of the images projected on the screen. "It was daring for TV to question the Bible," St. Joseph recalled. "You had General Kirk, Dr. Swain and Ann — fundamentalist, agnostic and atheist — contesting their convictions." ABC addressed their own concern after reviewing the first draft of the script. "Ann can retain a degree of scientific skepticism, but must not seem to ridicule or seem to be derogatory towards The Bible." The chapter closes with Dr. Swain writing the final verse, reaching a compromise between Kirk and Ann by saying, "Anything that creates faith is a miracle."

"Coping with miracles was difficult, but I solved the problem by allowing the TV audience to interpret these miraculous events in their own way," recalled Ellis St. Joseph. "Either God destroyed the walls of Jericho in the form of a cyclone, or it happened through a natural event, like a tornado. Who can say what history really is? It could be an enormous mass of gossip that has been twisted and changed to suit each usurping power. With 'Jericho,' I wanted to show, from a science-fiction viewpoint, how miracles could have happened in natural terms…I wrote an epic screenplay, not a teleplay. I went overboard and wrote a story that required a great director, great actors and great production. It was more than even a resourceful producer like Irwin Allen could afford. [James Darren and Robert Colbert] were as dependable as ever, and that helped, but I learned from writing 'Sky' not to make exceptional demands on actors. That way you won't be let down. Somehow, I didn't follow that reasoning with the 'Jericho' script."

Rahab, played by actress Myrna Fahey, was a prostitute who remained heroic and history records her brave deeds. In The Bible, the two spies stayed in Rahab's house, which was built into the city wall. When soldiers of the city guard came to look for them, she hid them under bundles of flax on the roof. After escaping, the spies promised to spare Rahab and her family after taking the city, even if there should be a massacre, if she would mark her house by hanging a red cord out the window. This scene remained intact, and accurate, although a number of scholars claim Rahab may have been an inn-keeper or food-seller, not a prostitute. General consensus claims she was the latter, and the character of a prostitute was not only taboo for television, but rarely covered except on programs such as *Gunsmoke* (ala Miss Kitty). "The production was very daring and censorable," Ellis St. Joseph recalled.

"Rahab actually describes in two speeches the indignities to which her body was submitted. There was a very good New York stage actress at the time, Louise Troy. I discussed the role with her and even suggested her for the part, but the next thing I knew, this unknown girl was cast. This girl couldn't act. Rahab was a tremendously dramatic part. The role required a top actress of deep emotional power, like Meryl Streep, but instead they brought in

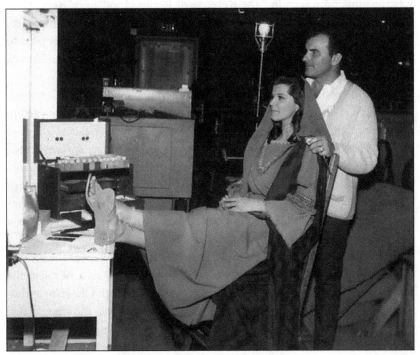

Lisa Gaye in make-up before going out on stage.

this inexperienced young actress who lacked the requisite qualities. She was a pretty thing, physically right for the role, but she was hardly a towering heroine and didn't project the heroic quality of this Biblical Jewish prostitute who saved Jericho."

Adding criticism to the production, Ellis St. Joseph disliked the costumes used in this episode. "I was horrified when I saw what the soldiers were wearing. Paul Zastupnevich is a very nice man and a talented costume designer, but Irwin has to keep the budget down. Paul wasn't given the time or money, so I don't blame him. But when I saw the soldiers, I thought I was watching Wagner. They looked like Vikings who had stepped off an iceberg!"

Conflict overseas almost threw a monkey wrench in the broadcast schedule and ABC expressed a realistic issue to Irwin Allen, weeks before the scheduled telecast: "Just a general caution that, if the present day strained relations between Israel and Jordan break into open conflagration, the theme and scheduling of this episode will have to be evaluated in the light of any such development."

The set used for the torture chamber is the same (including the door) that is featured in "The Revenge of Robin Hood." The iron maiden in the dungeon was the same prop seen in "The Revenge of Robin Hood" and "Revenge of the Gods." The torture rack is the same featured in "Revenge of the Gods." The tent in which Joshua resides is nothing more than a few drapes used to simulate a tent. The same drapes were again used to simulate a tent in "Attack of the Barbarians" and "Night of the Long Knives."

The stone god Chemosh, which Malek attempts to perform a human sacrifice, was a prop housed at 20th Century-Fox. This same prop is featured in the cave of artifacts in the *Lost In Space* episode, "Follow the Leader." The false idol can also be seen throughout the motion picture, *The Story of Ruth* (1960).

Rhodes Reason, who played the role of Colonel Travis in "The Alamo," returned for his second of two appearances on *The Time Tunnel*, in the role of Joshua, the Israelite leader. "Rhodes Reason was magnificent in his all-too-brief scenes," St. Joseph lauded to author Mark Phillips in 1992. "He gave a superb performance that helped the episode immeasurably."

Frank Griffin, who was a make-up stylist for this episode, was the brother of actress Lisa Gaye. "Those stunt guys had to wear every style of mustache and beard. It was just wild," recalled makeup artist Kenneth Chase, to author Tom Weaver. "After work, there was a certain cantina across the street called the Back Stage which was the scene of a brawl or two. I never got into one there; I came awfully close, but never actually landed a punch. Those kind of things [after-hours brawls] were not uncommon. When Frank Griffin and I were doing *The Time Tunnel*, one night at a bar near 20th Century-Fox, I saw Frank, a real big, strong, muscular guy, get into a fight for about 20 minutes and neither of them ever landed a punch [laughs]!"

Michael Pate had worked with Nathan Juran in *The Black Castle* (1952) and recalled working with the director for their *Time Tunnel* collaboration to author Tom Weaver. "Nathan was still trying to shoot television as he would shoot a feature," recalled Michael Pate. "And of course, Irwin came down on the set and rapidly changed that idea! [laughs] Nathan was a very talented man."

"He was kind and considerate to his staff but gently ruthless when it came to getting things done properly," Pate recalled to author Mark Phillips. "He would allow his directors great liberties, but if they didn't get it right, he took over. Time was always money."

According to inter-office memos, casting suggestions included Gia Scala for the role of Rahab and Sam Jaffe in the role of her blind father. "The cast was something for television," recalled Michael Pate. "Arnold Moss and Abraham Sofaer were fine actors. Myrna Fahey was a delicious lady but not easy to get to know. She wasn't used to working in the TV format — brief rehearsals and set-ups, etc. She was a bit uptight so we helped her along in

Myrna Fahey as Rahab.

some of the scenes. Debra Paget's sister, Lisa Gaye, was an old friend. She was a very nice, gregarious girl."

Fahey had done more television than motion pictures, so her experiences on the set should not have been a problem, especially since she played the role of Maria Crespo in four episodes of *Zorro* (1958), and the role of Katherine Banks on every episode of *Father of the Bride* (1961-62). Her appearance on *The Time Tunnel* was one of her final screen appearances, following three more television roles (including the recurring role of Jennifer Ivers on *Peyton Place*) and a made-for-TV movie.

Nathan Juran was sick and unable to report to the set one day and Irwin Allen filled in for him, most likely for the Time Tunnel Complex scenes.

A columnist for the TV Highlights column in the January 27, 1967, issue of the Connecticut *Hartford Courant* pointed out an interesting factoid: "For once Tony and Doug have stumbled across someone with enough faith to actually believe their incredible tale of time traveling. It is the prophet Joshua who is besieged outside the city of Jericho."

PRODUCTION #9622
IDOL OF DEATH

INITIAL TELECAST: February 3, 1967

SHOOTING SCRIPT DATED: December 21, 1966, with revised pages dated December 23, 1966 and January 4, 1967

DATES OF PRODUCTION: December 27, 28, 29 and 30, 1966 and January 3 and 4, 1967

FILMING LOCATIONS: The Moat, Stage 18, Stage 19 and Stage 21

GUEST CAST: Peter Brocco (Retainer); Anthony Caruso (Hernán Cortés); Patrick Culliton (Time Tunnel guard #1); Amapola del Vando (Chief's mother); Abel Fernandez (Bowman); Orwin Harvey (the first soldier); Rodolfo Hoyos (Castillano); Lawrence Montaigne (Alvardo); Teno Pollick (Young Chief); Pedro Regas (Chief's father); Eddie Saenz (the second soldier); and Paul Stader (Time Tunnel guard #2).

Stunt Doubles
Paul Stader (double for Alvarado)
Glen Colbert (double for Doug, Bowman *and* Young Chief)
Dave Perna (double for Tony)
Eddie Saenz (double for Tony *and* Young Chief)

PRODUCTION CREDITS
ART DIRECTORS: Jack Martin Smith and Rodger E. Maus
ASSISTANT DIRECTOR: Fred R. Simpson
DIRECTOR: Sobey Martin
FILM EDITOR: Alex Hubert
MUSIC: stock
MUSIC EDITOR: Sam E. Levin
Teleplay by Bob and Wanda Duncan.

STORY: Landing in the South American jungle during the 16th Century, in Veracruz, Doug and Tony find themselves facing the wrath of Hernán Cortés and his men, seeking a symbolic golden mask that would not only allow him to overthrow the Aztec Empire, but gain strength in demoralizing the Aztecs. When Tony and Doug witness Cortez and his men brutally murder the family of Young Chief, they rescue the lad and help him seek the landmarks pinpointing the location of the mask, while at the same time convincing the boy to seek revenge against the murder of his family and servant. An enterprising archaeologist, meanwhile, is brought to the Time

Tunnel Complex to identify landmarks that would allow Ray and Ann to pinpoint Doug and Tony's coordinates and bring them back. After a harrowing attempt to steal the mask brought through the tunnel for his personal collection, the archaeologist is taken into custody. Doug and Tony find the cave and battle Cortés' men once again, convincing Young Chief to set out on his own and fight against the invading Spaniards.

STOCK MUSIC: Color Bumper (by Johnny Williams, :03); The Boiler Room (by Williams, :29); Wild Anxiety (by Alfred Newman, :35); Saved to Perish (by Hugo Friedhofer, :35); The Quarrel (by Bernard Herrmann, :35); Mock Mysterioso (by Lionel Newman, :35); Deceitful Alexis (by Paul Sawtell, :35); Trial Curtain (by Lyn Murray, :35); Main Title (a.k.a. Time Tunnel Theme, by Williams, :37); Plague (by Friedhofer, :22); The Consecration (by Friedhofer, :22); The Mountain Pass (by Friedhofer, :19); Portola Returns (by Friedhofer, :19); Tell Them to Come (by Friedhofer, :19); The Paperhanger is Still Alive (by Daniele Amfitheatrof, :49); The Underground Complex (by Lennie Hayton, :21); The Mountain Pass (by Friedhofer, :21); Volcanic Island (by Robert Drasnin, :32); Tunnel of Slow Return (by Drasnin, :32); Louise's Discovery (by Sawtell, :32); The Boys' Escape (by Sawtell, :32); Destroying the Complex (by Lennie Hayton, :17); Boy Attempts to Escape (by Sawtell, :17); The Spearmen (by Herrmann, :17); First Test Part Three (by Leith Stevens, :17); The Name (by Sawtell, :07); Survival in Limbo (by Sawtell, :17); Two Drop In (by Drasnin, :17); He Won't Budge (by Drasnin, :16); Tidal Wave (by Drasnin, :45); Bumper (by Williams, :03); That's Bomb Biz (by Drasnin, :32); The National Razor (by Stevens, :31); A Dark Night (by Lionel Newman, 2:38); The Marshal (by Lionel Newman, :15); Eve of Suspicion (by Drasnin, :29); Death of Ula (by Friedhofer, 1:28); Destroying the Complex (by Lennie Hayton, 1:28); Countdown (by Sawtell, :34); Time is Short (by Sawtell, :21); Stalking (by Lionel Newman, :35); Fight (by Stevens, :35); Escape (by Stevens, :35); Careful Citizen (by Stevens, :35); Death of Christian (by Friedhofer, :35); Time Transfer (by Williams, :35); Wild Anxiety (by Alfred Newman, :35); The Fens (by Franz Waxman, :35); Volcanic Island (by Lionel Newman, :32); A Complex Problem (by Drasnin, :32); Bomb Warp (by Drasnin, :35); Boy Attempts to Escape (by Sawtell, :35); Plague (by Friedhofer, :28); The Awakening (by Herrmann, :28); Footsteps in the Dark (by Sawtell, :28); The Paperhanger is Still Alive (by Amfitheatrof, :28); The Fens (by Waxman, :28); Sniper (by Friedhofer, :28); The Marshal (by Lionel Newman, :28); Tony's Frustration (by Sawtell, :28); Time Transfer (by Williams, :02); Flying Chord (by Drasnin, :02); The Boiler Room (by Williams, :15); Death of Ula (by Friedhofer, :25); Volcanic Island (by Drasnin,

:25); Time Transfer (by Williams, :25); The Paperhanger is Still Alive (by Amfitheatrof, :25); The Cave (by Lionel Newman, :25); Next Week (by Murray, :09); End Credits (a.k.a. Time Tunnel Theme, by Williams, :40); and Fox I.D. (by Alfred Newman, :05).

SET PRODUCTION COSTS
Exterior of Jungle $3,000*
Cliff and cave $475
Interior Cave $2,820
Construction Foreman $945
Amortized $1,500
Total $8,740

Suggested Casting
Alvarado: Rudy Acosta
Castellano: Joseph di Santis

STORY PROPOSAL

The Duncans were paid $4,000 for their story "The Treasure Story," and for scripting the first and the final teleplay draft of "The Golden Mask." The entire production was filmed under the title of "The Golden Mask," including the shooting script, dated December 21, 1966. By the time the film was submitted to ABC on January 12, 1967, it has been re-titled, "The Idol of Death."

The official plot synopsis does clear up one absurdity in this episode, which is that the corrupt Castillano inexplicably throws the mask back into the Tunnel after he has forced the Time Tunnel personnel to retrieve it; in the story description, it is supposed to have been Kirk who does this, which makes much more sense. The synopsis also refers to the young chief as Quexcotl, but no one refers to him by name in this episode. It is possible that no one could pronounce the name, so they chose not to.

ABC CENSORSHIP CONCERNS

Please make the shot of the dying men struck with arrows, not grotesque or shocking to view.

Scream not over-done, please.

Caution that human cries are not added to sound of arrows hitting target. Also please be sure that we do not see them at the stake after this show, scene 39.

---

*This included logs, rocks, two walls with vines, a practical fire, trail areas, rocky promontory, Spanish camp, etc.

Scene 119. Please delete direction that "the body shudders."
Caution on how "cut" is indicated, blood, etc. to minimum.
No close up of the choking.

HISTORICAL MISTAKES

It is mentioned that Doug and Tony were transported to October 1, 1519, while Hernán Cortés was invading Veracruz. History records that Hernán Cortés took over Veracruz in July of 1519 and by October, accompanied by about 3,000 Tlaxcalteca, he marched to Cholula, the second largest city in central Mexico.

Tlaxcaltec (spelled Tlaxcaltapec in the shooting script) was an indigenous group of Nahua ethnicity that inhabited part of Mexico, and served as allies to Hernán Cortés and his fellow Spanish conquistadors. In this episode, however, Cortés was combating the Tlaxcaltec, completely the opposite of what history records.

NOTES

This episode marked Lawrence Montaigne's second of two appearances on *The Time Tunnel*. "The great thing about *Time Tunnel* was that it wasn't afraid to experiment with technology," Montaigne recalled. "We always think of TV

Above: Chief's father (Pedro Regas) arms himself in defense. Below: Actors Teno Pollick and James Darren display the new bumper sticker.

was being the bastard child of motion pictures, but today's film technology came from wonderful shows like *Star Trek*, *Time Tunnel* and *The Invaders*…I had been a stuntman in Europe. When I had a sword duel in *Time Tunnel*, producer Irwin Allen said to stunt coordinator Paul Stader, 'You'd better get a stunt double for Lawrence.' Paul, who knew of my background, said, 'Irwin, that's the craziest thing I have ever heard!' Paul and I worked out a sword routine, and it turned out beautiful."

The external cave entrance in this episode was the same set used for the episode "Kill Two By Two."

The visitor's badge is number 3137, the same one Admiral Killian wears in "One Way to the Moon."

On January 3, 1967, stuntman Charles Picerni cut his finger and had to visit the doctor before returning to the set.

The stock footage of Cortez and his men marching originates from the 1947 motion picture, *Captain from Castile*.

REVIEWS

The columnist for the Missouri *St. Joseph News-Press*, after watching this episode, remarked: "All the gore and excitement of those old Cesar Romero adventure movies is re-captured in with much slashing about in the throbbing, steamy jungle." Joan Crosby, in the syndicated *TV Scout* column, made the remark, "Scientists Newman and Phillips, who are still ricocheting around in time and space because of that goofed-up time machine, materialize in the 16th century, just in time to encounter Hernando Cortez (Anthony Caruso). It is history distorted for the adventure buffs."

BLOOPER!

The sword Tony holds on Cortez is a 19th century U.S. Navy cutlass.

PRODUCTION #9623 [FINAL SHOOTING #9684]
BILLY THE KID

INITIAL TELECAST: February 10, 1967
SHOOTING SCRIPT DATED: January 4, 1967
DATES OF PRODUCTION: January 5, 6, 9, 10, 11 and 12, 1967
FILMING LOCATIONS: Desilu 40 Acres, Stage 18 and Stage 19
GUEST CAST: Allen Case (Sheriff Pat Garrett); Phil Chambers (Marshall); John Crawford (John Poe); Patrick Culliton (a cowboy); Pitt Herbert (Tom McKinney); Harry Lauter (Wilson); and Robert Walker (Billy the Kid).

Stunt Doubles
Mike Picerni (double for Tony *and* Wilson)
Charles Picerni (double for Tony)
Glen Colbert (double for Doug *and* Pat)

PRODUCTION CREDITS
ART DIRECTORS: Jack Martin Smith and Rodger E. Maus
ASSISTANT DIRECTOR: Steve Bernhardt
DIRECTOR: Nathan Juran
FILM EDITOR: James Baiotto
MUSIC: stock
MUSIC EDITOR: Sam E. Levin
Teleplay by William Welch.

STORY: Lincoln County, New Mexico Territory, 1881. Tony and Doug find themselves caught in front of a gun barrel owned by William H. Bonney, alias "Billy the Kid." Carefree and reckless, Bonney makes a daring jailbreak and then sets his sights on Doug, who shoots the notorious gunman in the chest before fleeing the scene. Believing he shot and killed the outlaw, Doug is later relieved when he learns that the bullet deflected off his belt buckle. Bonney tracks down the two strangers and before he has a chance to kill them, is distracted by a voice transmission from General Kirk. Doug and Tony apprehend Bonney. Tony, wearing Billy's hat and gun, rides into town to alert Sheriff Pat Garrett of the news — only to be the victim of a case of mistaken identity. Tony is captured and locked up. The town citizens believe Tony is "Billy the Kid" and demands justice, attempting to mob the sheriff's office. Pat Garrett arrives and informs the mob that the prisoner is not William Bonney. Bonney, meanwhile, escapes Doug's custody as a result of quick thinking from his notorious gang and rides back into town to find

Doug, who is ultimately forced into a shoot-out with the gunman, but is saved by Pat Garrett at the last minute.

STOCK MUSIC: Color Bumper (by Johnny Williams, :03); The Boiler Room (by Williams, :25); Death of Ula (by Hugo Friedhofer, :35); Volcanic Island (by Robert Drasnin, :35); Complex Problem (by Drasnin, :35); Time Transfer (by Williams, :35); The Cave (by Lionel Newman, :35); Pursuit and Ambush (by Lionel Newman, :35); The End of Chico (by Lionel Newman, :35); Wild Anxiety (by Alfred Newman, :35); The Paperhanger is Still Alive (by Daniele Amfitheatrof, :35); Main Title (a.k.a. Time Tunnel Theme, by Williams, :37); The Mountain Pass (by Friedhofer, :45); Pursuit and Ambush (by Lionel Newman, :25); The Marshal (by Lionel Newman, :27); The Underground Complex (by Lennie Hayton, :27); Another Wagon Load (by Leith Stevens, :27); Eve of Suspicion (by Drasnin, :30); Paternal Squeeze (by Drasnin, :30); The Cave (by Lionel Newman, :49); Pursuit (by Friedhofer, :49); The Quarrel (by Bernard Herrmann, :49); Target Practice (by Lionel Newman, :19); The Arrest (by Lionel Newman, :30); The Paperhanger is Still Alive (by Amfitheatrof, :49 and :49); Bomb Warp (by Drasnin, :49); Pursuit and Ambush :39); The Cave (by Lionel Newman, :39); The Marshal (by Lionel Newman, :39); The Cave (by Lionel Newman, :39); Search and Find (by Drasnin, :03); Bumper (by Williams, :03); Target Practice (by Lionel Newman, :42); The Cave (by Lionel Newman, :42); Lots of It (by Lionel Newman, :34); Escape (by Lionel Newman, :34 and :34); The Underground Complex (by Hayton, :34); The Cave (by Lionel Newman, :19); Pursuit and Ambush :10); The Awakening (by Herrmann, :10); The Quarrel (by Herrmann, :09); Take Him Away (by Joseph Mullendore, :10); Wild Anxiety (by Alfred Newman, :31); Death of Ula (by Friedhofer, :31); The Rescue (by Lionel Newman, :31); Escape (by Lionel Newman, :31); Desperados (by Friedhofer, :12); The Gun Fight (by Lionel Newman, 1:40); Pursuit (by Friedhofer, :24); A Dark Night (by Lionel Newman, :24); Pursuit (by Friedhofer, :10 and :12); The Paperhanger is Still Alive (by Amfitheatrof, :19 and :19); Bomb Warp (by Drasnin, :19); Time Transfer (by Williams, :02); Brandon Take Over (by Lyn Murray, :26); The Boiler Room (by Williams, :17); Pursuit and Ambush (by Lionel Newman, :28 and :28); The Gunfight (by Lionel Newman, :33); The Cave (by Lionel Newman, :33); Next Week (by Lyn Murray, :09); End Credits (a.k.a. Time Tunnel Theme, by Williams, :49); and Fox I.D. (by Alfred Newman, :05).

EPISODE BUDGET
Story Rights & Expense $1,900
Scenario $5,908
Producer $6,461
Direction $3,000
Cast $19,092
Extras $5,504
Music $3,675
Staff $3,121
Art $2,642
Sets $8,540
Operating Labor $5,242
Miniatures $1,500
Camera $3,044
Sound $1,625
Electrical $3,949
Mechanical Effects $1,400
Set Dressing $3,579
Animals & Action Devices $855
Women's Wardrobe $404
Men's Wardrobe $1,429

Series budget $167,757
Estimate $171,296
Over budget $3,539

SET PRODUCTION COSTS
Western Street $875
Shack $1,245
Sheriff's Office #1 $1,465
Sheriff's Office #2 $1,775
Construction Foreman $975
Amortized $1,500
Total $7,835

Makeup & Hairdressing $1,246
Process $40
Production Film & Lab Charges
    $8,809
Stills $150
Transportation $4,100
Re-recording $3,700
Photo Effects $1,170
Opticals, Fades & Dissolves $3,150
Titles $585
Post Production & Lab Charges
    $15,084
Projectionists $205
Editorial $7,826
Fringe Benefits $15,240
Miscellaneous $1,525
Amortizations $3,253
Contract Overhead $15,000
General Overhead $7,343
Total Picture Cost $171,296

HISTORICAL ERRORS

Ann claims the history books report William H. Bonney was shot by Sheriff Pat Garrett on July 23, 1881. He died on July 14.

ABC CENSORSHIP CONCERNS

Just a caution that the arm choke grip does not cause any distended features or gurgling sounds.

Standard caution on the fights. No close up of blow with the gun barrel. Also, usual caution on how "gash" indicated: blood, etc. to a minimum.

NOTES

Many of the scenes in this episode were filmed at the Desilu Studios 40 Acres, the same Western Street seen in other episodes of *The Time Tunnel* including "The Alamo" and "The Death Trap." The first three days were filmed at Desilu Studios 40 Acres, and the remainder of the days were filmed on Stage 18 and 19. The same buildings can be seen in multiple episodes of television's *The Californians*, *The Texan*, *The Adventures of Jim Bowie*, *The Real McCoys* and *Yancy Derringer*, which were also filmed on 40 Acres.

Some of the stock shots of the cattle stampede were also used in "Visitors From Beyond the Stars."

John Crawford once recalled in an interview how, in order to get the role, he had to convince Irwin Allen that he could convincingly play the role of a cowboy, after having played the role of King John in the "Robin Hood" episode. "Irwin considered me a Shakespearean actor," recalled Crawford. "I used to carry a portfolio of photographs with me when I went to work in case someone wanted to check out my various profiles and consider me for a job. Larry Stewart was the casting director and I was at Fox being filmed for something at the time. Larry came up to me and asked if I had the photos. I went out to my car and returned with the portfolio in hand. One of those photos was handed to Irwin Allen and I was hired for the part. It was just one photo that convinced him."

Many fans of the program believe the best performance in this episode came from Robert Walker. Even a columnist at the Florida *St. Petersburg Times* remarked in "The Lively Arts" column, "One of this evening's best performances comes from Robert Walker as the old western favorite hero-villain, Billy the Kid, on *Time Tunnel*."

William Welch was paid $4,000 for his story, and the first and final draft of the teleplay.

Robert Walker as Billy the Kid.

BLOOPER!

Even dismissing the historical fact that Billy the Kid did not gain any notoriety until after his death…The name of Sheriff Pat Garrett is spelled with only one 't' when painted on the window outside the sheriff's office. But towards the end of the episode, Garrett is spelled correctly. Could the error have been noticed during filming and later corrected?

TRIVIA

The theme for *The Time Tunnel* was composed by John Williams (credited as "Johnny Williams"), who would go on to become one of film's most celebrated composers. Among his credits are *Jaws* (1975), *Star Wars* (1978), *Raiders of the Lost Ark* (1981) and *E.T. The Extra-Terrestrial* (1982).

PRODUCTION #9610
PIRATES OF DEADMAN'S ISLAND

INITIAL TELECAST: February 17, 1967
SHOOTING SCRIPT DATED: August 25, 1966, with revised pages dated September 9 and 12, 1966
DATES OF PRODUCTION: September 12, 13, 14, 15, 16 and 19, 1966
FILMING LOCATIONS: Stage B, Stage 18 and Stage 19
GUEST CAST: James Anderson (Mr. Hampton); Charles Bateman (Captain Stephen Decatur); Pepito Galindo (Armando Del Giddeo); Victor Jory (Captain Beal); Harry Lauter (Johnson); Alex Montoya (the Spanish Captain); and Regis Toomey (Dr. Ben Berkhart).

Stunt Doubles
Gil Perkins (double for pirate fight *and* Hampton)
Frank Graham (double for Tony)
Paul Stader (double for Doug)
George Robotham (double for Captain Beal)

PRODUCTION CREDITS
ART DIRECTORS: Jack Martin Smith and Rodger E. Maus
ASSISTANT DIRECTOR: Fred R. Simpson
DIRECTOR: Sobey Martin
FILM EDITOR: Alex Hubert
MUSIC: stock
MUSIC EDITOR: Sam E. Levin
Teleplay by Barney Slater.

STORY: Tony and Doug find themselves prisoners of Captain Beal, a Barbary Pirate, on an island stronghold along the Barbary Coast in North Africa, April 10, 1805. Armando, the ten-year-old nephew of the King of Spain, is held for ransom and pleads with Captain Beal to have them for servants, saving the lives of Tony and Doug. They use their reprieve to make the earliest possible attempt to escape with the child, vanishing into the jungle, beyond which they think is a city. Instead they find open water and are almost instantly recaptured. Captain Beal loses his patience and orders them killed, but changes his mind when he learns that three American Naval vessels are headed this way with the recently promoted Captain Stephen Decatur and his men to attack the pirate stronghold, in response to the frequent piracy of American vessels in the Mediterranean

Sea. Captain Beal, meanwhile, is accidentally transported to the present, jeopardizing the life of Ann MacGregor until he is returned to his own time. A retired Army doctor from the present is sent back in time to treat Doug, believing he was having a heart attack, only to discover he was suffering from shock. The good doctor from the complex wants to retire in the past, when times were more simple, and he lets Doug and Tony know that the complex has yet to find a way to bring them back...but they are working on it. Thanks to Doug and Tony's bravery, however, Armando will survive to tell his tale.

MUSIC CUES: Color Bumper (by Johnny Williams, :03); The Boiler Room (by Williams, :25); The Rescue (by Lionel Newman, :29); The Cave (by Newman, :29); Kreuger Comes Back (by Lennie Hayton, :03); Main Title (a.k.a. Time Tunnel Theme, by Williams, :37); The Fens (by Franz Waxman, :06); Val Escape (by Waxman, :56); Try it Again (by Paul Sawtell, :13); The Fade Out (by Sawtell, :23); The Marshal (by Newman, :32); Time Transfer (by Williams, :32); Take Him Away (by Joseph Mullendore, :32); The Cave (by Newman, :32); Stalking (by Newman, :39); The Quarrel (by Bernard Herrmann, :11); Bomb Warp (by Robert Drasnin, :11); That's Bomb Biz (by Drasnin, :11); A Fool (by Sawtell, :03); Take Him Away (by Mullendore, :03); Complete Destruction (by Sawtell, :13); The Paperhanger is Still Alive (by Daniele Amfitheatrof, :13); Total Surprise (by Sawtell, :13); Urgent Detergent (by Lionel Newman, :13); Pursuit (by Hugo Friedhofer, :13); Bumper (by Williams, :03); The First Chase (by Waxman, :30); Someone Moved (by Newman, :30); Sniper (by Friedhofer, :30); Someone Moved (by Newman, :21); You Call Me, Brother (by Mullendore, :21); The Cave (by Newman, :21); Boys Survived (by Sawtell, :13); The Jungle (by Williams, :07); Time Transfer (by Williams, :02); Tony Enters Machine (by Williams, :45); Tony's Tall Tale (by Williams, :45); Wild Anxiety (by Newman, :45); Control and Stalk (by Lyn Murray, :49); Complete Destruction (by Sawtell, :49); Control and Stalk (by Murray, :53); Time Transfer (by Williams, :53); Tony Rescued (by Sawtell, :53); Time Transfer (by Williams, :06); Jerry Collapse (by Murray, :17); Bomb Warp (by Drasnin, 1:04); Time Transfer (by Williams, :02); No Pursuit (by Stevens, :06); Time Transfer (by Williams, :03); Total Surprise (by Sawtell, :11); Ensign Beard (by Murray, :11); Time Transfer (by Williams, :02); The Telegraph (by Williams, :21); Time Transfer (by Williams, :02); Louise's Discovery (by Sawtell, 1:32); Pursuit (by Friedhofer, 1:32); Jettison (by Murray, :35); Time Transfer (by Williams, :02); Jerry Collapse (by Murray, 1:39); Saved and Disappear (by Murray, :11); Time Transfer (by Williams, :02); Flying Chord (by Drasnin, :04); The Boiler Room (by Williams, :18);

Target Practice (by Newman, :31); The Shot (by Sol Kaplan, :31); Pursuit and Ambush (by Newman, :31 and :12); Control and Stalk (by Murray, :12); Next Week (by Murray, :12); End Credits (a.k.a. Time Tunnel Theme, :48); and Fox I.D. (by Newman, :05).

EPISODE BUDGET
Story Rights & Expense $1,500
Scenario $5,808
Producer $7,215
Direction $3,000
Cast $16,890
Extras $6,037
Music $3,500
Staff $3,445
Art $2,649
Sets $10,506
Operating Labor $5,165
Miniatures $3,000
Camera $3,344
Sound $1,625
Electrical $3,949
Mechanical Effects $1,717
Set Dressing $5,109
Animals & Action Devices $135
Women's Wardrobe $229
Men's Wardrobe $3,789

Makeup & Hairdressing $1,511
Process $285
Production Film & Lab Charges
    $8,500
Stills $150
Transportation $2,900
Re-recording $1,784
Photo Effects $1,430
Opticals, Fades & Dissolves $2,150
Titles $745
Post Production & Lab Charges
    $14,304
Projectionists $205
Editorial $5,875
Fringe Benefits $15,588
Miscellaneous $630
Amortizations $1,002
Contract Overhead $15,000
General Overhead $6,850
Total Picture Cost $167,521

Series Budget $167,757
Pre-Production Estimate $167,521
Under Budget $236

SET PRODUCTION COSTS
Sandy Beach at Pirate Camp $1,100
Pirate Camp $475
Pirate Captain's Cabin $3,890
Pirate Captain's Cabin Wrecked $350
Decatur's Cabin $660
Total $6,475

STORY TREATMENT

Barney Slater received $3,370 for his teleplay, based on a story treatment he proposed: $1870 upon delivery of first draft, $1500 upon delivery of the final draft. Slater's original story treatment is not too much different from the finished teleplay except for the personality of Armando, and a strained relationship between him and the time travelers. When Doug and

Doug and Tony are taken captive by pirates along the Barbary Coast.

Tony find themselves at the mercy of an imperious young boy who treats them like equals one moment...like slaves the next. When the wrestling champion of the pirates issues a challenge, it's Armando who accepts and puts Tony up as an opponent. And he is angry when Tony wins, having bet on the other man.

Doug and Tony have been in communication with The Time Tunnel and now receive some very disturbing information. Admiral Bainbridge of the United States Navy is on his way with an American fleet to destroy the pirate stronghold. Realizing they will be under naval bombardment, Doug and Tony plan to escape by stealing a small boat. They urge Armando to come with them. The boy immediately informs the pirate leader. He doesn't want to go to sea in a small boat and he doesn't believe there is to be an attack. Furious over the planned escape, the pirate leader orders Tony and Doug to be strung up and lashed. The beating has just started when three American naval vessels appear off the coast and begin to shell the pirate stronghold. As buildings explode and catch fire, the pirate leader orders his men to their ships. He takes Doug, Tony and Armando with him.

During the naval battle between the pirate and the American ship, Armando is seriously wounded by a shell fragment. A few moments later, the Time Tunnel zeros in on Tony and the injured boy and an attempt is made to bring them both back to the present. Unfortunately, only Armando is picked up and he is brought only half-way back from the past. The wounded boy lies in the tunnel dying. A Naval medical doctor, who has viewed the proceedings in The Time Tunnel with skepticism, is asked to risk his life by walking into the tunnel and taking care of Armando. At first, he refuses. Why should he risk his life for a boy who doesn't even exist except in the past? But the groans of the wounded boy have their effect and medical bag in hand, the doctor walks back into the past to save Armando.

Doug watches the destruction and sinking of the pirate flagship with a deep sadness. But then a strange event takes place. Armando, shoulder bandaged, appears on the deck of Bainbridge's ship. He doesn't remember anything about his trip through time. He thinks there was a man...the man who fixed up his shoulder, but he got lost somewhere. At that moment, a sailor reports someone in the water; a survivor of the pirate ship. Doug looks over the side. Clinging to some wreckage is Tony.

ABC CENSORSHIP CONCERNS

Please be sure that cutlass is not pressed against Ann's throat or face. Caution that scream is not over-done and that Beal's handling of Ann does not seem unnecessarily brutal or sadistic.

Your usual care in seeing that wounds, effects of beating, are not over-done. Blood etc. to minimum.

Of course, no close ups of blows with shovel or karate blow or hammer blow which stops Mali.

As usual, hypo injection off-camera or completely "covered."

NOTES

Two old friends were warmly reunited on *The Time Tunnel* when Irwin Allen signed Victor Jory and Charles Bateman as guest stars for this episode. Jory plays the notorious Barbary pirate Captain Beal, and Bateman plays his arch-enemy and ultimate conqueror, American naval hero captain Stephen Decatur. Jory and Bateman were by no means strangers. They had appeared together many times in the *Manhunt* television series, which was about stories of the San Diego police. Jory was Police Lieutenant Howard Finucane, Bateman was his trusted right-hand man, Detective George Peters.

"Pirates of Deadman's Island" was the tenth episode filmed, and the 23rd episode broadcast. It was assigned production number 9643 during filming, but was ultimately re-assigned production number 9610.

Doug is taken captive by the pirates.

This episode used the same beach seen in prior episodes including "Devil's Island" and "Crack of Doom."

During the scene in which Captain Beal runs about the Time Tunnel Complex, stock footage from the pilot episode is re-used.

In this episode, we discover that Tony has relatives in Philadelphia, Pennsylvania.

The writer for the TV Time column in the February 18, 1967, issue of *The St. Petersburg Times* remarked: "*Time Tunnel*, with its inexhaustible supply of locations, lands its travelers Tony and Doug onto the deck of a pirate ship. The year is 1805. Just as they are about to meet a nasty end off the Barbary Coast, they are befriended by a twelve year-old youngster who is conveniently the nephew of the King of Spain. Pepito Galindo in the role will surely win the hearts of all the young viewers who have ever dreamed of adventure on the high seas while fighting buccaneers."

Columnist Joan Crosby thought more of the guest star who agreed to play the role of a cut-throat. "Victor Jory does a nice, nasty job as Beal, the sadistic Captain of a pirate ship off the coast of Barbary in 1805."

"Victor Jory was another one of my favorites," recalled Robert Colbert.

Director Sobey Martin and actor Victor Jory.

"He was a man who ran with John Wayne and Ward Bond and all those guys back in the hard-hittin' Western days — hard-drinkin' guys. Victor was a wiry, thin guy, but he was the toughest of all of 'em. When Victor got a little bit in his cups, nobody wanted to mess with him, and if they did, they ended up goin' through a wall some place, 'cause Victor was the toughest, meanest son of a gun that ever walked the planet. When he hit you, you stayed hit. So Victor and I became good friends."

"One-dayers and two-dayers aren't even worth talking about," Victor Jory recalled shortly after filming was completed. "Five-dayers begin to separate the men from the boys and a 10-dayer, if it's dark and thick enough, can look like a lot more. The big stuff, however, begins with the one and two-monthers. The sky's the limit from there." What Jory was talking about was beards. He considered himself an unofficial expert on adornment, chin-style. Villains were more likely to be the bearded ones. He would not allow a fake beard to be added. Jory grew his own for this episode. "It took nothing extra to be real," he remarked, "just a little notice from the producer and the rest came naturally."

Lee Meriwether later recalled Victor Jory being a bit too rough on her, during the scenes in which Captain Beal was running through the Time Tunnel Complex, and uses Ann MacGregor as a human shield. He apparently did not know his own strength and she later discovered black and blue bruises on her.

Stock footage of the pirate battles originate from *Anne of the Indies* (1951).

RECURRING THEME

Often characters from the past are brought forward to the Time Tunnel and characters from the installation are sent back in time. However, for some strange reason, Time Tunnel personnel can't get both Doug and Tony back, without complications (like a time warp), even though every time transfer does succeed, somehow, in transporting both of them to the same time period and nearly, but not exactly, the same geographical location.

Storyboard panels for the episode "Pirates of Deadman's Island."

PRODUCTION #9624
CHASE THROUGH TIME

INITIAL TELECAST: February 24, 1967

SHOOTING SCRIPT DATED: January 12, 1967, with revised pages dated January 13, 16 and 19, 1967

DATES OF PRODUCTION: January 16, 17, 18, 19, 20, 23 and 24, 1967

FILMING LOCATIONS: Stage 5, Stage 18 and Stage 21

GUEST CAST: Ann Dorre (a technician at Time Tunnel); Robert Duvall (Raoul Nimon); Gary Epper (Tic Toc guard); Lew Gallo (Vokar); Bart La Rue (Tic Toc intercom voice); Wesley Lau (Master Sgt. Jiggs); Vitina Marcus (Zee); Joe Ryan (Magister); and Hal Torey (the technician, a.k.a. Dr. Alfred Stiles).

Stunt Doubles
Charles Picerni (double for Tony)
Glen Colbert (double for Doug)
Polly Bergen (double for Zee)
Larry Hold (double for Nimon)
Paul Stader (double for Vokar)

PRODUCTION CREDITS
ART DIRECTORS: Jack Martin Smith and Rodger E. Maus
ASSISTANT DIRECTOR: Fred R. Simpson
DIRECTOR: Sobey Martin
FILM EDITOR: Dick Wormell
MUSIC: stock
MUSIC EDITOR: Sam E. Levin
Teleplay by Carey Wilber.

STORY: A foreign saboteur, Raoul Nimon, replaces a bus-bar in the Phase Synchronizer with one he has with him, a timing device set to detonate a nuclear bomb planted somewhere in the Time Tunnel Complex. Alarms go off and a chase is quickly organized as Nimon flees through the Complex and, in desperation, makes his escape through the Time Tunnel. Tony and Doug, in the Grand Canyon in 1547, learn what happened and soon find themselves drawing Nimon to them by making a fire, then they trap him. The Time Tunnel is reset and Nimon is transferred first and the time travelers a moment later. Arriving a million years in the future, Tony and Doug discover they are prisoners of a society as rigidly structured as that of honey bees.

Soldiers, workers and drones live among a complex honeycomb structure shaped like a bee hive, without any feelings or concern except what is best for the nest. Nimon is there, too, but he has gone through a time warp and has been with Vokar's people for ten years — busy trying to replicate a time machine so the futuristic society can expand to other eras. Doug and Tony are to help with the project, but the time travelers are only interested in learning where the bomb or the detonation device is located. In the extremity of the effort to move them, the Tunnel overshoots and the men, with Vokar and Zee, are transferred to One Million B.C. There, in dodging a prehistoric monster, Nimon falls into quicksand and will not reveal anything until rescued. They all but lose their lives doing it, only to then be menaced by Vokar, who is armed. Struggling against giant lizards, quicksand, volcanic disruption and a giant underground beehive during the Paleozoic Period, Vokar learns a little about human emotion and forces a confession out of Nimon, revealing the location of the time fuse that detonates the bomb. Swain and Ann manage to send the future residents back to where they came from, Tony and Doug to a new era, but run out of power and are unable to save Nimon before the approaching giant prehistoric honey bees arrive to attack their intruder.

STOCK MUSIC: Color Bumper (by Johnny Williams, :03); The Boiler Room (by Williams, :27); Target Practice (by Lionel Newman, :09); The Shot (by Sol Kaplan, :25); Pursuit and Ambush (by Lionel Newman, :25); Control and Stalk (by Lyn Murray, :33); Brandon Take Over (by Murray, :15); Control and Stalk (by Murray, :15); Wild Anxiety (by Alfred Newman, :18); Sneaky Pete (by Alexander Courage, :18); Theme from Voyage* (by Paul Sawtell, :18); Main Title (a.k.a. Time Tunnel Theme, by Williams, :37); The Fens (by Franz Waxman, :37); Jerry Collapse (by Murray, 1:32); The Cave (by Lionel Newman, :20); The Marshal (by Lionel Newman, :20); Escape (by Lionel Newman, :20); Time Transfer (by Williams, :07 and :17); Down in the Mine (by Murray, :17); The Spearmen (by Bernard Herrmann, :13); The Storm (by Herrmann, :23); Tony Suits Up #2 (by Murray, :23); The Quarrel (by Herrmann, :27); No Word (by Murray, :32); Moon Fuel (by Murray, :35); The Mirror (by Herrmann, :35); Booby Trap (by Friedhofer, :05); The Storm (by Herrmann, :05); The Mirror (by Herrmann, :05); Tony Enters Machine (by Williams, :05); The Mirror (by Herrmann, :19); Panic (by Herrmann, :19); Take Off (by Murray, :19); Impact (by Murray, :19); The Telegraph (by Williams, :05); Stalking (by Lionel Newman, :25); Bumper (by Williams, :04); Booby Trap (by Friedhofer, :13); Brandon Search (by Murray, :13); The Message (by Herrmann, :29); The Ruins (by Herrmann, :29); The Message (by Herrmann, :23); The Ruins (by Herrmann, :23); Panic (by Herrmann, :07); No Exit (by Courage, :07); Target Practice (by Lionel Newman, :07); Meteor (by Murray, :35); The Mirror (by Herrmann, :35); Bomb Wrap (by Robert Drasnin, :35); Fright, Flight, Fight (by Drasnin, :35); A Dark Night (by Lionel Newman, :35); Someone Moved (by Newman, :41); Time Transfer (by Williams, :06 and :37); Tony's Tall Tale (by Williams, :37); Booby Trap (by Friedhofer, :32); The Jungle (by Williams, :32); Total Surprise (by Sawtell, :07); The Fight (by Herrmann, :33 and :33); The Ruins (by Herrmann, :33); The Fight (by Herrmann, :33); The Iceberg Cometh (by Williams, :33); Terror (by Herrmann, :33); Millard's Death (by Friedhofer, :33); The Shot (by Kaplan, :33); Pursuit and Ambush (by Lionel Newman, :33); The Time Lock (by Sawtell, :19); Louise's Discovery (by Sawtell, :19); The Fight (by Herrmann, :19); Danger (by Herrmann, :19); The Storm (by Herrmann, :19); The Rescue (by Lionel Newman, :19); Pursuit (by Friedhofer, :27 and :21); Time Transfer (by Williams, :21); Control and Stalk (by Murray, :21); The Quarrel (by Herrmann, :21); The Cave (by Lionel Newman, :53); The Paperhanger is Still Alive (by Daniele Amfitheatrof, :53); The Cave (by Lionel Newman, :31); Time Transfer (by Williams, :15); The Paperhanger is Still Alive (by Amfitheatrof, :07); The Visor (by Herrmann, :07); The Boiler Room (by Williams, :17); A Dark Night (by Lionel Newman, :37); Urgent Detergent (by Lionel Newman, :43); Someone Moved (by Lionel Newman, :43); Next Week (by Murray, :08); End Credits (a.k.a. Time Tunnel Theme, by Williams, :48); and Fox I.D. (by Alfred Newman, :05).

* This is a music cue from Paul Sawtell's score for the motion picture, *Voyage to the Bottom of the Sea* (1961).

EPISODE BUDGET

Story Rights & Expense $1,900	Sound $1,625
Scenario $5,908	Electrical $3,949
Producer $6,461	Mechanical Effects $1,305
Direction $3,000	Set Dressing $4,576
Cast $16,200	Women's Wardrobe $404
Extras $5,198	Men's Wardrobe $2,079
Music $3,675	Makeup & Hairdressing $1,251
Staff $3,121	Process $40
Art $2,642	Production Film & Lab Charges $8,881
Sets $11,450	Stills $150
Operating Labor $4,822	Transportation $2,900
Miniatures $1,500	Re-recording $3,475
Camera $3,044	Photo Effects $3,890

Opticals, Fades & Dissolves $3,150
Titles $585
Post Production & Lab Charges
$14,817
Projectionists $205
Editorial $8,826

Fringe Benefits $16,295
Miscellaneous $630
Amortizations $3,253
Contract Overhead $15,000
General Overhead $7,681
Total Picture Cost $173,888

Series Budget: $167,757
Pre-Production Estimate: $173,888
Over: $6,131

SET PRODUCTION COSTS
Hive Complex $3,320
Teleport Room $530
Rocky Area $400
Jungle Areas $2,600
Bee Hive Cell $650
Construction Foreman $975
Amortized $1,500
Total $9,975

STORY DEVELOPMENT

This episode marked the switch from historical dramas to far-out futuristic adventures — which ultimately divided the writers. Carey Wilber created an original story of a saboteur who runs into the tunnel and Tony and Doug have to find him and force a confession before a detonation device triggers an explosion, sealing the time travelers to a permanent home out of place and out of time. Wilber was paid a total of $2,755 for his story, and the first and final draft of the teleplay. William Welch was paid $500 to polish the teleplay by a loan-out agreement and Welch's contribution was not credited on screen. (Welch had no agent so the check was paid to him at the studio.)

In Carey Wilber's first draft of the script, Tony and Doug are not motivated to find Nimon while misplaced in the Grand Canyon in 1547. Nimon simply appears and starts firing at them. At the suggestion of Jerry Briskin, who felt the script was about five pages short, a chase sequence was to be added of Tony and Doug attempting to find Nimon when he has sent himself back in time and the Tunnel has alerted the boys as to who he is and what he has done. "I think it makes heroes out of Tony and Doug if they jeopardize their lives and attempt to get information that would not only aid them in possibly returning to the complex, but at the same time try to get information that would keep the complex from being blown up," Briskin wrote. His suggestion was implemented in the final draft.

The first draft also had Jiggs explain that they searched Nimon's room and discovered "his bags are packed." Briskin remarked, "This seems pretty obvious and makes Nimon, in my opinion, stupid. I believe we just have

The cast gets ready for filming "Chase Through Time."

to make mention of the fact that they searched his room, found nothing, but in checking security, learned that Nimon was starting a furlough that evening."

Another concern Briskin wrote in a letter to both Wilber and Allen: "If in One Million A.D. they use force fields to keep people in and out of areas, why don't they have same on the door to the Teleport room rather than a lock which is now indicated? Having a lock on the door doesn't sound like One Million A.D. as far as I am personally concerned."

At one point during story construction, Carey Wilber and Jerry Briskin were at odds and Irwin Allen was forced to make a decision. They needed a concept approval or disapproval from Allen as to whether or not the people of the future were going to speak without their lips moving. But moving forward, this was only one problem with the overall switch to "far out" futuristic concepts for *The Time Tunnel*. "On reflection I think we have over-reacted to Hal Graham's suggestion for the revision of this script along the lines of the new sci-fi concept. I believe a revision would be ill-advised for the following reasons: The script *as is* is as 'far out' or more 'far out' than any of the new scripts yet to be written will be. It is futuristic (One Million A.D.);

James Darren hugs director Sobey Martin.

it has a futuristic heavy; it is prehistoric; it has prehistoric dinosaurs. To make it *more* sci-fi is unnecessary; it already conforms to Hal's new formula. The agreed upon revision (making Nimon an alien) is probably not correct; Vokar as a character is already the equivalent of an alien — he is a being of One Million A.D. Making Nimon an alien will necessitate large changes in incident and structure as well as character. Two similar heavies in one script are one too many."

In another letter to Irwin Allen, dated December 20, 1966, Jerry Briskin remarked: "I don't find any real drive in the first half of the script (future years) as after the boys are sent to get Simon, they are no longer heroes, in my opinion, as they are captures, they learn about the 'Bee Hive' existence of the future years, that life means nothing, and by means of the Tunnel Complex, and not their own ingenuity, they are saved and removed to another time period."

ABC CENSORSHIP CONCERNS

Your usual care in seeing that the "writhing in agony," that Nimon's screams are not "over-done."

Caution that the quicksand scene, generally, is not too horrifying for family viewing.

Of course, various close up of clocks not identifiable as to actual trade/brand names.

Standard caution on the choking. Usual care that features are not distended. No gurgling sounds. No close up of hands on throat or victim's face.

NOTES

During filming, the production number was briefly changed from 9624 to 9679. The production number reverted back before filming was completed.

The time machine capsule in the center of the Master Control Room is the same prop used for the experimental time machine in "Secret Weapon." The same prop used as a "homing post" in the Robin Hood episode can be seen hanging on the walls in the future society. The gun used by Vokar in this episode was among the many guns featured on seasons two and three of *Lost In Space*. Other props originate from past *Lost In Space* productions, including the costumes worn by the aliens and the red space suit vests now colored purple.

When Doug and Tony first arrive in the Paleozoic Period, the footage used originates from the unaired pilot. Because of the time difference between the two productions, additional footage that followed had Doug wearing a torn shirt and dirt smudges on his face to reproduce the way he looked in the footage shot half a year prior. The smudges are not exact, nor are the stains on the torn shirt, but they were close enough that most viewers caught up in the story would not have noticed.

Footage from the pilot was recycled for this episode. The giant lizards originate from Irwin Allen's 1960 production of *The Lost World*. Some of the footage featured in this *Time Tunnel* episode was never used in the motion picture, while the scene with the lizards fighting each other was in the movie, but presented here with the left side of the screen cropped off so television audiences would not see David Hedison and Jill St. John behind the rocks, avoiding the lizard fight. They failed. At the very beginning of the dinosaur fight, a glimpse of David Hedison can be seen on the bottom left of the screen, courtesy of stock footage!

The lizard fight in this episode of *Time Tunnel* might not have appeared had it not been for a production problem in 1960 during filming of *The Lost World*. "There was an actors' strike," Robert Mintz, post-production coordinator, recalled. "Rather than shut down production, Irwin brought in dozens of lizards and shot dinosaur fights with them until the last lizard was dead from exhaustion. Irwin never missed a beat."

Arthur Weiss felt the story was "fine as it is," after reading Carey Wilber's script, but Herman's proposed changes concerned Weiss. "It's more 'far out' than any *Time Tunnel* ever written. It's futuristic, it has a heavy and ends in

Vitina Marcus and Lew Gallo clown around back stage.

a prehistoric era with dinosaurs. It already conforms to our New Concept formula." Weiss did object to making Nimon a space invader. "Turning Nimon into an alien is a mistake. To do so will require major revisions to this character and the resultant story changes will jeopardize our preparations for filming. The secondary character of Vokar [Nimon's silver-skinned ally] is already the equivalent of an alien." Weiss won his argument and "Chase Through Time" ends with the human Nimon meeting a horrific fate from giant prehistoric bees.

The Florida *Evening Independent* featured the following review: "This one is a fast paced story for all of its followers. Robert Duvall ably plays the killer and of course it all ends well for our time heroes." *The Milwaukee Journal* reviewed: "It's an outstanding episode and is very convincing."

VITINA MARCUS

By coincidence, Vitina Marcus, who had played the role of a cave girl in Irwin Allen's *The Lost World*, played the role of Zee in this *Time Tunnel* adventure. She also made guest appearances on *Voyage to the Bottom of the Sea* and *Lost In Space*, and is perhaps best known to television audiences for her role as the enticing green lady, Athena, in the *Lost In Space* episode, "The Girl from the Green Dimension." Years later, she recalled an incident with Robert Duvall. "Robert saved my daughter's life when a few of us went horseback riding," she recalled. "We were in North Hollywood and the horse she was on took off and Robert galloped after them. I remember he stopped the horse just in time before it was going to run into a block wall, or maybe jump over it. Thank goodness he was there at the time. It terrifies me about what could have happened to her if he had not intervened."

THE DEATH MERCHANT

INITIAL TELECAST: March 3, 1967

SHOOTING SCRIPT DATED: January 24, 1967, with revised pages dated January 25, 26 and 27, 1967

DATES OF PRODUCTION: January 25, 26, 27, 30, 31 and February 1, 1967

FILMING LOCATIONS: Fox Ranch, Hunter Ranch, Stage 3, Stage 4 (both considered Western Avenue), and Stage 18

GUEST CAST: John Crawford (Major); Kevin Hagen (Sgt. Maddox); Denver Mattson (Union soldier #2); Kevin O'Neal (Corporal Perkins); Paul Stader (Union soldier #1); "Storm" (the dog); and Malachi Throne (Michaels).

Stunt doubles

Paul Stader (doubled for Michaels *and* Doug)

Charles Picerni (double for Tony)

Glen Colbert (double for Doug)

Denver Mattson (double for Michaels)

PRODUCTION CREDITS

ART DIRECTORS: Jack Martin Smith and Rodger E. Maus

ASSISTANT DIRECTOR: Steve Bernhardt

DIRECTOR: Nathan Juran

FILM EDITOR: Alex Hubert

MUSIC: George Duning

MUSIC EDITOR: Sam E. Levin

Teleplay by Bob and Wanda Duncan.

STORY: July 1863. Gettysburg, Pennsylvania. Tony suffers amnesia when he is knocked unconscious from an explosion and is mistaken for a Confederate courier. Doug, meanwhile, masquerades as a Union Major to help the Union find Michaels, a man who has stolen gunpowder and plans to sell it to the Rebs. While dodging bullets and cannon fire, the time travelers ultimately meet up with Niccolò Machiavelli, an Italian historian and philosopher who believes war is only interesting when both sides are evenly matched. Machiavelli was somehow transported from 1519 to 1863 because his frequency matches that of Doug's. Hoping to encourage more bloodshed, he combats the time travelers by manipulating others into acts of violence. During a fight between Doug and Tony, the latter's memory returns and, moments before the stockpile of gunpowder is blown up, the Time Tunnel

Complex manages to connect a special power supply from Hoover Dam to transfer Machiavelli, presumably back to his proper time, and Doug and Tony into another adventure.

MUSIC SCORE BY GEORGE DUNING *(dated February 27, 1967):* Color Bumper (by Johnny Williams, :03); The Boiler Room (by Williams, :17); In the Battle (1:38); Lost Trail (:25); By Choice (:13); Main Title (a.k.a. Time Tunnel Theme, by Williams, :37); Ann Worried (1:50); Michael's Dog (:34); No Signs (:57); Omens (:43); Corporal Shot (1:45); Tricky Michael (:24); Tools of Death (:15); Bleeding Major (:19); The Trunk (:46); Doug's Duels (1:23); Mike's Dog (:15); Tony Returns (:44); Tony Angry (:15); Bumper (by Williams, :03); Doug Chased (1:39); Time Transfer (by Williams, :08); Tony Again (1:00); Tony Threatens (:25); Kirk's Problem (:33); They Ride (:38); Tony Attacked (1:07); Why Did You? (:59); Maddox Exhausted (:47); Maddox Killed (1:06); The Powder (:23); Powder Cave (1:39); Pal Fight (:52); More Pal, Fight (:42); What's Happened? (:38); Stand Back (:58); Time Transfer (by Williams, :07 and :07); The Boiler Room (by Williams, :16); A Rainy Night (by Franz Waxman, :23 and :24); The Rescue (by Lionel Newman, :24); That's Bomb Biz (by Robert Drasnin, :24); Fright, Flight, Fight (by Drasnin, :24); Next Week (by Murray, :08); End Credits (a.k.a. Time Tunnel Theme, by Williams, :48); and Fox I.D. (by Alfred Newman, :05).

EPISODE BUDGET
Story Rights and Expense $1,900
Scenario $5,908
Producer $6,461
Direction $3,000
Cast $17,713
Extras $6,159
Music $3,675
Staff $3,121
Art $2,642
Sets $3,267
Operating Labor $5,378
Miniatures $1,500
Camera $3,306
Sound $1,625
Electrical $3,949
Mechanical Effects $1,875
Set Dressing $4,284
Animals and Action Devices $1,025 (horses)
Women's Wardrobe $404
Men's Wardrobe $3,209
Makeup and Hairdressing $1,221
Process $40
Production Film & Lab Charges $8,845
Stills $150
Transportation $8,940
Re-Recording $3,700
Photo Effects $970
Opticals, Fades and Dissolves $3,150
Titles $585
Post production Film & Lab Charges $15,443
Projectionists $205

Editorial $8,826

Fringe Benefits $14,345

Miscellaneous $2,290

Amortizations $3,253

Contract Overhead $15,000

General Overhead $7,855

Total Picture Cost $175,219

Series Budget $167,757

Pre-Production $175,219

Over $7,462

SET PRODUCTION COSTS

Various Forest Areas and Log Cabin* $675

Interior Cabin $100

Construction Foreman $117

Amortized $1,500

Total $2,392

STORY DEVELOPMENT

The origin of this episode dates back to 1964 or 1965 when Irwin Allen conceived of a premise titled "The Distant Past." Peter Phillips (not Doug) found himself in 1863 finding aid for wounded soldiers, while witnessing the maturity of a young man and young woman who discover what their purpose in life was. The story was then verbally tossed around between the script writers and Irwin Allen. Ample use of stock footage from movies that took place in the American Civil War were available and Allen felt the subject would be of interest to television viewers.

The initial intention was to have a Civil War story among the earliest adventures, as evident by a number of interviews Allen consented to in the summer of 1966. Even the September 10, 1966, issue of *TV Guide* described the new series: "One week they're back in prehistoric times, another week they're on a rocket to the moon, or aboard the Titanic, or at the Battle of Gettysburg."

Bob and Wanda Duncan were paid $1,245 for the final draft of "The Death Merchant" (formerly "Explosion at Gettysburg"), and $2,755 for their story and first draft of "Explosion at Gettysburg" (formerly "The Civil War"). These stories have been reprinted in Appendix D.

On January 9, 1967, Jerry Briskin wrote to Irwin Allen: "In my opinion the Duncans have written a good, solid script. This is something we could go with, in my opinion, in a hurry if need be." Briskin then created a list of

---

*Includes split rail fence, burning haystack, smoldering wagon, cannons, tents, dog, suspension bridge, etc.

inconsistencies in the first draft, which reveal a number of scenes that were obviously eliminated or revised for the final draft.

"How is it that Maddox just happens to have a Lieutenant's uniform in his field pack which fits Tony?"

"Tony's last speech in the scene — Tony is all of a sudden giving orders and Maddox and the others accept same although they know this is a man

Robert Colbert as Doug Phillips and Malachi Throne as Niccolò Machiavelli.

who can't remember anything that has happened to him in the past."

"Scene 154. Tony fires his pistol in this scene and in scene 155 we see a Union Cavalry rider fall off his horse. I take it this means our hero has killed someone and this is something that we haven't done with our leading men up to this time."

"I am not quite certain how Tony happens to come out of his amnesia. Is this the result of the complex having switched the boys in time or is it just time for Tony to come back to normal? Maybe we could set this situation up a little better."

"There are numerous battlefield explosions called for in this script and most of them are listed as off screen explosions with debris falling on our cast or characters. I would like to suggest that the explosions be made as on-camera explosions which we can do on the stage and which, I believe, will make the situations appear much more effective and believable when they appear on the screen."

ABC CENSORSHIP CONCERNS

Please keep the Corporal's eyes closed in death.
When the Major fires point blank, not at the head please.
Same for Doug who fires point blank at Michaels.
When Tony points gun straight at Doug, not at the head please.

NOTES

To accomplish a number of camera angles outside the Gunpowder Cave and the exterior of the cabin, a Mark II with 10 to 1 zoom was rented and used. This allowed for a greater depth for long shots that might not allow images at a distance to appear sharp enough on the screen.

The interior and exterior of the cabin where Machiavelli resides were located on the 20th Century-Fox lot, and were the same used for a number of *Daniel Boone* television episodes. The difference between the two cabins is evident when the amount of mud packed between the logs varies from interior shots versus exterior shots. The same cabin sets are used in "The Lost Patrol."

Machiavelli makes a comment that he is writing a book he titles "The Art of War." The real life Machiavelli did write a book of the same name, documenting his theoretical observations of military science. His works were sometimes said to have contributed to the modern negative connotations of the words *politics* and *politician*, and it is sometimes thought that it is because of him that *Old Nick* became an English term for the Devil and the adjective *Machiavellian* became a pejorative term describing someone who aims to deceive and manipulate others for personal advantage.

Machiavelli is shot at many times and doesn't die, laughing at Sgt. Maddox. He's beyond his time, he explains, and therefore already dead and cannot be killed. He believes he is immortal. Except for this one scene in the episode, nothing further is described or detailed to explain why he cannot die, leaving the audience to ponder just how he came to be immortal.

It was proposed that the character of Machiavelli on *The Time Tunnel* would return in a future episode, a recurring villain Doug and Tony would find themselves combating — an admirable foe.

Electronic equipment and props in the Time Tunnel Complex were also used on *Lost In Space*. A sound effect used in this episode (in the Time Tunnel Complex) was originally from *Lost In Space*, the sound of the Jupiter 2's engines.

Tony's dialogue when revealing his name is "Andrews" was obviously looped.

Extras playing both Union and Confederate soldiers: Steve Howell, John Moio, Louis Paul and T. Winslow. Extras were instructed not to shave. Stuntmen on hand during the fight on Wilson's Bridge and the exterior of the Gunpowder Cave: Glen Colbert, Bill Graeff, Charles Picerni and John Vick. Extras playing both security and Time Tunnel personnel at the Time Tunnel Complex: Glen Colbert, Ann Dore, Gary Epper, Charles Picerni, Paul Stader and John Vick.

BLOOPERS!

In the opening scene, one of the soldiers begins to fall to the ground before the bomb blows up behind him.

When Doug and the major are at the campsite by the stream, the trees are bare and dead leaves are on the ground, signifying the winter months during which this episode was filmed. Bizarre since the Battle of Gettysburg was in July.

In the scene where the Major tosses Doug a set of clothes, a modern day highway can be seen behind the tents.

PRODUCTION #9626
ATTACK OF THE BARBARIANS

INITIAL TELECAST: March 10, 1967
SHOOTING SCRIPT DATED: February 1, 1967, with revised pages dated February 1 and 7, 1967
DATES OF PRODUCTION: February 2, 3, 6, 7, 8 and 9, 1967
FILMING LOCATIONS: Fox Ranch, Stage 18 and Stage 19
GUEST CAST: Arthur Batanides (Batu); Paul Mantee (Ambahai); Vitina Marcus (Sarit); and John Saxon (Marco Polo).

Stunt Doubles
Paul Stader (Doug)
Dave Sharpe (Tony)
Glen Colbert (Doug)
Charles Picerni (Tony)

John Moio and Mary Statler were stand-ins for the exterior plains and clearing at Fox Ranch.
Mongol warriors: Al Cavens, Orwin Harvey, Denver Mattson, Gil Perkins and Charles Picerni.

PRODUCTION CREDITS
ART DIRECTORS: Jack Martin Smith and Rodger E. Maus
ASSISTANT DIRECTOR: Fred R. Simpson
DIRECTOR: Sobey Martin
FILM EDITOR: James Baiotto
MUSIC: stock
MUSIC EDITOR: Sam E. Levin
Teleplay by Robert Hamner.

STORY: Mongolia, 1287. Tony and Doug tumble into alien territory in time to discover they are in the midst of another war — this time involving Mongol warriors, the men of Genghis Khan. The Golden Horde, under the leadership of Genghis Khan's grandson, Batu, attempt to conquer Volga Bulgaria and the Kievan Rus by uniting all of the Mongolian tribes. To accomplish this, Batu needs Sarit, daughter of Kublai Khan. The time travelers are captured and taken to Batu's tent, where Doug is rendered unconscious, while Tony is questioned by Batu, mistaken for one of Marco Polo's men. Batu demands to know the weaknesses of the fort where Marco Polo and his men are holding out. Doug regains consciousness and manages to free Tony and drag him to safety. Marco Polo takes them to a nearby fort. There, Tony is cared for by Sarit, a beautiful girl. Tony and Sarit fall in love. Back at the Time Tunnel Complex, Ann is trying to hold the fix on the men and is deeply impressed by Tony's declaration of love. She ponders whether they should leave him with true love in 1287. Sarit is abducted and Tony and Doug succeed in rescuing her while Batu, determined to take the fort, is gathering thousands of tribesmen for an assault. Doug, recognizing their desperate situation, borrows Marco Polo's black powder and fashions some home-made bombs. Kirk, watching the image area, realizes they need fuses (percussion igniters) for their home-made artillery and is successful in making a transfer through the Time Tunnel. Tony and Doug attach the fuses and launch the explosives from catapults on the parapets as the Mogols attack. The Mongolians are crippled as a result of the explosions. Marco Polo and his men set out to finish the job as Tony and Doug vanish into the vortex.

STOCK MUSIC: Color Bumper (by Johnny Williams, :03); The Boiler Room (by Williams, :20); A Rainy Night (by Franz Waxman, :24); Maddox Killed (by George Duning, :26); The Rescue (by Lionel Newman, :26); Fright, Flight, Fight (by Drasnin, :26); That's Bomb Biz (by Drasnin, :26); Shoot Them (by Leith Stevens, :26); Main Title (a.k.a. Time Tunnel Theme, by Williams, :37); Prelude (by Bernard Herrmann, :25); Hammer of God (by Herrmann, :13); The Spearmen (by Herrmann, :29); Tony Again (by Drasnin, :29); The Awakening (by Herrmann, :23); The Message (by Herrmann, :23); Escape (by Waxman, 1:51); The Cave (by Lionel Newman, :07); Coda (by Leith Stevens, :07); The Cave (by Lionel Newman, :40); Coda (by Stevens, :40); Volcanic Island (by Drasnin, :37); Sniper (by Friedhofer, :37); Shalimar (by Lionel Newman, :37); Complex Problem (by Drasnin, :37); Kirk's Problem (by Duning, :23); Stand Back (by Duning, :23); Tony Angry (by Duning, :23); Doug Chased (by Duning, :43); The Powder (by Duning, :17); They Will Do (by Sawtell, :11); Doug's Duels (by Duning, :50); Tony Threatens (by Duning, :17); Omens (by Duning, :17); Trapped Underground (by Murray, :15); By Choice (by Duning, :03); Bumper (by Williams, :03); Hat Bridge (by Drasnin, :19); House of Bamboo (by Leigh Harline, :19); Tunnel Trip (by Drasnin, :24); Rabbit Rouser (by Drasnin, :24); Shalimar (by Lionel Newman, :24); The Gunfight (by Lionel Newman, :19); Pursuit and Ambush (by Lionel Newman, :19); The Gunfight (by Lionel Newman, :09); The First Chase (by Waxman, :57); Doug's Duels (by Duning, :32); Shalimar (by Lionel Newman, :24); Tools of Death (by Duning, :15); Death of Christian (by Friedhofer, :17 and 1:11); Time Transfer (by Williams, :05 and :33); House of Bamboo (by

Harline, :15); The Pass (by Herrmann, :15); The Rescue (by Lionel Newman, :27); House of Bamboo (by Harline, :27); Flying Chord (by Drasnin, :02); The Boiler Room (by Williams, :05); Saved and Disappear (by Lyn Murray, :23); The Quarrel (by Herrmann, :23); A Stitch in Time (by Drasnin, :29); Chilling Reception (by Drasnin, :29); The Quarrel (by Herrmann, :29); Next Week (by Murray, :09); End Credits (a.k.a. Time Tunnel Theme, by Williams, :48); and Fox I.D. (by Alfred Newman, :05).

EPISODE BUDGET

Story Rights and Expense $1,900
Scenario $5,891
Producer $6,461
Direction $3,000
Cast $17,440
Extras $4,632
Music $3,675
Staff $3,186
Art $2,681
Sets $12,380
Operating Labor $4,833
Miniatures $1,500
Camera $3,108
Sound $1,693
Electrical $4,147
Mechanical Effects $1,300
Set Dressing $4,865
Animals and Action Devices $180
  (horses)
Women's Wardrobe $554
Men's Wardrobe $4,149
Makeup and Hairdressing $1,690
Process $40
Production Film & Lab Charges
  $8,845
Stills $150
Transportation $4,900
Re-Recording $3,556
Photo Effects $650
Opticals, Fades and Dissolves
  $3,150
Titles $585
Post Production Film & Lab
  Charges $15,093
Projectionists $215
Editorial $9,267
Fringe Benefits $16,145
Miscellaneous $1,565
Amortizations $2,753
Contract Overhead $15,000
General Overhead $8,427
Total Picture Cost $179,606

SET PRODUCTION COSTS

Batu's Tent, with torches and powder explosion $1,100
Interior Marco Polo's Quarters and Corridors $2,165
Base of Fortress $100
Parapet with scaling ladders and catapults and clay containers $3,300
Construction Foreman $1,000
Amortized $1,500
Total $9,165

STORY DEVELOPMENT

With each episode of *The Time Tunnel* exploring a different aspect of the boys' travels through time, a time traveler falling in love with someone of the past had to happen sometime. And a beautiful woman was at the root of that. Robert Hamner was paid $2,755 for his story and a first draft teleplay of "Marco Polo," and $1,245 for final draft of "Marco Polo."

Robert Hamner wrote a lengthy plot proposal titled, "Siege of Xanadu," which told the story of Tony and Doug's adventures in the midst of a thirteenth-century Mongolian war camp. They soon discover an adversary, the formidable-looking Mongolian chieftain, Jamukha, the oldest son and heir of the now dead Genghis Khan. Tony and Doug are apparently Europeans and the only other European the Mongolians have ever seen is Marco Polo, who is now a captain in the service of the Kublai Khan — Jamukha therefore maintains that Doug and Tony must be friends and allies of Marco Polo, must also be in the service of the Kublai Khan, must also be blood enemies of Jamukha and his tribesmen. Jamukha questions Tony about the fortress to the North, probing for its weaknesses but Tony doesn't have any of the answers Jamukha is after. Jamukha quickly tires of the questioning and signals two Guards, who drag Tony off to one side of the tent and strap him to the torture wheel there. Tony screams in pain as the wheel is tightened and Jamukha again questions him. After each question Tony doesn't have the answer so the wheel is tightened again and after several sharp cries of pain, Tony loses consciousness.

Inside the tent, Doug is still on the floor, unconscious as Tony (still on the rack) is revived. Just barely conscious now as Jamukha resumes his intensive questioning. Tony cannot answer the questions and the wheel is tightened again. Tony again screams in pain and lapses into unconsciousness. Jamukha disgustedly decides to let Tony revive before again resuming the questioning and leaves with one of the guards for business in another area of the camp. While the remaining guard has his attention on Tony, Doug jumps the guard, knocking him out. Doug then unties Tony, gently lifts him over a shoulder, carries him to a rear panel of the tent side, slits it with the knife he'd taken from the unconscious guard and then carries Tony off.

Tony wakes to find himself in a castle with the beautiful Sarit tending to his bruises. Doug tells Tony how they'd taken a horse from Jamukha and managed to escape his camp in the middle of the night. They'd ridden North, been picked up by a patrol of Marco Polo's cavalry and taken to the fort. Marco Polo explains that he'd been escorting Princess Sarit to Venice where she could study European civilization and manners and report on it to her father, Kublai Khan. They'd gotten as far as this central plains area and could go no further as Jamukha and his Mongol horsemen have the area completely terrorized with a series of hit-and-run attacks. Jamukha has some of the hill tribes all stirred up and is trying to get the whole countryside engaged in another war of conquest to regain the lands his father, Genghis Khan, had conquered.

Arthur Batanides as Batu.

Marco Polo, as Kublai Khan's ranking officer in the area, has assumed command of the fort and can only hope they'll be able to hold out long enough for word of the rebellion to reach Kublai Khan, who'll then send enough soldiers to crush Jamukha.

Later that evening, a table is set for dinner in the fortress room (which is Marco Polo's quarters and the command nerve center of the fort) and Tony, Doug, Sarit and Marco Polo sit down for the evening meal. Doug and Marco Polo are engrossed in talk of the fort's defense but not so much so that Doug doesn't notice that Tony (now feeling a little stronger) and Sarit are becoming more and more attracted to each other.

After dinner, Sarit retires to her own quarters. Marco Polo goes off to check the night watch and Tony and Doug are alone in the room. Doug tries to feel Tony out, stressing that Sarit and Tony could never have any life together; they're of different worlds, different times. Tony still won't heed Doug's words of caution and angrily exits from the room. Sarit is captured and the time travelers return to Jamukha's tent to rescue her. Using firecrack-

John Saxon as Marco Polo.

ers Doug creates with Marco Polo's black powder, they throw the Mongols into momentary confusion. The firecrackers also panic the tethered camels and they stampede through the camp knocking tents down and running right over them (stock). The camp is thrown into confusion as camels, tents and running men go every which way.

Back inside the safety of the fort, Sarit thanks them all but both Doug and Marco Polo exchange a worried glance as they see that her eyes return again and again to Tony.

In the tent, Jamukha is furious as he gathers all his forces together for an all-out attack on the fort.

It's later that day as Tony, Doug and Marco Polo stand on the parapet looking off as a horde of Mongols gather on the plain before the fort. An aide of Jamukha is escorted to them and offers Jamukha's pledge of safety for every man in the fort in exchange for the return of Sarit. The offer is refused and the aide then adds Jamukha's vow — should his offer be refused, no man in the fort will be left alive.

James Darren and Vitina Marcus.

The Mongols attack the fort twice; the second time in a stronger, more intense assault. On the parapet, Doug suddenly tells Marco Polo to send a cavalry unit out to divert the Mongols and buy them some time. He's just had an idea and needs some time to implement it.

Doug begins creating a percussion of explosives. As they talk, both Tony and Doug suddenly realize that they're missing one very essential item — something to detonate the shells.

In the Time Tunnel Complex, Ann, Swain and Kirk are watching Tony and Doug, just as caught up in their dilemma. Kirk suddenly turns to Swain and asks that they send percussion caps. Doug and Tony use the caps and then watch from the parapet as the attack is repelled. When victory seems assured, they turn to each other and exchange a smile. They've had their disagreement but their friendship is strong enough to prevail. Tony agrees and says he wants to find Sarit. In answer to Doug's look, Tony adds that he just wants to find her to say goodbye. Tony starts to walk from the

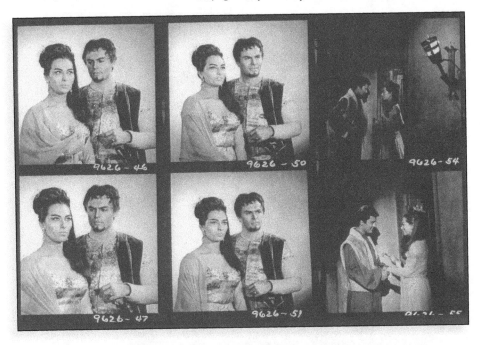

parapet, but doesn't get more than a step of two before he and Doug suddenly de-materialize and both are transported back into the infinity of the Time Tunnel.

With but noticeable differences, "Siege at Xanadu" was revised in the first teleplay (of four), dated December 28, 1966, now titled, "Marco Polo." On January 6, 1967, Les Warner wrote to Irwin Allen, concerned about the expense in producing such an episode. "Although the number of sets was held to a minimum according to Rodger Maus, their nature and scope for action involved will bring the cost up to the danger line; we should not consider additional sets in any future script revisions." To accomplish the budget figures, Warner proposed all sets be on stages, with no exterior shooting. "Although we are not in trouble with the number of cast, we will be in trouble with the number of fighters and fight doubles if any additional situations are written into future script revisions...The catapults will have to be built. Two are called for — and needed, for a story point."

On January 4, Arthur Weiss expressed his concern to Irwin Allen: "The stock footage for this picture is probably the best we have had available for any of our shows. It should be used more extensively throughout the story. In the script, as written, it is used only at the end of Act Three and in Act Four… Tony must fall in love with Sarit in a way which will not make him appear immature. As written, there is no underpinning for the Act One curtain love

Arthur Batanides as Batu.

scene…Tony's character in one scene is written as though he were a guy on the 'make' rather than a mature man falling in love."

"There is no satisfying resolution of the love affair between Tony and Sarit," Weiss explained. "Scene 173 between Tony and Doug leaves me in doubt as to whether Tony is giving Sarit up, or not. Nothing is said again about the love affair…This *Time Tunnel* story is composed of two beats which occur intermittently throughout the script. One, the Time Tunnel's attempt to get a fix on Tony and Doug. Two, discussion concerning Tony's love affair in which the question is: should Tony be allowed to remain with Sarit, or not. We should reduce drastically the Time Tunnel's intermittent attempts to get a fix on Tony and Doug. We should develop more intense conflict between Ann and the others in the Time Tunnel concerning the love affair."

The teleplay underwent additional revisions (third draft dated January 26, 1967) and the final draft was dated February 1, 1967, with revised pages dated February 1 and 7. The entire episode was produced under the title of "Marco Polo," and the title was not officially changed to "Attack of the Barbarians" until February 17, 1967.

ABC CENSORSHIP CONCERNS

Usual care in seeing that the stock shots are not too frightening or horrible for family viewing.

Caution in this torture rack sequence. Please be sure that the pain aspect in what we see and what we hear is not over-done.

NOTES

In the first draft of the teleplay, it was scripted for Batu to be killed as a result of the explosions but the network, fearing retribution from concerned parents who witnessed our heroes causing the death of another human being, asked that the scene be removed. Instead, Marco Polo and his men race out to combat the attackers. No mention of Batu's death is given at the end of the episode.

"I played Genghis Khan's grandson and I loved the makeup," Arthur Batanides recalled to author Mark Phillips. "It took over two hours to put it on and they had a whole stretch cloth over my head to bald me. It was a great role to play."

Stock footage of the Mongol warriors and battle scenes originates from *Taras Bulba* (1962), a Harold Hecht Production.

Rolly Harper and Ralph Green, a company specializing in motion picture catering, located in Glendale, California, served food to cast and crew on location for this and all episodes of *The Time Tunnel* that required filming on location (including the Fox Ranch).

The tent in which Batu resides is nothing more than a few drapes used to simulate a tent during production. The same drapes were again used to simulate a tent in "Night of the Long Knives" and "The Walls of Jericho." Most of the props in Marco Polo's room — the medicine cabinet, the throne, the wooden table and the candle holders — are the same props used in the episode "The Revenge of Robin Hood." The same candle holders can be seen in the bizarre world of "The Magic Mirror" on *Lost In Space*. A few of the colored packages in Batu's tent are seen in the back room of Machiavelli's cabin in "The Death Merchant."

The footage of security personnel placing weapons into the time tunnel to send back to help assist Doug and Tony was originally filmed and used for "Revenge of the Gods." Observant television viewers might have experienced a sense of déjà vu and wondered whatever became of the modern-day weaponry that was sent back in time and never used.

The TV Previews column in the March 10, 1967, issue of *The St. Petersburg Times* reviewed: "Tony Newman discovers love in the 13th century tonight and he finds that it can have the same devastating effects as it does today. Zipping all the way back to 1287, the time-sturdy adventurers are caught up in a barbaric battle for power between Kublai Khan and the grandson of Genghis Khan. The historic happenings mean little to Dr. Tony Newman, however, after he meets one of the prizes of the battle, a beauteous Mongolian princess (Vitina Marcus). Just to make matters complete, the TV author throws in Marco Polo to tie things together. John Saxon ably portrays that part."

Vitina Marcus as Sarit.

According to the February 3, 1967, issue of *The Ottawa Citizen*, columnist Dick Kleiner reported: "In an effort to juice up the ratings of *Time Tunnel*, they will be giving James Darren more love interests in subsequent episodes."

HISTORICAL INACCURACIES

If any episode of *The Time Tunnel* butchered historical facts, "Attack of the Barbarians" is at the top of the list. Genghis Khan's grandson Batu and the Golden Horde led the Mongols to conquer Volga Bulgaria and the Kievan Rus in 1237, concluding the campaign in 1240. Batu died in 1255. But this time travel adventure takes place in 1287.

Only two daughters of Kublai are known by name; he may have had others. While the names of sons were documented, daughters were not. No documents have survived that definitively provide the number or names of daughters born to the wives and consorts of Kublai Khan. In this *Time Tunnel* episode, however, Sarit is referred to as the only daughter of Kublai Khan. The name "Sarit" was pure fiction for this episode.

Marco Polo was indeed traveling through Asia gathering riches and treasures, and Polo would have been 34 years old at the time this adventure takes place, played by actor John Saxon, who was 30 years old when this episode was produced.

At 11:40 a.m. on February 2, 1967, stuntman Gil Perkins caught his left foot in the stirrup as he fell from his horse, sending him to Dr. Tom R. Hodges at 1:30 p.m., when it was discovered that Perkins suffered an injury that was beyond a minor sore. The hospital advised the crew to take Perkins home in the company station wagon. An ambulance was unnecessary. No apparent fracture, but there were torn ligaments.

Gil Perkins was a champion athlete and trackman in his native northern Australia. He ran away from home and went to Hollywood where he established himself as a stuntman for William Boyd in numerous Hopalong Cassidy westerns. He also appeared in a number of iconic horror movies including doubling for Bruce Cabot in *King Kong* (1933) and Spencer Tracy in *Dr. Jekyll and Mr. Hyde* (1941). He replaced Bela Lugosi as the Frankenstein monster in *Frankenstein Meets the Wolf Man* (1943). He was the co-founder of the Stuntmen's Association of Motion Pictures in 1960. During his tenure on *The Time Tunnel*, Perkins was a treasurer for the Screen Actors Guild (1964-1979). His television and movie credits are too numerous to completely document.

BLOOPERS!

When Doug tosses the shield away after rescuing Tony, the shield reveals itself as flimsy and bounces when it hits the floor. Apparently it was not made of metal.

Dirt on the front of Tony's sweater during his scene on the torture rack disappears later in the episode with no explanation.

Arthur Batanides as Batu.

TRIVIA

Despite the tacit understanding that recorded history cannot be altered, sometimes Doug and Tony's actions are essential in causing history to unfold as it did, and the lives of individual people could be influenced by the actions of the Time Tunnel time travelers and scientists. In this episode, Marco Polo tells Doug Phillips that Tony and the Princess Serit can fall in love with each other despite their being from different times because they can then and there see and touch each other. Dr. MacGregor points out to Gen. Kirk and Dr. Swain that history itself might allow for Tony and Serit to marry.

MERLIN THE MAGICIAN

INITIAL TELECAST: March 17, 1967

SHOOTING SCRIPT DATED: February 8, 1967, with revised pages dated February 10 and 16, 1967

DATES OF PRODUCTION: February 10, 13, 14, 15, 16, 17 and 20, 1967

FILMING LOCATIONS: Stage 16, Stage 18, Stage 19 and Stage 21

GUEST CAST: Vincent Beck (Wogan); Mr. Bowman (a Viking Guard); Skip Burnham (Viking #4); Christopher Cary (Merlin); Steve Howell (Viking #3); Lisa Jak (Guinevere); Paul Kessler (Viking #2); Seymour Koenig (Viking #5); Jim McMullan (Arthur Pendragon); Gene Silvani (Viking #1); and T. Winslow (Viking #6).

Stuntmen

Paul Stader (stunt soldier #1)

George Robotham (stunt soldier #2)

Charles Picerni (double for Tony)

Glen Colbert (double for Doug)

Paul Stader (double for Arthur)

Pete Peterson (stunt soldier #3)

Chuck Hicks (stunt soldier #4)

Denver Mattson (stunt soldier #5)

Hubie Kerns (double for Doug during sword fight sequence)

Bill Graeff (stunt Viking)

John Drake (stunt Viking)

Virginia Semon (stand-in for Lisa Jak)

PRODUCTION CREDITS

ART DIRECTORS: Jack Martin Smith and Rodger E. Maus

ASSISTANT DIRECTOR: Steve Bernhardt

DIRECTOR: Harry Harris

FILM EDITOR: Dick Wormell

MUSIC: stock

MUSIC EDITOR: Sam E. Levin

Teleplay by William Welch.

STORY: The Coast of Cornwall, England. 544 A.D. By command of Merlin the Magician, Tony and Doug materialize in a rocky glade and are immediately attacked by Vikings. Arthur Pendragon and Tony are captured by the invading

Vikings, led by Wogan, a Viking chieftain with a reputation as a human butcher. Doug is seriously injured, but is miraculously saved by the magic of Merlin. On their way to the castle where Arthur and Tony are being held captive, Doug and Guinevere are apprehended by Wogan and his horde. Tony manages to escape and, disposing of the prison guards, finds Arthur unconscious. Doug, determined to rescue his friend, starts out alone for the castle. Meanwhile, Wogan, searching for the escaped prisoners, discovers a dagger and recaptures them. Guinevere has followed Doug, offering to show him the way, but they are both taken captive by Vikings and Doug is chained to the dungeon wall alongside Tony and Arthur. A bowman, under orders, sends an arrow through Arthur's heart, but Merlin appears and reverses the action, restoring Arthur to life and freeing them from their chains. Guinevere, meanwhile, is held captive in the hopes of being traded to England monarchy for loyalty to the Vikings. With Merlin's assistance, the Vikings are forced to flee England and Arthur is given a reward for his bravery — the hand of Guinevere and a round table. Doug and Tony will become the first men knighted by the soon-to-be King Arthur, but they never have a chance because they vanish courtesy of the Time Tunnel.

STOCK MUSIC: Color Bumper (by Johnny Williams, :03); Time Transfer (by Williams, :05); Saved and Disappear (by Lyn Murray, :23); The Quarrel (by Bernard Herrmann, :23); Chilling Reception (by Robert Drasnin, :43); A Stitch in Time (by Drasnin, :43); Appear Sting (by Herrmann, :07); The Quarrel (by Herrmann, :07); Escape (by Herrmann, :04); Time Transfer (by Williams, :10); Paternal Squeeze (by Drasnin, :31); Main Title (a.k.a. Time Tunnel Theme, by Williams, :37); Doug's Duels (by George Duning, :10); Tricky Michael (by Duning, :10); Tony Again (by Duning, :10); Appear Sting (by Herrmann, :07); Take Him Away (by Joseph Mullendore, :08); Saved and Disappear (by Lyn Murray, :08); Doug's Arrival (by Williams, :08); That's Bomb Biz (by Drasnin, :27); Fright, Flight, Fight (by Drasnin, :27); That's Bomb Biz (by Drasnin, :29); The Trunk (by Duning, :29); Corporal Shot (by Duning, :45); Destroying the Complex (by Lennie Hayton, :45); First Test Part Two (by Leith Stevens, :22); Tunnel Lights (by Murray, :13); Tony and Comet (by Murray, :13); Louise's Discovery (by Paul Sawtell, :41); No Word (by Murray, :03); Escape (by Herrmann, :04); The Paperhanger is Still Alive (by Daniele Amfitheatrof, :37); Booby Trap (by Hugo Friedhofer, :37); The Paperhanger is Still Alive (by Amfitheatrof, :37 and :33); How Did It Go? (by Mulledore, :18), Appear Sting (by Herrmann, :07); Escape (by Herrmann, :03); Flying Chord (by Drasnin, :03); Bumper (by Williams, :03); Althea's Attack (by Williams, :18); Appear Sting (by Herrmann, :07 and :05); Tony Attacked (by Drasnin, :29); Powder Cave (by Duning, :22); Tony Attacked (by Duning, :22);

The Powder (by :22); Death of Christian (by Friedhofer, :31); Try It (by Stevens, :31); Try It Again (by Sawtell, :13); The Cave (by Lionel Newman, :13); The Jungle (by Williams, :13); The Marshal (by Lionel Newman, :17); The Cave (by Lionel Newman, :17); The Rescue (by Lionel Newman, :17); Tony Enters Machine (by Williams, :17); Appear Sting (by Herrmann, :07); Tony Talks (by Sawtell, :19); The Boys' Escape (by Sawtell, :19); Louise's Discovery (by Sawtell, :19); Volcanic Island (by Drasnin, :52); Complex Problem (by Drasnin, :52); Deceitful Alexis (by Sawtell, :11); They Will Do (by Sawtell, :11); Corporal Shot (by Duning, :59); The Fight (by Herrmann, :38); First Test Part Two (by Stevens, :33); First Test Part Three (by Stevens, :33); First Test Part One (by Stevens, :33); The Horse (by Stevens, :33); Torturak (by Stevens, :17); Fire the Camp (by Stevens, :35); Tricky Michael (by Duning, :22); Doug's Duels (by Duning, :22); The Rescue (by Lionel Newman, :55); The Neal Mansion (by Sawtell, :28); Time Transfer (by Williams, :02); Senior (by Leigh Harline, :10); Ensign Beard (by Murray, :17); Let's Go (by Stevens, :11); The Fight (by Herrmann, :27); Moon Fuel (by Murray, :27); Impact (by Murray, :27); Beard and Dove (by Murray, :27); Next Week (by Murray, :09); End Credits (a.k.a. Time Tunnel Theme, by Williams, :48); and Fox I.D. (by Alfred Newman, :05).

EPISODE BUDGET

Story Rights and Expense $1,900	Process $40
Scenario $5,891	Production Film & Lab Charges $8,845
Producer $6,461	Stills $150
Direction $3,000	Transportation $2,900
Cast $16,940	Re-Recording $3,556
Extras $5,595	Photo Effects $1,600
Music $3,675	Opticals, Fades and Dissolves $3,150
Staff $3,142	Titles $585
Art $2,681	Post Production Film & Lab Charges $15,743
Sets $8,625	Projectionists $215
Operating Labor $5,092	Editorial $9,267
Miniatures $1,500	Fringe Benefits $15,550
Camera $3,228	Miscellaneous $1,130
Sound $1,693	Amortizations $2,753
Electrical $4,147	Contract Overhead $15,000
Mechanical Effects $1,790	General Overhead $7,741
Set Dressing $4,958	*Total Picture Cost* $174,349
Women's Wardrobe $554	
Men's Wardrobe $3,504	
Makeup and Hairdressing $1,748	

$167,757 Series Budget
Pre-Production Estimate $174,349
Over $6,592

SET PRODUCTION COSTS
Countryside $600
Castle Courtyard $650
Dungeon Cell $750
Bedchambers (both) $500
Corridor $850
Watch Tower $2,000
Set Total $5,350
Construction Foreman $800
Amortized $1,500
Total $13,000

STORY DEVELOPMENT

William Welch was paid $4,000 for his story, and the first and final draft of the teleplay. His initial story proposal was titled "Raiders From The North." On February 1, 1967, he completed a revised story proposal titled, "Merlin, the Magician."*The differences between the version we see on film today and the initial proposal includes the introduction of Merlin, who first makes his appearance when Doug requires medical help, and not Merlin's visit to the Time Tunnel Complex. Doug, stabbed by a Viking, wakes to find himself in a castle recovering from his near fatal wound. He has been brought there the night before by a mysterious old man and is now being cared for by the daughter of King Leodegan. Doug learns that her name is Guinevere and realizes she is fated to become the wife of Arthur and the Queen of all England. It is here that Doug meets the old man who saved both Tony and Doug, and miraculously healed Doug's wound. The old man, of course, is Merlin. The magician reveals how he has a plan for them, but the Time Tunnel now has fixes on both Tony and Doug. They prepare to shift them through time when Merlin magically appears in the Complex to stop them. He demonstrates his magic to the Tunnel scientists, then tells them the time travelers cannot be moved until they play their part in the rescue of the future King.

Returning to the 6th Century, Merlin so arranges matters that Guinevere and Doug are also captured by Wogan, who decides to torture Doug to death,

---

*At one point in time, this episode was going to be titled "The Vikings" but changed back to "Merlin, the Magician."

along with Tony and Arthur. He will then make Guinevere his Queen and become England's Monarch.

With an assist from Merlin, the boys and Arthur escape their torture chamber. (In the film, Merlin merely reverses time to save the life of Arthur. Doug and Tony figure the way out of the dungeon.) Tony and Doug get away to raise an army while Arthur remains at the fortress to see that no

Guinevere (Lisa Jak) is rescued by Dr. Tony Phillips of the future.

harm comes to Guinevere. The army attacks the fortress at a pre-arranged signal from Arthur. (In the film, it was Tony who created the signal.) In the battle, Arthur sabotages the defenses permitting the castle to be over-run. In a personal duel with Wogan, Doug avenges himself for his near fatal wound.

At last the Vikings are conquered and Merlin is about to make Arthur king by having him draw the sword from the stone. He also plans to arrange the youth's marriage to Guinevere who will bring, as a dowry from her father, a great round table. Tony and Doug prepare to watch Arthur draw the sword from the stone, after which they will be made the first of Arthur's knights. But at this dramatic moment, they vanish to go on to some new adventure.

ABC CENSORSHIP CONCERNS

Standard caution that fights are not necessarily prolonged or brutal. Telescope as much as possible.

No close up of sword buried in Doug's body or Wogan impaled on Tony's sword. Effects of flogging, what we see and hear, not over-done.

No close up of chain hitting attacker's face and no close up of victim with chain around neck.

Caution on the drowning sequence.

We can see the figure fall but not hitting the rocks.

No close up of torch hitting wagon.

No shots of burning men.

Generally, any cries of pain held to a minimum. These sequences and stock shots can only be approved on film.

Merlin (Christopher Cary) conjures up a spell for Doug.

NOTES

Dan O'Herlihy was originally cast as Merlin, the magician. After two days of filming, he quit and never returned to the studio, due to artistic differences. Christopher Cary replaced him. The casting of *Time Tunnel* fell primarily to Larry Stewart. "Irwin loved big name movie stars and he wanted them on his TV shows," Stewart recalled to author Mark Phillips. "I had to explain to him that feature film stars require feature film salaries. It was very frustrating when Irwin's friends like Red Buttons, Victor Mature, Edward G. Robinson or Groucho Marx visited the set and were genuinely excited by what we were doing but they wouldn't even consider doing guest appearances. I had a difficult time even getting journeyman type actors to do shows. Fred Gwynne was very offended when we approached him to do a *Lost In Space*. He took it as an insult. Many actors felt Irwin's shows, particularly *Lost In Space* and *Land of the Giants*, were beneath them and could hurt their careers. At Irwin's bequest, Richard Basehart did a voice cameo on *Lost In Space* ["The Derelict"] but he was adamant that nobody ever find out. We also had a famous dancer, Cyd Charisse, signed up to do *Land of the Giants* ["Doomsday"] and at the last minute she got cold feet. Francine York replaced her."

"A coach taught me how to do the sword fighting," recalled actor Jim McMullan. "*Time Tunnel* was a heck of a good show. I loved the whole concept of going back in time. It would be a good series to revive as a motion picture."

Stock footage in this movie originates from *Price Valiant* (1954). This also explains why young Arthur is wearing a wig that is more becoming of a comic strip character, such as Prince Valiant, so it would match the stock footage used in this episode. (The wig, however, really did not need to be used since the only stock footage of Prince Valiant to feature the title character was his stunt double sliding down the rope to the window, and the costume didn't even match anyway.)

Since Valiant fought against Vikings in the movie, it also explains why Arthur, Tony and Doug are combating Vikings instead of knights in armor. Stock footage from the movie features Primo Carnera in the role of the villainous Sligon, but only for a couple seconds as Tony peeks through the curtain.

Television viewers watching the show weekly might not have observed the reuse of sets and props, but with the convenience of today's technology, episodes of *The Time Tunnel* can be seen back-to-back, revealing such factoids as the dungeon set in this episode: it is the same one seen in "The Revenge of Robin Hood," "The Walls of Jericho" and other episodes. The top of the castle where Tony gives the signal using the flaming torch is the same castle set used for "The Walls of Jericho."

Once again, the electronic console Ann and Swain are using are now different from the lighted boards featured on prior episodes.

THE REVIEWS

Joan Crosby, an actress herself as well as a syndicated TV columnist, reviewed: "It's hard to say where the drama ends and the comedy begins in this *Time Tunnel* episode. In one scene, Merlin woefully explains to Tony and Doug that they must now help Arthur become King because the famed wizard has used up too many of his miracles and he may need what he has

James Darren and Lisa Jak.

left over for an emergency. But it's all in good fun, with Christopher Cary playing a sprightly Merlin and Jim McMullan a youthful Arthur. The powerful wizard has time-napped the boys to help Arthur defeat the Vikings and to gain power."

The March 11, 1967, issue of the Florida *St. Petersburg Times* reviewed this episode: "With this continuing tunnel gimmick, that opens the pages of history to whatever chapter a TV writer chooses, there is no telling where Tony and Doug will land or who they'll meet. So tonight the ol' tunnel spins around and out pops Merlin, the legendary wizard of Sixth Century, England. He commands our two heroes to fight the Vikings."

Above: Merlin tries to cast a spell on Guinevere.
Below: Lisa Jak and Jim McMullan.

LEE MERIWETHER PULLS DOUBLE DUTY

All of the scenes at the Time Tunnel Complex were usually shot on the first or last day of production. For this episode, the scenes were shot on February 10, 1967. As soon as filming was completed on Stage 18, Lee Meriwether had to race to Stage 15 for an appearance on television's *Batman*. Meriwether played the role of Lisa in an episode titled, "King Tut's Coup," which was filmed in five days, beginning Monday, February 6, 1967. Meriwether was needed on the set all five days. On the fifth and final day, filming was completed at 2:45 p.m. with Victor Buono. The director and crew filmed a number in insert shots and other gimmicks until later in the afternoon when Lee Meriwether arrived. Her scenes were shot from 5:00 to 6:00 p.m., completing production on schedule.

Lisa Jak as Guinevere.

"Due to the unforeseen conflict of shooting schedules for both shows, I had to report to the *Time Tunnel* set, shoot my scenes there and then dash over to the *Batman* set to be made up and have my hair done like Cleopatra before filming that episode," Meriwether recalled. "If I had really been able to exert much control over the Time Tunnel, I would have been able to use it to make it much easier on myself by having the Batman part all done before I had even started."

Christopher Cary as Merlin, the magician.

PRODUCTION #9627
THE KIDNAPPERS

INITIAL TELECAST: March 24, 1967
SHOOTING SCRIPT DATED: February 14, 1967, with revised pages dated
February 16 and 22, 1967
DATES OF PRODUCTION: February 20, 21, 22, 23, 24, 27 and 28, 1967
FILMING LOCATIONS: Stage 5 and Stage 18
GUEST CAST: Michael Ansara (the curator); Ray Didsbury (intercom voice);
John Drake (the Renaissance scholar); Bart La Rue (computer voice); Bob
May (Hitler); Del Monroe (OTT (Official Time Traveler)); and Bob Todd
(the Roman Senator).

Stunt Doubles
Gary Epper (stunt guard #2) Interior Dispatching Chamber and Interior
Corridor
Glen Colbert (stunt guard #2) Interior Scientist's Office
Paul Stader (stunt guard #1)
Glen Colbert (double for Doug)
Charles Picerni (double for Tony)

PRODUCTION CREDITS
ART DIRECTORS: Jack Martin Smith and Rodger E. Maus
ASSISTANT DIRECTOR: Fred R. Simpson
DIRECTOR: Sobey Martin
FILM EDITOR: Alex Hubert
MUSIC: stock
MUSIC EDITOR: Sam E. Levin
Teleplay by William Welch.

STORY: When Ann MacGregor is kidnapped by an aluminum-colored
figure from the future, Tony and Doug are transported to the coordinates
on a data card dropped by the intruder in the hopes of rescuing her. They
soon find themselves in 8,433 A.D. in the planetary system of the Star
Canopus and discover Aliens are gathering information on the history of
the planet Earth, along with the memory and personality of various important scholars and tyrants by kidnapping them from their own times. Ann
was kidnapped simply to lure Tony and Doug to the planet for extraction.
At the Time Tunnel, OTT reappears and steals the time-space converter,
leaving them to work desperately to replace the part. Back on Canopus,

Doug and Tony discover they will live in a vegetable-like state after their memories and knowledge is extracted. After discovering the Aliens exist in the same manner as plant life on Earth, and go dormant when their closest star (similar to our own Sun) shines on the opposite side of the planet, the time travelers trick the aliens into thinking they swallowed a sedative. While Doug and Tony combat OTT, the alien security officer and official time traveler, Ann figures out how to operate the Aliens' time machine and transports herself back to the Tunnel Complex. Before Doug and Tony can return home, the machine is destroyed to ensure the Aliens do not continue their intergalactic kidnapping and Doug and Tony are whisked away to another time.

STOCK MUSIC: Color Bumper (by Johnny Williams, :03); Let's Go (by Leith Stevens, :11); Moon Fuel (by Lyn Murray, :31); Spack Work (by Murray, :31); Impact (by Murray, :31); The Spearmen (by Bernard Herrmann, :31); Jettison (by Murray, :31); Main Title (a.k.a. Time Tunnel Theme, by Williams, :37); The Boiler Room (by Williams, :15); Escape (by Herrmann, :41); Outer Space (by Herrmann, :23); The Marshal (by Lionel Newman, :37); Terror (by Herrmann, :37); Tony Suits Up (by Murray, :37); The Mirror (by Herrmann, :47); The Knife (by Herrmann, :47); Time Transfer (by Williams, 1:01); Tony Talks (by Paul Sawtell, :19); Drugged Interrogation (by Sawtell, :19); Tony Remembers (by Sawtell, :19); The Quarrel (by Herrmann, :19); Time Travel (by Murray, :25); Doug's Count Down (by Williams, :25); Time Transfer (by Williams, :25); The Fight (by Herrmann, :25); The Mirror (by Herrmann, :25); Althea's Attack (by Williams, :07 and :39); The Pass (by Herrmann, :39); Doug's Arrival (by Williams, :11); The Storm (by Herrmann, :11); Tony Threatens (by George Duning, :15); Time Travel (by Murray, :46); Brandon Stalked (by Murray, :46); Tony Missing (by Murray, :46); Control and Stalk (by Murray, :46; Tony Suits Up #2 (by Murray, :16); Plastic Device (by Murray, :23); Tony Angry (by Duning, :09); Bumper (by Williams, :03); A Fool (by Sawtell, :08); Beard and Doug (by Murray, :40); Time Travel (by Murray, :51); Beard and Doug (by Murray, :51); Time Travel (by Murray, :18); Beard and Doug (by Murray, :18); Moon Fuel (by Murray, :27); The Marshal (by Lionel Newman, :27); Moon Fuel (by Murray, 1:30); Moon Approach (by Murray, :14); Moon Walk (by Murray, :43); Brandon Search (by Murray, :43); The Pass (by Herrmann, 1:35); To the Tunnel (by Williams, :31); The Telegraph (by Williams, :31); Tony's Tall Tale (by Williams, 1:06); Tony Suits Up (by Murray, :22); The Jungle (by Williams, :22); Time Transfer (by Williams, :37); The Storm (by Herrmann, :37); Time Transfer (by

Williams, :02); Flying Chord (by Robert Drasnin, :03); The Boiler Room (by Williams, :23); First Test Part Two (by Stevens, :17); Coda (by Stevens, :17); Take Off (by Murray, :15); Next Week (by Murray, :09); End Credits (a.k.a. Time Tunnel Theme, by Williams, :48); and Fox I.D. (by Alfred Newman, :05).

EPISODE BUDGET
Story Rights and Expense $1,900
Scenario $5,891
Producer $6,461
Direction $3,000
Cast $16,690
Extras $5,487
Music $3,675
Staff $3,142
Art $2,681
Sets $11,350
Operating Labor $4,660
Miniatures $1,500
Camera $3,108
Sound $1,693
Electrical $4,147
Mechanical Effects $1,130
Set Dressing $4,785
Women's Wardrobe $404
Men's Wardrobe $2,904
Makeup and Hairdressing $1,628

Process $40
Production Film & Lab Charges
    $8,845
Stills $150
Transportation $2,900
Re-Recording $3,556
Photo Effects $4,120
Opticals, Fades and Dissolves
    $3,150
Titles $585
Post Production Film & Lab
    Charges $14,243
Projectionists $215
Editorial $9,267
Fringe Benefits $16,455
Miscellaneous $1,130
Amortizations $2,753
Contract Overhead $15,000
General Overhead $8,047
Total Picture Cost $176,692

SET PRODUCTION COSTS
Interior Complex, corridor, scientists office, dispatching chamber and cell $5,800
Interior Limbo Set $700
Construction Foreman $975
Amortized $1,500
Total $8,975

STORY DEVELOPMENT

William Welch was paid $4,000 for his short story, the first draft and the final draft of "The Kidnappers." Jerry Briskin wrote to Irwin Allen on February 13, 1967, with concerns about the first draft of the script. Briskin's comments reveal much about the initial intention of scenes that were never produced and/or revised. A list is reprinted below.

> "Before Kirk speaks, could OTT say something to Ann about having come to the Complex to take her away? In the same scene, I believe we should have a photo effect when Kirk almost touches OTT's arm so that the viewers will see a visual effect on the screen and know what is happening."

> "Again, I believe we should have a photo effect when OTT's arm approaches Swain and hurls him to one side."

The Time Tunnel cast with Bob May as Adolf Hitler and Michael Ansara as the curator.

"If the scientist has set a buzzer alarm so that Tony and Doug won't escape from his office, why doesn't it go off when they open the door rather than when they run off?"

"Kirk's last speech, scene 71, Kirk threatens OTT by telling OTT that if he takes one step towards any of the people in the Complex, he will be shot. I don't understand Kirk's reasoning as on page 3, scene 8, when the Security Guard in the Complex fired at OTT and couldn't kill him. How does Kirk think he can overcome this situation?"

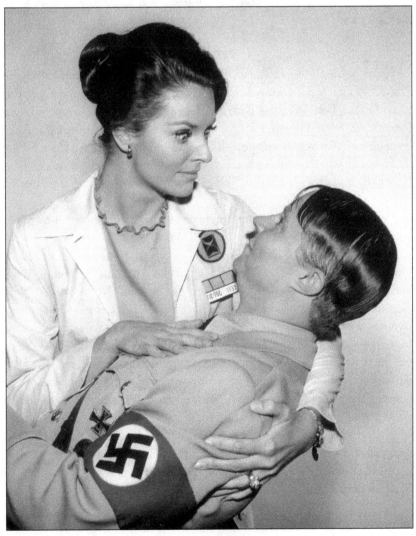

Lee Meriwether clowns around with Bob May.

"If the scientist had the ability of using mental telepathy, why doesn't he know what our people have done in the way of faking the taking of the cubes?"

"The description of the colored cubes that our group is supposed to take reads like the description of how LSD is taken when explained in our daily newspapers."*

ABC CENSORSHIP CONCERNS

The body, in relation to the beam, can stiffen but please delete the direction "convulsively."

NOTES

Extras inside the Time Tunnel Complex: Skip Burnham, Ann Doree, John Drake, Bill Graeff, Steve Howell, Paul Kessler, Charles Picerni, Virginia Semon, Gene Silvani, Bob Todd and Barbara Washington. Hatmos Guards in Silver: John Drake, Steve Howell, Paul Kessler and John Moio. Stand-ins for Alien complex included Skip Burnham, Bill Graeff, Virginia Semon and Gene Silvani.

It is referenced in this episode that Tony Newman left Philadelphia in 1954 to Boston on a Scholarship. This may have been an in-joke. James Darren was born in Philadelphia.

Some of the stock music cues originate from Bernard Herrmann's music score for *The Day the Earth Stood Still* (1951).

Del Monroe (as OTT), wears parts of outfits that can be seen in *Lost In Space*, including Verna's top from "Revolt of the Androids" (March 8, 1967) and a head piece later used in "Deadliest of the Species" (November 22, 1967). (Monroe once recalled how the makeup was uncomfortable.) Other aliens wear space suits from prior *Lost In Space* outfits. Many of the electronic props in this episode originate from prior *Lost In Space* episodes. The space aliens use the same guns a different race of aliens use in "Town of Terror." The glass desk Michael Ansara sits behind can also be seen in an episode of *Land of the Giants*, "The Secret City of Limbo," *and* two episodes of *Voyage to the Bottom of the Sea*, "Time Lock" and "Flaming Ice."

On February 20, as soon as production for "Merlin, the Magician" was completed (about 4 p.m.), production for this episode began that same afternoon, most notably the Time Tunnel Complex scenes.

The beams in this episode were animated.

---

* These same cubes are featured in the opening scene of "The Mechanical Man," a second season episode of *Voyage to the Bottom of the Sea*, featuring James Darren as the title character.

LEE MERIWETHER

"I've never thought of Lee [Meriwether] in any relationship terms other than friendship, but we had this one moment," recalled Robert Colbert to author Kyle Counts. "She was married to Frank Aletter at the time, when we were rehearsing a scene where I was supposed to kiss her; just a peck. My lips touched hers, and, honest to God, you would have thought Krakatoa went off in my dressing room — the sparks flew. We knew that, under the circumstances, we shouldn't touch each other. That was the end of that, but I've never forgotten it to this day."

Lee Meriwether clowns around with Bob May.

Critics were harsh when it came to their reviews. "Michael Ansara is the only believable part of this program," wrote Joan Crosby in her syndicated *TV Scout* column. Columnist Hal Humphrey, after watching the summer re-run, wrote in the August 10, 1967, issue of *The Los Angeles Times*, "Lee Meriwether, as Dr. Ann MacGregor, has had very little or nothing to do on *Time Tunnel*, except to maybe utter things like, 'We had better intensify the probe.' She starred in 'The Kidnappers' episode last night, where she was kidnapped from the Time Tunnel Complex by a time traveler from 6,000 years in the future. Lee Meriwether deserved so much better than that in this series, which, thank heaven, went off after one season."

BLOOPER!

OTT's silver makeup wasn't complete. In one scene when he raises his hand you can see the actor's skin tone where the paint did not cover.

Director Sobey Martin poses with Bob May.

RAIDERS FROM OUTER SPACE

INITIAL TELECAST: March 31, 1967
SHOOTING SCRIPT DATED: February 27, 1967, with revised pages dated March 2 and 8, 1967
DATES OF PRODUCTION: March 1, 2, 3, 6, 7 and 8, 1967
FILMING LOCATIONS: Moat, Red Rock Canyon-Mojave, Stage 7, Stage 18, and Western Avenue
GUEST CAST: George Barefoot* (Android #2); Jerry Catron (Android #1); John Crawford (Captain Henderson); Kevin Hagen (Planet Leader); Gil Perkins (Sergeant); and Paul Stader (Stunt Arab).

Stunt Doubles
Glen Colbert (Doug)
Charles Picerni (Tony)
Paul Stader (stunt Slave #2)
Mike Donovan (stunt Slave #1)
Eddie Saenz (stunt Arab)

PRODUCTION CREDITS
ART DIRECTORS: Jack Martin Smith and Rodger E. Maus
ASSISTANT DIRECTOR: Steve Bernhardt
DIRECTOR: Nathan Juran
FILM EDITOR: James Baiotto
MUSIC: stock
MUSIC EDITOR: Sam E. Levin
Teleplay by Bob and Wanda Duncan.

STORY: November 2, 1883. Tony and Doug land in a desert in North Africa, within earshot of the 1883 battle during the Siege of Khartoum, and after defending themselves against Arabs, quickly encounter an alien race from the planet Aristos bent on conquering the galaxy. Their plan is to launch a missile capable of destroying all of London, thus injecting fright into the human race who will surrender when encountering such force and power. After the Planet Leader warns the scientists at the Time Tunnel Complex not to try a pickup again or he will destroy the Tunnel, and upset because Tony and Doug are interfering, the Aliens plant a detonation device in the Time Tunnel

---

* George Barefoot also doubled for an Arab. Jerry Catron also doubled for a soldier.

Complex, set to go off in 60 minutes, unless they provide knowledge of their time travel capabilities, which the Aliens plan to use in their conquest. Tony and Doug manage to escape the Aliens and, after helping the British fight against the Arabs, the time travelers convince British Captain Henderson about the existence of the extra-terrestrials. Henderson urges Tony and Doug to go to Khartoum with him to get help to destroy the Alien Complex. But the final battle between the Arabs and the Sudanese under British command impedes their progress and they can only gather up some ammunition and try to stop the Planet Leader themselves. The three of them attack the cave while Kirk and Swain send the detonation device through the tunnel, exploding the secret missile base and cave moments before Doug and Tony, escaping with their lives, vanish to another adventure.

STOCK MUSIC: Color Bumper (by Johnny Williams, :03); The Boiler Room (by Williams, :23); First Test Part Two (by Leith Stevens, :46); Coda (by Stevens, :46); Take Off (by Lyn Murray, 1:51); Brandon Take Over (by Murray, :05); Main Title (a.k.a. Time Tunnel Theme, by Williams, :37); No Word (by Murray, :25); The Arrest (by Lionel Newman, :33); Meteor (by Murray, :35); Appear Sting (by Bernard Herrmann, :03); Althea's Attack (by Williams, :37); Escape (by Herrmann, :11); Moon Fuel (by Murray, :11); The Quarrel (by Herrmann, 1:01); Impact (by Murray, :09); Tony Suits Up (by Murray, :23); Brandon Take Over (by Murray, :23); Saved and Disappear (by Murray, :05); Take Him Away (by Joseph Mullendore, :09); The Cave (by Lionel Newman, :15); The Paperhanger is Still Alive (by Daniele Amfitheatrof, :35); Someone Moved (by Lionel Newman, :35); The Rescue (by Lionel Newman, :35); Volcanic Island (by Robert Drasnin, :35); Complex Problem (by Drasnin, :35); Moon Approach (by Murray, :12); Jettison (by Murray, :12); Brandon Take Over (by Murray, :12, :03 and :16); Doug's Count Down (by Williams, :16); Time Transfer (by Williams, :05); The Paperhanger is Still Alive (by Amfitheatrof, :53); Time Transfer (by Williams, :05); Maddox Killed (by George Duning, :23); Time Travel (by Murray, :23); Powder Cave (by Duning, :23); Appear Sting (by Herrmann, :23); Stand Back (by Duning, : 26); Corporal Shot (by Duning, :26); The Powder (by Duning, :26); The First Chase (by Franz Waxman, :30); The Bombing (by Paul Sawtell, :30); Bumper (by Williams, :03); Doug's Duels (by Duning, :43); Maddox Killed (by Duning, :43); Plastic Device (by Murray, :38); The Mirror (by Herrmann, :38); The Cave (by Lionel Newman, :38); Trapped (by Waxman, 1:01); Escape (by Waxman, 1:01); Wild Anxiety (by Alfred Newman, :45); The Rescue (by Lionel Newman, :45); More Pal Fight (by Duning, :45); House of Bamboo (by Leigh Harline, :55); Main Title (by Waxman, :22); Death of Ula (by

Hugo Friedhofer, :22); The Cave (by Lionel Newman, :22); What Now? (by Friedhofer, :22); More Trouble (by Lionel Newman, :35); The Quarrel (by Herrmann, :35); The Marshal (by Lionel Newman, :35); A Dark Night (by Lionel Newman, :35); Destroying the Complex (by Lennie Hayton, :35); The Paperhanger is Still Alive (by Amfitheatrof, :35); Doug's Count Down (by Williams, 1:45); Fright, Flight, Fight (by Drasnin, :30); Bomb Warp (by Drasnin, :30); Urgent Detergent (by Lionel Newman, :30); Moon Survival (by Murray, :15); Time Transfer (by Williams, :07); The Boiler Room (by Williams, :35); Plastic Device (by Lyn Murray, :23); No Word (by Murray, :23); Fight (by Stevens, :23); Stand Back (by Duning, :23); Moon Walk (by Murray, :23); Next Week (by Murray, :09); End Credits (a.k.a. Time Tunnel Theme, by Williams, :48); and Fox I.D. (by Alfred Newman, :05).

Note: All Budgets Prepared by Paul De Herdt.

EPISODE BUDGET
Story Rights and Expense $1,900
Scenario $5,891
Producer $6,461
Direction $3,000
Cast $17,440
Extras $4,911
Music $3,675
Staff $3,230
Art $2,681
Sets $5,565
Operating Labor $5,042
Miniatures $1,500
Camera $3,496
Sound $1,693
Electrical $3,440
Mechanical Effects $2,045
Set Dressing $4,777
Animals and Action Devices $560
Women's Wardrobe $404
Men's Wardrobe $3,619
Makeup and Hairdressing $1,453

Process $40
Production Film & Lab Charges
    $8,845
Stills $150
Transportation $5,900
Location Expenses $2,710
Re-Recording $3,556
Photo Effects $2,996
Opticals, Fades and Dissolves
    $3,150
Titles $585
Post Production Film & Lab
    Charges $14,993
Projectionists $215
Editorial $9,267
Fringe Benefits $15,430
Miscellaneous $1,130
Amortizations $2,753
Contract Overhead $15,000
General Overhead $8,175
Total Picture Cost $177,678

Series budget $167,757 per episode
Pre-Production Estimate $177,678
Over $9,921

SET PRODUCTION COSTS

Cave and rocky area, cave corridor, sand in moat and solar mirrors cost $1,000
The cave corridor and missile room was $2,100.
Set Total $6,500
Construction Foreman $975
Amortized $1,500
Total $12,075

STORY DEVELOPMENT

Bob and Wanda Duncan were paid $4,000 for their story, and the first and final draft of the teleplay. Their initial story conception was titled "The Gladiators."

In the first draft of the teleplay, the aliens were not seen protecting the entrance to the cave. When rational common sense dictated that a scene should be added to reveal the guards, it was added. The initial draft also called for the android to wear a strange-looking bracelet, which he uses at various times, including removing the invisible force field that protected the entrance to the cave. In the original script, this device was a ring and because the studio was building one in the prop shop, the bracelet was replaced with a ring.

Tony is pushed into the "extractor," a prop that appears in episodes of other Irwin Allen shows.

Because Doug was being held in place by an invisible beam, it was questioned why he had to be strapped to the chair. This was later revised to the "extractor" that is used in this episode.

On February 21, 1967, Jerry Briskin wrote to Irwin Allen, questioning a suggested script revision. He questioned the fact "that the Aliens would proceed with their plans of 1883 when the Alien planet leader appears on the Time Tunnel Image Area in the year 1968, which would automatically inform the Aliens that they never destroyed or conquered Earth in 1883."

Briskin also questioned: "I wonder why the Aliens never call upon their slave beings to help them protect the missile base in the latter part of the script when Tony and Doug break into the base and eventually destroy it."

ABC CENSORSHIP CONCERNS

Your usual care in seeing that fights are not unnecessarily brutal or prolonged.
Standard caution on your choice of battle stock shots. Can only be approved on film.
Androids' appearance should not be too frightening for family viewing.
Gun can be pointed at, but not pressed against Tony's head.
Special caution on effects of "exotic chair" on Doug and Tony: Pain reaction, etc. not overdone.

Doug fights back against aliens in disguise.

NOTES

The un-credited roles of Arabs were played by Skip Burnham, Bill Graeff, Steve Howell, Paul Kessler, John Moio and Gene Silvani. The un-credited role of three British Soldiers: Skip Burnham, Steve Howell and John Moio. The un-credited role of four Slave Beings: Skip Burnham, John Drake, Steve Howell and Gene Silvani.

On March 3, 1967, Vic Lundin appeared on the set to play the role of Android #1, a.k.a. the Planet Leader. Beginning March 4, actor Kevin Hagen reported to the set to replace Lundin, who was told not to report to the set. The reason for Lundin's replacement remains unknown. Kevin Hagen recalled, "I almost went up in flames when my giant alien brain caught fire in a special effects stunt gone awry!"

Miss Lynette Kentwell wrote to the Australian *TV Times* magazine in October 30, 1968, after watching this episode on her local television channel. "In all my life I have never seen a historical bungle like the one in the *Time Tunnel* episode, 'Raiders from Outer Space'...All the battle shots in this *Time Tunnel* episode were taken from the film, *Khartoum*, and we even saw Charlton Heston, as General Gordon, striding 'round the place. How utterly bungled and ludicrous can you get!" In the November 20 issue, the editor commented that "at no time did viewers see Charlton Heston as General Gordon striding around the place."

The costumes and hats worn by the British in this episode don't match those of the stock footage from the movie, *Khartoum* (1966).

The columnist for the *TV Scout* column in the *Utica Observer-Dispatch* remarked: "The producers of *Time Tunnel* must have their problems finding locations to go along with their way-out scripts. This one is set in a desert, the Sahara to be exact, where the boys are getting ready to witness the battle for Khartoum. While the British and Arabian forces are gathering for the assault, figures appear that would have made Kipling rush for gin and beer. They are aliens who are using the location as an arsenal for an Earth takeover. You don't have to be a genius to know they fail."

The "extractor" prop used on James Darren in this episode can also be seen in the following Irwin Allen productions: "The Cyborg" (*Voyage to the Bottom of the Sea*), "Condemned of Space" and "The Phantom Family" (*Lost In Space*), and "The Mechanical Man" (*Land of the Giants*).

The aliens that first greet Tony and Doug in the beginning of this episode is the same as the green demon in the *Lost In Space* episode, "A Visit to Hades," and the *Voyage to the Bottom of the Sea* episode, "Deadly Amphibians."

HISTORICAL ERRORS

In this episode, the British are fighting against the Arab uprising, with Egyptian forces led by British General Charles George Gordon and a Mahdist Sudanese army led by the self-proclaimed Mahdi Muhammad Ahmad. But that event did not begin until March of 1884. This episode takes place in November 1883, when history records the Egyptian army suffered a bloody defeat at the hands of the Mahdist rebels at El Obeid. The script writer was off by a year in the time table of events.

If one wants to be critical, the script at no time mentioned General Gordon or the Mahdi, the two main opponents in the fall of Khartoum in 1885, except for the final scene. The battles featured in the story were not necessarily meant to be that final tragedy, but an earlier skirmish in the area. It was Doug and Tony who "assumed" where and when they were when they initially landed.

The set outside the fort is the same where the Seaview docks at the Nelson Institute of Marine Research, featured prominently on *Voyage to the Bottom of the Sea*.

BLOOPER!

When Tony is pushed against the "extractor," the entire prop wobbles and moves more than once!

During the fight scene in the fort, an explosion sends rocks flying behind the barricade, landing behind Tony and Doug. As the scene progresses, the rocks disappear and reappear.

During the fight sequence in the cave, Doug lands on the pipes that are supposedly rooted deep in the Earth, but they clearly wobble.

PRODUCTION #9630
TOWN OF TERROR

INITIAL TELECAST: April 7, 1967
SHOOTING SCRIPT DATED: March 8, 1967, with revised pages dated March 9, 10 and 14.
DATES OF PRODUCTION: March 9, 10, 13, 14, 15 and 16, 1967
FILMING LOCATIONS: Peyton Wharf, Stage 4, Stage 18 and Stage 19
GUEST CAST: Mabel Albertson (Sarah Pettinghill, the old lady); Vincent Beck (Alien Leader at space station); George Burrafato (frozen townsperson); Fred Carson (frozen townsperson); Ann Doree (frozen townsperson); Gary Haynes (Pete); Bart La Rue (voice of Andro One); Kelly Thordsen (Sarah Pettinghill as an Alien); and Heather Young (Joan).

Stunt Doubles
Charlie Picerni (double for Tony)
Glen Colbert (double for Doug)
Gil Perkins (stunt villager)
Denver Mattson (stunt alien)
Chuck Waters (stunt alien)
George Robotham (stunt alien)

PRODUCTION CREDITS
ART DIRECTORS: Jack Martin Smith and Rodger E. Maus
ASSISTANT DIRECTOR: Fred R. Simpson
DIRECTOR: Herschel Daugherty
FILM EDITOR: Dick Wormell
MUSIC: stock
MUSIC EDITOR: Sam E. Levin
Teleplay by Carey Wilber.

STORY: September 10, 1978. Doug and Tony encounter a waspish little Sarah Pettinghill who soon turns into Alien Sarah, a hideous Android, who is in charge of a project to remove all of Earth's oxygen and take it to another planet. To this end, she and her Androids have immobilized everyone in the small fishing village of Cliffport, Maine, and set up laboratories for the project that begins in an hour. Their force field surrounding the town prevents the Time Tunnel Complex from picking up Doug and Tony, whom they finally have an accurate fix on. After meeting two young kids, Joan and Pete, who have been hiding out in town, the time travelers learn of the plot and they plan to dynamite the Alien control center in the cellar of the local New England hotel. Back at the Time Tunnel Complex, oxygen is being drained through the tunnel as the Aliens begin their intergalactic theft. Meanwhile, Doug and Tony obtain some explosives and hurry them to the control center while a violent storm caused by the draining of the Earth's oxygen begins. Pete is taken over by one of the Aliens and tricks Joan into revealing Doug and Tony's plans. The Aliens rush to stop the time travelers, but they are successful in fighting them off and blowing the control center to pieces, thus foiling the scheme, restoring the citizens of Cliffport and saving the lives back in the Time Tunnel Complex in 1968. They are whirled away from the recovered village and into the time vortex.

STOCK MUSIC: Color Bumper (by Johnny Williams, :03); The Boiler Room (by Williams, :27); Plastic Device (by Lyn Murray, :25); No Word (by Murray, :25); Fight (by Leith Stevens, :25); Moon Walk (by Murray, :25); Moon Survival (by Murray, :25); Stand Back (by George Duning, :25); Tony's Tall Tale (by Williams, :25); Althea's Attack (by Williams, :25); Moon Approach (by Murray, :17); Saved and Disappear (by Murray, :05); The Big Whew (by Alexander Courage, :05); Moon Approach (by Murray, :05); Main Title (a.k.a. Time Tunnel Theme, by Williams, :37); Take Off (by Murray, :57); The Mirror (by Bernard Herrmann, :57); Time Transfer (by Williams, :57); Tony's Tall Tale (by Williams, :57); The Marshal (by Lionel Newman, :57); The Marshal (by Lionel Newman, :52); The Paperhanger is Still Alive (by Daniele Amfitheatrof, :52); Beard and Doug (by Murray, :52); The Paperhanger is Still Alive (by Amfitheatrof, :08); Terror (by Herrmann, :19); The Boiler Room (by Williams, :09); Wild Anxiety (by Alfred Newman, :12); The Paperhanger is Still Alive (by Amfitheatrof, :12 and :12); Time Transfer (by Williams, :12); The Jungle (by Williams, :12); Time Transfer (by Williams, :10); What's Happened (by Duning, :10); Appear Sting (by Herrmann, :10); No Word (by Murray, :19); Saved and Disappear (by Murray, :08); Appear Sting (by Herrmann, :08); The Glowing (by Herrmann, :41); Count Down (by Paul Sawtell, :14); Making Contact (by Williams, :23); Doug's Arrival (by Williams, :23); Control and Stalk (by Murray, :23); Tony Suits Up (by Murray, :29); Appear Sting (by Herrmann, :24); The Glowing (by Herrmann, :21); Saved and Disappear (by Murray, :04); Moon Approach (by Murray, :06); Bumper (by Williams, :03); Moon Approach (by Murray, :32); Moon Fuel (by Murray, :32); Saved and Disappear (by Murray, :04 and :04); Appear Sting (by Herrmann, :04); Moon Fuel (by Murray, :06 and :37); The Marshal (by Lionel Newman, :37); Voice in the Sky (by Robert Drasnin, :37); The Marshal (by Lionel Newman, :57); Voice in the Sky (by Drasnin, :57); Doug's Count Down (by Williams, :59); Mock Mysterioso (by Lionel Newman, :17); Comet Tail to Explosion (by Murray, :03); Appear Sting (by Herrmann, :03); Tony Enters Machine (by Williams, :29); The Titanic (by Williams, :29); Saved and Disappear (by Murray, :11); Althea's Attack (by Williams, :29); Tony Talks (by Sawtell, 1:27); Trying to Remember (by Sawtell, 1:27); The Jungle (by Williams, :17); Take Off (by Murray, :36); First Test Part Two (by Stevens, :36); Bomb Warp (by Drasnin, :36); Voice in the Sky (by Drasnin, 1:27); Time Transfer (by Williams, 1:11); Escape (by Lionel Newman, :09); Meteor (by Murray, :19); Tony Enters Machine (by Williams, :19); The Iceberg Cometh (by Williams, :19); The First Chase (by Franz Waxman, :19); Disappearing Act (by Williams, :19); Doug's Arrival (by Williams, :19); Brandon Take Over (by Murray, :19); The Paperhanger is Still Alive (by Amfitheatrof, :13); Voice in the Sky (by Drasnin, :08); The Paperhanger is Still Alive (by Amfitheatrof, :27 and :27); Moon Walk (by Murray, :27); Stand Back (by Duning, :27); Jerry Collapse (by Murray, :27); Time Transfer (by Williams, :02); Flying Chord (by Drasnin, :02); The Boiler Room (by Williams, :24); Approaching the Berg (by Williams, :05); The Iceberg Cometh (by Williams, :05); The Rescue (by Lionel Newman, :05); Next Week (by Murray, :09); End Credits (a.k.a. Time Tunnel Theme, by Williams, :48); and Fox I.D. (by Alfred Newman, :05).

EPISODE BUDGET

Story Rights & Expense $1,900
Scenario $5,891
Producer $6,461
Direction $3,000
Cast $17,440
Extras $4,911
Music $3,675
Staff $3,142
Art $2,681
Sets $12,575
Operating Labor $5,125
Miniatures $1,500
Camera $3,376
Sound $1,693
Electrical $4,147
Mechanical Effects $2,090

Set Dressing $5,581
Animals & Action Devices $0
Women's Wardrobe $404
Men's Wardrobe $1,854
Makeup & Hairdressing $1,453
Process $40
Production Film & Lab Charges $8,845
Stills $150
Transportation $3,200
Re-recording $3,556
Photo Effects $2,000
Opticals, Fades & Dissolves $3,150
Titles $585
Post Production & Lab Charges $14,243
Projectionists $215

Editorial $9,267
Fringe Benefits $16,730
Miscellaneous $1,130
Amortizations $2,783

Contract Overhead $15,000
General Overhead $8,214
Total Picture Cost $178,007

Series Budget $167,757
Pre-Production Estimate $178,007
Over Budget $10,250

SET PRODUCTION COSTS
Laboratory-Hotel $1,935
Alien Control Center $1,825
Main Streets and Buildings $1,900
General Store $875
Town Hall Corridor $715
Foremen $1,100
Total $8,350

STORY DEVELOPMENT

On March 9, 1967, Carey Wilber was paid $4,000 for story, and the first and final draft of the teleplay. The original title of Wilber's story was "Tomorrow's Past."

After reviewing the first draft of the script, Jerry Briskin created a list of notes on February 22. "I wish I knew where to begin commenting on this particular script because of the numerous inconsistencies, holes in the story, lack of characterizations, unbelievable situations, etc.," he wrote. "There is over a page of process called for in the script which covers Doug and Tony and the police officer while they have dialogue in moving cars. We need process plates to match the location that the other exterior action takes place in. In addition, we need mock ups of the two cars that are utilized in the sequences that they work in. As we are dealing in the year 1978, what kind of car do we use when the boys make their first escape in town and what kind of a car do we use for the police officer?"

"In the interior of the Time Tunnel Complex, there are a couple of occasions when a paper is lifted off one of the consoles and gently and slowly drifts into the Tunnel and disappears. This sounds like wire work and can't be done with any speed insofar as shooting time is concerned."

"There are a couple of cuts of the interior alien complex and to sell the vastness of this room and the machinery contained therein, I am of the opinion that we could have to have a couple of matte shots."

"There are going to be numerous wardrobe costs involved in the making of this show as practically all the outside cast members are seen in Alien wardrobe at one time or another."

"I believe that the dialogue in this script should be given a complete going over starting with page one. In addition, it is my opinion that the corny, small-town kind of dialogue that is written into the script will get us nothing but laughs…Jumping to the back end of the script at this point, I don't understand how this story can hold together. My reasoning is that the action takes place in 1988, yet our Time Tunnel has warned Washington about the incident that is to take place 20 years later and Washington obviously has done nothing to prevent the incident. I am sorry to say, I don't follow this logic."

Tony and Doug arrive in a "Town of Terror."

"It is very difficult for me to accept the fact that the police officer would handcuff Tony and Doug together and put them in the back seat of his car while he casually got in the front seat to drive them. This kind of action would make it very simple for Tony and Doug to overpower the policeman. The fact is that patrol cars normally have two officers in them so as to prevent situations such as this."

"As Dan (the police officer) is actually an alien, who and what are the people in the police station that he spoke to when he first captured Tony and Doug? By the way, is Dan posing as a police officer of Cliffport (the town the aliens occupy) or some other community?"

"An example of the kind of dialogue I would like to see eliminated from the script is as follows: Page 28, scene 134: Tony's last speech on the page (this follows a period of time that Tony and Doug have been handcuffed to a post in the Sheriff's office) — 'Just as luck would have it, we meet a State Trooper...We'd better get out of here'."

Doug offers an explanation of what is happening.

"I am still at a loss to figure out why the Aliens, with their viewing screen, don't know exactly what Tony and Doug are up to at all times. Also, if Earth is going to be a dead planet in 20 hours or less, I don't know why the aliens even bother to keep our guys alive. Why don't the aliens freeze Tony and Doug like they have done to all the other people in the town?"

"The idea of Tony and Doug escaping from the Sheriff's office by using a paper clip to unlock their handcuffs is too much for me to accept."

"Jumping back to the latter part of the story again, I am at a loss to believe that once Kirk found the oxygen bottle in the medical cabinet in the Tunnel Complex (which, by the way, we don't have), he never gets onto the inner Complex speaker system and informs the others in the Complex, who are slowly dying of asphyxiation, to go to the medical supply room once they can get around through the use of the bottled oxygen and get out larger quantities of oxygen so as to continue their work."

"It seems that no matter where we are in the town, we never seem to find the aliens around searching for Tony and Doug."

"When Tony and Doug discover Pete and Jean, the kids tell our boys they have been hiding out for the last three weeks. As the Aliens have the viewing screen, how in the world did these people hide from them?"

"On page 45 of the script after Tony and Doug have left Pete and Jean to see what they could do, they depart the Sheriff's office and go into the hotel where the entrance to the alien complex can be found. I don't understand why they would go through the front door of what they know is the aliens' headquarters, nor do I understand why the aliens, who know Tony and Doug are loose, would not have guards surrounding the area."

"When Pete runs to help Tony and Doug and runs into the aliens who look like Dan and Sam Crawford, it would seem to me that the aliens would simple freeze him at that point and throw him into some room where he couldn't bother them any longer rather than changing him to an alien at a later point."

Joan (Heather Young) flees from the clutches of an Alien being.

"The final sequence in which Tony and Doug enter the alien complex in an effort to destroy it is, to me, completely unbelievable. How the aliens could have one man working in this tremendous complex is bad enough, but not having any guards around it when our boys are running around footloose and fancy free is something that I can't comprehend."

NOTES

Robert Colbert cut his forehead on March 15, 1967, while attempting to jump through a breakaway window. He was treated by the studio hospital and returned to set at 2:15 p.m. It's possible the injury was not the result of him jumping through the window, but from the bench moments before. Robert Colbert remembers the scene where he and James Darren rammed a big bench through the window, or at least tried. The bench hit him in the head and Colbert received a severe cut. Because they could not stop the bleeding, they stitched him up at the hospital and then applied makeup to cover the scar, so they could continue filming. "I do remember I ended up with a gash in my forehead that required me to leave the set immediately and go have

Doug and Tony examine the body of a man they think they killed.

about 20-some stitches," recalled Colbert. "Of course they were very small stitches, because nobody wanted to damage my beautiful face [laughs]. I was gone a very short time, maybe a couple of hours, and then I was back on the set working — I'm sure they didn't even miss me!"

The same Peyton Wharf used for this episode was also used for Manitou Junction in the *Lost In Space* classic, "Visit to a Hostile Planet." It was known as Peyton Wharf on the back lot because it was featured prominently in the television program *Peyton Place*. The director made sure instructions were given not to shoot the wharf from the reverse angle, which is what they did for *Peyton Place*, hoping television audiences would not notice the similarity. It was during the third season of *Peyton Place* that the wharf was fully dressed, but *Time Tunnel* fans probably took note of the signs of "Cliffport" throughout the show, to dress it up and match this episode. (The same wharf can be seen in "The Shell Game" and "The Mechanical Man" episodes of *Land of the Giants*.)

This episode aired not with a preview of next week's episode, but with scenes from "Rendezvous With Yesterday," so that summer reruns could pick up where the season began.

The Aliens in this episode use the same guns the other outer space visitors use in the episode "The Kidnappers."

Tony, Doug and Joan must prevent a storm that is brewing.

Exactly whatever became of the alien device that was planted in the Time Tunnel Complex?

The purple alien masks in this episode are the same red masks in the *Lost In Space* episode, "The Phantom Family."

The pipes sticking out of the ground in the basement floor was the same prop seen in the reactor room of the Seaview in many episodes of *Voyage to the Bottom of the Sea.*

The radiometer featured prominently in "End of the World" also appears on the top shelf in the laboratory in this episode.

PRESS RELEASE: FACT OR FICTION?

According to a press release, the scene set in the small hotel lobby offered an unusual bit of trivia…if the information is true. "Behind the desk were the usual pigeon holes used for mail. But if anyone had checked the prop mail sitting in those holes, they would have found it was real mail. Postcards and empty envelopes that went back 20 years were actually used by the prop department. It was all old fan mail letters — three old letters to Betty Grable

Heather Young arrives at the parking lot for the day's filming.

circa 1944, two Jeanne Crain letters circa 1949 and other letters and postcards to Lon McAllister, Rory Calhoun and Victor Mature."

BLOOPER!

In the background, near the 40 minute mark, you can see 20th Century-Fox studios behind "Cliffport Garage."

The storm was created with giant fans positioned behind the cameras. This causes shrubbery and trees in the foreground to move and sway but not the ones in the background.

When Pete is touched by the alien, he doesn't remain frozen like a statue, like everyone else.

Michael Ansara sleeps while Lee Meriwether receives instructions from the director positioned off camera in the episode, "The Kidnappers."

APPENDIX

APPENDIX A
ALTERNATE ENDING

Scene 136 CONTINUED *(Alt.)*

TONY: It could be anywhere, anytime. They had to move us in a hurry. Wherever we are, it's better than where we were.

DOUG: I hope so. Look…

They turn their heads toward the edge of the jungle. A swirling, blinding fog is billowing out, already starting to engulf them.

Scene 137, TWO SHOT–DOUG AND TONY *(Alt.)*

As they stare around at the white blanket of churning mist. When they speak, their voices echo hollowly.

TONY: Everything's fading again!
DOUG: Don't lose sight of me this time. They're switching us.

Tony cranes his neck, trying to penetrate the fog.

TONY: Can't see a thing...
ANN'S VOICE: *(far off–echoing)* Doug...can you hear me?
DOUG: *(reacting)* Ann...*(up)* We're here!
TONY: *(grabbing Doug's arm and pointing)* Look!

Scene 139 P.O.V. SHOT *(alt.)*
Through the thick, turning fog is the faint glow from the end of the Time Tunnel.

Scene 139 ANGLE ON TONY AND DOUG *(alt.)*
They turn to congratulate each other.

TONY: They did it! We're back!
DOUG: *(calling)* Ann...Ray...General! We're home!

The two men start through the mists, hurrying toward the light at the end of the Tunnel as the music builds to a curtain.

FADE OUT

The End

FORMAT
THE TIME TUNNEL PILOT SEGMENT
BY IRWIN ALLEN

Teaser

The gigantic tunnel-like device created by Phillips and Newman to cross the boundaries of time, is finally ready for a first "live" test. A tiny mouse is placed in the convergence chamber, the power build-up initiated and held and then, with the stators screaming, the laser switches are thrown. One millisecond later, the mouse is gone, sent coursing back through the dark tunnels of time. But the mouse cannot be returned. Only a being with the intelligence of man can wear the tiny ion generator ring and activate it when its power build-up is adequate. Without this cooperation from the time traveler — there can be no return. Now Phillips and Newman stand on the brink of what must be history's most revealing moment — man's first journey into time. Preparations and tests continue and finally, with everything checked and re-checked, the decision is at hand. Phillips deliberately picks up the ion ring, slips it onto his finger and steps into the convergence chamber. Moments later, the glaring white spot of light in which Phillips was standing reveals…nothing! The most incredible journey since the dawn of geological time has begun.

Act One

With the first test planned for just a few minutes duration, Newman now starts the power build-up that will effect Phillips' return. Over and over he runs the check list and throws the switches. But he cannot rescue his partner from the warp of time.

Phillips shakes himself out of the near-hypnotic state created by the empty, shadowless grey of the time mist to find himself on a pleasant Pennsylvania farm in mid-summer. He is attempting to orient himself when suddenly he finds he is staring down the barrel of a loaded musket in the hands of a frightened and exhausted youngster wearing the uniform of the Confederacy.

Phillips gradually becomes aware of the fact that he has arrived at that point back in time known as the second day of the Battle of Gettysburg. The young Confederate, trying to desert, finally is convinced that Phillips is not a Northern spy. Together, they head for a nearby farmhouse seeking shelter and a way to get to the Union lines. As they approach the house they are suddenly fired on. They hit the dirt and are held down by the witheringly accurate fire.

Act Two

With the young rebel, Phillips plans a daring attack on the farmhouse and finally they take it. They suddenly discover that their "enemy" is a frightened young girl desperately determined to fight either army to keep her father's land. With the girl and the young rebel, Phillips remains holed up in the farmhouse throughout the bloody second day of the battle. Finally, after devising a way to aid the wounded, Phillips heads for the Union lines. When he returns, the girl tells him the boy is gone. His outfit was Pickett's Brigade.

Meanwhile at Silvermine, Newman continues trying to bring Phillips back to the present. At the same time, he has his own problems concealing the disastrous result of the experiment without having his efforts to reach Phillips curtailed. Finally, contact is made. With his ion ring activated, Phillips is swept back into the nothingness of the time warp. For a moment, Newman can see Phillips' vague outline on the monitor plate. They converse for an instant — the man locked into another dimension of time and the man desperately trying to bring him back. Then, the shadowy image is gone. Only white light and silence remain.

Act Three

Now Phillips finds himself in the ancient past — the year is 200,000 B.C. Here he encounters the staggering experience of dinosaurs and pre-historic man in a series of adventures that defy the imagination. Finally, after fighting for mere survival as no modern man ever has, he activates his ring and contact is made. He is lifted from the Paleolithic slime to what he at first believes is the present when he finds himself in the middle of Grand Central Station during the five o'clock rush.

Act Four

Certain that he has finally traveled all the way back in time, Phillips heads for the institute. But as he makes his way there, he comes to the realization that it is not his present, but instead, the not-too-distant past: 1956. At this moment in time, he has not yet even met Newman and begun their long association. He is not yet on the staff at the Institute. He is unknown there. Finally, he gives up in Silvermine and heads for home. But when he reaches his home town in central Ohio, he stands in the street and sees himself as a much younger man leaving the house. He realizes bitterly he can't go home again, either.

At the Institute, Newman continues to fight the agonizing frustration of repeated failure. But he remains dedicated to the proposition that Phillips can be returned. Finally, Phillips is once again moved in time towards some as yet unknown destination. Again there is a fleeting moment of contact between the two men but an instant later it is ended — with Phillips once again floating through the grey limbo of warped time towards some unknown moment in the blackness of infinity.

APPENDIX C
ON-THE-AIR
TELEVISION ANNOUNCEMENTS

The following are four audio announcements for intermission breaks between television programs, promoting *The Time Tunnel*. A photo capture (often provided by a television slide) was presented on the screen for 20 seconds while the local announcer delivered the following audio:

(30 seconds) The wonders of the future open up…the mysteries of the past unfold…when you enter *The Time Tunnel*! You can be inside the first rocket to Mars…or inside the Trojan Horse. See the discovery of a new planet…or the discovery of fire. For the vast spectrum of time is revealed when two daring scientists are cast adrift in the fourth dimension — time! Be with them when James Darren and Robert Colbert star in *The Time Tunnel, (beginning) (day) (tomorrow) (tonight) (date)* at ___ p.m. *(in color)* on Channel ___ !

(20 seconds) The Time Tunnel — it can project you back to yesterday, or to a million years from now! Take an incredible trip through *The Time Tunnel* with two daring scientists. You might find yourself in Cleopatra's Egypt, or in King Solomon's time. Travel through limitless time with James Darren and Robert Colbert…via *The Time Tunnel, (beginning) (day) (tomorrow) (tonight) (date)* at ___ p.m. *(in color)* on Channel ___ !

(20 seconds) Would you step into yesterday…or tomorrow…or a million years from now? Two daring scientists do…and their incredible adventures within the vast spectrum of time are recorded in *The Time Tunnel*! Follow James Darren and Robert Colbert as they travel from the remotest part to the distant future *(beginning) (day) (tomorrow) (tonight) (date)* at ___ p.m. *(in color)* on Channel ___ !

(20 seconds) The Time Tunnel — the incredible machine that can project a man back into the battle between David and Goliath! Or to the future — a future that man's mind cannot as yet grasp! Explore unimagined mysteries as two men are sent out into time through *The Time Tunnel*. Starring James Darren and Robert Colbert *(premiering) (in color) (day) (tomorrow) (tonight) (date)* at ___ p.m. on Channel ___ !

Television Slides Inserted Between Programs to Advertise *The Time Tunnel*.

APPENDIX D
TWO
"GETTYSBURG" PLOT SUMMARIES

Dated December 9, 1966
GETTYSBURG
by Bob and Wanda Duncan

Revise on New Concept

The heavy in the story as now written is a man who is willing to sell 150 barrels of gunpowder to North or South — whichever side bids higher.

The idea: We make this heavy a reincarnation of Machiavelli whose only interest is in selling death to either side and if possible, both sides. Although Gettysburg cannot be historically changed, the few additional thousands of lives which would be otherwise lost if the merchant of death succeeds in his effort, would be saved through the efforts of Tony and Doug.

The heavy has a number of super-human characteristics because he is a reincarnation of a centuries-old historical figure. He can appear; disappear; re-appear. He can be sent back to his own time only if his effort to sell death is frustrated. Our buys succeed in doing this.

The Time Tunnel acting remotely — like a long-range time-gun helps the boys' battle against the reincarnation.

Dated December 28, 1966
EXPLOSION AT GETTYSBURG
by Bob and Wanda Duncan

Teaser

The Time: July 2, 1863. The Place: Gettysburg, Pennsylvania, on the eve of the battle that will be the turning point in the Civil War, and Doug and Tony materialize in the middle of a fierce battle between the Confederate and Union troops. They come down separately and some distance apart and, just as each starts to run for cover, there is a burst of cannon fire and Tony goes down. Doug checks Tony hurriedly and believes that he is dead. A Union

Major comes out of the brush, throws him a gun and tells him he needs all the help he can get, just as another Confederate attack sends them into the brush, running for their lives.

Act One

In the Time Tunnel, Ann is still getting a signal from Tony, faint but unmistakable, so she knows that he is still alive. The battlefield is deserted now except for the bodies of Tony and a few soldiers. Smoke is still clinging to the trees as a Confederate patrol comes out of the brush, picks up Tony and carries him off. The patrol is under the command of a Sergeant Maddox and they have been sent out to meet a courier in civilian clothes who has been on an intelligence mission for the South. Maddox has never seen the courier before and is certain that since Tony was at the designated rendezvous position, he is the courier.

They manage to bring Tony around. He is suffering from concussion and a minor head wound, conditions which have brought on amnesia. He can give them none of the information which they think he was sent out to collect, intelligence concerning the location of a cache of gunpowder which has been offered at auction to both sides by a profiteer names Stevens. Stevens is a neutral who has taken advantage of the misery of war to enrich himself and he is known to have the cache somewhere in this area. Tony is issued a Confederate uniform and he sincerely believes that he is a part of this Confederate unit.

As Doug goes with the Union Major, he finds himself in a predicament. The Major was sent out to stop the southern courier and the Major saw him killed during the skirmish. Doug tells the Major that he is a civilian who just happened to get caught up in the battle, but the Major insists that there are no civilians in this war; every man must take sides. Doug agrees, out of expediency, and the Major gives him a highly important mission. There is no time for the Major to get anybody else. All of his men have been killed and he desperately needs help. Doug goes along.

Now that the courier is dead and that part of the Major's assignment is over, he has to deal with Stevens and to keep the South from getting the gunpowder. They arrive at Stevens' cabin in the woods, and they find Stevens to be a complete scoundrel. He does not care how many people die or which side wins or loses. He has 150 kegs of gunpowder to sell. The Major insists that this gunpowder was stolen from a Union arsenal near Washington, that it is Union property and he is here to reclaim it.

Stevens just laughs. When the Major makes a move against him, Stevens gives a signal and one of his men fires from the brush and the Major goes down. Stevens refuses him medical attention and orders Doug and the Major thrown into a room until he decides what to do with them.

The Major is dying. He tells Doug that Stevens must be stopped and that Doug himself is the only man who can do it. But Doug is already completely involved, so angry at the cold blooded cruelty of Stevens that he will do anything to stop him. Doug tells the Major that he will do his best. The Major dies; Doug is on his own.

Doug knows he can do nothing until he finds out where the gunpowder is so he decides to bluff it through. He tells Stevens that he is empowered to act for the Union Army and that he will make a bid for the gunpowder as soon as he verifies its existence and tests its quality. They are just about to come to terms when the Confederate patrol finds the cabin. Tony and Sergeant Maddox spot Doug in his Union uniform through a window and Tony raises his rifle to kill him as we: FADE OUT.

Act Two

The shot misses and the fight is on, a fierce battle as the Confederate patrol moves to take the cabin which is defended by Doug, Stevens and Stevens' two men. During the fight, one of Stevens' men is killed and the other severely wounded. Finally, the Confederates capture the cabin and Doug comes face to face with Tony, startled to find that he's alive, delighted to see him. But suddenly, Tony rushes at him with a knife, determined to kill him.

The fight is halted by Stevens, who still has the upper hand. The South needs the supply of gunpowder even worse than the North does and if Stevens is harmed, the South certainly will not get it. Stevens is the only man who can lead them to it but he cannot be threatened into cooperation. He wants money. Sergeant Maddox and Tony are seething but there's nothing they can do about it. They agree to meet the price.

Now there is the question of what to do with Doug. Tony sets out to interrogate Doug, quite fiercely, and Doug tries to re-establish Tony's identity and to reason with him. Doug knows that what happens to the gunpowder will make no difference in the long run because the North is going to win. But Doug wants to destroy the gunpowder, just to keep Stevens from profiting by it. Tony won't listen to any of this. He is convinced that Doug is lying, and after a short but bitter scene, Doug is condemned to death.

The Time Tunnel has brought in a military expert to fix the location so they can try for a retrieve, but the military expert's job is an impossible one because of the undergrowth and the lack of identifiable landmarks. Too, even if they could make a fix now, they could not make a transfer. It's possible that Tony's amnesia is temporary, but to switch him would certainly make it permanent.

Back in the cabin, the decision is made to kill Doug immediately and Tony himself volunteers to carry out the execution as we: FADE OUT.

Act Three

Before Tony can carry out the execution, Doug appeals to Sergeant Maddox. "Is this the way the gallant South is going to win the war?" he asks. "By shooting down unarmed men?" Maddox decides not. As a non-commissioned officer, he is not qualified to handle these things and he decides to take Doug and Stevens back to the Supply Train and hand them over to his superiors.

As they leave the cabin, Doug manages to escape and Tony goes after him. Tony has the advantage because he is out for blood and Doug is not. Nevertheless, Doug soon finds himself in a position of either killing or being killed and the fight is halted only by the commencement of a stock battle as the Union troops attack the Supply Train toward which Sergeant Maddox is heading. Tony rushes off to join in the battle which is a spectacular one with the cannons firing on both sides, the supply wagons being blown up and the Union cavalry charging up the hill.

Stevens takes a position of safety while the Sergeant and his men fire at the advancing horsemen.

In the Time Tunnel, Ann is very upset. Tony is in a highly hazardous position and is likely to get killed before they can do anything. Swain comes up with a daring plan, something which has not been tried before, and starts working it out with the military expert.

Now, on the battlefield, it appears that it will be too late for Tony. He is charged by a Union soldier with a bayonet and while he is fighting him, another Union soldier charges from the opposite direction. Tony's death is certain as we: FADE OUT.

Act Four

But Doug can't sit back and see Tony killed. He rushes in, takes on the other soldier charging Tony, saves his life, and then is forced to move away as Sergeant Maddox and his men rush in. Tony is puzzled, confused. For a moment during that fight, it was almost as if he knew Doug from somewhere else, and Doug did save his life. But Sergeant Maddox doesn't believe it. It's possible Doug rushed in to make sure that Tony was killed and was attacked by his own man in the confusion.

The battle is over and the Sergeant's superiors are all dead, so the decision is still his to make. With the destruction of the Supply Train, the South needs the gunpowder more than ever. The Sergeant finds a metal paymaster's box in the debris and knows that it contains ten thousand dollars which had been sent to pay the troops. He makes the deal with Stevens. He will give him ten thousand dollars for the gunpowder. Stevens agrees.

Back in the Time Tunnel, Swain starts to put his plan into operation. They will fix on the signal of a known landmark on the Gettysburg battlefield and then superimpose the signals on the Gettysburg battlefield and then superimpose the signals of Tony and Doug. By using a burst of power, critically timed, Swain hopes for a secondary special transfer, putting the boys in position for a retrieve. It's a risky business, but they have to try it. Kirk gives his permission. They pick a spot on Cemetery Ridge known as the "Bloody Angle," the apex of the heroic and futile Confederate charge which General Pickett will make tomorrow. "The bloody Angle" is relatively deserted now. Swain makes his settings. Stevens leads the Confederates to the decrepit-looking wagon where he has the gunpowder and is given the moneybox in exchange. But now Doug comes out of the brush with a lighted touch, warns them to stand back. The Confederates back up, all except for Tony who has a rifle and a clear shot at Doug. Maddox yells at him to fire, but Tony cannot bring himself to do it. His memory isn't clear yet, but it's beginning to return. Doug orders Stevens to put the money box next to the wagon, and then he throws the torch. The wagon begins to burn. Stevens makes a mad dash for the money box just as the wagon explodes. When the smoke clears, the moneybox has been blown open and Stevens lies dead, his body half-covered with a shower of Confederate money, all worthless.

Just at that moment, Swain makes the switch, but something goes wrong. Doug is transferred to the "Bloody Angle" all right, but there is an unpredicted switch in Time as well, and now it is the next afternoon, in the middle of Pickett's charge. In the Tunnel, the military expert advises them to make the next transfer quickly, because in this most famous of all Civil War battles, the Confederates were massacred, one regiment losing 90 percent of its members, Pickett's own division losing 3,393 officers and men out of 4,800. And Tony is there, with the advancing Confederates, coming into certain death.

But as Tony advances among the charging men, his memory returns. Spotting Doug among the Union sharpshooters, he calls his name, advances toward him. Doug tells the sharpshooters to hold their fire and he makes his way to Tony. And then they freeze and change into their traveling clothes and de-materialize to go spinning off into their next adventure as we: FADE OUT.

End of Episode

THE PAPERBACK NOVELS

In 1964, Pyramid Books published a novel titled *Time Tunnel* (sans *The*), written by Murray Leinster, a nom de plume of William F. Jenkins. It tells the story of Professor Carroll and his associate, Harrison, who discover a

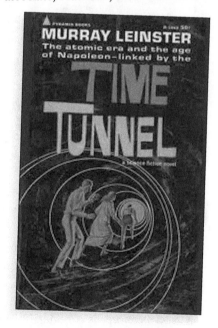

time tunnel with a fixed connection between the present and the Napoleonic era of 1804. Dubois, owner of a profitable antique store, used the tunnel to deliver exotic perfumes to Paris in which very few people bathed. It was not unreasonable for the return-traffic to be ornamental snuff-boxes, out-of-date newspapers and flint-lock pistols to be sold in his shop. Harrison, attracted to the condition of the antiques, soon discovers Dubois' secret. The tunnel could have been used to prevent the destruction of the human race. But it was actually used to keep a shop going. The tunnel itself was an odd natural phenomenon created as a result of large masses of iron, which formed the temporal connection between decades. With the threat of immediate atomic war from the Chinese, Harrison knew that Dubois had somehow caused damage to the past and a correction was needed to prevent the future destruction of all mankind. The result of Harrison's efforts was purely self-preservation. When he could not find a solution, he attempted to convince his love to come through the tunnel and take up permanent residence in the past as an atom-bomb-proof shelter. It is in decades past that Harrison then discovers what he can do to prevent the future from growing into a nightmare. After taking the necessary steps, he travels back through the tunnel to the present. Things are now different. The Chinese never had an atom bomb. There was no threat to the world and therefore no time-tunnel. Many of the characters ceased to exist but with the threat eliminated, Harrison decides to live content with the knowledge that the horrible events of the past never happened.

For the record, Irwin Allen's concept of a television series at about the same time Leinster was drafting his novel was purely a coincidence. It has been argued that, in regard to simultaneous invention, science and art are

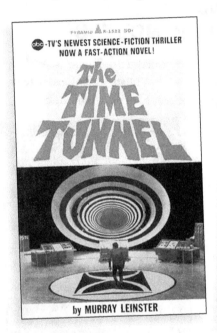
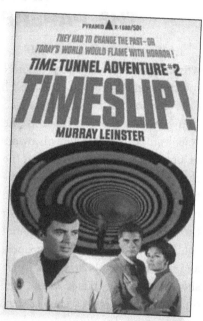

similar. When two scientists independently make the same discovery, their papers are not word-for-word identical, but the core ideas in the papers are the same. Likewise, two novelists may independently write novels with the same core themes, though their novels are not identical word-for-word. Leinster's concept is considerably different from Irwin Allen's and finding comparison between the two is a waste of time. Allen himself revised his concept more than once; including later revisions from Shimon Wincelberg and Harold Jack Bloom. Both the initial concept and the filmed adventures bears little (if any) similarity to the Leinster novel.

In January 1967, Pyramid Books published the first of two paperback novels based on the television series. Murray Leinster was also the author. Neither of the two merchandising tie-ins bore any resemblance to his 1964 novel other than the name. The first novel, simply titled *The Time Tunnel*, started out as an adaptation of the pilot episode. A few changes were noticeable. Tony greeted Senator Clark, not Doug, to Century City which housed the Time Tunnel Complex. Kirk's past was briefly explored: he was one of three ranking generals in the Air Force when he applied for early retirement and then quietly vanished. Kirk had a large share in the construction of Project Tic-Toc. He used strictly confidential orders by the executive branch of the government to hornswoggle contractors into believing they were at work on something relatively commonplace.

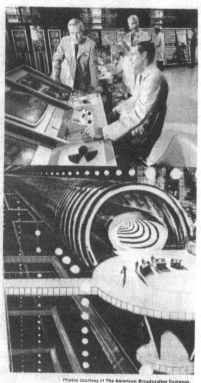
Advertisement promoting one of the paperback novels.

The construction of the Time Tunnel was explained briefly in the novel: *"Project Tic-Toc has been set up in secrecy because it would not be possible to convince Congress of the need for it. More than that, public opinion in America would not permit it. No member of Congress would dare to vote for it. The nation would lose every friend it had, if the project — and especially its success — was revealed. And it wasn't a matter that a group of nations could undertake together. There could only be one Project Tic-Toc. More than one was unthinkable."*

Instead of the radiation bath demonstrated in the premiere episode, Tony straps on a metal harness so the technicians at the Time Tunnel Complex could bring him back whenever they wanted. In an effort to demonstrate to Senator Clark the importance of the project, and to prove the tunnel works, Tony transports himself into the past. May 31, 1889. Johnstown, Pennsylvania. The day of the famous Johnstown Flood. When Tony attempts to warn the townspeople of the pending flood, he is temporarily thrown in jail. Doug straps on a harness and travels back to the same point in time to help get Tony out of jail. Soon after, failure of the South Fork Dam and the flooding begins. Doug and Tony make an effort to save as many citizens from a watery grave. When Ann MacGregor attempts to bring Doug and Tony back to the present, something goes afoul with the controls and the time travelers find themselves amongst a massive Indian attack at Adobe Walls in 1874. After meeting Hanrahan, Billy Ogg and Bat Masterson, Tony and Doug help save the life of a young woman named Elena. Ann MacGrgeor once again attempts to bring Doug and Tony to the present and the time travelers find themselves in the future where most of mankind has mysteriously become extinct as a result of a strange alien force field. Wandering through the deserted futuristic city of St. Louis, Doug and Tony visit the library and look up Elena's obituary to discover she lived a good old age with four sons, three daughters and twelve grandchildren.

After discovering where the alien pressure wall originated, the time travelers destroy the generator and potentially save the surviving human race from extinction. Tony is disillusioned by what the future holds and wonders if the Time Tunnel could possibly be used to thwart future attacks from visitors from outer space. Ann MacGregor finally succeeds in bringing the boys back to the present and Tony briefs General Kirk and Senator Clark about all that he and Doug witnessed during their travel. Senator Clark agrees to persuade gray hairs in Washington to keep Project Tic-Toc in operation. "No other man like Hitler will be able to attain to Hitler's power," Clark explains. "The Time Tunnel can sway and incline and guide the events of the world so that the whole planet may some day be ruled for the benefit of humanity." Tony agrees.

In July 1967, Pyramid Books published a sequel, *Timeslip*, also written by Murray Leinster. When an experimental nuclear missile was being transported to a new location — with the guidance of the Time Tunnel — something went wrong, and it wound up buried in the capital of a great nation, over a century ago. Vera Cruz, Mexico. Now, in the present, excavation equipment was moving toward the site. Any day a bulldozer blade might set the bomb off, destroying a mighty city and plunging the world into war. Tony Newman had only one chance to head off the disaster. He had to go through the Time Tunnel and make the accident "unhappen." The trouble was, there was a war going on in 1847 and the bomb was in enemy territory. (Oddly, Ann MacGregor was now referred to as "The MacGregor.")

It remains uncertain why Leinster wrote the two paperback tie-ins. It is most likely that Leinster was hired to do the tie-in books as compensation for the fact that Pyramid was going to retire his original novel from their catalog. It was also most likely a means of making sure that he had no claims on the ABC-TV series, as far as general concept was concerned.

In May 1966, Westminster Press published a novel, *Tunnel Through Time*, written by Lester Del Rey. Marketed to a juvenile audience, it tells the story of young Bob Miller whose scientist father, Sam Miller, has invented a "time ring" from which anyone could walk through and travel to another time. Sam fails to return, "Doc Tom" (an archaeologist) takes over the controls. Bob and Doc Tom's son travel into the past in an effort to bring Sam back to the present. They visit the Mesozoic era, combat large reptiles, fight off an ice storm during Earth's ice age and befriend a female cave dweller before they accomplish their mission. This novel, similar in concept, was published months before Irwin Allen's television series premiered on ABC.

APPENDIX F
STORYBOARDS FOR "RENDEZVOUS WITH YESTERDAY"

The following are storyboards for the pilot episode. A film storyboard is essentially a large comic of the film or some section of the film produced beforehand to help film directors, cinematographers and television commercial advertising clients visualize the scenes and find potential problems before they occur. Often storyboards include arrows or instructions that indicate movement.

CAR APPROACHES ELECTRIC FENCE
IN A CLOUD OF DUST —

GUARD AT ELECTRIC GATE — CAR
APPROACHES

GUARD SEEN IN REARVIEW
MIRROR OF CAR AS M.P. DRIVER
SHOWS I.D. CARD.

#7   EXT. DESERT.

CAR MOVES TOWARD RAMP
(2ND UNIT)

(2ND UNIT
PHOTO EFF.)

#7   CONT'D. B   EXT. DESERT TUNNEL ENTR.

CAR MOVES DOWN INTO RAMP
RAMP DOOR CLOSES   2ND UNIT
PHOTO EFF.

A-121   CONT'D. A.   EXT. DESERT TUNNEL ENTR.

ANGLE ON RAMP — DOUGS CAR DRIVES
UP AND OUT.

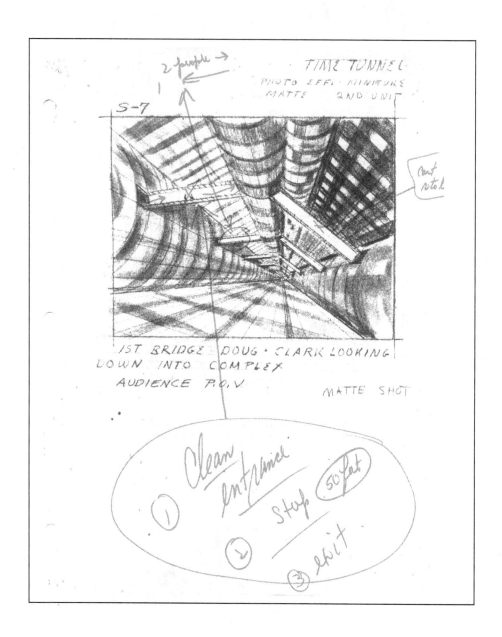

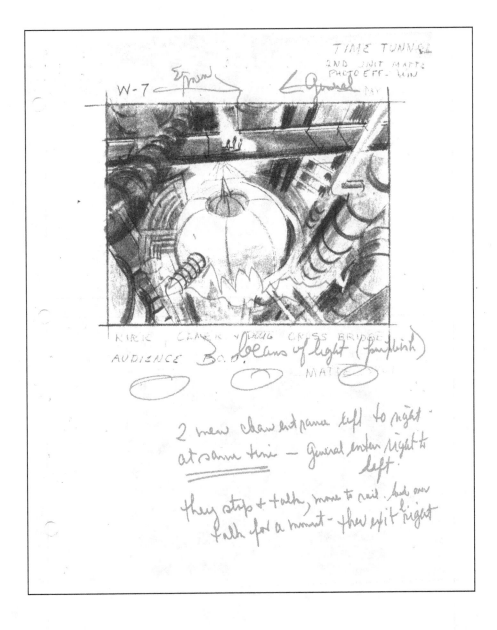

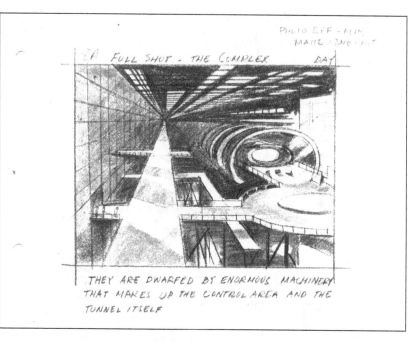

PHOTO EFF - MIN
MATE - 2ND UNIT

5A FULL SHOT - THE COMPLEX　　　DAY

THEY ARE DWARFED BY ENORMOUS MACHINERY
THAT MAKES UP THE CONTROL AREA AND THE
TUNNEL ITSELF

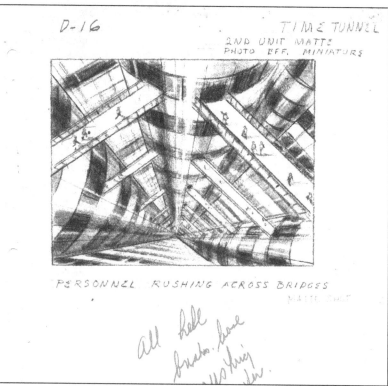

D-16　　　　　　　　　　TIME TUNNEL
2ND UNIT MATTE
PHOTO EFF. MINIATURE

PERSONNEL RUSHING ACROSS BRIDGES
MATTE SHOT

all hell
breaks loose
us thing
der.

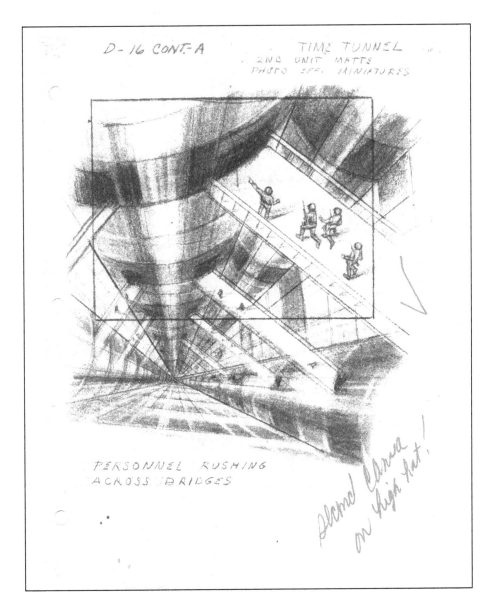

F-18

TIME TUNNEL
2ND UNIT
BLUE BACKING

TONY IN A VIOLET MIST - THRU
WHICH HE CAN BE SEEN IN SILHOUETTE

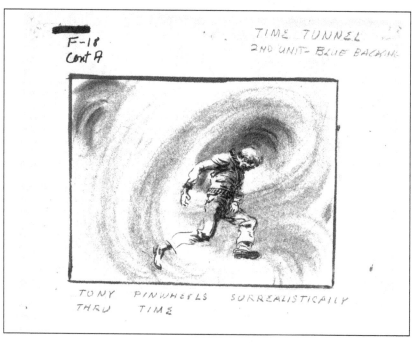

F-18
Cont A

TIME TUNNEL
2ND UNIT- BLUE BACKING

TONY PINWHEELS SURREALISTICALLY
THRU TIME

PETE'S BODY MATERIALIZES IN
DESERT, HE RUNS TOWARD CAMERA

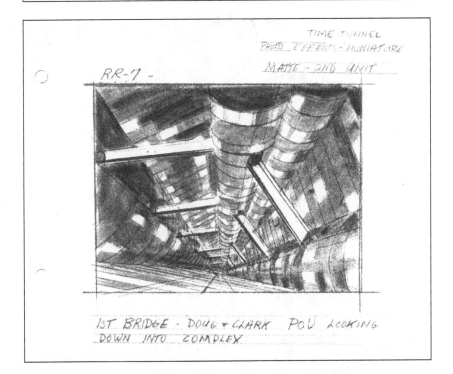

TIME TUNNEL
PHOTO EFFECTS-MINIATURE
MATTE-2ND UNIT

RR-7 -

1ST BRIDGE - DOUG + CLARK POV LOOKING
DOWN INTO COMPLEX

SELECTED BIBLIOGRAPHY

Amory, Cleveland. *TV Guide* magazine (October 29, 1964)

Barnes, Alan and Marcus Hearn. *Kiss, Kiss, Bang! Bang!* (B.T. Batsford, 2000)

Brooks, Tim and Earle Marsh. *The Complete Directory to Prime Time Network and Cable TV Shows, 1946-Present* (Ballantine Books, 1995)

Clark, Mike. *Starlog Magazine* (#159), interview with Shimon Wincelberg.

Clark, Mike. *Starlog Magazine* (March 1992), "The Master of Disaster"

Counts, Kyle. *Starlog Magazine* (June 1992), "Time Traveler"

Counts, Kyle. *Starlog Magazine* (July 1992), "A Time to Remember"

Gardner, Paul. *The New York Times* (September 13, 1964), "Drafted to Serve — On Land, Sea and TV"

Grams, Martin. *I Led 3 Lives: The True Story of Herbert A. Philbrick's Television Program* (Bear Manor Media, 2007)

Grams, Martin. *The Twilight Zone: Unlocking the Door to a Television Classic* (OTR Publishing, 2010)

Leinster, Murray. *Time Tunnel* (Pyramid Books, 1964)

Leinster, Murray. *The Time Tunnel* (Pyramid Books, 1967)

Leinster, Murray. *Timeslip!* (Pyramid Books, 1967)

Philips, Mark and Frank Garcia. *Science Fiction Television Series: Episode Guides, Histories and Casts and Credits for 62 Prime Time Shows, 1959-1989*, (McFarland, 1996)

Phillips, Mark. *Starlog Magazine* (September/October 1991), "Time & Time Tunnel Again"

Phillips, Mark. *Dreamwatch* (April 2002), "Time Tunnel Reopens!"

Phillips, Mark. *Starlog Magazine* (#363), "Secrets of the Time Tunnel"

Rosin, James. *The Invaders: A Quinn Martin TV Series* (Autumn Road Company, 2010)

Salerno, Al. *World Journal Tribune* (December 4, 1966) "We May All Fly Away in a Yellow Submarine"

Weaver, Tom. *Starlog Magazine* (January 2007), "Rendezvous With Yesterday"

Weaver, Tom. *Starlog Magazine* (October 2007), "Timely Destinations"

Weaver, Tom. *Starlog Magazine* (October 2007), "Tunnel Vision"

Weaver, Tom. *I Talked With a Zombie* (McFarland Publishing, 2008), interviews with cast.

INDEX

ABOUT THE AUTHOR

MARTIN GRAMS, JR. is the author and co-author of more than twenty books about old-time radio and retro television including *The Twilight Zone: Unlocking the Door to a Television Classic* (2008), *The Green Hornet: A History of Radio, Motion-Pictures, Comics and Television* (2009), *The Shadow: The History and Mystery of the Radio Program, 1930-1954* (2010), *The Have Gun-Will Travel Companion* (2000), *I Led 3 Lives: The True Story of Herbert A. Philbrick's Television Program* (2007) and *Science Fiction Theatre: A History of the Television Program, 1955-57* (2011). Martin is the recipient of numerous awards including the 2008 Rondo Award for "Best Book of the Year" (The Twilight Zone). Martin currently lives in Airville, Pennsylvania.

The author has a weekly blog. Every Friday afternoon, Martin Grams offers essays and postings about all things nostalgic from old-time radio, vintage movies, retro television, pulp magazines and much more. Essays of the past included the origin of Have Gun-Will Travel, "The Mystery of Greta Garbo," plot summaries for lost Green Hornet radio adventures, Bela Lugosi on Quick as a Flash, and Jean Harlow in the tabloids.

www.martingrams.blogspot.com

It's free to subscribe via e-mail or check out the web-site every week for the latest offering!

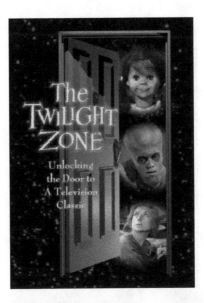

THE TWILIGHT ZONE: UNLOCKING THE DOOR TO A TELEVISION CLASSIC

BY MARTIN GRAMS, JR.

Very few television shows withstand the test of time, and Rod Serling's *THE TWILIGHT ZONE* is one of the notable exceptions. Proven to be an important part of American culture since its debut on CBS in October 1959, many Hollywood producers, screenwriters and directors have been inspired and influenced by this series. Comic books, magazine articles, numerous television revivals, a major motion picture and even modern audio productions have been produced, showcasing the continuing popularity of this television classic. This definitive history presents a portrait of the beloved Rod Serling and his television program, recounting the major changes the show underwent in format and story selection, including censorship battles, production details, and exclusive memories from cast and crew. The complete episode guide recalls all 156 episodes of the series in detail that has never before been accomplished in any publication. This book will make you want to look back at the episodes once again, whether you are a casual fan or serious enthusiast of the series. Unlock the door to a television classic by reading about the in-jokes, bloopers, and other trivia associated with the behind-the-scenes production of...*THE TWILIGHT ZONE!*

Available from BearManor Media, *www.bearmanormedia.com*
and *www.martingrams.com*

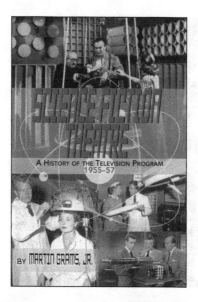

SCIENCE FICTION THEATRE: THE HISTORY OF THE TELEVISION PROGRAM, 1955-57

BY MARTIN GRAMS, JR.

From 1955 to 1957, *Science Fiction Theatre,* a semi-documentary series, explored the "what ifs" of modern science. Placing an emphasis on science before fiction, television viewers were treated to a variety of complex challenges from mental telepathy, robots, man-eating ants, killer trees, man's first flight into outer space and the possibility of visitation from outer space. Hosted by Truman Bradley, a former radio news commentator, *Science Fiction Theatre* became an influential program for the time, courtesy of Ivan Tors, a man with a healthy regard for science and nature. Hollywood actors Gene Barry, Ruth Hussey, Gene Lockhart, Basil Rathbone, Howard Duff, William Lundigan and Vincent Price are but a few who lent their talents. For the first time ever, this 530-page book documents the entire history of the television program with biographies about Fred Ziv, Ivan Tors and Truman Bradley; behind-the-scenes production details; over 150 exclusive never-before-published photographs; and an episode guide for all 78 episodes including dates of production, fake science props, cast list, salary fees, location shooting, and much more!

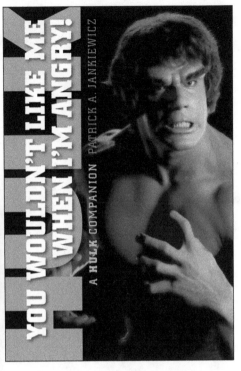
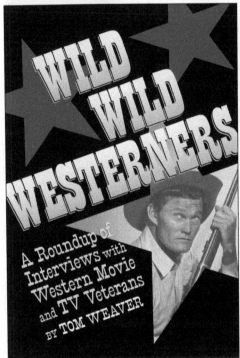

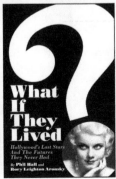
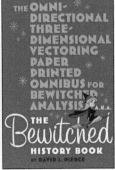
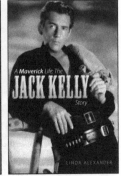

CPSIA information can be obtained
at www.ICGtesting.com
Printed in the USA
BVHW050937201021
619398BV00001B/19